COMPARATIVE LEGAL REASONING AND EUROPEAN LAW

Law and Philosophy Library

VOLUME 50

The titles published in this series are listed at the end of this volume.

COMPARATIVE LEGAL REASONING AND EUROPEAN LAW

by

MARKKU KIIKERI

University of Turku, Finland

KLUWER ACADEMIC PUBLISHERS

DORDRECHT / BOSTON / LONDON

A C.I.P. Catalogue record for this book is available from the Library of Congress.

ISBN 0-7923-6884-3

Published by Kluwer Academic Publishers,
P.O. Box 17, 3300 AA Dordrecht, The Netherlands.

Sold and distributed in North, Central and South America
by Kluwer Academic Publishers,
101 Philip Drive, Norwell, MA 02061, U.S.A.

In all other countries, sold and distributed
by Kluwer Academic Publishers,
P.O. Box 322, 3300 AH Dordrecht, The Netherlands.

Printed on acid-free paper

Printed in the Netherlands.

TABLE OF CONTENTS

ACKNOWLEDGEMENTS

The following argument was first defended as a doctoral dissertation in March 1999 in the Department of Law at the European University Institute Florence. The criticism, the comments and the support received during and after the defence have shaped this text to its contemporary form. The text is considerably shortened, but as well some new chapters have been included. Some work related to the correction of the various fallacies unfortunately embedded in the thesis and to sharpening of the argumentation.

I would like to thank the readers of the thesis, Aulis Aarnio, Massimo La Torre, John Bell, Marie-Jeanne Campana, and Günther Teubner, for their help in this project. Especially the support and the encouragement of Aulis Aarnio and Alexander Peczenik have been essential for this publication. Aulis Aarnio has shown his deep broad-mindedness during this process and I hopefully have learned something from it.

I also want to thank Susan Lamb again for her short introduction to public secrets of the English language. The comments of the (unfortunately) anonymous Kluwer referee have also been instructive and he (she?) has given me inspiration to review and make additions to the text. Furthermore, many additions are due to the discussions I have had with Kaj-Henrik Impola, Olavi Sulkunen, Jari Hellsten and Heikki Larmola in the Finnish Parliament library during the endless "breaks". Three of us have already defended, so these breaks have not been obstacles for the work but obviously some kind of intellectual "gymnastics" necessary for scientific thought.

The Finnish Parliament provided me work place in the researchers' hall and help in research. Especially I want to thank Eila Rantala. The University of Turku provided me valuable experience by having me as a substituting professor of International and European Law in the Faculty of Law during 1999-2000, and various discussions there were very inspiring. I hope I would have the possibility to return some day to this University rich in tradition.

I would like to acknowledge the scholarship provided me for the Doctoral research by the Finnish Academy. The Finnish Cultural Foundation (Heikki Haapaniemi fund) gave me financial support for finishing the thesis. However, the work after the defence has been possible only because of the scholarship I received from the Emil Aaltonen Foundation. I sincerely thank all persons involved.

My friend Antti Lähteinen has patiently and with high professional skill provided me assistance with all the matters relating to computers, programming. The publishing editor Sabine Wesseldijk and her assistants Anny Burer and Ireke Ravesloot have patiently helped me and directed this publishing process in a friendly ambience.

Because this has been so long project I want to thank also Ilkka Kangasniemi, Tero Lahdes, Harri Pennanen, Merja Pentikäinen, Risto Wallin for the great moments together. My family, including my brother Mika, my parents Paavo and Anna-Liisa, Eeva Gaebel, Jussi and Pirkko Kiikeri, Orvokki Vuori, Jaana, Roosa and Pietu, and Ulla Aaltonen supported me in my defence, which I remember with joy.

My wife Anu and sons Justus and Walle have, like during this fathers' day, created the good humor, atmosphere and everything else for all this. I find no adequate words to thank you, so I dedicate this book to you.

In Rome, Tomba di Nerone, 12th November 2000,

Markku Kiikeri

"Spoken words are symbols for different states of mind and the written words are symbols for speaking"

ARISTOTLE

CHAPTER 1

INTRODUCTION

1. GENERAL REMARKS

European law is an extremely confusing phenomenon[1]. This is so even though the discourse in legal theory, in international law, and in different national systems all seem to reflect the traditional concept of modern positive law.

European law, consisting of internal and external relations and the discourses of all legal institutions in Europe, seems to exceed the limits of predictability and understandable explanation[2]. Furthermore, if one asserts that the relative legitimacy of these institutions is connected to this explanation, one may say that this phenomenon requires clarification. One has to "get to the bottom" of European law.

On the other hand, it is not difficult to notice that, in general, the discursive and democratic idea of law is in crisis and that institutional corporate instrumentalism is coming to the fore.[3]

Comparative law comprises a part of this obscure phenomenon of European law[4]. Indeed, the main argument of this book is that comparative law seems to be at the heart of the modern European law or even its postmodern brainchild. Furthermore, the idea here is that by studying it, in theory and in practice, one may bring to light certain key questions relevant to the present analysis of European law.

A preliminary issue for consideration is: what is meant by comparative law? Why does the problem of comparative law arise?

The machinery which is put in place to guarantee the smooth functioning of social

---

[1] 'European law' may be defined, in this connection, as a phenomenon consisting of the law of European countries and the law of the European Union and the European Human Rights System. European institutions are the institutions of national and European level legal systems (orders). European level legal institutions are the courts of European Community (Union) and the European System of Human Rights.

[2] The question is about traditional legal structures and dynamics within them. In Europe, states are legislating as they always have, but at the same time, the basis of their legal and political existence is changing rapidly. This type of phenomenon will obviously generate certain changes in conceptualization; both during and after the transitional period.

[3] Unger, R.M., 1976, pp. 200-203.

[4] One of the interests of the study springs from the fact that "internationalization" and the "Europeanization" of law, also in its nationally implemented form, underline the role of (innovatory) judicial interpretation. This is connected to the role of comparative law. Comparative law functions in these situations as a "reason of innovation".

cooperation can be called legal order. In a more systematized form, it is a legal system[5]. It may be said that the main aim of contemporary comparative law is the systematization of different legal orders and legal systems.

These legal orders and legal systems, manifested in institutional forms[6] and having their own particular geographical, linguistic, and "cultural" outlooks, have a close and practical impact upon our lives. Legal norms of these orders play a part in guaranteeing different freedoms and possibilities. What seems to be natural predictability in social cooperation depends, in the end, on the possibilities for systematized legal orders to intervene in cases of the malfunctioning of societal interaction through positive laws[7] On the other hand, the use of force and restrictions upon our freedom of movement and action do not usually occur, in a visible way, in a society, which seems to function well, and which seems to satisfy individual demands of equality.

The idea that different people think differently seems to be the rudimentary idea behind comparative law. Why is this so? Do all social systems have their own "ethos"? Are they "worlds apart"? What is "another" social system, legal order, or legal system"? Why are they compared and studied and even used as the basis for different types of justifications of acting? Moreover, how is it possible that, even if comparative law seems to be a somewhat haphazard account of individual experiences, there have been attempts to formalize and systematize comparative legal research and practice?

It may be observed that, at one time, at least the distinctions between different social systems and their processes (and, consequently, distinctions between laws) appeared clearer. People were attached to their physical and intellectual-historical environments, and information derived from elsewhere did not seem to appear so relevant for the daily life, at least for traditionally-oriented peoples. At the same time, influences, both received and

---

[5] Brusiin, O., 1938, p.195. By 'legal system' one can understand a system based on the cognitive legal scientific process of knowing. 'Legal order', on the other hand, can be defined as a volitative system related to power relationships. He
Raz, J. (1971, p.795 ff.) has considered the problem, why one needs the "systems" of law (as unity and identity). He maintains that the term "a legal system" is not a technical term. It is basically an ideal term (used in thinking about law). The unity of municipal legal systems can be divided to material and formal unity. This distinction relates to the problem of the identity of legal systems (ibid., p.796).
The answer to the question of identity can be found when posing the question of what is *"criterion or sets of criteria that provides a method for determining whether any set of normative statements is, if true, a complete description of a legal system"* (ibid., p.797). According to Raz, the three main issues, in this respect, are 1 The relationship between the existence and efficacy of law, 2. The distinction between making (a new) and applying (an old) law, 3. The relation between law and the state (ibid., p.801). One may call them the questions of legal science and the identity of legal systems.
[6] On legal institutions, MacCormick, N., Weinberger, O., 1986. *"What we call necessary institutions are no often more than institutions we have grown accustomed"* (Alexis de Tocqueville, 1970, p.76).
[7] *"By the attraction of pleasure as they preserve their species. They have natural laws because they are united by feeling; they have no positive laws they are not united by knowledge. Still, they do not invariably follow their natural laws; plants, in which we observe neither knowledge nor feeling, better follow their natural laws"* (Montesquieu, The Spirit of Laws, I.1.1.)

given, were more visible.

In this day and age, the world seems to be full of coexisting and overlapping social and legal orders and systems. The nature of these rules and legal systems does not show itself clearly or distinctively, to a not specialist. One thus has to be more careful in speaking of about particular or general features. This may be related to the value and instrumental rationality prevailing in post-industrial (information-based) societies.

On the other hand, nor does it appear easy any longer take to notice the traces of these constant influences. Adaptations, influences, imitations, and copying are the basic canons of the (post)modernist world[8]. In this sense, traditional identities, for example, do not appear clear. People seem to identify themselves more with the information channels hitting the headlines. Discussions concerning nations, legal orders and systems, discussions on ideal identities, do not seem to be particularly important, or even attractive. They appear, instead, as self-evident notions.

At the same time, the traditional (meta-)classifications of legal systems within comparative law do not seem to be plausible any longer. Cultural, political, and institutional structures have changed and are changing so dramatically that no basic and acceptable classification can be proposed. It seems that a grouping based on one idea can be outdated rapidly after the passage of time. In an "information society", the interpretational value of these distinctions is not self-evident. All that seems to be permanent is the dynamics and the change itself.

Nevertheless, one may claim that, in our contemporary society, the differences of "systems" could be found in the interpretations of these seemingly similar systems and their rules. This idea is based on the observation that as and when experiences accumulate in daily life or, when following the decision-making of legal institutions, these differences strike us. One may notice that these differences are based on differences in day to day life and practical discourses. The differences within daily life and in legal interpretations appear in more careful observations of the acting of various people and groups of people. Observation of the laws, institutions, and the behaviour of people is part of the hard core of contemporary comparative law. On the other hand, even if there are methodological and traditional forms of observation, the basic idea is that of individual inspection.

Why are these "comparative" observations made and expressed?

---

[8] Generally speaking, "modern" is seen as a contradistinction to the traditional (Lash, S., 1987, p.355). Yet, modernity can be seen as renaissance 16th and 17th century rationalism, whereas modernism is a 19th century arts' paradigm. The logic of modernity could be seen as a form of an ideal possibility. In its concrete form it is a process. (Modernity in law, see Weber, M., 1969, pp. 284-321 For more recent discussion of this, Unger, R.M., 1976, pp.192-222.)
   Contemporary social practices can be seen in terms of modernism, as a transformation of modernity into instrumental and substantive rationality (Lash, S., 1987, p.356, and 364, Weber, M., 1969, pp.304-305). For modernism as anti-rationality, see ibid., p.357 ff.). This is so especially in its institutionalized form.
   For imitation in law, see Sacco, R., 1991, pp.394-395. Imitation is a form of social learning (see for example, Miller, N.E., Dollard, J.,1941).

As maintained, one makes these observations because they strike us and because they are interesting. On the other hand, one tries to avoid them if they seem to be too frustrating. Nevertheless, whenever these differences appear, it seems that, almost automatically, one starts to use these observations as narratives in order to amaze or to achieve some other purpose. By using these observations, one may try to alter our behaviour in order to adapt ourselves or other people to changes or to contrast behaviour so as to make a statement regarding the correctness of another form of behaviour[9]. One takes them up, as arguments, within a social discourse.

Is there thus something special in the observation of legal behaviour?

"Our" form of "behaviour", in general, seems to be the form of behaviour which we feel to be the binding and correct one - except when we are convincingly told otherwise and we tend to fall in with that. This seems to be based on the identity emanating from societal discourses. However, in the field of law, the binding character of our form of behaviour is categorical. This binding character is connected to the social and binding nature of law as a social discourse. One cannot change law(s) solely based on personal preferences. This applies also to those who interpret and apply the law. Courts, for example, must apply the rules as they are directed to apply them. Administrators and police, on the other hand, cannot deviate from the types of behaviour which is binding upon them in terms of these social discourses.

If one already has categorically binding laws, what would be the purpose of observing the legal behaviour of others? Furthermore, why should this be done according to certain formal criteria? Moreover, why would this be a relevant factor within a discourse? Here one does no longer discuss the situation where one has to adapt behaviour to the laws of another country, for example, because of our physical or mental attachment to it. The basis of such reasoning has to be examined.

This is the basic theoretical question of this book. One may say that by concentrating on these dynamic processes of comparative observation and reasoning in legal systems and legal orders one may begin to recognize certain constant issues in contemporary legal discourse, and to see traces of the dynamics of law. In this sense, one does not look into the changes of some ideal legal rules as such, but instead gains an insight into normative ideologies of legal institutions and their actors in general[10].

In conclusion, the preliminary and basic concrete questions of this study are: why (other) legal systems are observed? How they are observed? What is done with this information? Why the information is used as it is used in legal institutions? Finally, what seems to be the results of these uses to the legal systems, institutions and individuals? Our specific focus is

---

[9] On phenomenology and the role of comparative law, see Mössner, J.M., 1974, p.205.
[10] This is in accordance with general neo-institutionalist theories of law and politics.

European law.

This book starts also from the idea that there is, and has to be, a change in the way comparative law is to be seen in the context of contemporary law. The change can be explained in the following way.

Traditionally, comparative law has been comparative law of legal orders. This means that it is still determined by the tradition of 19th century legal thought, where law is seen a system of positive legal orders. The 20th century comparative law has been concentrating on the comparison of these strong positive cores of legal orders in order to avoid the problems of more discursive approach to the law.

In the context of contemporary legal theory, law is seen discursively determined phenomenon. This means, as maintained before[11], that law can be seen not only as positive legal orders, but also more as legal systems determined by the systematization discourses in the context of these positive legal orders. Consequently, comparative law has to take into account this development in the contemporary legal thought, and define itself more as comparison of legal systems in the sense of systematization discourses.

This idea is strongly related to the European law. Namely, the evolutive aspects of European legal system are based on the observation of legal discourses, not only related to the underdeveloped and institutional systematization discourse of autonomous European level legal orders (European Community law and European system of Human rights), but also to the examination of the systematization discourses of law in the context of, for example, each domestic legal systems related to the European law. These legal systems include also the law of United States and some other extra-community legal systems, which have traditionally had a strong influence to the European law, especially after II World War.

2. COMPARATIVE LAW IN THE CONTEXT OF EUROPEAN LAW

The contextualization of comparative reasoning[12], as described above, means its contextualization as a practical phenomenon. This requires an examination of the

---

[11] See, note 5.

[12] The term "comparative reasoning" is used here because the intention of this study is to examine the argumentative, even "contextually argumentative", forms of the use of comparative observations. These comparative observations are used for arguing in favour of certain legal interpretations, and this reasoning can be studied in legal theoretical terms, which are to be developed below.

The term *"harmonizing interpretation"*, proposed by some, gives the impression that the use of comparative material has as its objective the harmonization of laws in different legal systems (Against the use of "comparative", see Kisch, 1961, p.168) This argument applies also against another alternative conceptualization *"unificatory interpretation"* (Idem.). To call this process comparative reasoning emphasizes the idea of process rather than the idea of an aim or a result of an exercise.

consequences of the comparative legal reasoning in concrete decision-making, and an examination of its value for contemporary legal discourse (and in particular for European law).

The argument of this book is that comparative considerations play an important role on many levels of the European legal discourse, especially in so called "hard cases".[13] On the other hand, the claim is that comparative law has become "institutionalized".[14]

Secondly, the argument is that a step has to be taken towards the idea of comparative law as a category of "sources of law" in order to ensure that the contemporary European legal discourse remains traditional and value-based, instead of legally instrumental.

One could assert that this reevaluation has importance for both legal science and legal practice, and an impact upon the development of the concept of European law and European socio-normative systems as a whole.

Related to the latter perspective, it is suggested, in the end of this book, that the relationship between different European legal orders and "systems" is a "discursively reflexive" one. This idea of "discursively reflexive European law" includes, however, the discursive "opening up" of legal justifications in European legal orders and certain changes in the orientation of European legal research.[15]

---

[13] The "hard case" nature of comparative law related considerations has been explained by Otto Brusiin (1962, pp.43-48). The idea is expressed as follows.

According to Brusiin, comparative considerations and research are perhaps the most important a *stimulus* for the legal theorist to achieve intellectual liberation from the perspective of one legal order. Unless such liberation takes place, the legal phenomena in "one´s" system are, for the observer, only illustrations, exemplifications, useful for the development of purely theoretical problems. Brusiin refers, for example, to the remarks of Hans Kelsen that one of the foundations of his legal theory has been the comparative research.

Brusiin says, consequently, that for a legal theorist the comparative research is never an end in itself, but only valuable means. One may say that because valuable legal research is based on the theoretical perspective of a legal phenomenon under consideration, comparative research seems to be a preliminary step in getting to this theoretical perspective. (On this point, see Strömholm, S., 1972, and Klami, H.T., 1981, p.123.)

Consequently, a study of legal theory is a study of a legal phenomenon in the larger sense, concerning its psychological, logical, behavioral, and argumentative elements, beyond the norm in question.

[14] A description of the characteristics of legal institutionalization is given by Weber, M., 1969, pp.299-300. He maintains, for example, that

"*If the legal profession of the present day manifests at all typical ideological affinities to various power groups, its members are inclined to stand on the side of order. Which in practice means that they will take the side of the legitimate authoritarian political power that happens to predominate at the given moment. In this respect, they differ from the lawyers of the English and French revolutionary periods and of the period of enlightenment in general*" (ibid., p.300).

[15] One may relate the observations of Brusiin's ideas (see, note 13) to this study too. This study has been built upon comparative observations on the uses and non-uses of comparative law. This way is gained a theoretical perspective, which tries to focus on the use of comparative law from the "psychological" (or, rather "phenomenological") logical, behavioral, and argumentative points of view. Consequently, the analysis will include some considerations of the (quasi-) psychological, (quasi-)logical, behavioral, and argumentative aspects of the uses of comparative law, as the structure of the work indicates. All this takes place in realm of the legal theory, as is explained below.

On the other hand, following the logic of Brusiin, one may say that what is observed is, in fact, also the behavior of (legal) actors in their attempts to liberate themselves from the narrow perspective of the one legal system. We, in fact,

3. THE RELEVANCE OF THE STUDY

As mentioned above, the basic theme of this work is to view law from the point of view of legal discourse theory. However, this evaluation is made within empirical context. This empirical survey establishes the background for the consideration of the functionality of European law. Hence, the study appears more "holistic" than traditionally dogmatical. In the end, the focus is on European law from the point of view of the theory of comparative legal reasoning.

In this sense, the investigation is expected to tell something about the "evolutional" side of the law as a system rather than the evolution of a particular doctrine or interpretation of a legal rule. Consequently, the results of the inquiry must be understood in the context of a specific legal phenomenon, namely "European comparative law".

In European law, comparative reasoning has gained additional relevance, for example, because of the reintroduction of principles like subsidiarity into legal terminology.[16] This type of "prudential" dimension is certainly unthinkable without the consideration of comparative aspects, though it is not guaranteed that even comparative law can extricate the European law in its contemporary "prudential" crisis[17].

Comparative aspects are also related to the discussion on federalism. The discussion on federalism is becoming more and more attractive in European law due to the tendencies toward the increasing competencies of the European Union[18].

---

analyze the intellectual move to the theoretical perspective. At the same time, one also follows a process, in which a person who has taken this theoretical perspective applies this analysis to a legal phenomenon in a legal decision. Indeed, it seems that there is a genuine attempt to make a complete legal analysis in a decision-making process!

Moreover, one also follows this reasoning process to the final normative conclusion, if possible. This seems to be an observation of a complete process of legal consideration. What one may say, in other words, is that this study concentrates on the institutional solutions to legal theoretical questions.

However, these observations on these different stages of analysis and generalized. This is so because one needs to make a theoretical analysis of the legal phenomenon of comparative legal reasoning and not only look into the individual and particular process of comparative legal decision-making.

The final synthesis at the end of this book relates to the analysis of the relationship between discursive legal theory and the theory of the institutionalized law. This way one ends up with an evaluation of the relationship between these two. This serves as a basis for a theoretical perspective on European law, which is presented in the conclusions of the study. (Regarding the need for and importance of a final synthesis of the 'microsystem' and the 'total preliminary system', see Brusiin, O., 1962, p.44)

[16] Some analysis, see Ward, I., 1995, pp.28-30.

[17] Discussion, see Weiler, J.H.H., 1998.

[18] One example of the latter is seen in the Amsterdam Treaty from 1998, where the European Court of Justice was given a right to interpret basic right instruments. This seems to bring the European law towards European constitutionalism.

Mr. Ward has analyzed the relationship between federalism and integrity of legal systems from the point of view of Kantian philosophy in a following way (Ward, I., Kant and the Transnational Order: Towards a European Community Jurisprudence. A draft of the paper presented in European Law seminar in 1993 in Edinburg, Scotland):

"Kant's identification of economics and commerce as the ultimate impulses behind any such future order was indeed prophetic. What Kant advocated therefore was a world order of the confederal type which exists in the Community today. What he did not advocate, of course, was the federal order which some perceive the ultimate ideal of the

Furthermore, it has been suggested, at the institutional level, that comparative law should "assist" in the construction of the European system.

In general, the similarity of European aims and objectives combined with the deviating traditions and interests is the a notable contemporary phenomenon. This is why comparative law, or comparative reasoning, is a relevant subject. It seems to be a form of justification for practical syntheses and choices, which are made at different levels of different systems and orders in Europe.[19]

On the other hand, by examining the contextual and justificatory uses of comparative law, one may be able to glimpse the legal-discursive identity of European law and European legal culture. This may augment the idea of legal identity, which is determined only by a focus upon positive rules and institutions. The doctrinal approach to European law often represents only the facade of the phenomenon. By way of contextualization, one may commence looking into the selection of "European essentials"which are, in many ways, the basis of the European legal identity.[20]

Legal research on comparative law in this century has aimed at the examination of the role of comparative law in practice. Yet, a genuine and extensible discoursed analysis of the uses of comparative law has not been produced. It seems that the nature of comparative reasoning in legal decision-making has not been authentically considered in contemporary legal literature. The relevance of the study is increasing because of the expansion of use of comparative law in legal drafting, reasoning and interpretation.

The fact that studies of the phenomenon of comparative reasoning are lacking may be connected to the claim, made by many scholars, that comparative law is not an essential element in legal practice, or that it is a marginal phenomenon in the practice of law. The argument is that comparative law aspects are seldom considered in legal interpretation ("cognitively"), and that their use is not explained explicitly (argumentatively)[21]. Consequently, the idea seems to be that comparative considerations are not phenomena of modern positive law. Furthermore, there is some support for the view that comparative law can hardly be classified as a source of law and legal norms, as traditionally defined.[22]

Community, and which has also been detected as the underlying trend of the Community judiciary. Kant's suspicion of fully federal orders lay essentially in the pragmatic, because any such orders can challenge the integrity of discrete communities, chiefly, by their tendency to institute politically sovereign bodies. However, if a federal order was once established, in the European Community or indeed in any political system, then Kant would have vigorously continued to stress the fundamental importance of maintaining the integrity of the normative order". The concepts of legislative, political and adjudicateive integrity, see Dworkin, R., 1991.

[19] On the new enthusiasm, see Riles, A., 1999, p.221 ff.

[20] See, note 5. On the historical cultural identity, Häberle, P., 1994, p.26. Good analysis, see Legrand, P., 1996, p.56 ff., with a different type of argument.

[21] For example, Kamba, E.J., 1974, p.499. One can call this "contextual comparative law".

[22] See, Koopmans, T., 1996, p.545, and de Gruz, P.,1993.

These viewpoints regarding comparative law emphasize the "quantitative", dogmatic, and institutional dimensions of law.[23]

One could declare that most of the non-contextualist approaches to law preserve this idea of the "marginality" of comparative legal considerations. This may be one of the reasons why there have not been general studies on the role of comparative legal considerations in several legal systems[24].

However, the question of marginality cannot be clearly resolved solely on the basis of quantitative and dogmatic observations. Quantitative marginality does not necessarily imply "material" marginality. In other words, there is a need for an alternative perspective to the phenomenon. This may break new ground in the field of comparative law. The alternative approach consists of empirical approaches to the quantitatively marginal legal conceptualizations, deviations, creations and confirmations in connection to comparative considerations.[25]

---

[23] With regard to the "quantitative" approach in comparative law, see Yntema, H.E., 1978, pp. 167-168. She stresses the point that there is no fundamental disparity between the quantitative and qualitative method of inquiry (ibid., p.196). The differences between these approaches derive from the types of data collected and the "mechanics" of manipulation of the data (idem.). Quantitatively analyzed situation and some remarks on lack of use, Zimmermann, R., 1995, p.24 (referring to Drobnig, U., 1986, p.610 ff.).

For quantitative and qualitative aspects in Comparative law, see Merryman, J.H., 1977, p.475. The qualitative study refers to a study with a purpose of identifying elements on which an unidentified substance in the law is composed. One does not understand substance *a priori* but attempts to identify it with the help of some elements.

On the qualitative interest in comparative law, see Sacco, R., 1991, p.388.

A study of comparative legal reasoning is a qualitative study because it aims at revealing the context of the comparative legal argument and at determining the aims of the comparative reasoning.

On the general perspectives and comparative law, see Neumeier, K., 1973.

(On the idea that without qualitative research, orders would seem "natural", see Perelman, Ch., Olbrechts-Tyteca, L., 1969, p.508.)

[24] One could say that no comprehensive and compound study has been produced on the role of comparative considerations in different legal systems. Considerations seem often to be based on "beliefs" on the general and factual situation (see, for example, Koopmans, T., 1996, p.555).

The fact that one can see comparative reasoning taking place mainly in the dissenting and concurring opinions is also part of the "marginality" of the comparative argument. However, the role of these dissenting opinions for legal evolution has not been really considered.

[25] When speaking about analogy, Perelman observes (Perelman, Ch., Olbrechts-Tyteca, L., 1969, p.372) by referring to Hume, D., A Treatise on Human Nature), that

"*It is true that some philosophies - notably those of Plato, Plotinus, and St. Thomas Aquinas - have justified the use of analogy in argumentation because of their particular conceptions of reality, but in such cases the use of analogy has been linked to the metaphysical conception, with which it stands or falls The empirists, on the other hand, for the most part look on analogy as a resemblance of quite minor importance because of its weak and uncertain character. It is more or less explicitly accepted that analogy constitutes the least significant member of the series identity-resemblance-analogy. Its sole value is that it makes it possible to formulate a hypothesis for verification by induction*".

However,

"*Any complete study of argumentation must therefore give it a place as an element of proof*".

It looks, at first blush, like the closer one gets to concrete legal interpretations - interpretations, which are directly issued to the parties in a process - the more "rare" comparative considerations are. The "power of law" does not seem to be based on comparative law. The power of comparative law seems to be in the legal discourse in general and in its connection to

On the other hand, the short glimpse to the history of comparative law enables us to understand contemporary forms of comparative reasoning[26]. Namely, at the heart of the history of comparative law there seems to be a phenomenon of legal institutionalization[27]. This forces legal research to take a more empirical approach to the comparative reasoning within legal institutions. One has to turn to analyses of particular aspects of the use of comparative law in different legal institutions so as to explain why it is attempting to use comparative reasoning in international and regional legal systems and orders. One has to find values embedded within the use of comparative law in legal decision-making.

---

dogmatic and scholarly works.

[26] "... our understanding of an analogy will often be incomplete unless we take into consideration the earlier analogies, which one amends or replaces" (Perelman, Ch., Olbrechts-Tyteca, L., 1969, p.392).

[27] The legal theoretical formulation of this concept can be found in Weinberger, O., 1998. Weinberger maintains that "neo-institutionalism is ... a synthesis based on a philosophical construction of a specific action theory with a theory of legal institutions (p.2). Central to this theory is an idea of "institutional facts".

CHAPTER 2

SOME HISTORICAL AND
THEORETICAL OBSERVATIONS

1. PRELIMINARY REMARKS: THE RHETORICAL NATURE OF THE COMPARATIVE LEGAL ARGUMENT

Legal justification is, in general, based on generality argument and pro-arguments of a solution. It is a kind of an analogy between the result and the argument, which appears to be the decisive part of a justification.

Comparative legal arguments are, on the other hand, generality, disparity and, and example types of arguments. The theme of the comparative legal argument is the domestic legal system(atics), which is related to the "phoros" of the comparative counterpart of the argument (foreign system or systems).

The decisive comparative legal argument is usually in a comparative legal generality form (analogy as such). It may be within a rich (i.e. analytical) or more synthetic type of generality argument. If it is an example type of argument, it usually is a representation of a more analytic attitude in reasoning and in interpretation. In its illustrative form, it is kept separate from the phoros. If it is not analytic or illustrative, it comes close to pure modelling.

One has to remember, however, that the analytical quality of comparison may be irrelevant to its persuasiveness[28].

If comparative (legal) disparity arguments - whether rich or non-rich, analytic or synthetic - appear as decisive parts of the justification, the justification is not based on any generalizable premises, except on the comparative disparity as such. The justification is then, basically, a justification of these disparities (non-analogies in relation to the phoros, i.e. other legal systems). Then it moves in the realm of the tradition of comparative law.[29]

However, this type of disparity argument may appear also as a justification in an *e contrario* form. Then the generality is somehow autonomously resulting from the disparity as an unacceptable or rejected premise. Then we are close to an argument by identity or coherence. This may also be in a form of example or illustration. Usually, the latter type of argument is based on the idea of anti-modelling.

Same type of phenomenon can be seen in the case, where any other type of generality is used in *e contrario* form. Then one is basically speaking about a justification by comparison by

---

[28] Perelman, Ch., Olbrechts-Tyteca, L , 1969, p.245
[29] For more discussion, see below

opposites. These two types of arguments may appear in synthetic or in analytical, rich or non-rich forms.

One may say that, in some ways, the identities and the "nonidentities" belong also to the realm of comparative legal argument and justification. They seem to function as presumptions for comparative reasoning as such.[30]

In general, an adoption of a legal norm, without an analytical and "rich-analogical" approach, may be called the value-based establishing of a comparative justification. As maintained, this can be an argument by comparative generality or disparity. These value-based justifications are often established on the identity of some kind,[31] and on concepts and "dogmas" internal to the value -based comparative argument and legal tradition. Here the idea of "coherence" is contacted.

These types of reductions should be, nevertheless, justified.[32] Usually, however, these identities are not analysed and reproduced explicitly.[33]

In comparative legal reasoning, the question is usually about partial identity (as opposed to complete identity)[34]. This is due to the closed system character of legal orders and systems. This, on the other hand, can be associated with the idea of normative legal culture. In the case of nonidentity, which can be, for that matter, used as well a legal argument, the elements can stimulate a disparity of approaches. In this case, the elements are "nonidentifiable".

The fact that certain arguments can be arguments by "nonidentity" does not mean necessarily that they are based on paradoxical thinking. Generalities are not necessarily determined by the "tautologies of identity".[35]

The analysis of the partial identities as "common" terms - the enquiry into the criteria, upon which the comparison is based - transfers the problem of comparison to the comparison of the elements themselves. This is a highly complex exercise. Ordering and opposition become often devalued, when one seeks to do justice to various elements in a comparison.[36] The analyses of the criteria uncover the argumentative structures, that is, the elements upon which

---

[30] Nonidentity can be called "negation of a term by itself" or "an identity of contradictories" (Perelman, Ch., Olbrechts-Tyteca, L., 1969, p.218). Here in the beginning the terms are capable of being identified, but after interpretation, difference arises, which can be known before argumentation (Idem).

[31] Perelman, Ch., Olbrechts-Tyteca, L., 1969, p.210. Identity is a result of a relation to something Identity is itself an abstraction.

[32] Here the interesting question is about nominal and real definitions. In law, nominalism - as an extreme idea of formalism - could be neglected as such, for nominalism assumes arbitrariness. One should instead speak about real definitions as such, for in law they are a matter of being either true or false, but not arbitrary (see, Perelman, Ch., Olbrechts-Tyteca, L., 1969, p.211).

[33] This has to be distinguished from the basic "identity" of law, which assumes certain criteria of being (see, Perelman, Ch., Olbrechts-Tyteca, L., 1969, p 393).

[34] For these terms, see Perelman, Ch , Olbrechts-Tyteca, L., 1969, p 211 ff.

[35] Perelman, Ch., Olbrechts-Tyteca, L., 1969, p 211.

[36] Perelman, Ch., Olbrechts-Tyteca, L , 1969, p.211 ff..

the ordering itself is based. The predominant - and often incompatible criteria then come to light.[37]

2. SOME HISTORY

2.1. Early comparisons

Both ancient private and public comparative law had radically contrasting function. Furthermore, it has been claimed that comparisons in the law of ancient times and the early middle ages were only comparisons of customs[38]. During this period, comparison as a systematic method seemed to be related to political theory, and not to any systematic studies of positive laws in the modern sense. Some exceptional "positive" comparisons were attached to different codifications during that time. One could say, for example, that because codifications were rare, the historical comparisons were accepted without criticism. The idea of a universal history of law prevailed. This feature can be related also to the difficulties entailed in acquiring sufficient information concerning societies and their laws.

It has been claimed that Jean Bodin's comparative approach demonstrated some kind of a theory of continuity.[39] One may say that Bodin stressed the importance of discourse. This may be seen, for example, in the fact that the comparative approach ran through all his works. In the ultimate analysis, he considered that the failures of one type of discourse could be replaced by other discourses, and by the discourse between religions (i.e. between those particular elements, which were to destroy the ultimate sovereign).[40]

In his comparative approach, Bodin did take part of a discourse, which was extremely value-based. He did not discuss possible alternative interpretations of the rules of different systems according to different writers, but made a selection of the "relevant" or "trustworthy" writers as sources *a priori* according to their background and nature as legal historians. Furthermore, even if "sociological" observations were part of his comparative method and approach, it was distinguished, in practice, from the main "legal" observations. It appeared mainly in theoretical and separate form as an indication of the methodological premises Bodin had. In some analyses, the climactical context was used in connection to analyses of legal

---

[37] Perelman, Ch., Olbrechts-Tyteca, L., 1969, p.211 ff..

[38] Valladão, H., 1961, p.99. For more detailed analysis, see Kiikeri, M., 1999.

[39] Reynolds, B., 1945, p.xxvii. ". . *ruling in rectitude and integrity*" (Bodin, J., 1979, Republic, 1. French ed, the preface I). "*There is nothing more dangerous to the commonwealth than that its subjects should be divided into two fractions, with none to mediate between them*" (Bodin, J., 1955b, V.2)

[40] For some analysis, see McRae, K.D., 1979, p.A24.

institutions.[41]

Bodin was the one attempting to throw light upon to the concept of sovereignty which had, in his time, been so badly confused in the abstract and which had also been muddled within the practice of the medieval feudal system.[42] This may also be the reason why he refused to see the concept of sovereignty in any functional sense (the idea of a mixed state etc.), and why he maintained a strict concept of 'sovereign' and monarchy.[43] On the other hand, his theoretical concept was morally neutral, accepting any type of sovereign as a sovereign.[44] The functional problems were the problems of (functional) rules rather than matters of fundamental premises.[45]

Bodin was modern in the sense that he associated the supreme political authority with the state. This authority was realized by lawmaking. His interest was apart from the judicial and administrative functions as such.[46] On the other hand, it has been maintained that Bodin was directing his attention to the real world rather than simply to the theoretical realm. His comparative approach must be seen part of his desire to apply his concepts to a "comparative" reality of a European legal world.[47]

In the practice of 16th and 17th centuries, the idea was that foreign authorities could be referred to (especially the *communis opinio totius orbis)* when the statutes, customs, and judicial and doctrinal determinations were in accordance with each other in the European area. This was so even if the case was clear according to the applicable municipal law.[48]

---

[41] Bodin, J., 1955b, V.1.

[42] Also, McRae, K.D., 1979, p. A13.

[43] Bodin, J., 1955b.

[44] This latter aspect is reminiscent of the Kelsenian approach to the question. Ethical qualifications appear in the concept of state, however (McRae, K.D., 1979, p.A20).

[45] For Bodin's problems in understanding any functionality in legal orders of his time, see McRae, K.D., 1979, p.A 20. McRae's constitutional idea is evident also in his analysis of Bodin's work.

[46] McRae, K.D., 1979, p. A 14.

[47] McRae, K.D., 1979, p. A 20.
One may say that Bodin's ideas on sovereignty were in line with the development of modern constitutional traditions in many countries (contrary to some opinions, McRae, K.D., 1979, p.A 21).
It has been claimed that his ideas suit well also to the idea of European federalism. It has also been maintained that *Republic* would provide many ideas for reformation of the national state (also in the form of European integration, McRae, K.D., 1979., pp.A 66-67) However, some ideas in the *Republic* may be difficult to adjust to the notion of supra-(national)state legal orders. "*If, however, the orders of the prince are not contrary to the divine and natural law, he [magistrate] must execute them, even if they are contrary to the law of nations, for the law of nations can be modified by the civil laws of any particular state provided natural justice and equity to which the prince is bound is not infringed, but public and particular utility only is in question"* (Bodin, J., 1955, III.4. p.86). In this passage Bodin seems to construct a hierarchy between the law of nations and the law of the sovereign. Equity and natural law seem to justify deviation from the law of nations.

[48] Gorla, G., 1982, 129. This was based on the practical and theoretical role those jurists (of each country), who were trying to show that municipal law was not based on arbitrary ideas (i.e. that it accorded with common experience and common reason, as represented in the *communis opinio totius orbis).* This is different from the idea that an idea be "in accordance with natural law" (idem.) There were no dominant authorities in England, however, (Schlesinger, R.B., 1995,

Comparative law was considered as a necessary ingredient in the practical and theoretical activities of jurists.[49] The main purpose was to find the "similarities". The differences were the "*varietas in unitae*".[50]

Many treatises and commentaries on municipal law included comparisons for various purposes, and were used mainly to illustrate and integrate municipal law within the framework of the common law of Europe. However, continental lawyers, with few exceptions, considered the "*orbis*" to be continental Europe, or regarded, for example, English law within a narrow perspective. This applied also to the practical jurisprudence, to the *Allegationes* and *Consilia* of lawyers.[51]

The "common law of Europe" has been defined as a juridical idea, according to which there was a concordance between the laws of states, especially among those emerging and developing between the 15th and 18th centuries. This accord related to the various feudal, canon, roman, commercial and international laws existing at that time. In this sense, it comprised a "Common European jurisprudence".[52]

One of those who applied a comparative approach to the consideration of the Lex Mercantile and the principles of European private law was George Joseph Bell.[53] He himself called it the "common jurisprudence of Europe".[54]

---

p.480).

[49] Gorla, G., 1982, p.129.

[50] Gorla, G., 1982, p.130. It was typical to compare municipal law with the Roman "*ius commune*" of the author. Also Gutteridge, H.C., 1944, p.3 ff.
Regarding *Ius Commune* and its reception in Europe, see Wiegand, W., 1991, pp.230-231. On the unified Europe of 17th century, Schlesinger, R.B , 1995, p.278.

[51] Gorla, G., 1982, p.130.

[52] Gorla, G., 1982, p.133. See also, Gorla, G., Moccia, L., 1981, p.144, 163. Regarding its disappearance and the consequences of this, see ibid., pp.153-154.

[53] Mr George Joseph Bell (1770-1843).

[54] Bell's writings are interesting, because they give some indication of the ideas prevailing during this period.
Bell explores the idea in his book that there is recorded evidence of the Universal Law Merchant, grounded upon principles of equity (Bell, G.J., 1870 [1810], p.xi).
His treatment of the subject is strongly Roman law based. However, he maintains that "*the object of this work ... [is] directed to an investigation into the differences ... between international law and conflicts of laws ... object mercantile usage .. to a common standard in different countries*" (ibid., pp.4-5).
He starts from Lord Mansfield's definition of the mercantile law as "*a branch of public jurisprudence, not restricting for its character and authority on private institutions or local customs of any particular country, but on the principles and usages of trade, which common convenience, and a universal sense of justice had recognized as fit to regulate the dealing of merchants. in all the commercial countries of the world*" (ibid., pp.3-4). "*the law merchant is universal. It is part of the law of nations, grounded upon the principles of natural equity, as regulating the transactions of men who reside in different countries, and carry on the intercourse of nations, independently of the local customs and municipal laws of particular states.. consist ... decisions of courts ... writing of lawyers in different countries (("not making law, but handing it down"). . recorded evidence of the application of the general principle ... guides towards the establishment of the pure principles of general jurisprudence*".
The comparisons in the book are Roman law based (according to him, others had "*peculiar forms and narrower maxims*"). He uses Scottish law and English law, American (adoptions based), French, Dutch law, and that of different

The modern comparative law - especially in its 19th century form - seemed to merge the legal and "natural" (non-relative) ingredients of Montesquieu's theory. At the same time Montesquieu's ideas on governance became "legalized".

One may maintain that the problem, in the reinterpretation of Montesquieu's approach, has been the overemphasis of the idea of a 'legal' nation and 'national law' within a modernist and holistic context. These ideas were considered long as notorious facts of law, sociology, and political philosophy. This led , within the study of comparative law and in the use of comparative law in legal and political institutions to an unanalytical approach to the characteristics of the "nation-law" as a process. One may claim that this has also engendered the possibility of the holistic instrumentalization of law.

Consequently, the Montesquieuan heritage seemed to give modern law a more "descriptive" direction. The repercussions of this approach have been, in the 19th and 20th centuries, the idea of the independence of comparative law as a legal discipline and the overemphasis upon the idea of the autonomy of comparative research[55]. In its ultimate form, one is faced with institutionalization of comparative law. The "scientification" of comparative law has reproduced, especially in its institutional form, one type of concept of legal system. One may say that this approach made comparative law turn away from the practical discursive sphere toward some kind of "cultural" approach, whereby other systems were seen, again, *a priori* to be in contrast.[56] It may be said that, in this paradigm, legal systems seem to have identities as socio-legal systems. This has resulted in practical self-maintenance of national legal systems in a process of similarity/disparity exploration, made without any normative aim in mind.

The Montesquieuan approach emerged as a perfect model also for the nationalist and ethnological comparative law of the 19th century. It had all the qualities of a persuasive socio-historical analysis. The claim regarding the autonomy of the nation suited many purposes perfectly.[57]

---

types of institutions ("*tribunaux de commerce*"). Russian cases are also quoted (Custom House Court of St. Petersburg, ibid., p.238). The use was basically "illustrative". There is no extensive comparative analysis in the modern sense of the word. The analysis of Roman, English and Scottish law is "reproductive" (descriptive).

At the end of the book, there is a kind of an analysis of conflicts of law situations. Interestingly, he speaks about "*integrity of our system of law*" .. "*still much caution is to be observed in the adopting of English judgements as authorities in Scotland*" (Bell, G.J., 1870, pp.x-xi).

Bell also wrote "*Inquiries into the contract of sale of goods and merchandise judicial decisions and mercantile practice of modern nations*" (Edinburgh, 1844), which referred to foreign authorities, institutions, and treatises (Bynkershoeck, *Questiones juris privati*, Statutes of New York, Law of Holland, French Law, and English law).

[55] On the struggle for independence, see Hug, P., 1932, p.1029.

[56] Some discussion on different periods in this respect, Schlesinger, R.B., 1995, p.477.
One of the contemporary misinterpretations of Montesquieu by Legrand, P. (1996, especially p.81) missing the discursive point of view.

[57] On ethnological approach, see Schmitthoff, M., 1941, p.102. It is based on ideas upon the "different evolutionary stages of mankind" and the primitiveness of societies.

One must remember, however, that the analysis in the *Spirit of Law's* was practical. Many interpretations of Montesquieu's approach do not do him justice. If his approach is to be understood properly, one has to interpret it in its own context. To interpret it solely as a for of a foreign transplant or as a categorical statement of theory is to put too much emphasis upon political dimension and to comparative law methodologization.

Montesquieu's idea seemed to be to produce an extensive argumentation on behalf of a type of "new" government in some historical context.[58] His aim was practical, and not methodological in theoretical terms. One may say that Montesquieu took part of the socio-political discourse, and he recognized his audience, even if he tried to universalize his basic arguments. In the end, one may claim that the idea of the autonomy of socio-legal systems he proposed created possibilities for fruitful receptions, and that he did not try to discourage this from happening.[59]

One may understand the nature of Montesquieu's approach also from the point of view of the comparative law discourse prevailing during this time. During his time, there was no systematic comparative law discourse in place. There was thus no real comparative law audience for Montesquieu. The audience was the political audience of a particular political system. Every use of comparative argument was instrumental in the sense that other legal systems represented a legitimate argument and even a legitimate model. This is why, one could claim, he did not see comparative law as a method, but as a practical argument. It is noteworthy that attempts to construct comparative law theory from the *Spirit of Law's* remain usually references to dispersed remarks by Montesquieu.

Consequently, Montesquieu's idea was to argue for the universality of the doctrine of the separation of powers in a particular context. To be able to do this comparatively, he had to maintain the existence of disparate systems. He started from the relativization of political systems as "natural", socio-anthropological and fundamentally political nations[60], and relativized in this way the legitimation on which the <u>existing</u> political systems were based. In this way he was able to use comparative argument. This should be remembered in the modern comparative law. By relativizing social systems in general, he made it possible to argue comparatively for a fundamental political change. Consequently, he saw systems as being "culturally" different but politically alike.[61]

---

[58] See, Cohler, A.M., 1989, p. xxiii, Montesquieu, 1989, 6.30.1 ff.\6 31.1 ff.. He clearly took part, in the final analysis, in fundamental discussions of that time.

[59] See, for example, Hug, P , 1932, p.1050.

[60] Montesquieu, 1989, I.1.3.

[61] Montesquieu maintains. ". *..some have thought that government by one alone is most in conformity with nature But, the example of paternal power proves nothing... it is better to say that the government most in conformity with nature is the one whose particular arrangement is best related to the disposition of the people for whom it is established"* (Montesquieu, 1989, I,1,3) (see, interpretation, Cohler, A.M., 1989, footnote q, p.8). (compare, Bodin, J., 1955b)
In his analysis of Bodin's *Republic*, McRae, K.D. (1979, p.A 22) makes the following remark:

In this way Montesquieu dispensed with prevailing religious and historical methods of argumentation.[62] It was possible for him to neglect the natural and universal legitimation of the existing paradigm and to challenge it as being static vertical (ideal), horizontal (historical), and "natural" political construction of that time.[63] This way, one could claim, he attempted to maintain the discursive integrity of the prevailing particular political discourse; one in which people were no longer convinced of the merits of "descending power". Whereas Aristotle saw comparability as being based on the uniqueness of the Greek city states and their ethnological essence, Machiavelli on the power of the ruler, and Bodin, ultimately, relied on the idea of plurality of religions, Montesquieu established the basis for comparability and the possibility of reciprocal discourse upon the universalist model of government in relation to the sociological and political essence of a nation and its individual people[64].

Montesquieu taught us an important lesson concerning comparative reasoning. In its "sociological" form, comparative reasoning makes it possible to maintain the internal political discourse of a particular social system, while simultaneously avoiding the problem of considering the specific political system under review as the only one which should prevail. This way Montesquieu aimed at a more open form of government.

It has been claimed that the elements defined by Montesquieu have lost to a certain extent their relevance, and that political and structural factors have gained importance in the legal

---

"*Bodin did not systematically relate the theory of climate to his theory of sovereignty and his classification of states, but its impact on this part of his thought may be clearly seen. The theory of climate served as a strong conservative force, depriving his political theory of its otherwise revolutionary implications. Bodin had a strong preference for the monarchical form of government, but he did not advocate its indiscriminate export The best form absolutely is not necessarily the best form for particular situations, and some people were plainly unfitted for a constitution on the French model. The whole tenor of the theory of climate was to justify existing forms of government, to promote broad tolerance for the world as it is, and to cast doubt upon the wisdom of deliberate political change.* [underlining author's] (ibid., p.A23 relating Bodin to Burke).*

[62] Comparative argumentation appears, in his work, as an alternative to this type of argumentation.

[63] Montesquieu, 1989, I.1.1., especially, p.4. He maintains that "*god has called him [man] back to him by the laws of religion. Such a being could at any moment forget himself. Philosophers have reminded him of himself by the laws of morality. Made for living in society, he could forget his fellows; legislators have returned him to his duties by political and civil laws*" (I.1.1.).
On the 'vertical' and 'horizontal' in this sense, see Zweigert, K., Kötz, H., 1977, p 8.

[64] See Montesquieu, 1989, I.1.3.
One should make the following comment. The idea of 'nation' for Montesquieu seems to be an idealized concept. This means that the nation and the differences between nations seem to refer to differences in how persons in different area and social communities see their possibilities, probabilities, and how and in what form they want to increase these opportunities. The different concepts and criteria of Montesquieu for distinguishing nations may be seen as the basic concepts of reflection, by which certain groups of people regulate their opportunities.

discourse[65]. However, one could maintain that, within traditional comparative law research, these elements maintain their role as important methodological premises.

2.2. Modern comparative law

The 19th century comparative law began to apply emerging system-concepts to different models of legal practice and to make distinctions, within law, philosophy and natural sciences, between different systems. This was due especially to the emerging of organismic theories of law and nationhood, and the step from rationalism towards romanticism[66].

Increasing interest in comparative law arose, in the second half of the century, in many countries in the western world[67]. Also, in some countries such as Japan an interest in European legal thought increased.[68] Modern comparative law took shape, in European countries, once a systematic study of legal systems emerged.

It has been claimed that 19th century comparative law had mainly role in the field of criminal, procedural, patent, and copyright law.[69]

19th century comparative law had two basic features. Firstly, comparative law had gained a relatively independent status as a methodology and science[70], and, secondly, the task of comparison was to construct, scientifically, common rules at the international level.[71] On the other hand, typical of this modern period was the increasing focus upon practicality of comparative law, even if a separate tendency seemed to be also the study of "system of

---

[65] This may be related to the fact that the state paradigm has concentrated more upon the politization and legalization of the concept of nation than upon its empirical and discursive nature.

For the state paradigm of law, see Raz, J., 1971, p.811 ff. He is interpreting, however, Kelsen's legal theory quite narrowly and seems to miss its "liberative" aspects (ibid., p.813, and n. 36).

[66] For a characterization of comparative law during this period in general, see Hug, P , 1932, pp.1069-1070.

One may claim that the distinction between mechanical and organic transplantations was a result of the development of the natural sciences. Before this, legal discourse was understood in a very practical way

One may say that this the period was characterized by a move from the modern to the modernist.

[67] Hug, P , 1932, p.1053.

[68] See, Igarashi, K.,, 1977, pp. 36-42

[69] Kropholler, J., 1992, p.702.

[70] One of the leading figures in this development was Anselm von Feuerbach. He was a strong "Kantian" rationalist, but emphasized the importance of empirical studies, and, for example, the idea that comparative studies must be guided by the philosophical method of jurisprudence (see, with direct references, Hug, P , 1932, p 1054, Constantinesco, J-L., 1971, p.97 ff.)

On the independence of comparative law, see Ancel, M , 1978, p.350, and de Gruz, P , 1993, p.1

[71] For the factual development in this respect, see Schmitthoff, M., 1941, p.109.

systems" in the realm of culturally and politically defined comparative law.[72] The focus of the latter idea seemed to be related to the "common origins'" approach.

Textual interpretation was the basic method of scholarships. This may be associated with the strong status granted to legislation as a source of law. As maintained above, the law was legislation, and comparative law, consequently, the comparison of legislation. The great codifications in Europe, from the 17th century on, had established the basis for the nationalization of law and for practical national legal science including comparative legal science.

The emphasis upon the idea of the independence of comparative law seemed to become stronger towards the beginning of the 19th century.[73] The "autonomy" was possible because of the recent codifications, especially in the field of private law[74]. Furthermore, comparative law became more "formalistic".[75] Its systematic features were stressed. The notion of its independence was to become related also to the fact that comparative law was well able to define its object, functions and methods in abstract. This generated the specialization of the comparative lawyer.[76]

In the 19th century one could, for the first time, also make the distinction between historical comparative law, which studied systems which had since, disappeared, and the study of living systems. Distinctions such as "ethnological"[77], "historical", "systematic", and "dogmatic" approaches to law were also introduced.[78] The general approach seemed to be interested in the practical and instrumental value of comparative law.[79]

One may assert that comparative law already occupied a central place in the European legal discourse in the pre-nationalistic period.[80] The highpoint of modern comparative law was unequivocally, however, at the beginning of 20th century, when the legal identity of the nationalistic systems seemed to be strongest. Comparative law appeared to be combined with this "construction" of legal identity and its interpretation. The identity comprised also forms

---

[72] The distinctions in comparative law have been based on different ideologies of the legal systems (David, R., 1950). This seems to be the reason for the difference between the common law and continental law being considered only as comprising a difference in technique.

[73] Lambert, È, 1978, p.36.

[74] The "independence" of a discipline has to do with the specific interests involved, which direct the research (see, Rotondi, M., 1973)

[75] One could say that the lack of codifications in the Anglo-Saxon world generated a more practical idea of comparative law.

[76] See also, Schlesinger, R.B., 1995, pp.479-480 on specialization and institutionalization.

[77] For example, Kohler, Sailles, R., Lambert, È. (See, Constantinesco, J-L., 1971, p.145 ff).

[78] Rabel, E., 1978.

[79] Lambert, È, 1978, p.44.

[80] For comparable development in the United States.

of "groupings"[81].

What else happened in 19th century law? The coherence of law based on the Roman tradition was dissolved, and European law at least came to be influenced by positivist pluralism.[82] The methodology of comparative law concentrated on the idea of the *tertium comparationis*. In the end, ultimate positivization seems to have caused the degradation of empirical research.[83] In the 20th century comparative law, at least in the first half of the century, has considered its methodological issues mainly in the context of private law[84]. One began also, from the beginning of the century onwards, to stress the economic and historical closeness of nation states, although sensitive points at the ideological and theoretical (philosophical) levels remained. This applied also to institutionalized comparative law.[85]

The breakthrough in system relationships took place after the second world war. "Universalist" concepts were introduced to the European states, and the inter-relationship of systems was build up on a supranational basis. All the same, legal discourse remained a matter for particular legal systems. National systems seemed to remain domestic in their focus and concern. It has been maintained that comparative law helped in getting rid of this national insularity, and served the practical purpose of assisting in the construction of, for example, new constitutions. This opening-up seemed to be, however, fairly temporary.[86]

The 'European' legal level was, during this era, designed as a system with a subsidiary character. Legal systemic relationships were established by semi-political considerations (i.e. ECHR), or the relationship was regulated by advisory systems (EEC). The universalist legal discourse remained, nevertheless, as a minor issue. On the other hand, the points of contact between legal systems were considered to be, necessarily, points in need of legal regulation, and "voluntary" legal consideration of other systems´ solutions seemed to remain as a specific matter for isolated comparative law professionals.

One could assert that 20th century comparative law was a direct descendent of the culturally "nationalistic" approach, and that it even went beyond. Cultural differences between legal systems were seen to be increasingly self-evident. However, some innovations during this

---

[81] Lambert, for example, made a distinction between *"groupe latin"*, *"groupe germanique"*, *"groupe anglosaxon"*, *groupe musulman"*, and *"groupe slav"*. On different "static" groupings, see Bogdan, M., 1990, p.82. On the centrality of the comparison to anglosaxon law in France, Zajtay, I., 1981, p.597.

[82] On this, see Zimmermann, R., 1995.

[83] Markesinis, B., 1990, p.20, Heldrich, A., 1970, p.441.

[84] Kropholler, J., 1992, p.702

[85] For some analysis see Constantinesco, J-L., 1971, p.159 ff.. For an example, see David, R., Brierly, J.E.C., 1978, p.16, stressing the idea of the *"experience of all nations"*. As Schmitthoff, M. (1941, p.103) maintains *"the parallelism of the reorganization of the international society and the revival of Comparative law found their visible expression in the constitution of the International Institute for the Unification of Private Law in Rome, which works under the direction of the League of Nations"* However, on the reality of the comparative law function, see Gutteridge, H.C., 1944, pp.6-7.

[86] Zagrebelsky, G., 1980, pp.89-116.

century render it different from the previous periods[87].

Contemporary comparative law reflects the basic features of 20th century globalization, economic, social, and cultural assimilation, and political differentiation.[88] Furthermore, the concept of what comprises a 'legal system' has become central. It has also been claimed that increase in capitalist production and economic activity, which served to break down national boundaries, changed the "aims" of comparative law. Comparative law became a matter for lawyers dealing with these questions.[89]

It has been contended that the interest in the peculiarities of each legal system, which had already emerged by the 19th century, had been replaced in the middle of 20th century by the interest in unified comparative law.[90]

After the second world war, the connection between comparative law and "transnational" doctrines was established. One may say that in the post-war period, there had been an increasing interest in transnationality in the realm of "universalized" legal principles.[91] "Transnationalism" was seen as the raw material from which "diffusions" or "distillations" were made to different legal systems as "general" law[92]. Transnational adjudication and legislation in the field of public law developed accordingly.

Consequently, one of the functions of comparative law in the 20th century has been the coordination function. This is especially the case in the regulation of private transactions (private law) and economic activities, in the coordination of macroeconomic aspects, and in the clarifying of the idea of the separation of powers[93]. The first area has been instrumentalized by international legal practice.

Scientifically, on the other hand, comparative law has, in theory, oriented itself towards sociological comparison, adopting a qualitative approach.[94] However, attempts to resolve its

---

[87] 20th century comparative law, see Zweigert, K., Kötz, H., 1977, pp.52-56, Zajtay, I., 1981, p.598 ff.

[88] Kahn-Freund, O., 1974, p.8. The latter idea may be contested in contemporary global development Some analysis, Capelletti, M., 1973, pp.74-75 On Globalization and comparative law, see Riles, A, 1999

[89] Peterí, Z., 1974, p.46, Ancel, M., 1971. See also, Zweigert, K., Kötz, H., 1977, pp.52-56
This is also due to the increasing importance of economic efficiency and integrated economic markets, which neglect the analytical approach, and which stress the relevance of the examination of the economic context of law and legal systems in comparative law

[90] Gorla, G., 1982, p.130. On transnationalization, Schlesinger, R B., 1995, p.479.

[91] Capelletti, M., 1989, p.119 ff
Contemporary legal positivism has been claimed to be a synthesis, with higher supranational principles connected to ordinary legislation (ibid., pp 130-132).
After the second World War, there is the phenomenon of an emergence of new principles, and also the positivization of principles. Consequently, courts started to apply different principles within different forms of judicial review (ibid., p 118).

[92] Mádl, F., 1978, pp.6-7, 35-40 (referring to Langen, E., Transnational commercial law (Leiden) 1973)
The idea of transnational private law was considered to be a central idea to the "socialist" comparative law, whereas the principle orientation may be seen more central to the western scholarship

[93] "Koordinierungsaufgabe", see Buxbaum, R.M., 1996, p.213.

[94] Buxbaum, R M , 1996, pp.222-223, Capelletti, M., 1973, p.68.

internal philosophical problems still appear in the discussion[95].

On the other hand, the internationalization and regionalisation of law has facilitated the use of comparative law also in the implementation of international and regional rules and its control.[96]

Post-wars comparative law reflected, from the outset, the "cold war" distinctions. Generally, these distinctions had highly political flavour[97]. Distinctions such as socialist countries/western democracies and developed/developing legal systems were the basic distinctions in the comparative law of this period.[98]

The idea of families-of-law was the main connecting factor, and the history and individual system structures came under close scrutiny[99]. Nevertheless, in the context of this development, comparative law gained greater practical significance due to the globalization of world markets and the emerging liberal economy in the west. Comparative law started to be connected, instead, to different branches of law[100].

It could be claimed that one of the major causes for the decline of the traditional comparative law approach and the confusion in the 1990's was due to the fact that some self-evident and fundamental categories of comparative law, such as the socialist group[101], disappeared. This revealed these categories' "political" nature. At the same time, after the second world war, the actors in European legal systems and European legal orders were directing their attention strongly towards the United States. During the latter part of the 20th century, European law

---

[95] Buxbaum, R.M., 1996, p.224.

[96] Buxbaum, R.M., 1996, pp.226-227.

[97] Kahn-Freund, O., has claimed that the "political factors gained importance in Montesquieu's strategy" (1974, p 9)

[98] See, Zweigert, K. Kötz. H., 1987, p.37, and Hazard, J.N., 1973, p.362.
On the development of the distinction between the socialist and non-socialist law, see Eörsi, G., 1973, pp 183-184 In United States, Hazard, J N., 1973, pp.360-361 The "iron curtain" in the field private law, see Schlesinger, R.B., 1968, p 67. The role of the socialist/non-socialist distinction, Tunc, A., 1964, p 285, 294. Some analysis on the comparability, Sacco, R , 1991, pp 5-6, and on Marxist theory, Klami, H.T., 1981, p.134 ff

[99] Lambert, É., 1978
The idea was that structural differences (sources of law etc.) deepened the identity of these systems (idem.). For a contemporary discussion, see Interpreting Statutes (Dartmouth)1991.

[100] Ancel, M., 1978, p.357. See also Ajani, G., 1995.

[101] See Zweigert, K, Kötz, H. (1977, p.16) who maintained in a perceptive way that "As the threat of war recedes, the relations between capitalist and socialist countries will become much closer and their ideological differences will probably diminish". This shows, nonetheless, how greatly the distinction between them was political.
On the other hand, the argument seems to assume the existence of a universal system of law, from which the "socialist" system was merely a deviation This idea seems to be related to a "non-empirical", logical, and categorical idea of comparative law. It also assumes a development of legal systems toward a more sophisticated, harmonized, and unified system of law However, in this system of law "environment.. social justice . These problems cannot be solved by any one state in isolation" (ibid , p.16). Finally, however, the state seems to be the basic category for analysis ".. they call for full cooperation of all state and people", idem.) Consequently, the idea of Zweigert and Kötz is "Bodanian"; i.e the idea that the study of comparative law would guarantee a more universal concept of law (see also, ibid., p.17)

has been clearly influenced by its relationship to United States (and vice versa).[102] The reasons for this may be numerous. One form of this influence has been the transplantation of American models to the European legal thinking (and systems) in a highly value-based manner.[103] This development was related to the inter-penetration of different forms of language, but it had also the jurisprudential and educational dimension.[104]

Internationalization has also generated the need for understanding of the global circumstances and international contexts of the application of law.[105] This has caused the revival of traditional comparative law. Comparative law has established itself once again as a practical measure.[106]

However, whereas the 19th century tendency was towards unification, the 20th century strategy seems to be instead the harmonization of law.[107] In this sense, relativism has entered into comparative law thinking. This has also been described as the "realism" of comparative law[108].

After the First World War, comparative law was "institutionalized" within various forms of international legal cooperation.[109] Comparative law, which was already ensconced in a scientific crisis, was adapted also to different legal institutions as a means of legitimation[110]. After the two world wars, global peace was to have been established by organizational cooperation between states, and this meant, to certain extent, and for a period of time, a step away from the legislative formalism and a move towards more substantive approach to comparative law.[111] This reflects the 20th century's so-called "state-centric universalism".

---

[102] The German constitutionalist influences in Europe (Koopmans, T., 1991, p 494) can also be seen as an indirect adoption of American constitutionalism in Europe.

[103] Pugliese, G., 1978, pp.100-101.

[104] Wiegand, W., 1991, pp.232-235. For some conceptual and "legal institutional" examples, see ibid., p.236 ff.

[105] On this, see Riles, A., 1999, 222 ff.

[106] De Groot, G-R., Schneider, A, 1994, p.53.
 For the discussion, in France, on the need for comparative research in practice, see Flécheux, G , Israël, J-J, 1996, p.319 ff., 325 ff.

[107] Winterton, G., 1975, pp 76-77 For the harmonization and unification of comparative law see Schlesinger, R.B., 1980, p.33
 Mouly, Ch. (1985, p.896 ff) has suggested three conceptions of European unification (integration) The first is the legislative one, which was the conception of the past century The second is the practical and educational conception, and it is more based on sociological analysis The third seems to be related to the (romantic?) revival of *ius commune* The fourth seems to be based on integration driven by some type of rational and discursive community.

[108] Capelletti, M., 1973, pp.74-75.
 It has been maintained that contemporary comparative law is, and should be, more realistic (ibid , pp.72-73).
 This realism has certain peculiar characteristics. Namely, for contemporary comparative law "closes" the systems with greater ease in order to be able to use them as legal arguments (for some discussion, see Ancel, M , 1973, p.5)

[109] Like *Société des Nations*, see Ancel, M., 1968, p.354. In Japan, see Igarashi, K , 1977.

[110] The "institutionalization" of comparative law may have been a result of the fact that comparative law was incapable of resolving the problems of legal cooperation prevalent at the beginning of the century

[111] Ancel, M., 1968, p.355

Recent changes within contemporary Europe have created an enormous enthusiasm for the trans-national and institutional transplantation of law. Many systematic and theoretical concerns have been supplanted by economic pragmatism, and eclecticism can therefore be seen. This applies not only to legislation, but also to adjudication and to legal training and education.[112]These types of transplants are ultimate examples of the pragmatism in contemporary comparative law[113].

Taken together, the tendency within the postwar period has been to shift from the inter-state character of comparative law toward the more pragmatic comparative law of international organizations. International organizations identify their competencies and norms based on comparative observations. Comparative law is used in the formation, formulation, interpretation, and application of norms. The international, even global, audience has to be convinced on comparative basis.

Comparative law has become in many ways, also in the sphere of education, a matter for institutions. This has moved the discussion on comparative law toward the institutional functioning of law.

From the scientific point of view, one could claim that during the 20th century sociological aspects remained only as declarations of the emerging theories of comparative law. More sociologically oriented approaches to law took the place of scientific comparative law[114].

2.3. Conclusions

It is unsurprising, that the works of all great comparativists were based on their own

---

[112] Ajani, G , 1995, pp.107-112. This transplantation has been encouraged, for example, by the European Community association agreements, and by different western countries, such as the USA, in the form of international commercial agreements. This can be called legally regulated transplantation. The so-called "specialist" transplantation, drafting of "western types of constitutions", is also a contemporary phenomenon (see, Venice Commission Bulletin on Constitutional Case Law, edition 3 (Council of Europe) 1994.

[113] We may recognize two tendencies in contemporary "applied comparative law". First of all, there is a tendency toward extreme pragmatism in the use of comparative law Secondly, this pragmatism is seen within the dynamic political changes in contemporary legal systems. Pragmatic comparative law is an instrument for the stabilization of dramatic political changes

[114] Consequently, contemporary comparative law has been obliged to consider sociology only as a "supplementary" part of comparative law. It is part of comparative law doctrine, but it does not have a real and essential application in it. Instead of following its methodological conclusions, comparative law has been institutionalized. It has become a matter of expertise, and a matter of restricted juridical thinking rather than a complete and applied method of law.
In this sense, contemporary comparative law cannot be identified as an adequate legal science, but as a practical form of argument within a legal discourse, a technique of law (See Capelletti, M., 1973, p.63).
The lack of a social dimension within contemporary comparative law makes comparative law a phenomenological legal argument rather than a scientific one.
For the evolution of legal systems and the role of comparative law from the point of view of contemporary French legal discussion, see Agostini, E., 1988.

experiences in foreign countries.[115] One could call this the phenomenological dimension of comparative law. It could be said that comparative law is bound to the experiences of individuals and that it is strongly inspirational.[116] On the other hand, these experiences were instrumentalized for practical purposes according to changing circumstances. All periods were characterized by revolutionary changes within legal and political life[117].

This is one of the most interesting features of comparative law. Namely, one could predict that the systematic study of other legal systems would be the most fruitful starting point for a comparative legal studies. However, the need to write about these observations arises from the fact that there is something in this individual experience which does not accord as such with previous experiences, as is the case in all social discourses.

The history of comparative law may be roughly divided into different cultural and political periods. These different "periods", on the other hand, correspond to unifying and separatist tendencies within these societies[118].

Comparative argument is often used in the context of political theory. It seems to be related to the justification of fundamental changes within the basic cultural system. It has to do with situations where internal arguments are somehow problematic from the point of view of societal communication[119]. This seems to be the basic feature of all comparative political theories.

This may be seen in all early approaches. One could claim that by providing observations upon several systems and combining them in the concept of constitution, Aristotle, for example, managed to create convincing arguments for the establishment of the constitutional tradition. This was in accordance with his general philosophy on the "middle road". On the other hand, Machiavelli followed the Aristotelian tradition, but towards the opposite conclusion. He advised the ruler to maintain disparities in order to be able to retain power.

---

[115] On this, see Jamieson, M., 1996, p.1

[116] It has been maintained that the "intuitive" model of comparative law cannot be called comparative law, Bogdan, M., 1990, p.27, Kamba, E.J., 1974.

[117] It seems that all the great comparativists worked in a context of disappearing social forms of life. It appeared as if they all were facing the decline of the traditional forms of legal order and social system. They saw comparative observations as essential for its conservation.
On this and the dialectical method, see Terrill, R.J., 1981, p.178.

[118] Hill, J , 1989, pp.109-111, referring for example to Schmitthoff, M., 1941, p.103, Bedwell, The Present value of Comparative Jurisprudence. In 29 Yale Law Journal, 1919, pp.512-515, Gutteridge, H.C., The Value of Comparative law, 1931, JSPTL, p.26, and . As a concrete program, Hazard, J.N., 1951, p.273.

[119] As it has been shown, comparative "law" is a way to challenge and reexamine the very basic premises of positive law. It functions in a process, whereby the basic presumptions of forms of government etc., are considered anew. On the other hand, it reproduces these forms and basic assumptions in another, and perhaps, more developed form. It is strongly connected, in its contemporary form, to the reexamination of institutional arrangements.
In its argumentative form, it challenges traditions of positive legal thinking. These features are balanced by legal theoretical devices.
One could claim, however, that comparative law and comparative observations, and their use as arguments in political philosophy, are often part of "realist" political theory, as opposed to political philosophical speculation.

However, in both approaches, one did not consider it important to stress any autonomous features of the system; the main interest was instead the effective and "good" way of using power. Any argument on substance would have decreased argument's persuasive power.

Bodin, on the other hand, following Aristotle put, to a large extent, emphasis on the idea of consensus. He stressed the importance of the balance between the contending powers of that time, both of which related to religious movements. In the beginning, he attempted to derive arguments from examination of laws, but in the end he understood the fundamental problems behind "legal disputes" and turned to the general legal themes of political philosophy[120]. Finally, he stressed the importance of dialogue between the religions and emphasized different moral ideals.

Whereas Bodin stressed, ultimately, the comparability of religions in a highly dynamic sense, Montesquieu saw the problem in the use of sovereign power in general. Unlike Bodin, he established (historically, and from the point of view of the normative sciences) a strong "natural" division between nations and their laws, and yet tried to maintain the dynamics of political discourse.

Modern comparative law has also changed according to political-social circumstances. Whereas early modern comparative law stressed the "similarity" of problems and solutions despite the differences in method[121], post war comparative law was characterized, quite evidently, by solutions in different political contexts vis-à-vis Eastern and Western legal systems.[122] The similarities and differences depended upon by different political factors.[123] Inside these different "comparative legal cultures", further distinctions were considered to be minor importance or as matters of "styles".[124] Perhaps the motive behind this was that further analysis would have required a detailed grasp of the application of individual rules and norms.[125]

The history of comparative law can be also characterized by categorizations of the *tertium comparationis*. This gives an indication of different "periods" of comparative law.

Early comparative law was determined by the distinction between natives and barbarians. It also expressed the supremacy of a system as a traditional form of government. On the other

---

[120] McRae, K.D., 1979.

[121] See Hill, J., 1989, p.107, Zweigert, K., 1966, p.17, David, R., Brierly, J.E.C., 1978.

[122] An example of this may be seen in the critical evaluation of the Zweigert, K , Kötz, H., 1987 by Hill, J (1989, p 108). He maintains that *"The Soviet legal system, for example, as a result of its ideological bases, faces the 'problem' of how to prevent citizens from acquiring unearned income through the purchase and resale of consumer goods at a profit"*.

[123] Zweigert, K., Kötz, H., 1987, p.48.

[124] For example, Hill, J., 1989, p.108. For post-war ideas of culture, see Schweisfurth, T., Cultural and Ideological Pluralism and Contemporary Public International Law. In: Reports on German Public Law and Public International law to XIIth International Congress of Comparative law (Heidelberg) 1986 (169-182). There is no clear definition of culture and ideology in contemporary public international law. It seems to be a pre-legal fact (ibid., p.179) related to peaceful coexistence of nations (ibid., p.180).

[125] Zweigert, K., Kötz, H., 1987, p.36. Some criticism, Hill, J , 1989, p.109

hand (for Machiavelli, for example) all socio-legal systems were utilizable in the same way, and, accordingly, comparable. Nevertheless, in all these types of comparisons, the common factor was their "internal" systematic point of view with regard to the issue of *tertium comparationis*. This "Romanist" perspective remained strong for centuries.

For Bodin, systems were comparable based on the theory of climate, and for Montesquieu as national "legal, climatic, and socio-cultural systems". These types of ideas expanded thought concerning *tertium comparationis* towards more sociological and universally oriented (non-historical) forms of *tertium comparationis*.

Western "modern" law has, however, over the centuries, defined its *tertium comparationis* by reference to Roman law. The break in this tradition has produced several "alternative" ideas on comparative law, and has resulted distinctions, such as the distinctions between continental and common law, socialist and liberal systems etc.[126] At the moment the fundamental distinctions seem to be related to institutionalized constitutional traditions, and also to different conceptions of democracy. The European legal systems seem to be comparable, within the institutional framework, as constitutional legal systems with their "own traditions".

Different ideas on comparability have also been determined by the different conceptions of dynamics and statics. These aspects have also been related ultimately to explanations of the acceptability of comparative observations.

Contemporary (modern) comparative law is problem-oriented in a quite peculiar sense. The *tertium comparationis* is the problem in itself. This is why, in contemporary comparative law, one is dealing with legal institutional solutions[127]. Modern comparative law is "functional" and "instrumental" in nature[128]. On the other hand, in contemporary "highmodern" comparative law, one may speak about distinctions such as professional, cultural and scientific comparative law.

Within the history of comparative law, on the other hand, one can identify a change away from practical discursiveness (natural law-oriented) toward the more positivist, system-oriented discourses.[129] In its ultimate sense, one may speak about institutional discursiveness.

This fact has caused many problems for the interpretation of the history of comparative law. One could claim that in the interpretation of the early classic and medieval writers, and even Montesquieu, one should stress the practical application rather than the systematic features of modern law. It was only during 19th century developments that autonomy of a legal system began to be recognized. This may have, on the other hand, generated contemporary ideas of

---

[126] The latter distinction has also been seen as a distinction between the planned economy and market economy, Bogdan, M., 1990, p.61. The function of this distinction, see ibid., p.64.
[127] Capelletti, M., 1990a, p.6, by referring to the impact of Merryman's thought on these ideas.
[128] Zweigert, K., 1972, p.465, and Pizzorusso, A., 1987, p.79.
[129] Capelletti, M., 1973, p.72.

critical comparison as a counter-reaction[130].

One may identify from this short description of the history of comparative law how legal systems and their rules have been used as arguments for some kind of "identity" of systems. This identity argumentation seems to be based on static presumptions concerning city states, civilization, "legitimacy" (or "rightness") of power, religion, natural law, nation, ethnicity, and, in the end, on the relative stability of positive and formal legal systems, legal rule, and legal institutional arrangements.

These presumptions concerning identities of law have enabled the dynamic use of comparative observations as an argument in legal discourse. The aim has been, as it has been maintained, to prove the existence of constitutions, the "goodness" of one system, different types of sovereign power(s), the existence of common norms, the superiority or uniqueness of a particular legal system, and, as in contemporary discourse, the relative autonomy and sovereignty of legal cultures, particular fields of law and, finally, the institutions and norms of supranational regional systems.[131]

On the other hand, it could be claimed that the increasing discussion concerning the methodological aspects of comparative law is related to the instability and unclear premises of law given the role of different "nonlegal" discourses to law in the 20th century[132]. The independence of comparative law was seen to guarantee the legitimacy of a situation, where legal systems clearly lacked a coherent idea of law. Methodological speculations were reflections of "modernist" ideals of law[133]. It could be argued that comparative law reflected a "crisis" within law, where an attempt was made to solve so-called "hard cases"[134].

In conclusion, one may say that the role of comparative law, within the history of law could be analysed in tandem with ideas concerning the role of natural law in the development of law:

".. it slings between the revolutionary and conservative function. While institutions are still stable and not too incongruous with existing demands, natural law tends to be found bolstering up the status quo. As the institutional status quo becomes increasingly incongruous with the changed economic, cultural and social conditions, this law

---

[130] Capelletti, M., 1973, pp.71-72.

[131] Even if one may claim that there are certain "phenomenological features" in each of the works mentioned above, there are many differences between them. It could be maintained that, from the point of view of contemporary ideas of law, Aristotle is a "dogmatic" comparativist, whereas Machiavelli, for example, seems to be more a "phenomenologist". Bodin can be placed more close to Aristotle. Montesquieu seems to be more a political sociologist and an empiricist.

[132] What one have faced during the last 30 years, and may be seeing increasingly in the near future, is the decline of the traditional political and democratic state and its deregulation, the decline of the political party system at national levels, increasing localization, European centralization, increasing corporativism, increasing governmental regulation, and the development of closed processes of rule-making and interpretation.

[133] Some seem to suggest that the modernist era has ended in the sense that there is a tendency to turn to a polycentric (international) law. One has failed in the modern (modernist?) reconstruction of institutional structures (Koskenniemi, M., 1997, pp.337-338).

[134] The history of comparative law is a history of legal identity; a history of legal systems.

may become a revolutionary instrument for challenging and demoralizing existing institutions"[135]

However, comparative law has had ultimately conservative function, and its revolutionary tendencies can be seen mainly in the substantial changes which have occurred in the interpretations of existing systems and institutions. In this sense, it can be called positivized natural law.

In modern comparative law, the conservative and revolutionary functions seem to coexist and to have some parallel functions. Comparative law may support the idea of the relative rationality of the systemic innovations under consideration, but many support also the up-holding (self-maintenance) of existing structures. Consequently, when at the beginning of the century states searched for their legal identities, now the state and supranational systems search for their procedural- and rule-identities. This process applies also to the segmented systems of law of post-industrial cultures.[136]

This is why the nature of comparative law has to be studied in the context of the discourse theory of law and theories concerning the sources of law.

3. TO THE IDEA OF COMPARATIVE LEGAL REASONING

3.1. Introduction

Many views on the best methods of comparative research and optimal usages of comparative observations can be found within the tradition and history of the comparative law discourse as well as in the contemporary discussions on comparative law theory.

Here the purpose is not to go critically into the details of these types of structures and functions of comparative law identified in contemporary comparative law theory within modern institutionalized comparative law. However, the idea is to present some conclusions of this type of examination and some ideas on the comparative legal discourse and comparative legal reasoning for the context of the empirical study.[137]

---

[135] Stone, J., 1968, chapter 2. See also Weber, M., 1969, p.288, Graveson, R.H., 1958, p.652. Furthermore, Hill, J., 1989, p.103 referring to the Roman *ius gentium*, "applied to all nations" One could see a direct link between the *ius gentium, ius naturale* and general principles of all nations (idem.). On natural law and comparative law, see Klami, H.T., 1997.
[136] Concerning "segmentation", see Weber, M, 1969, pp.301-303.
[137] For more details, See Kiikeri, M., 1999, pp. 97-154.

3.2. Traditional approach

Traditional comparative law examines contemporary forms of legitimation in law and legal systems. It tries to reveal the structure and functions of law in different societies, and seems to be able to deduce legal dogmatics from it, to a certain extent.

Ultimately, one can observe positive law and conceptual underpinnings of one system on the basis of the "law" of another system. Furthermore, one can, and one usually does, reveal the customs of the one's own system in the process of selection and choosing customs, institutions, concepts, and structures from the other systems. All discovered elements can be used in argumentation within the "internal" discourse.[138]

As it has been maintained, comparative legal research parallels every discipline, and can contribute concepts and ideas to the legal discourse. In this sense, it is part of legal systematization. It opens up systemic possibilities for the legal discourse. It brings legal arguments to the legal discourse of a system.[139] The more analytical, the better.

In this sense, comparative law seems to be the purest form of empirical <u>legal</u> research in general. Basically, it is not bound to practicality in any "normative sense", apart from its attachment to a political theory. Furthermore, it departs from the idea of social sciences in many ways.

On the other hand, comparative law research, if done properly, is burdensome, as it requires much time and dedication. It is linguistically and methodologically problematic, and irritating because of "cultural" barriers.[140] This is why comparative law has problems being "living comparative law", and why it tends to be only a professional matter, an issue for those who are obliged to undertake it or who are dedicated to it. This, on the other hand, may lead to a relatively superficial and frivolous comparative law discourse. Comparative explanations appear in rather abstract forms. Moreover, the contemporary professionalization and institutionalization has caused strong "stereotypical" observations of foreign legal systems and legal "cultures". This seems to lead more to misunderstandings than to understanding.

Traditional comparative law seems to be based on a 'rationality' assumption of legal systems. It takes it as given that legal systems are a guarantee of the rationality of law[141].

---

[138] This is the phenomenological side of comparative law This dimension has been identified by the tradition of comparative law by "understanding" and "developing" one's own system.

[139] For the idea that comparative law is a source of arguments (dialectic), Kekkonen, J., Legal research in changing Europe. In: Oikeus, 1992, p.345.

[140] Frankenberg, G., 1985, p.420, see also, Teubner, G., Legal Irritants: good faith in British law or how unifying law ends up in new divergences. In: Modern Law review, 1998.

[141] The basic feature of modern comparative law is the closing up of legal systems and the reduction of existing complexity of socio-legal systems to simple, legal formalism (Frankenberg, G., 1985, p.437, Sacco, R., 1991, p.401, Legrand, P., 1996, p 59 ff.)
The closing up of systems in comparative law enables instrumental uses of the legal systems as arguments. In this sense, modern comparative law is based on a closed system conception On the other hand, the use of comparative observations

Contemporary comparative law has taken, to a certain extent, many system distinctions for granted. This has, it may be claimed, affected the emphasis of the research of comparative methodology and comparative legal cultures.[142]

In addition, the comparative law discourse, based on these cultural spheres, has, as an autonomous branch of law, fallen into an internal crisis as a discourse. This can be seen especially in the spheres of law, where development is fast[143]. On the other hand, attempts have been made to establish the authority of comparative law by a massive endeavor to discover the system of the systems, a cultural classification of legal systems as a cultural project. The result has been a kind of legal-cultural-political science[144], based on legal material, which is attached, on the other hand, to the basic structural characteristics of the traditional nation state.

At the same time, comparative law seems also to be bound to the general rationality assumption. It assumes a separate rationality of the comparative legal discourse.

Consequently, the role of comparative law has been, in the sphere of legal systems, that of an imaginary and independent "legal systematic discourse", in which different influences appear at the back of one's mind, or in which comparative observations may be used in extremely abstract way. One may say that the practical value of the systematic interaction has been hidden within a scientification of system relationships, which has resulted, on the other hand, in an internal rationality problem for comparative law. It has failed to establish its own authority as an authoritative source of inspiration.

In this work, the functions of comparative law are evaluated and described more thoroughly in connection with the study of institutionalized European law. One could claim that the legal function of comparative law appears there more clearly. The abstract description of the functions of comparative law remains more or less ritualistic, until the normative targets and aims are revealed.[145] This makes it seem also instrumental.

---

in open legal discourses may open these closed systems.

The clear problem of comparative law is its the inability to recognize different levels of conflicts between different socio-legal systems (Loussouarn, Y., 1981, p.134).

[142] Zweigert, K., Kötz, H. claims, however, that comparative law has not concentrated extensively upon its methodology (1977, p.24). This statement sounds quite odd given the contemporary context.

[143] It is not sufficient to say that comparative law should go to case law to find its practical importance, see Markesinis, P., 1990.

[144] For example, David, R., Brierly, J.E C., 1978

[145] Jamieson, M., 1996. This "*suits the pedantic frame of mind* (ibid.)

It is quite generally recognized that until it is claimed openly what one wants and what is the aim, one is, in a discourse, trapped in a ritualistic use of words and sentences. Every form of "translation" is based on this fact (ibid., p.124) For the view that comparative law is essentially instrumental, see Pizzorusso, A., 1987, pp.79-84.

3.3. Comparative law argument and comparative legal culture

It can be claimed that comparative law and recognition of other legal systems as analogical systems create possibilities for other types of analogies. Ultimately, these possibilities are "formative" ones (they form the legal system).

On the other hand, if the results of comparative law are presented as types of strict rules of (cultural) incomparability or comparability, the necessary nature of this distinction introduces a static dimension to the "cultural" sphere. The strict rules of incomparability and comparability create cultural obstacles, which might be later difficult to remove. In practice, they may become unavoidable distinctions in the legal and general cultural discourses (popular "stereotypes").

Accordingly, comparative law makes it possible to find not only traditional legal arguments, but also the legal quality of different types of arguments, which were previously not considered to be particularly relevant. On the other hand, in this way comparative law creates possibilities for making the distinction between legally relevant and irrelevant arguments and considerations.

"Culture"based comparative considerations, not really part of the systematic dimension of deductive decision-making in law, on the other hand, are "cognitive" approaches towards other systems. This generates an inspirational and sources-of-ideas type of phenomenon within the traditional processes of state legal systems. This is a peculiar means of opening up the legal and social environments of legal systems.

Consequently, there are basically two dimensions to consideration of the "inspirational" use of comparative law: the consideration as to how society is seen in general, and consideration of the norms of the legal system in general and in particular.[146]

In practice, however, the interest in comparative observations seems not always to be determined only by these above-mentioned dimensions. A comparativist may also be interested in developing her argumentative expertise in a particular or general scheme. This kind of "instrumentality" is a phenomenon occurring in many fields of legal practice, but especially in the scientific realm of comparative law. Furthermore, the phenomenon can be visible in different types of organizations involved in normative decision-making. Comparative considerations, even systematic ones, enable the decision-maker to reflect alternative possibilities (as alternative as they appear to him). As one may understand, these kinds of comparative considerations are, in many ways, hidden from the public and explicit legal discourse.

During decision-making and practical comparisons, normative choices of comparability are

---

[146] The process of comparative consideration seems to be inspirational. On the other hand, because it is determined by an "intuitive" sense of "cultural comparability", it can be claimed to be also a "reproductive" operation.

based on a legal-cultural and educational prior understanding, and comparability as such are hardly analysed. There is a claim to understanding in the choice of the compared. This is why one is able to reveal the basic cultural attitudes of the decision-maker.

In the decision-making context, the ultimate question seems to be the comparability of the institutional decision-makers. If a legal decision-maker considers certain "comparative" aspects, he is actually asserting the comparability of the decision-makers he is referring to. He is thereby claiming that the institution in another system, which has chosen certain normative premises as the relevant premise in certain situations, is comparable to it[147].

This nature of the decision-making comparison makes it an "institutional" argument, i.e. an argument based on the qualities of the chosen external reference rather than on reasonable factors. Here comparative reasoning becomes problematic. Basically, the argument should not be based on a choice of authority (or "self-authority"). It has to be rationally based. The decision-maker cannot rationally use its own choices as a basis and the premise of a legal decision[148].

As it has been maintained, the modern comparative law is based strongly upon the modern paradigm of positive state law[149]. However, comparative law is disconnected from the informal rules of a political and sociological nature because they cannot be generalized within the contemporary comparative law paradigm. Only a comparative approach which would not have as its basic distinction a distinction between (national) legal systems could be able to also compare the socio-legal subsystems of national legal systems[150]. On the other hand, if comparative law could function at the level of social sub- or supra-systems, it would challenge the basic state paradigm of comparative law.

The contemporary idea of comparative law moves on the level of values by putting itself above the legal discourse. Comparativists seem to make generalizations, whether within legal

---

[147] In this type of functionalist comparison, one claims comparability in many ways. The choice of a "comparable" argument is combined with the choice of a comparable decision-maker.

In non-decisionist comparisons, there is, naturally, also a claim of comparability, but the comparability is not claimed to exist between the comparativist and the actor whose (legal) acts are compared but between those several institution whose decisions are compared.

This establishes, for example, the relationship between national legislatures and supranational courts (as a matter of political integrity).

[148] A problem exists in the fact that in comparison, an institution interprets another institution, which it is basically incapable of doing. The decision-maker assumes that he understands that particular system perfectly. This way one comes to the demand that comparative reasoning has to be either systematically analytical or practically analytical in order to comprise a valid argument, i e. to be transformed from an intuitive choice to a reasonable choice, and to be discursive rather than "analogical".

[149] It has been claimed that the idea of comparative law, based on the state paradigm of law, can easily cause "optical illusions" (Sacco, R., 1991, pp.345-346). See Jescheck, H-H., 1974, p.772

All the same, one may say that a shift in the paradigm is taking place. The segmented "sub"systems of law may be treated separately and, on the other hand, some dynamics may become visible. This question, however, is treated after the analysis of the "European" material, which can perhaps shed light on certain questions.

[150] For "Extra-national bodies", see Davis, F., 1969, p.628.

institutions or in academic debate or scholarship, which are above any genuine jurisprudential discourse. Contemporary institutionalized comparative law has become an obstacle for a genuine form of legal discourse by closing it up. The problem of comparative law seems to be that it has lost sight of social distinctions, which are used in actual legal discourses in order to make distinctions between different cases, and in order to be to facilitate reasonable distinction-making. The analysis in traditional discourses is directed to the sources of law, interpretative techniques, etc., in a value-based manner. Contemporary comparative law cannot recognize these forms. It is thus blind to the analytical capacity of the actual (genuine) legal discourses.

On the other hand, even if comparative law practitioner (judges, for example) may take into account the dogmatic discourses and different political analyses (eg. travaux preparatoires) and other contextual material in their decision making, they would still have only a very restricted idea of the integrity of law. In using this type of comparative approach, they are not able to take part - genuinely - to any dogmatic discourse and do not really aim at any adherence of the dogmatic audiences.

In this sense, contemporary comparative law does not, in reality, aim at the preservation of the discursive integrity of law. On the contrary, It refers to the "social" without being able to refer to anything else but "substance".

On the other hand, institutionalized comparative law seems to be based on the premise that the reproduction of law takes place on the basis of an ideal comparative discourse. However, by neglecting the importance and in a sense by usurping the role of actual legal discourses, it actually functions in the opposite way.[151]

Consequently, one may ask; is comparative law really needed within the legal discourse?

One could formulate this question in another way. Should comparative law studies start to compare its premises (*tertium comparationis*) with the contemporary ideas appearing in the theories of legal discourses? This would mean, in practice, that institutionalized and instrumentalized comparative law could and should be compared with particular legal discourses. Consequently, through an examination of these means of using comparative law in modern law, one may be able to reveal the prevailing idea on rational audiences of law.

3.4. Comparative law as comparative legal reasoning

Critical movements in contemporary comparative law stress the failure of ethnological

---

[151] One may ask, whether this could be the basic, even intentional, strategy of contemporary comparative law? Is the primary idea of current comparative law theory to make distinctions between different audiences? Does the basic idea of comparative law refer to audiences, which are seen as basic and "rational' audiences within the legal discourse?

comparative law and its former distinctions in general[152]. This kind of "postmodern" criticism of traditional modern comparative law stems from the insistence upon a more theoretical, methodological and in the normative sense, ethical approach to comparative law. This criticism claims that comparative law has been too greatly relied upon "common sense".[153] This phenomenology of comparative law has attempted to grapple with those issues speaking of the metaphorizing of comparative law as "traveling", or by seeing it as a "learning process".[154]

The critical approach goes back to basics, and seems to neglect any systematic component of comparative law[155]. This may be a result of the frustration caused by the contemporary institutionalization of the law and comparative law. The critical approach recognizes the dynamics of this neo-institutional law, which the "normal" lawyer does not dare or bother to recognize so explicitly.[156]

One could say, consequently, that because the "modernist" comparative lawyer has gone beyond the traditional legal discourse, the integrity of law has to be maintained by a different type of discourse. This is the reason why contemporary comparative law must orient itself differently.

The critical approach to comparative law, especially in the terms of the political theory of

---

[152] Frankenberg, G., 1985, p.415, Pöyhönen, J., 1992, p.62 ff.

[153] Frankenberg, G., 1985, p.420.
One could call 20th century comparative law "intellectually isolated" (for good analysis, see Maine, H.S., 1875. For some critical reflections on contemporary comparative law, Mayda, J., 1978, pp..361-378.

[154] Frankenberg, G., 1985, pp.412-413. For problems concerning this, see ibid. p.441. One of the problems is naturally that the comparative discourse is part of the legal discourse (ibid., p.441)
The problems of comparative reasoning are connected also to its legal-phenomenological nature. The comparative argument would need - in order to be rational - go through the systematic and cultural study of its relationship to the system where it is adopted so as to be systematically understood. This is so, because the argument does not carry with it, as a normal legal premise derived from the systemic legal discourse, the relationship with the system. Or, it does so in a negative sense (as a relationship with another system).
These problems of foreign connections bring also interpretational problems into the picture. Here the argument should be interpreted from the foreign premisses, which makes the arguments more difficult to understand.
The comparative argument should be, in this sense, understood with its restricted relationships with both systems The system holistic approach should not be taken

[155] See in this regard, Frankenberg, G., 1985, pp.452-453). He, however, seems to recognize ideas regarding the integrity and coherence of public discourses, and the distinction between the public and private etc.
The inability of the postmodern critics to combine comparative reasoning with the discursive attitude, undoubtedly embedded in the method of comparative law, results in unjustified criticism against the use of comparative law. For example, Watson strongly claims that comparative law is unsystematic almost by necessity (1974, p.11). This kind of criticism belongs to the non-discursive paradigm of law, which fails to see the rationality of comparative law based on the traditional restrictions of the sources of the comparisons.

[156] Frankenberg G., recognizes the problem, and that it might easily result in more ethnocentric interpretations of law (1985, p.421, and 428 ff.). The comparative lawyer is in a different position than the "normal lawyer", because he has to separate himself from the dominant legal consciousness (ibid., p.446).
Frankenberg has, in his presentation, some problems with ethnocentrism and "domestic legal consciousness" (ibid., p 442) and culture based language (ibid., p.443).
On the frustration in general, see Goodrich, P Reading the Law (Oxford) 1986, p.210 ff.

comparative law[157], would be a helpful approach in understanding the need for a new type of discourse. One could also propose new classifications for comparative law in the "high" modern paradigm of law. This would entail changes in two respects: in the object of the classification, and in the criteria of the classification. This idea could be connected to other phenomenon in "high modern" law: material and procedural segmentation. Nevertheless, as maintained, the nation state paradigm is still the modern basic unit of comparative law.

Another criterion of the classification could be found also in the "discursive" aspects of these systems. One could classify different systems according to their openness and orientation towards their environment. This essentially means the classification of different legal systems as either value-based, traditional, or instrumentally discursive[158].

Previously there was a inquiry into the tradition of comparative law based on the traditional distinctions, aims, and ideas concerning methodology. Accordingly, comparative legal discourse seemed to be a reproductive discourse having a partly separate function in modern legal discourse.

On the other hand, legal discourses can be classified on the basis of the quality of the discourse. This quality has been related also to the general societal discourse in the realm of values. However, on the basis of legal discourse theories one may distinguish three types of discourses: value based, traditional and instrumental discourses. These distinctions can be applied to the classification of the comparative discourses as well.

One may say that every comparative aspects introduced into systemic discourses involves a value decision from the systematic point of view. In this sense, in the introducing of comparative aspects into the discourse, one establishes a genuine relationship with the general legal discourse. Furthermore, if the comparative aspects remain only synthetically discussed, the adaption is genuinely value based. Here the comparative discourse is not founded on an attempt to evaluate analytically the relationship of the comparative observation and the general legal discourse in whatever form the latter appears. On the other hand, a more evaluative comparative discourse in the public legal discourse is based on an attempt to "traditionalize" the comparative aspects, concepts, rules etc.

The distinction between the value-based and traditional comparative approaches to the legal discourse are, consequently, based on the attitude of the comparative approach towards general legal theoretical assumptions concerning sources of law. The traditional type of comparative discourse seems to evaluate its relationship to the general discourse by focusing on the legal-sociological, legal-cultural, legal-philosophical, and legal-political connections of comparative observations. However, this takes place, as may be seen, not at first hand, but via the relationship to the value-based discourse of law, i.e. in the realm of legal sources.

---

[157] Frankenberg, G., 1985, p.452.
[158] The problem of the state paradigm of comparative law is in the strong idea of the homogeneity of national legal systems.

Moreover, the instrumental type of comparative discourse is in hand when the comparative "formant"[159] is adopted within a discourse not in order to sincerely establish discursive coherence but with instrumental purposes concerning the legal discourse. This type of comparative discourse uses the formant for purposes other than indicated by its legal nature as a source of law.

Basically, all uses of comparative reasoning are like the same, as maintained. Nevertheless, the difference lies in the type of traditionalization which takes place. In an instrumental comparative discourse, the formant is intentionally given an independent context in a separate discourse, for example, by strongly "sociologizing" it. On the other hand, instrumentalization may take place by not revealing the observations in the legal discourse in general (i.e. by the maintenance or creation of a separate audience). This does not "traditionalize" comparative discourse on a larger scale, and maintains possibilities for critical evaluations other than that of the particular "value" discourse. This indicates an abandonment of the principle of the discursive integrity of law[160].

As it has been maintained, comparative law is, in a way, comparable with the legal dogmatics (scholarly opinions) as a source of law. It looks actually to be continuation of the legal dogmatic discourse. As in dogmatics, one has different possibilities of interpretation. One presents hypothetical suggestions for rules and interpretations. All the same, in the comparative "dogmatics" the interpretation is more imbedded in the process, and the justificatory aspect is needed due to legal, political, and cultural reasons, and because of the lack of systematic connections.

How does comparative legal dogmatics, then, differ from traditional dogmatics, and what is the principal characteristic of this relationship?

The basic idea is that both the comparative and the traditional dogmatist use the idea of sources of law. However, the understanding of these and their use can differ, especially in the case of an ordinary legal academic or practitioner, who does not have a theoretical "comparative" legal education. In practice, comparative arguments are usually presented by a person, who is not educated in another legal system. He is, *a priori*, considered not to have knowledge of the social rules existing in that society. This makes a difference also to the "socio-political" validity of the dogmatic argument.

Furthermore, a comparativist may be unfamiliar with other types of arguments and rheto-

---

[159] Sacco, R., 1990.

[160] In this type of reasoning and comparative discourse, comparative reasons are used in order to maintain the internal institutional coherence or consensus between the participants within the closed discourse. One also attempts to formulate a convincing justification only towards the public audience. The rationality is based on the value of the institutional actors as such. At the same time, the direct relationship of the comparative discourse to the general legal discourse is not established. Indirectly this may take place, for example, *a posteriori*, between different actors within the same institution. There is no sincere relationship between the institutional comparative discourse and the legal discourse in general.

rical and non-rhetorical elements which may be somehow relevant elements (even if non-legal) within a (discursive) system.

These are some of the reasons, why the comparative lawyer is not considered to be an authoritative expert. There seems to be an idea that one cannot be a master of many social systems. This is based on the assumption of "life formative" homogeneity. The stability of interpretations is not backed up by firmly established ideas deriving from societal discourses, but the comparative dogmatist is considered as one who is doomed to compare constantly different societal forms of behaviour. This might render his statements unpredictable and unreliable[161], and thus problematic from the legal point of view.[162]

One of the characteristics of comparative dogmatics is that when the political, general and legal dogmatic contexts cannot be strongly emphasized, one has to rely more on practical legal statements on the interpretations of certain types of situations rather than upon general statements concerning the meaning of particular rules. This may be one of the reasons, for example, why comparative dogmatics is oriented more to case law and concrete decisions as sources of its interpretation, than to statements in the traditional legal systematic dogmatics.

Consequently, socio-cultural expertise is the main argument which distinguishes the comparative and traditional dogmatics from each other[163].

Comparative law seems to be related also to the "custom of the land" as a source of law. Namely, these two spheres seem, in theory, to qualify each other. This custom seems to be also a "substantial source of law"[164]. In some situations, it can also be an "unprivileged" source[165].

Custom of the land seems to relate to comparative method of interpretation, because essentially, it seems to need some "reasonability".[166] This reasonability may be provided by comparative observations. This may be motivated also by the fact that custom of the land is

---

[161] This is definitely also the problem in international and regional organizations The phenomenon is related to the polycentric qualities of the institutions. In other words, matters concerning some states and legal systems are dealt with by the persons coming from those "systems". This is seen as the solution and actually one of the major characteristics of the daily functioning of regional and international organizations.

Towards the outside, however, this polycentrism is manipulated to look homogeneous (as one can see in justifications of the European Court of Justice, for example). The question is a matter of the combining specialist knowledge and institutional authority.

In this sense, traditional comparative law seems to be more universal in nature, because, as a scientific approach, strong cultural distinctions cannot be recognized - as in legal institutional arrangements.

[162] Values in legal dogmatics, see Aarnio, A., 1997, pp.83-86 (especially, pp. 83-84).

[163] This is reflected in the instrumentalization of national lawyers in international legal interpretation. (For some analysis, see below.)

[164] See Aarnio, A., 1986, p.93.

[165] Aarnio, A., 1986, p.98. This means that if the question concerns only the "gap" in a statute, other sources of law become decisive, even if the "custom of the land" is given strong priority in general and in filling the "gap" in the law

[166] Aarnio, A., 1986, pp.80-81, referring to the writings of Alanen, A., Jurisprudence and private international law, [Yleinen oikeustiede ja kansainvalinen yksityisoikeus] (Vammala) 1965, and to the Finnish Code of Procedure, Chapter 1, Section 11.

sometimes more general (or also restricted) than the borders of modern state legal systems. In this sense, the criteria of "the legal convictions of citizens" (presented by the historical school) or of the tacit acceptance by the legislator do not apply.[167]

Custom of the land, on the other hand, seems to counteract the arbitrariness of the comparative observations to a certain extent.[168] There is going to be some discussion on the relationship between comparative law and *travaux preparatoires* below.

Furthermore, the pertinent question within the idea of legal source theory is the principled obligatoriness of the use of a source and arguments deriving from it[169].

In the case of comparative law, there does not seem to be such an obligation. The obligation is based on a practical discourse in the comparison itself. On a contrary, one could say that there are even systematic and practical obstacles to the use of comparative analysis as a basis for a justificatory decision, as maintained. On the other hand, if the exception is made, it should be explicitly justified[170]. This is due to the fact that if the comparative derivations were to become the central issue of the system, as one may imagine in some situations of legal transplantation[171], comparative law would no longer function as a rational source of law, but as a source with no *a priori* defined possibility for a rational choice. The increasing use of comparative aspects abolishes the possibility of achieving a balance in a legal discourse, which is fatal to the rationality of the system, as explained.

One could thus maintain that there cannot be a general obligation to use comparative law in legal reasoning.

Can one say that if comparative law would be capable of being a source of law, and that it belongs to the category of "allowed" legal sources?

As noted, it is difficult to imagine the role of comparative law as an *a priori* established legal source in systematic decision-making context[172]. Even the basic ideas on comparative law as an argument for integration, understanding, etc. do not appear convincing.

As has been maintained, in practice, arguments deriving from comparative law seem to be merely some unsystematic arguments without any *a priori* status of legal, they are used in the

---

[167] On the idea that the custom has been instrumentalized in order to govern the native cultures, see Pöyhönen, J., 1992, p.67 (referring to Said, E., Orientalism, 1978)

[168] As it will be seen later, the "customary" borders of law seem to correspond strongly to the scope of comparative observations.

[169] See Aarnio, A., 1986, p.89.

[170] This can be seen in connection to many legal systems.

[171] This is so also in some international legal systems.

[172] Basically the legal system functions as a ultimate source of legal norms. All these "legal" arguments derive from this legal system based on the ""Grundnorm"". The law, *de lege lata*, is traditionally interpreted by legal arguments based on systematization discourses.

Comparative law does not basically systematize anything, at least not traditionally, if one does not consider it systematizing tradition as a subject in the discourse itself. Then the comparative argument seems to be capable of systematizing anything connected to the discourse, also the discourse itself. This seems to be problematic.

legal discourses for any purpose, with the ultimate aim of establishing a connection between legal systems and in confirming the authority of legal systems and orders, in general, as a source of law. In this sense, comparative reasoning could be seen as a symptom of a one-sided practice of adaption of a legal statement within relatively autonomous legal systems (and discourses). Furthermore, the comparative discourse does not seem to exist, as such, in the discourse on the discourses, but it only seems to be a process of learning which takes place in a one-sided fashion[173].

Nevertheless, the comparative argument could be defined as a relatively consistent (and even quite static) argument because of its political-traditional context[174]. This is so despite of the fact that one cannot ignore the legally non-systemic and autonomous nature of comparative law as a source of law. Comparative law gives discursive dynamics to the law and legal systems, by still keeping the discourse in certain limits of rationality.

It also makes legal discourse more general. It is strongly connected to the international-ization and regionalisation of law, which, in contemporary society, seems to be more law than any other form of law. Furthermore, the use of comparative law may be even extremely important, because it is used in the cases, where one has to react "to serious needs of the community"[175].

Thus, one could suggest that comparative law is, at this stage, an additional source of law[176] - with qualifications. Because comparative analysis is difficult to classify as a normal source of law in domestic legal systems, one could make a hypothesis that it is a critical source in law. It reflects certain aspects of the "common law" of more general legal community, and it serves as a reflective, unsystematic and critical model of argumentation and reasoning in legal decision-making, requiring, however, also constant critical reflections itself.

In conclusion, it can be claimed that comparative law should be considered more seriously as a source of law than any other form of legal source in the contemporary discourse of law. Indeed, it is asserted that it's "source" nature is more evident than that of any other types of

---

[173] In this context, one should actually speak of legal learning instead of legal transplantation The learning processes takes place internally within the law, and there is no other instance, which would be capable of "transplanting" legal institutions into a legal system than the one-sided legal discourse itself

Transplantation refers to a political-authoritative process of adaption of legal ingredients, and to the relationship between political and social systems in general, which is only reflected in legal systems. It does not refer to the relationship between legal systems (comparative law). On this, see Watson, A., 1974, Sacco, R., 1991, and some analysis, Kiikeri, M , 1999, p.141 ff.

[174] The question concerns rules and interpretations of rules, which have been openly argued and justified in one system, and then adopted within another system. Comparative arguments, despite their nature as learning processes or external systematic arguments, have, in other words, gone through a democratic process, and interpretations on the validity and correctness have been tested in a legal audience. They belong to some discourse, though they would not be part of the particular discourse in which they have been used.

[175] Watson, 1978b, p.522.

[176] As Koopmans, T., 1996, p.550

legal sources because "comparative" observations and arguments, theoretically, assume an "existence" of an (institutional and positive) legal system. In other words, where there is a strong assumption of an existence of a legal order that is applying rules and creating norms, one can justify a need of a possibility for an alternative and affirmative argumentation (relating to the need of clarification and criticism). In fact, in the application of comparative observations in legal discourses one is speaking about qualitative systematization of a legal system and its rule and norms, contrary to a "quantitative" idea of creation and institutional ordering (by institutional authority) without any motives for systematization.[177]

This is why the application of comparative rules and norms have to be justified by some "qualifying" criteria. When studying comparative law as a legal source, one has to observe the motives for their application in particular context and focus upon the discursive nature of these arguments.

Comparative reasoning, as the all discursive legal instrumentalizations, as it has been already maintained in connection to the comparative discourse, can be divided into the instrumental, value-based, and traditional instrumentalizations according to the quality of the reasoning as a social communicative action. The distinction between these different types of uses can be associated with interests (or principles) of interpretation the user is having.

By traditional comparative reasoning is meant the use of comparative legal information in an analytical way. This means consideration of all elements which may be relevant according to the tradition of comparative law. Traditional comparative reasoning entails the analytical presentation of general and particular features of the legal phenomenon in question. These types of presentations are traditionally analytical (legal or legal-sociological) studies, which refer to all systematic features relevant to the legal audience. Traditional comparative reasoning can be claimed to be a neutral use of comparative observations, an attempt to maintain the legal "balance" and the existing structural arrangements. It also reveals the basic values of the legal decision-maker in the comparative legal discourse and legal discourse in general. It functions as a basis for further discussion (the idea of discursive integrity). It is based on communicative rationality.

By value-based comparative reasoning one refers to the use of comparative information in a non-analytical, strongly principled way. Comparative information is determined "auto-poietically", i.e. only by reference to the "internal" conceptualization of the legal system (or

---

[177] In fact, one could claim that comparative law is already a legal source by definition In the history of legal positive law it seems to be - in addition to "jurisprudence" - a "primary" legal source, whereas in contemporary state-paradigm it is a secondary source due to the institutional-contextual discourses which have transferred "finer" distinctions for our legal-analytical stock of instruments. However, in the discursively democratic system there does not seem to be any obstacles for its use except some qualitative restrictions.

order) concerned, which is assumed to be understood by the audience.[178] Value-based comparative observations are characterized by disregard of comparative generality or disparity as premises of the discourse.[179]

The instrumental approach means the use of comparative information in the internal reasoning processes of the institution in a manner which is invisible for the general legal (dogmatic-scientific) audience. This instrumentality of comparative law can be related to the search for forms of argumentation *a priori* by way of justification. This is why one may call it, in the ultimate sense, institutional reasoning. In various ways, comparative legal studies help the decision-makers find persuasive and convincing forms of reasoning (arguments), and to achieve aims which are not directly part of the interpretation of a rule ("system maintenance"). The instrumental use of comparative law leads to instrumental reasoning in general.

This instrumentality is apparently connected to the teleological intentions or to the internal coherence of the institution. By looking into individual systems, in particular and general, one may design such norms and reasons, which make flexible interpretation of law possible. In this way the system may implement its norms in a prudent way, depending on all particular circumstances.

The aim of internal comparative reasoning is the justification as such, not the adherence of the legal audience in a value based or traditional way. In this case, the premises of reasoning are based on the aim of achieving the adherence of the "internal" interests of some audiences, which also means, in fact, that a distinction between different comparative and general audiences is reproduced.

The instrumental use of comparative law and instrumental reasoning can be divided into following concrete types.

The first type of instrumental (comparative) reasoning is the individual action type, which is connected to the contextual heuristics of the individual decision-maker as a person. This can be defined as an inspirational type of comparative reason search and reasoning. It is basically the comparative interpretation as such. It is determined by the personal qualities, characteristics, interests, and the social context of an individual. These types of "reasons" could be found only by interpretation of the heuristics of a person[180], but also by examining different internal discourses.

The second type instrumental argument is the affective one, where comparative observations are used extremely situationally within a closed discourse. The basis of this use is rather the

---

[178] Generality, etc. This type of "internal" value based distinction seems to be based on "good/bad" distinctions as criterion of relevance, instead of the legal/illegal distinction used in the systems theory.

[179] This value-based reasoning can be called the restructuralization of a comparative argument.

[180] For certain problems in this regard, see Aarnio, A , 1986, p.22.

emotional affection toward certain arguments. In the same way as the former type of use, it is strongly connected to the basic values of the user, and argumentation is characterized by argumentation "*ad hominem*". These types of instrumentalizations are not rationally directed toward any genuine audience.

Both these forms may include extensive analytical observations and be "traditional" from the point of view of comparative law.

The third type of instrumental (comparative) reasoning is systematic institutional reasoning. This takes place in the internal, institutional, and contextual discourse. It is connected to the context of the discovery of the justification by the institution. It is usually made in the form of systematic research internal to the institution, resulting in the systematic formation of the legal justification. This can also be made in the traditional or value based comparative law form.

Instrumental uses of comparative law lead usually to argumentation and justification by means of general features or disparities without any analytical quality. On the other hand, instrumental comparative reasoning can depart from strict general features, or disparities, and remain on the traditional level of reasoning. Here the method for analysis of the generalities or disparities is related to traditional methods of legal sources and arguments.

Furthermore, if one goes to the deep analysis of systems by stressing the particular features and problematizing the whole idea of the comparability (strong systematic "polycentrism" as its ultimate form), one is dealing with strongly value-based forms of comparative observations in the instrumental sense. Here the general reasoning usually results in coherence - or similar kind of - reasoning.

In the case of traditional analysis, legal theory and comparative law meet in the concept of legal sources. With reference to legal systems as general or disparate, comparative reasoning implies values of the legal system as a basic form of value.

It can be maintained that an explicit reference to a particular legal system as a source of legal argument is not a necessary condition for the rationality of comparative reasoning (an original source).

A special type of phenomenon must also be mentioned.

Instrumental reasoning takes place also in a case, where reasons are revealed in an open justification, but only as institutional "additional" material (value based or traditional way). Many "opinion" types of comparative observations are of this type. As it will be seen, they may function in guaranteeing the convincing force of the "main" reasoning. This type of instrumentalization, as a kind of contextual justification, may also attempt to guarantee the integrity of a legal order and an institution. However, from the point of view of value based and traditional reasoning, these additional comparative observations may be relevant also to the development of the system.

The procedural and persuasive nature of comparative reasoning seem to be connected. This idea can be explained in the following way.

One may claim that comparative legal reasoning is as persuasive, as the ability of its user to create a bridge between the system from which the argument is deriving and the system in which it is used. This is related to the reasoner's ability to apply the idea of the "discursive integrity of law". In this sense, the original context of the rule, including the sociological, historical or other socio-political "bridges", are, or should be, stated in the reasoning.

In this sense, one may parallel "normal" legal reasoning and comparative legal reasoning. In traditional legal reasoning the context is taken, in many ways, for granted because of social systematic assumptions, or because the context is a possible source of further distinctions within a discourse. The context seems to be part of socio-legal systematization directly. In the case of comparative legal reasoning, this is not necessarily so. This discourse has to be explicitly reconstructed.

On the other hand, in traditional rule application (as in the comparative interpretation as well) the decision maker has to create the link between the decisional norm statement, and the legal sources deriving from sphere external to that institution and from the legal systematic "framework". For example, if socio-political considerations have been traditionally seen as valuable for decision-making, by examining them one attempts to connect the existing social practice to the norm proposed. If the *travaux preparatoires*, for example, have been traditionally considered as a valid source, the reasoning is merely an expression of the linkage between this material and the norm applied.

In this sense, there seems to be an interesting difference between comparative interpretation and traditional legal interpretation.

In traditional comparative law research, the comparative legal sources (foreign law etc.) have been seen only as a process of constructing bridges between the legal systems, without any *a priori* idea of systematization or norm interpretation. However, for example in adjudicative comparative interpretation, the linkage should be made between two norms in two systems and between their contexts.

Now, because it is understood that this latter bridge cannot be made in any "genuine" sense (because of the different socio-systematic ontology of these norms), the bridge building has to be based on qualities other than in the traditional common (discursive-social) system-framework decision-making. It has to be based on the framework of the comparative perspective itself, or on a system of systems (a substantive legal theory).

The fact is, however, that these types of frameworks and substantive theories do not seem to exist in the traditional sphere of law. A value decision seems to be meaningless to an audience, which is not directly involved, and which is not affected by the decision, as in the case of comparatively-reasoned norm. This is due to the fact that the comparative reasoning is not reasoning concerning a norm in the transferring system, but rather in the adopting system. There is no reciprocal interaction in the legal sense. No systematization takes place, and no systematic framework is created, or maintained, as it has been observed before.

Consequently, one can maintain that the comparative reasoning cannot be based on any genuine value similarity in different systems. The analysis of the comparative reasoning has to be seen in its "own" context, i.e. based on its quality as a process. However, at the same time one loses any "correctness" dimension, and the formal evaluation becomes a matter of legal "aesthetics" or moral perspectives.

The problem could be solved by some kind of ideal legal audience theory. Namely, one may imagine, that although the comparative reasoning nearly always lacks, as indicated, the general audience (lack of reciprocal communication, influences, and genuine relationships), it can be maintained that if the reasoner is using comparative arguments, she has to at least ideally try to orient herself towards audiences which do not, in the traditional comparative or systematic framework, appear important. In other words, the reasoner has to keep in his mind the ideal audiences of the national systems in general (their dogmatic and legal theoretical framework) in addition to the situational and systematic audience composed of parties and participators in the particular and general institutional processes. Even if this seems to be problematic, one has to assume this construction as a regulative idea of comparative reasoning.[181] This is the "ideal comparative perspective" of comparative reasoning in legal decision-making.

This means, in the end, that, even if the audience of the foreign legal system is not an audience in the genuine sense of the word, the arguer has to approach the foreign legal audience mainly on the basis of the "correctness" of the interpretation of the foreign norms, but not by trying to interpret the norms of the system. The audience of the sincere legal interpretation is, on the other hand, the genuine audience in the institutional and legal discursive (dogmatic) nature. The comparative audience, on the other hand, appears relevant only to the extent of "correctness".

This idea leads to the second rule, to the "material" rule of transitivity.

As maintained, the function of comparative law, and arguments deriving from it, is to bring into a system an external norm. On the other hand, other "external" elements connected to that particular foreign norm, may also follow. This makes the comparative argument, as such, a source of new elements. This means that the comparative argument may open up the legal discourse to the structures, forms, and practices of "another system" in general. It actually reveals a new sphere which needs to be to be clarified and taken into account.

As maintained, as much comparative observations create clarification, they may create confusion and misunderstandings in an explanatory sense. In the context of reasoning, this may be the situation where the comparative aspects contain both general and particular

---

[181] This discursive opening up means, at a minimum, that even if the reasoning is not explained the material has to be public.

elements. Contrary to the idea of comparative law as a way of arriving at legal solutions - in which sense it could be even be called comparative <u>law</u> - one should stress the fact that comparative law is rather a collection of legal information from which inventive arguments <u>can</u> be derived. It is, in other words, a collection of arguments as such. This is so, however, not in the sense of the traditional doctrine of the source of law, as seen. Comparative arguments, as sources of arguments, are heterogenous arguments. As much as there seems to be a coherence presumed in connection to normal legal argument, there may be possible generalities, as well as disparities, embedded in a comparative legal argument.

In this sense, comparative law must be considered to be a transitive [182] source of arguments. The nature of the argument in the transferring and the receiving systems is not identical. However, if an element belongs to the "original" argument (original rule or norm) which is derived by comparative means, it should be adopted also in the application of the argument (by the "receiver") or it should be at least be considered. On the other hand, no additional elements should be connected to the application of the argument in the receiving system (as arguments belonging to the original argument) if they were not originally part of it. This concerns also arguments which may seem to belong to the original arguments, but which actually are not general arguments at all[183].

It seems that <u>transitivity is the logical and formal "material" rule applying to the uses of comparative arguments (comparative reasoning).</u>

Some final remarks may be produced related to these remarks above.

Comparative reasoning is as analytical as much as it supports certain functions. This means that the extension of the argument to particular and general features is determined by the functions of the user of the argument. On the other hand, distinctions between irrelevant and

---

[182] Transitivity has to do with the "large" and "strict" application of the comparative method. As explained above, the more strict one is in the comparison, the more one comes into the field of conceptualization, which is connected to the particularities of one's own system. This leads to instrumentality. This is why transitivity is a condition for the existence of a traditional and value based comparative argument in its modern form.

In mathematics and logic the transitive law means that if A bears some relation to B, and B approximates some relation to C, the A bears it to C (A=B, B=C,> A=C).

This means, in our context, that if a norm B is a comparative law argument in the justification C, and if, originally, A belonged to this rule, A belongs (explicitly or implicitly) to C.

One may continue with the analysis. If A is essential element of B, one may say that it has to be considered in C. If it is a minor point, it may be considered. On the other hand, if A is in conflict with C, there is a fundamental problem of transitivity.

Intransitivity exists, when, for example, an element x is attached to B (and C), though x does not belong to B. This means that the situation is intransitive if A's relationship to B is determined by different qualities that B:s relationship to C. This kind of situation may exist, as explained, if, to the relationship between B=C, is attached x, even if it is not in the relationship A=B

The transitivity can also involve modified transitivity (conditional transitivity) However, from the point of view of the discourse theory, this is a matter of discourse This brings a dynamic character to the transitivity relationship.

[183] This phenomenon is visible especially in cases, where the "main" generality derives from many legal systems and from one legal system.

relevant features are made on the basis of the audience to whom one is speaking. One chooses arguments which are accepted by the reasoner's legal audience. Furthermore, because in the case of comparative reasoning arguments are generalizations of legal systems, one can satisfy the legal audience with lesser analytical observation than in the case of genuine national discourses. All the same, the comparative opinion concerns the individual systems has to satisfy the national legal audience, and it has to be based, consequently, on national discourse and opinion. It has to be transitive.

In this sense, when one does not use analytical comparative observations as a basis of comparative generality reasoning, one could claim that the normative issue is disputable. On the other hand, where generality is forsaken absolutely and explicitly, the normative issue seems to be very unclear.

The justification for the non-analytical approach can be that one attempts to avoid the claims of irrelevancy or inefficacy. These claims are allowed according to the discourse theory. When this is assumed, there is lack of relevant information, or one expects inefficacy claims to be made on the basis of a too deep analysis[184].

Nevertheless, in case comparative law reasoning is effected, one may say that the comparative legal analysis must be supported at least by the traditional analysis based on the idea of the main and generally accepted legal sources and standards of reasoning. This way one may satisfy the ideas of legal efficacy in the audience, but also maintain the coherence of the reasoning. On the other hand, here the general legal opinion and the comparative opinion can be reasonably connected.

Because, in this type of reasoning, one also speak of the "method" of comparative law ("canons of interpretation"), some consideration has to be given to the issue of selection of legal sources[185]. This means that there is a consultation of the general legal opinion.

---

[184] In this case, one usually would depart from the idea of legal sources. However, the problem of the lack of information is not a genuine problem, because the dogmatic analysis could be made, and the comparative and national audiences consulted.

The justification by generality approach seems to be only a rhetorical device.

The claim of irrelevance of the information based on the lack of information cannot justify the "generality in legal systems" approach.

The autonomous legal actor and the comparative self-referentiality of law are interconnected. One can identify one with a help of the other. If the legal decision-maker is referring to the generality or disparity in legal systems, it has to have a *tertium comparationis* as its premiss. It defines the criteria for common features, and this way its premisses. In this sense the system is self-referential. Where the generality or disparity argument is used, the legal decision-maker is relatively free to determine the *tertium comparationis*, because it is not legally regulated. This is where the relative autonomy of the legal actor is visible.

[185] This is where comparative dogmatics comes into play (comparative legal sources). In this type of reasoning, the comparative reasoning is legally self-referential also in the way that it has to satisfy the ideas of legal sources in order to be acceptable.

What is claimed here is that if one uses "generality in legal systems", one should also reason and consider also the question on what type of legal comparative generality the substantive generality is based (comparative legal sources). Naturally, one could claim that the reference to an established idea of comparative legal sources could also satisfy this

Furthermore, if the arguer wishes to depart from the legal sources-approach in the comparative "generality" argumentation, for example, by deriving arguments from non-general sources of law, she has to justify the departure, if she wants to maintain the approach and to be seen as reasonable[186]. On the other hand, if one argues on the basis of allowed and non-obligatory sources, one has to do it in general, i.e. in relation to all systems used. One cannot use only some systems as obligatory, and other merely permitted, etc. One has to apply the rule of generality also in the choice of different types of sources. If departure from this idea occurs, it must be justified. This idea may guarantee also the visibility of the "transitiveness", which has to be maintained in relation to foreign legal systems and comparative law opinions.

Moreover, one may make some concrete concluding remarks related to traditional standards of reasoning[187] regulating the grammatical, extending and restricting, analogical, and *e contrario* approaches in reasoning. These aspects seem to be at the centre of comparative reasoning.

It could be maintained that one should interpret comparative law observations by taking into account the text as it stands. All elements of the text should be given significance. On the other hand, if the same text appears in different connections, it should be given the same meaning, unless sufficient reasons are given to justify a departure from this presumption. This applies also to the assumption concerning the ordinary meaning of words. Nevertheless, if technical or special expressions prevail, one should interpret the text according to them. These are the standards of reasoning which appear also in relation to "normal" legal reasoning.[188]

However, one can maintain that all "modifying" ideas related to comparative reasoning cannot be applied. Accordingly, any extending, restricting, or analogical modes of reasoning referring to the "internal" systematic interpretation do not seem to be applicable. This can be related to the fact that a comparative interpretator may - commonly - lack the idea of the "analogical key"[189] which prevails in the system.[190] This idea applies also to any

---

demand. In dogmatic sense, one can abandon further analysis on the basis of the self-clearness ("generally accepted opinion").

[186] Practice also seems to confirm that these argumentative models are used interchangeably. Namely, one either uses the traditional legal sources analytically, or one justifies the non-analytical approach by introducing principles or philosophical arguments (general opinion) in connection with comparative observations

[187] See Aarnio, A., 1986, p 101 ff.

[188] See Aarnio, A., 1986, pp.101-103.

[189] Aarnio, A., 1986, p.104. *"The key is not objective"*. Analogical relationship seems to be a matter of values

[190] This seems to relate also to Alexy's rule that *"different speakers may not use the same expression with different meanings"*, and that *"every rule must be universally teachable"*. Furthermore, comparative rules, attached strongly to value (or even moral) standpoints, may be evaluated by the rule that they must *"stand critical testing in the terms of their historical genesis"*. (Alexy, R., 1989, p 193.) For problems on formulating these types of "interpretative" reasons in relation to comparative arguments, see ibid , p.301 In this sense, other arguments take also *"precedence over"* them.

transformation of the sources of law doctrine. One should not be able to challenge the prevailing idea concerning the preferences of the sources.

Nevertheless, in any *e contrario* reasoning by comparative means one may be able to stress the "systematic" coherence and even historical integrity of interpreted systems and their rules. Namely, if one is able to identify the systematic coherence and historical continuity by some analogical key, one can do it. This may be related to the stress upon predictability in legal decision-making in general. However, this type of reasoning seems to apply more to comparative legal science than to practical reasoning by use of comparative source of law.

As far as the technical form of the reasoning is concerned, one could maintain that comparative observations should be kept separate from the analysis of one's "own" laws, and the other legal systems to be studied in separately.[191]

In conclusion, it can be stated that comparative reasoning seems to be justified when the question is about quite "new" laws and exceptional rules. This may related to the fact that social situations, not supported by internal systematic and integrative interpretations, may be balanced by comparative observations.[192] One may say also that in introducing interpretative methods and rules of procedures, the modes of comparative reasoning depend strongly on the discursive qualities of the procedure and legal development in general. This is related more to the justificatory dimension of comparative law uses, and will be discussed more thoroughly in the general conclusions of the work.

3.5. Conclusions: the basic structure of practical comparative legal reasoning

In conclusion, one can divide comparative legal reasoning into two spheres. The first sphere is the sphere of adoption. This includes the real adaption argumentation, which transitively argues on the rule itself, but also analyzes the rule within the framework of the theory of legal sources of the transferring legal system. It is transitive systematization argumentation according to the source theories of the original system. As maintained, to this analysis applies the rules of transitivity, but also the prohibition of taking, as a starting point any "analogical" rules from the transferring system.

The second sphere of the adoption reasoning is the systematization reasoning within the

---

[191] In fact, however, if comparative analogical argument is used as a "conclusive" argument in a legal discourse it may reveal some problems in the communicative situation, and this sense lead to an "*e contrario*" solution in very fundamental sense. On the other hand, by revealing value problems it may also stimulate the discourse.

Aarnio maintains that "*as an interpretative doctrine, it follows the same principles of reasoning and uses same type of source material as the domestic legal dogmatics. The distinction is that comparative study of law considers foreign legal rules instead of the national legal order*" (Aarnio, A., 1997, p.77).

[192] This seems to be contrary to the "analogical" interpretation, see Aarnio, A., 1986, p.106 (referring to Alexy and Petczenik).

sources theory framework of the recipient system. There is the real comparative analysis, where the formal rule and the above described transitive analysis is systematized within the legal peculiarities of the recipient system. In other words, it is the systematization analysis of the transitively adopted rule. In this analysis, the transferred rule is situated to the framework of the adopting system, and any systematic unsuitability or "illogicality" is revealed and evaluated. This means that the nature of this reasoning (discourse) is not really logical, but dialogical in the sense that the any deviancies do not necessarily result the rejection of this rule, but the nature of this "abnormality" is evaluated and balanced with other characteristics of this rule.

The second part of the comparative reasoning one could describe the critical part of the comparative reasoning. One could call this social systematization reasoning, but it is also the social philosophical part of this comparative reasoning. This reasoning can take place in two different ways. The first approach is the sociological approach, which usually aims at the rejection of any adoption. In it, one examines analytically the peculiarities of the recipient social system, and attempts to motivate the idea, why the adoption is not really suitable for the social system in general. This is the analytical critique against the legal analytical transplantation. It can be used also in more positive or confirmative form, but in legal analysis, it is usually excluded, and the following type of approach is chosen.

This second approach is not really an analytical and discursive approach at all. It is phenomenological in the sense that it either assumes, perhaps based on different heuristic and phenomenological processes, the suitability or the unsuitability of this analytically motivated legal adoption in the first place. It is value based reasoning in the sense that it is not analytical and explicit in relation to the social systematic suitability of the legal comparative analysis.

The so called phenomenological, value-based approach can be extended so far as to exclude also the internal systematization discourses from the scope of analysis. This can be called a legal phenomenological approach (vs. the socio-phenomenological approach explained above). In relation to the original system analysis, this type of approach is extremely value-based in the sense that the selection of the elements from the original system is highly arbitrary and contingent, and it does not represent the criteria of the selection in any visible sense. If this exclusion is related to the systematization discourse of the recipient system, the reasoner takes as granted her knowledge on the recipient system, but does not consider necessary the evaluation of the relationship between the systematization in those two systems.

CHAPTER 2

4. GENERAL CONCLUSIONS

Comparative reasoning is an extremely paradoxical phenomenon. It <u>seems</u> to be the most persuasive form of legal reasoning and to be connected always to the hard cases, though it is clear, in theory, that it is an extremely weak and problematic form of reasoning.

Nevertheless, one knows that in every type of reasoning there is always a lack of a syllogistic model as a normative premise in hand - *a priori*. The choice of arguments takes place in some "sphere". The rationality of legal reasoning does not seem to be based on the idea of "one possible answer", but there is instead a range of possible reasons for which decision-makers can choose and which are, on the other hand, reasonable in relation to a particular context.

On the other hand, it may be correct that comparative argument is one of the most powerful and misused arguments in law. As contended, it can be hidden within the institutional context without granting any possibility for further development and analysis. If this use is conscious, the system and its actors are communicatively manipulating the discursive audience in the most problematic way possible.[193] On the other hand, because, in comparative reasoning, one is simultaneously referring to the functionality of social institutions and because one is also directly searching for the acceptance within the legal discourse without prior "relevance" - having been accepted in advance - the "legality" is searched all over again. Its relevance is, in this sense, determined mainly by its "practicality" and "functionality", and its results and aims and teleological qualities. Its persuasiveness is related to choices and acceptability, and to the interpretation it produces (or is supposed to produce).

One could also argue that it is actually untrue that comparative reasoning is persuasive. The persuasiveness of comparative reasoning can be a fiction, which will be revealed by comprehensive analysis concerning comparative reasoning itself. Furthermore, one could think that comparative law considerations do not result at all in "just" and "equitable" solutions in relation to state paradigm of law. One could profess that comparative reasoning is directed to the ultimate general legal auditories, for which the national legal systems provide the ultimate forms of legitimacy (including national dogmatic, comparative, and general legal opinions). By comparative reasoning, international institutional actors, for example, seem desire the support of this type of legal audience in order to justify only the institutional opinion. However, they do not necessarily try to maintain it as a genuine tradition. Comparative reasoning does not really seem to be reasonable in social context (a critical "high"-modern argument).

Furthermore, the claim that modern comparative argument is not rational at all could be based on the claim that modern society is increasingly segmented through its normative

---

[193] On the misuses of comparative law, see Kahn-Freund, O., 1974, p.20.

systems (a critical "post"-modern argument). Moreover, it seems that when comparative observations are employed, in different contexts and within different systems, the discourses on legal systems and their rules seem to become ever more differentiated. The homogeneous nature of the legal discourse in a legal system gets heterogenized. There is an increasing number of interpretational possibilities for the consideration of the legal system, its rules, and its processes.

It seems that comparative law fails to provide, as an autonomous discipline, value criteria for the choice among competing alternatives.[194] Consequently, comparison in contemporary world is highly unpredictable and is forced to rely upon sources of norms and rules connected to systems which have no democratic political character.

Subsequently, this type of postulate would mean, for example, that comparative reasoning within international institutions, as some system and sociological theories of law seem to suggest, actually decreases the legitimacy of these legal arrangements, although the reasons for this would not be visible in the legal discourse. On the other hand, one may say that the strongly principled and value-based comparative justifications are related to these questions in international and regional law, which comprise the most problematic cases from the political and legal point of view. Namely, in these cases one is confronted with question to which one seems to be unable to find a suitable solution in regional and international levels - and where many problems remain in and between different state legal systems of law. On the other hand, "comparative cases" may be the possible cases causing drastic institutional changes.

Reasoning by way of comparative argument appears in different levels of adjudication and legislation. What seems to take place in comparative argumentation and justification in legal decision-making is the process of moving from the legislative integrity to the adjudicative integrity in the context of the general political action. Whenever this analogical move is made, expressed and analysed, the political integrity is possible to assume. In concrete terms, only when the comparative analysis is expressed in a reasonable way, can one assume that marginal legal systems, not belonging to the general sphere, can be integrated into the majority systems.

One may say that if one could argue according to the principle of discursive integrity the discursive tradition and evolution would be respected. This would maintain the discursive integrity of different levels (adjudication and legislation) of law. Decisions would be made in a way that (political) integrity would not be unbalanced. This postulate may be combined also with comparative law research.

It is evident that this type of idea of integrity of legal systems is problematic, for example,

[194] Hill, J, 1989, pp.104-105 criticizing the conclusions of Zweigert and Kötz in the case of comparative law and contracts (1987, II, pp.42-43).

for an international judge. She is, by making a normative decision, in the process of "developing" the system. Accordingly, a strict application of the idea of discursive integrity works better for a comparative lawyer making a "descriptive" analysis, because its employment results ultimately in maintenance of the system *status quo*.

All the same, there may be also some room for the development of law in an integrative sense. This would demand, as generally coherent argumentation always entails, an extensive of preunderstanding of different national histories, philosophies, styles, and social conditions - just as the tradition of comparative legal theory suggests. This involves a move away from the phenomenon of institutionalized comparative law.

Consequently, it can be asked, why comparative observations are used in contemporary legal orders, and why the study of comparative law could be also relevant from the non-critical point of view - from the point of view of the positive law? Can there be "comparative dogmatics" of law?

As noted, the use of comparative arguments has traditionally been justified by a need to fill *lacunae*, integrate legal systems, etc. On the other hand, as maintained, comparative law is an essential element of regional and international legislation and adjudications. However, what are the why's and wherefore's of its use in contemporary national legal systems and orders?

The fact that law has become positively "internationalized" and "regionalised" during this and the previous century (ultimately in the form of international orders) the role of national legislation has decreased. Parliaments are not presently the sole or the main sources of law, at least, not if one looks at the origins of different international and regional rules.

This has brought national adjudication to a peculiar situation. The national courts and legal processes actually have to strike a balance between different valid norms. Namely, regional systems and their norms can be a source of valid arguments before national courts (even if national courts cannot usually interpret the content of these regional norms!)[195]. Furthermore, these regional norms can be used as arguments, even if they <u>may</u> be contrary to valid national

---

[195] See, for example, the operation of Article 177 (the new Article 234) of the EEC Treaty, and the EC system in general On the other hand, national courts do add additional arguments to the discourse by having recourse to competent European institution. It balances these European interpretations with other arguments deriving from national systems in coming to a concrete decision. To a certain extent, Article 177 (the new Article 234) functions as a legal basis for the arguments, but not for norms as such.

The basic idea, however, seems to be that the European arguments direct the choice of norms in national legal systems. Some norms are valid, some not in relation to European law. The European Court extends or restricts the interpretation of European law on an *ad hoc* basis in relation to the national systems and its norms (in the national context) depending on what result is desirable. Because this interpretation is of an *ad hoc* nature, i.e, it is related to the legislation in that particular system, it must usually refer to the basic principles of constitutional type so as to legitimate the general application of law in European context. At the same time, the decision tends to reinterpret national constitutions (the constitutionality of a norm) in relation to the norms of the system. Article 177 (the new Article 234) provides basically for the reinterpretation and "resubstantiation" of national constitutional law in this way.

This one can claim that the European law in many ways functions as a legal basis and an argument for a open constitutional control of the legislation by the national courts.

norms (thus creating internal conflict). On the other hand, because national norms are *a priori* contestable and can be invalid the substance of the decision of the court may depend on the "right choice" of norms. In fact, it seems that it is the <u>possibility</u> for a valid interpretation of a regional norm which is sufficient to establish the rationality of the decision.

One could claim that the fact that parliamentary (or governmental!) legislation has a strong international and regional character has forced the courts to seek support from "external" sources to enable them to deal with the task they are entrusted with: to function as a balancing of power. One may say that courts seek to find the best arguments at the same rationality level as the legislator. Only these arguments can compete with the regionalised and internationalized national legislation. In this sense, there would be no objection to the use of comparative observations, if one wishes to maintain the traditional modern idea of balance of power in a political system.

Consequently, it is the breaking-up of the modern and traditional state system rationality, which has brought, and may bring, comparative law into the center of national legal practice. When using comparative law, adjudication can to go beyond the strict formal validity of the decision, and, to a certain extent, attempt to find the best interpretation. This way it could reasonably persuade the legal audiences by reference to the rightness of the choice of a norm.

Nevertheless, as noted, here the adjudication no longer functions within the traditional modern rationality of the systemic thinking. Furthermore, the adjudication no longer necessarily reproduces the traditional validity of the system, provided that the system is considered as a formally coherent and discursively integrated national legal system. This applies also to the reproduction of the political integrity etc.[196]

On the other hand, this sense the adjudication is not absolutely independent of the national legal system. The national legal system and its discourse function as alternative possibilities for the adjudicative system.[197] In other words, the question is about, what kind of generality one is seeking.

The problem of the expansion of all types of legal sources and possible arguments is that it may result in communication problems. Functional arguments cannot justify the use of special professional language rules in law.

The ideas presented above seem to be visible in legal reality, as we come to see. Some courts do refrain from public analysis, and use contextual comparative law. Some do demonstrate, via sweeping statements, why analytical reasons can be ignored. On the other hand, some use

---

[196] In the light of the doctrine of sovereignty and the enlightenmentian tradition, one may say that where in the traditional doctrine (Bodin, Montesquieu) the governments and courts had functional, if not even direct, relationship with the parliamentary legislator, in the Europeanized law the separation of these spheres of sovereign powers has taken place. Courts, by having their relationship with European level, have got more independent, as well as the governmental bodies are increasingly attached to the European Council as an "autonomous" bodies.

[197] As it has been maintained, it is the national legislator, who has produced such a system in contemporary Europe.

comparative considerations as inspirational material and these considerations may be discussed within closed discourses. Furthermore, pure "translations" take place between all these methods in some form or another.

Consequently, one is inclined, for example, to enter into an institution-centred system of, for example, European adjudication, whereby the legal discourses encounter difficulties in producing the relevant material and analysis required for reasonably justified legal decision. The traditional systematization via the genuine legal discourses is comprehended secondary exercise in many ways. This leads to the professionalized and institutional interpretation of law[198].

Next our aim is to set forth and interpret comparative reasoning mainly within "legal" institutions.

This study, henceforth, analyses and connects two types of knowledge. The first type of knowledge consists of open comparative reasoning, and the second of comparative considerations in context and in some dogmatic opinions in different fields of law. In this way one may explain the forms of the use of comparative law in contemporary European legal decision-making.

Many different institutional "legal actors" and their opinions are taken into account in this inquiry. This idea is related to the claim that legal borrowings take place through intermediaries in highly complex reflexive processes, and that many of these institutional actors "play second fiddle" to the final decisions-makers[199] and to legal development, in general terms. The argumentation by parties, interlopers, individual judges, administrators, judges etc. are all relevant for the study of comparative reasoning within a particular legal institution. Through all these intermediaries comparative aspects are filtered, until they appear, if they appear at all, in the institutional justification.

Consequently, the next part comprises an analysis of the actual relationships between legal systems and orders, different normative solutions, and the role of institutional actors in terms of the ideas presented above. The study moves towards the examination of legal reasoning in more a "value-based" and instrumental sphere. In a legal sense, the question of "how" institutions think is combined with the question "what" they think.[200] Finally, some remarks are made concerning "how they should" think, both in legal dogmatics and legal adjudication.

Most of the ideas developed in this chapter will be directly and explicitly "applied" in the following analysis, but not all. This chapter remains, consequently, relatively independent theory of comparative legal reasoning.[201]

---

[198] This is typical of European-level legal adjudication.
[199] Sacco, R., 1991, p.395.
[200] "What" means here the audience, the solution etc. in the legal context.
[201] For more comprehensive treatment, see Kiikeri, M , 1999.

CHAPTER 3

COMPARATIVE LAW
IN EUROPEAN LEGAL ADJUDICATION

1. INTRODUCTION

1.1. Preliminary remarks

The objective in this part of the book is to consider the "practice" of comparative reasoning in law from the point of view of the ideas developed in the previous chapters. This means an examination of the value-based argumentative and justificatory restrictions and the determination of the scope of the use of comparative observations in legal decision-making institutions. In this way one may be able to determine the limits of traditional uses of comparative law in the traditional theory of legal discourse. Only by making some conclusions on the instrumental and value-based adjudicative uses on these empirical basis, one is able to check the validity of the premises developed in the previous chapters, and, on the other hand, to consider the validity of comparative considerations from the point of view of the value-based theory of legal justifications.

On the other hand, the empirical study will, in the end, raise certain issues for the traditional "classificatory" comparative law to be reconsidered, and, furthermore, it will offer reasoned possibilities to rethink the "European" paradigm of law.

Before going into the details of the European level case law, there is a short discussion on the context of this comparative legal interpretation in European legal culture, namely, discussion on the use of comparative law in some European national legal systems.

The examination of the use of comparative law in other types of international organizations is excluded from the scope of this study.[202]

1.2. Some "legal" bases for the use of comparative law in adjudicative legal reasoning

The interest of interpreters of law in its comparative aspects has been recognized in modern legal history, though many explicit references are lacking. Comparative law has been used in public law (international and national), in private law (international and national), in

---

[202] For some analysis, see Kiikeri, M., 1999, pp.312-317.

conflicts of law, in international and national arbitration, in regional and various "issue-based" organizations. Its use extends from legal drafting to interpretation and justification - and to legal education to legal cultural and political studies. On the other hand, there are differences in approaches to comparative legal interpretation, which may be depend upon, for example, whether one is speaking about fields of public or private law, and that of national or international law.

One may assert, for example, that premises in international systems are, to a certain extent, contrary to those of national adjudication. In international and regional legal systems, comparability is usually assumed to exist, and the use of comparative studies is considered occasionally and virtually necessary.[203] In the realm of comparative interpretation of national law, on the other hand, the basic premise of the adjudicative function seems to be the non-comparability of legal systems. That is to say, in practice, comparative legal arguments - arguments deriving from other legal systems - are not relevant or perhaps not even permitted[204]. This may be related to the idea that in an interpretation by comparative observations, as in legal drafting too, the question is about the development and improvement of (national) law[205]. This is puzzling for the national adjudication having, as its basic premise, the idea that it is contrary to the concept of a legal system to introduce and emerge *ad hoc* considerations and new rules and interpretations into the system in an unsystematic and unpredictable manner.[206]

On the other hand, in modern legal systems one does not expect judges to know the law of another country.[207] Moreover, comparative interpretation may be seen only as a luxurious form of legal analysis[208].

As one may notice, however, the reality is more complicated than these assumptions may suggest.[209] One may say that if knowledge exists, there are no principled obstacles to use it or,

---

[203] As one could see, however, to this "rule" there are both normative and practical exceptions.

[204] In the case of disallowed sources, a system cannot function as a source of law alone or with some other system. Usually this leads to the maintaining of existing conditions as they are (coherence, comparison by opposites types of argumentation, margin of appreciation). On the other hand, a system, for example, a regional court, gain additional importance because of its institutional actors.

[205] See, Markesinis, P., 1990, p.5 ff.

[206] One may also establish a common denominator to these "legal spheres" of reasoning for the purpose of this study. This common denominator shall be the idea of "legal order", which can be described, in general, as a "sphere" of positive laws and interpretative traditions, which is regulated by the obligation to justify the decisions on the basis of legal sources, in a form or another, in order to maintain the discursive integrity of law.

[207] Markesinis, P., 1990, p.4.

[208] Marsh, N.S., 1977, p.655.

[209] Comparative interpretation plays a practical role in many states, see the remarks on the use of comparative legal analysis in private law in Greece, Turkish, Dutch, Luxemburg, French, Belgium, Swiss, German, Austria, Czech Republic, Marsh, N.S., 1977, p.656 The basic use has been seen in *lacunae* filling.
    Swiss courts refer sometimes to German, Italian, Austrian law, Marsh, N.S., 1977, and references. Remarks on wide use of comparative material in Swiss Courts, see Aubin, B., 1970, p.480.

at least, to consult it. On a contrary, in some cases, it may even be the case that the knowledge of another legal system must be considered positively.

It has been maintained that the legal use of comparative law is connected to the purpose of filling up *lacunae* in the law.[210] In contemporary adjudication, the practical interpretation of law, on the basis of comparative law, can be also based on common legislation, but for that matter, upon the fact that all countries have undergone similar type of social changes.[211]

The use of comparative law in legal interpretation can also be legally regulated. The legal basis for comparison establishes the *a priori* comparability of certain systems. The legal regulation of comparative law, as a necessary form of consultation in legal interpretation, establishes comparative law as a relatively obligatory source of law in a particular system[212].

For uses of English law in United States, see Winterton, G., 1975, p.73, and in general, Riles, A., 1999, p.221 ff and Zaphiriou, G.A., 1982.

For uses in Holland, see Koopmans, T., 1996, p.545, 551. For example, Hoogeraad, *Van Greuningen v Bessem*, 21 May 1943, Nederlandse Jurisprudentie, N.J. 1943, 455, May, 21, 1943., Advocate General Hartkamp in product liability case, material damage, Hoogeraad 9 October 1992, N.J. 1994, p.535, referring to Supreme Court of California, 607, P.2d, 949 (Cal. 1980), where the Court finally denied the doctrine. Also. Kisch, I, 1981, Supreme Court of Netherlands, Civil division, April 2, 194, Supreme Court of the Netherlands,, Civil Division, p.23, 1950, NJ 600, (Austria, France, Germany, Italy, Switzerland used in case on 'promise as a gift').

The application of foreign law in socialist states has also been discussed (Erezinsky, C., 1978). "Modellings" can be identified.

On Austria, for example, see Schwind, F., 1973.

One can make distinctions between the informative function and interpretative function. The informative function does not have a role in the justification as such ("passive comparison"). The interpretative function there is a penetration of the comparative observations to the legal justification ("active comparison"). (Boult, R., 1977).

This idea is problematic in many ways. It assumes that the information as such cannot have any normative role. It also neglects the analysis of the contextual discourses, on which the representation of the passive information is only a sign. According to this idea, one considers the passive side of the comparison only declaratory. Furthermore, one seems to forget system maintenance and systems relationship-creative functions. In other words, it does not take into account the discursive nature of the "declarations".

[210] In European legal history, the prevailing theory of *lacunae*-filling has been more or less connected to the use of Roman law in the absence of explicit rules. This idea derives from the Bologna School's analysis of medieval practices. (Winterton, G., 1975). For examples in practice, see Coing, H., 1973, p.505.

[211] Marsh, N.S., 1977 pp.664-665.

[212] There are many questions related to these types of legally regulated comparative observations. One may ask, for example, if there an obligation to explicitly analyse these observations in the justification, and secondly, to what extent one has to look into these observations in the internal work of the court?

The Article 1 of the Swiss Zivil Gesetzbuch has been seen a kind of a normative basis (Zweigert, K., Kötz, H., 1977, p.14). It states that

"*Das Gesetz findet auf alle Rechtsfragen Anwendung, für die es nach Wortlaut oder Auslegung eine Bestimmungen enthält.*

Kann dem Gesetze keine Vorschrift entnommen werden, so soll der Richter nach Gewohnheitsrecht und, wo auch ein solches fehlt, nach der Regel entscheiden, die er als Gesetzgeber aufstellen würde.

Er folgt dabei bewährter Lehre und Überlieferung".

In Israel the case of lacunae in one's own law has been also regulated on legal basis (Friedmann, D., 1975, pp.350-355).

One can find certain legal rules establishing comparative law as a source of law from some international systems (International Court of Justice, Treaty establishing the European Community). In general, see Bogdan, M., 1990, p.33, Zweigert, K., Kötz, H., 1977, pp.7-9, David, R., 1950, pp.100-104, Gutteridge, H.C., 1944, pp.1-10, 1949, pp. 61-71. It has been seen also "common for the worlds civilized nations" and part of the practices of some Regional Courts like the

Nevertheless, in adjudication the idea of sources tends to be more liberal than the theory of legal sources often suggests. There can be considerations which do not necessarily appear in the justification and argumentation and which cannot be, in a systematic way, grasped by the legal sciences. Comparative law seems to be one of these "extra" sources. Courts seem to use comparative law, though no explicit obligations or permissions are formulated in the systematic discourse. Consequently, comparative law is an example of a legal source where there are more controversies and difficulties when it is considered at the theoretical level than when it is used in practice[213]. Reasons for this feature have already been given in the previous chapters.

These aspects give the study two directions: one has to consider the use of comparative law both in context and in relation to open justification.[214]

1.3. Some observations concerning the material of the study

The "empirical" material of this part consists of interviews of the judges and administrators, and some legal cases. Furthermore, some literature is consulted.

On the other hand, the idea is also to focus on the roles of different discursive actors in the realm of the use of comparative law[215]. As maintained above, the role of the different organisational actors as comparativists can be evaluated by a study of the interaction between these actors. The role of the administrators, reporters and advocates is essential to allocate the different uses of comparative law. This is necessary in order to understand the role of comparative law in the realm of institutionalized law. Because of this, moreover, some

---

European Court of Justice (Pescatore, P., 1980, pp.337-359, Lando, O., 1986, pp.101-102). See also, for example, Pescatore, P., 1983, pp.337-359, Bogdan, M., 1990, p.93, and p.34, referring to Eustathiades, Droit comparé et méthode comparative en droit international public. In: Xenion. Festschrift Zepos, Vol 2 (Athene) 1973, pp.133-139. Also, Schlesinger, R.B., 1968, p.72.

[213] Trindade, A.A.C., 1977.

[214] One should be aware of the problem of the different types of "openesses", which may exist in different legal orders. One should see some legal orders in a "large" sense by including, to the "publicity" of the judgment, also the arguments of the parties and other "players" in the written and even in the oral part of the procedures. Some systems, like English legal system, are discursive and open already in relation to their form of judgment.

This idea would need, however, further development. Nevertheless, what one may say that the written justificatory form is the most decisive from the dogmatic and legal discursive point of view. Furthermore, it is clear that some systems are argumentatively and discursively more open than the others (see, for example, Legeais, R., 1994, pp. 257-258).

[215] The inquiry as to the "informal" uses of comparative law requires consideration of two aspects. Firstly, one has to study the practice of its use in both internal and external argumentation and justification. This requires two different methods; one has to make qualitative studies about the "inspirational" and internal use, and, on the other hand, one must identify comparative practical arguments from the justification of different decisions.

remarks are, at times, made upon the organizational principles.[216]

The results of the interviews have been mainly merged into different analyses of the practical phenomenon and the explanations. Interviews are not reproduced and explicitly referred to.

It must be mentioned also that in relation to some legal institutions, it was easy to obtain access in order to interview judges[217], and that the entry to some systems was more difficult. In some systems it seemed to be problematic to interview judges, and the interviews had to be made with functionaries.[218] This may be due to many reasons. Analysis of this aspect is not, nevertheless, made here.

The interviews were based on a questionnaire which included certain question related to the subject[219]. The interviews themselves created further questions. It was not possible to ask all

---

[216] Comparative arguments may appear, in adjudicative processes, in statements of the parties, in the oral hearings, in personal preliminary considerations of judges, in advisory opinions (before hearings), in advisory opinions internal to the institutions, in research internal to the institution, in internal closed discussions, in justificatory judgments, and in dissenting opinions.

[217] Finland, Sweden, Germany, England, European Courts.

[218] Italy, France.

[219] Questions were:
Introductory questions:
1. Have you been interviewed before on reasoning in this court and internal research within it?
General part:
2. Could you describe shortly the processes of this court?
3. What material is there available?
4. How is internal research made in general? How is it restricted?
5. Do you ask for statements from external experts?
6. Are there external experts used in the course of the proceedings?
7. How long does the procedure last (on average)?
Comparative law:
8. Is comparative law research part of the work of this court?
9. How do you see the role of comparative law in this court in general?
10. How is a comparative study limited, if it is made?
11. What type of information belongs to a comparative survey (sociological, systematic, cases, rules, etc.)?
12 From which countries are there material available?
13. Do the judges have a general interest in comparative law?
14. How much comparative law (cases, rules etc.) is discussed in this institution?
15. Are comparative studies presented by the parties? What is the reaction to these studies?
16. Could you describe the situation where comparative studies are made/reasons for making comparative studies?
The "internal" argumentation in courts:
17. Are comparative arguments used in the internal discourses of the court?
18. What kind of role do they have there?
19. In what form are these arguments used?
20. Are legal systems discussed "technically" or "culturally" ("systematically")?
21. How "distant" are the cases or systems used?
22. How do you see the effect of these comparative observations upon interpretation?
23. Could you give some examples of cases, where comparative law has had a role?
24. What countries are discussed in particular?
Specific questions in international institutions:
25. Do judges compare the laws of their own countries in the internal discussion?

the questions connected to the issue. Some questions, which seem to be essential, remain unasked[220]. All the same, the free flowing nature of the interviews, although structured around the formal questions, revealed some characteristics of the use of comparative law. These observations have reproduced in this study.

One of the basic ideas in the methodology of the interviews was to let the interviewed define the topic themselves. In other words, the question was defined as a question about the "use of comparative law", but the content of 'comparative law' was let open and unexplicated. Consequently, an interesting phenomena was observed: for example, many of the interviewed connected use of the decisions of some supranational courts to the use of comparative material, or at least the "comparative" nature of these latter decisions was many times recognized even if, however, all those interviewed emphasized in the end the "specific" binding nature of the systems and decision deriving from supranational institutions. The confusion related also to system of "intervening" (by third) parties in European courts.

The interviews played also some role in the selection of cases.

The presentation of the information achieved in the interviews is not explicitly connected to any particular person interviewed. The idea is to speak about legal systems, orders and institutions, and not to give reason for the speculation as to the correctness or wrongness of the answers of those interviewed. The presentation of the remarks is generalized already in the explanation.

It is a fact that the interviews represent quite weak and subjective knowledge in this context. Not all personnel was interviewed, even if the attempt was made to have at least two persons interviewed from one institution. However, one could claim that the conclusions may be generalized, to a certain extent, because of the nature of the questions and supporting analysis

---

26. How could you explain the fact that comparative observations appear usually in dissenting and advisory opinions?
General questions:
27. Who is the audience of this court?
28. Do you think comparative law is useful, or not, necessary or not and relevant or not?
29. Do you think comparisons are made for integrative purposes or for the purposes of the case only? Is it important "internally" to the legal system, or "externally" to legal systems?
30. Do you see any obstacles for making comparative studies in this court?
31. What could be the obstacle for using comparative reasons in the course of reasoning?
32. Do the lower courts use comparative observations in their justifications?
33. How do you see the development of databases from the point of view of the use of comparative law?
[Some additional questions:
34. What kind of role could comparative law have in contemporary law?
35. What kind of comparative studies would be "useful"?]
    Many modifications upon this questioning took place during the interview in order to maintain the "coherence" of the interview.
[220] One of these questions was for example; when are comparative studies made by those, who give dissenting opinions? Are these made before or after the internal decision has been taken place (relating this to the internal procedural rules and practices)? Questions related to the application of the Article 177 (new 234) both in European and national level remained unasked too. Furthermore, one could have specified the role of comparative studies related to the examination of the possible breaches in implementation (*bona fide*, see below).

from the literature.

No phenomenological approach to legal institutions was applied, that is, there was no participation.

On the other hand, it has to be noticed that the main focus, in this part of the book, is in the functioning of comparative legal reasoning within the European level institutions. This can be motivated, thinking about the results in the theoretical perspective, by the fact that in these institutions the role of comparative observations is more explicit and easier to investigate. Furthermore, in these institutions, the basic question of the use of comparative law is connected on a more visible way to the hard cases of law and legal interpretation. On the other hand, it can be claimed that the forms of comparative interpretation of law in national systems and even different traditions are reflected, in a more open form, at the European level. Consequently, the characteristics of comparative interpretation of law can be more easily shown by way of examples deriving from European level.

The analysis of the European Court of Justice and the European Court of Human Rights in their relation to each other, however, differ considerably because of the "comparative" institutional differences. One has to remember, as far as the structure of argumentative processes is concerned, that there are remarkable differences between the European Court of Human rights and the European Court of Justice. For example, in the former dissenting opinions are allowed and preliminary (Commission) decisions are given, in the latter this does not occur.

However, the function of the Commission in the European Court of Human Rights (and, in a way, the expressions of the dissenting opinions) can be, to a certain extend, discursively identified with the role of the Advocate General in the European Court of Justice, even if these institutional arrangements remain essentially different. Nevertheless, the opinions of the Advocate General and the opinions in the European Commission of Human rights can be situated within the "context" of legal justification.

1.4. The use of comparative law in some national legal orders

1.4.1. General remarks

The philosophies of the European legal orders, or the legal "cultures", differ considerably from the discursive point of view[221]. As noted, in some systems the processes are highly "inquisitorial" (i.e. the continental approach), other systems are more passive (especially the

---

[221] Also, Summer, R.S., Taruffo, M., 1991, pp.508-509. The philosophy may also be related to the philosophy of history in these systems, see Legrand, P., 1996, p.71 ff.

English system as an accusatorial or adversial system). In the former type of system, one makes the examination of the law and facts (doctrine, social, comparative conditions etc.) in a functional institutional administration, and in the latter type of system, the arguments put forward derive mainly from the argumentation presented by the parties. One may say that the basic philosophies seem to be remarkably different. The procedural difference is related to the non-inquisitorial nature of common law processes.[222]

This distinction is not, however, as clear as it seems. In both types of systems these elements overlap. On more discursive (adversial) processes, some experts have occasionally been used. On the other hand, in the inquisitorial systems, the administration may be sometimes separated from the main "court", and, for example, the opinions of the Advocate Generals (or commissaire du gouvernement in France) are not the "official" part of the decision-making as such, but part of the oral procedure.

In some systems, on the other hand, the importance of the parties and expertise is recognized, and in some systems there is no "external" research needed. This all, however, depends naturally on the type of cases examined and also on the different levels of the "hierarchy" of the court, though the hierarchical status of the court is not always decisive factor.

Nevertheless, the basic features seem to be clear. Some systems' (or courts') administration is constructed so, that there is great use of *a priori* research before the hearing of the case, and this is to be encouraged organizationally. On the other hand, in some systems (such as the House of Lords and in the Court of Appeal, for example) the parties are considered to be the only sources of the arguments and the role of the administration has, and *should* not have, anything to do with the "substance" and argumentation of the case.

Here the interest is not to focus on the classification of different legal systems and concentrate on the analysis of their differences and similarities, but to consider the relevance of this distinction from the point of view of the ideas on the sources of law and ideas concerning standards of legal reasoning.[223]

---

[222] The legal process is discursive in the sense that the task of the judges is not to make any preliminary studies or *ad hoc* studies on the correct material for the law. The material is more or less presented in the legal processes. This seems to differ, to a certain extent, from the idea in continental systems. (Lawson, F., 1977, pp.365-366.) This related to the differences in the significance of systematization (Legrand, P., 1996, p.65 ff.).

[223] See, for example, David, R., Brierly, J.E.C., 1978, Zweigert, K., Kötz, H., 1977, Schlesinger, R.B., 1980 and 1995 (pp.480-481 on reasoning and structural differences in general (for example, law and equity)). Gorla, G. (1980, p.308) maintains that what is often forgotten is that the distinction between common law and continental (civil law) was being used already in 16th century English legal literature. Furthermore, the return to this discussion was a phenomenon of the nationalistic English historiography of the modern age. Moreover, this distinction was taken by the continentals as an self-evident distinction from the beginning of 19th century.

See also, Gorla, G., Moccia, l., 1981, p.146, and Moccia, L., 1981, pp.158-159 on the pre-modern and modern concept of 'civil law'. Ingredients of differences, see Lobban, M., 1995, p.34 ff.

For some differences between French and common law, see Koopmans, T., 1991, pp.493-494. One of the characteristics of French law is the strict division between private, criminal and administrative law, and the deductive method of

Very generally, however, continental law can be described as the Roman-Germanic tradition, whereas the common law has originated from the English type of legal system.[224] Nordic systems have been seen as a distinctive "legal group".[225]

Where Talcott Parson, for example, viewed the English legal system as an integrated system of universal norms, Max Weber, on the other hand, saw the common law, one may say, less rational than the law of other European systems[226]. Weber saw capitalism establishing itself in England almost despite the legal system.[227] Nevertheless, the traditional idea, which seems to indicate something essential to the differences between these "philosophically" distinctive spheres of law and is connected directly to the traditional problems of comparative law, is the institution and function of trust.[228] One could maintain that the trust is a case in point for more "holistic" thinking about abstract legal institutions in common law countries. It seems that the regulation of trusts is related to their social-economic functions.[229] Unlike many "comparable" regulations of the use of capital in continental systems, the law of trusts seem to be an example of "liberal" regulation, which, however, is directly related to many dimensions of social life.

This kind of conceptualization of trusts would be quite strange for continental philosophy of regulation, as many authors have maintained. In continental systems, these aspects are separate from the regulation of family, contact, property and succession law, and the social functions are not seen holistically. This is an example of how different types of regulations take into account the social dimension of the regulated objects in modern liberal law.[230]

Some differences may be found also in relation to meaning of rights in these systems. This

---

reasoning.

[224] For some definitions, see Gorla, G., Moccia, L., 1981, pp.143-144

[225] Zweigert, K., Kötz, H., 1977, 284 ff.

[226] Weber. M., 1969, pp.294-297, pp.317-318.

[227] Weber, M., 1969, p 318.

Weber's idea on the English system can be criticised. One may say that predictability and flexibility are not necessarily the features of a positive and formal legal system. Namely, if the positive and formal system does not meet the requirements of social development, the informal system will (Friedman, L.M., 1975, pp.207-208).

I believe that the basic problem of Weber's analysis of common law was the problem of not recognizing the "informal formality". This means that he saw the English legal system through the lenses of his own tradition. It can be claimed that formality in the English system is much more formal in the social sense, i.e., the authority of law is seen from the point of view of the "ruler". It is institutional (on the institutional theory of law, see Weinberger, O., MacCormick, N., Institutional Theory of Law (1995). The Benthamite approach to law explains a lot. On the other hand, the concept of property , extremely central to the Anglo-Saxon legal philosophy, refers more to some kind of a 'holistic" approach of property and capital, which can be seen in the trust institutions and their history.

[228] See, Zweigert, K., Kötz, H., 1977, p 274 ff., referring to Keeton, G.W., Social Change in the Law of Trusts (1958), without, however, a thorough historical-contextual study concerning the "public" dimension of the institution.

[229] Zweigert, K., Kötz, 1977, p.278 ff.. See also, Drobnig, U., 1972, p.124.

Basically, people applied to the central power, as requested it to take over the church function of the administration of bodies of property which had been established by a testament or a will etc.

It is interesting that this type of explanation is not emphasized by most of the comparative lawyers.

[230] For some discussion, see Rabel, É., 1978, pp.88-90.

may be related to the absence of written constitutional rights in English legal system, for example.[231]

One could try to search for differences in interpretative techniques, between common and continental law, by examining historico-political forms of reasoning in different contexts. In this sense, the differences may relate to the emphasis of the natural law in continental and common law countries.[232]

It can be asserted, on the other hand, that one of the common denominators for these different legal philosophies seems to be the need for a dynamic, yet coherent, developer of the law. In modern continental countries judges were, historically, mistrusted and provided with codified standards, which led to the glorification of the legislature (and sovereign) in this regard. Judge-made law had no place in the hierarchy of sources of law. In the common law, on the other hand, the only possibility for creating law, historically, seemed to be through the judiciary.[233] The general differences in interpretative techniques between continental and Anglo-Saxon systems could be explained, accordingly, by the different (public law) assumptions concerning the separation of powers, and by the roles of statutes and precedents as sources of stability.[234] The strictness of the legal norms in the common law has been

---

[231] See, Legrand, P , 1996, pp.70-71. This makes a distinction, at least formally, between English and the United States legal systems.

[232] Pollock, F., Sir, The expansion of the common law (South Hackensack, N.J) 1974, p111 ff. Maitland, F.E., The constitutional history of England : a course of lectures delivered by F. W. Maitland (Cambridge).

However, the same tendencies can be found in the attempt to "secularize" natural law thinking during the modern era, even if the context and forms of realization of this objective was different (see, Capelletti, M., 1989, pp.127-128). For the United States, see ibid, p.130.

[233] See Herman, S., 1981, p.337.

[234] The most important source of argument is the precedent. This was given in this century, at the House of Lords a horizontal binding force (the so-called "self-limitation" rule, Case *Young v Bristol Aeroplane Co.,* 1944, KB, p.718.). In 1966, however, the self-limitation rule was not considered as an absolute basis for decisions (*Practice Direction,* House of Lords, (1966) 1 WLR p.1234). This has had some practical consequences. It seem that this rule is not obeyed strictly in English courts. The unity of the Common law has been to be preserved by vertical binding qualities. However, there seems to be a tendency, in the contemporary case-law, to challenge vertical binding force (See, Prott, L.V , 1978, p.425. Cases *Broome v Cassell & Co* (1971) 2 QB, p.354, *Schorxch Meier v Hennin* (1974) 3 WLR, p.823, *Miliangos v Georg Frank (Textiles) Ltd* (1975) QB, p.487,and *Harper v National Coal Board* (1974) QB, p.614).

The comity -doctrine, based on the idea of the unity of Common law, has kept this horizontal binding force within Great Britain in general terms (Prott, L.V., 1978, p.425).

Legrand, P. (1996, p.74 ff.) has spoken about the difference in the idea of the separation of powers (by referring to works of Kahn-Freund, O.). The idea is that in *"England the executive cannot justify any course of action unless it can rely on conferment of a power by the legislature"*. On the other hand, continental governance is based on an inherent power to govern.

The relationship between executive and the judiciary is also interesting. One can claim, namely, that the executive is more independent in English system in relation to judiciary than in continental countries. This is based on the observations that the executive branch seems to act quite progressively in English system, being, however, in the full control of judiciary. (This observation is based on the study of the cases against England in European Court of Human rights, and on the cases of *Horseferry* (1993) and *Pinochet* (1998), see below). This could be explained by the fact that where the executive's powers are confirmed by the Parliamentary authority, it may play an effective role under the supervision of the judicial branch. Interesting is also that where the judiciary is confirming the powers of the executive to act, it also relates strongly

contrasted with the broader formulations in the civil law systems[235].

Consequently, one of the basic differences seems to be, or at least has been till now[236], the idea of a source of law bound to the different emphasis of the case law. In the continental countries - or, more explicitly, in civil law systems - case law has often been considered as an "informal" source of law.[237] This may be related in general, as have been mentioned already, to the historical role of the court in these systems[238], and to differences in the professionalization of law.

The methods of reasoning are remarkably different between the continental and common law courts. The use of few interpretative techniques is not as strongly stressed in the common law as in continental countries. In fact compared to the continental systems in the common law, there seems to be a diversity of accepted modes of reasoning[239]. Where, in continental law interpretation, one usually concentrates on the analysis of a single legal institution, in the common law analysis one takes into account a bundle of specific problems connected to the

---

the justification to the intention of Parliament (*Pinochet*). This type of interaction between politically and legally clearly separate bodies seems to function as described despite of the sphere of law one is speaking about (European law, international law, or purely internal sphere of law).

This type of interaction seems to be really "action" based, whereas in Finland, for example, some recent cases have show (*Campoy* case, child kidnapping, KKO 1998) that the Supreme court of Finland decides the case strictly on statutory basis, but on the same time tries to put pressure on (and generate discussion in press etc) the Parliament to reconsider the statutory measures (also international agreements (Hague Convention)!) in order to maintain the systematic solution "politically" correct in general. This Finnish example suits to the description of Kahn-Freund on the role of judiciary in continental systems. (This case in Finland is, nevertheless, an extreme example of this type of function.)

[235] Sacco, R., 1991, p.387. In fact, one could say that there are no legal "rules" at all in common law (Legrand, P., 1996, pp.67-68). Judicial decisions may occasionally "appear" as a set of rules (ibid., p.68).

[236] The contemporary British system, for example, seems to be precedent-based Common law, but, more and more, also based on the modern statutory law. Furthermore, there seem to be less dissenting and additional reasoning in justifications. Weber saw this development in a following way: *"As the bureaucratization of formal legislation progresses, the traditional position of English judge is also likely to be transformed permanently and profoundly"* (1969, p.320).

[237] Capelletti, M., 1989, p.144, Markesinis, P., 1990, p.20. See also, Sacco, 1991, p.321, 346. For some historical analysis, see Gorla, G., Moccia, L , 1981, p.147. For judicial precedents in some continental countries in legal history, see ibid. p.150.

[238] See for further analysis, Capelletti, M., 1989, pp.144-146.

[239] Prott, L.V., 1978, p.435.

The main methods of reasoning in British systems are: linguistic, philosophical (or logical), historical, traditional and sociological (Cardozo, B., 1947, (ed. Hall, M.E. and Patterson, E.W.,), p.117). This appears in the forms of precedent based arguments, the development of procedural substantive law (by examining underlying principles and reason), and judicial logical arguments.

Logical arguments are not formal logical arguments, but consist in a search for basic underlying principles. There is a tendency to use less historical and judicial logical arguments. The doctrinal writings and theory of interpretation are also considered (Prott, L.V., 1978, p.421 and 429). The importance of these writings has increased (Cases *Broome v Cassell, Sweet v Parsley* (1970) AC, p.132, and *Miliangos v Georg Frank (Textiles) Ltd* (1975) QB, 487. (Prott, L.V., 1978, p.430)).

The sociological method has its place in the system probably because of the nature of the historical character of Common Law (See case *Herrington v British Railways Board* (1972) AC, p.902), and the influence of academics such as Roscoe Pound (On the latter, see Prott, L.V., 1978, p.430). The application of these sociological arguments mainly supports exceptions to precedents. There is a tendency to use increasingly sociological arguments.

plurality of legal institutions[240].

On the other hand, the idea of stability seems also to be related to this question. In the common law, stability may be based on the strict distinction between making law and discovering the law (Blackstone). The former seems to be a complicated process, where the establishment of *stare decisis* depends on the explicitness, the width, or narrowness of the reasoning (in substantive sense). One may say that because law-making is more complicated, the cases are more "isolated", and the inductiveness of the law relates to a discursive attitude towards new factuality and the establishment of rules in general.

The biggest difference may lay exactly in the approach to the principles (rules) and the facts; while continental judges approach the instances from principles, the common law judge goes from the instances to principles. There is therefore a difference in the need for and nature of systematization.[241] Another notable difference relates to the numerous separate justifications given in a judgment. This seems to indicate also the general discursive characteristics of the English legal system.

In conclusion, it has been claimed that the written judgments of English courts do not aim at exposing the motivation, conscious or unconscious of a judge, but rather to reconcile an audience with the use of power that such a decision authorizes. It attempts to persuade the public to fall in with the court's activity.[242] This may be the reason why judgments of English courts are verbose[243]; this is a way to avoid giving an impression of arbitrariness to the public[244].

It is clear that there are also many differences in methods of interpretation and justification also between so called continental countries. In countries where the *travaux preparatoires* have a role, interpretation may be derived from the preliminary material produced by parliament as a legislator in its open publications. In continental countries, the open analysis of this type of material does not seem to be as relevant as in Nordic systems.[245]

---

[240] Zweigert, K., Kötz, H., 1987, p.34, Goutal, J.L , 1996, p.117. Legrand, P. (1996, p.65) has suggested that the reasoning on common law is analogical, and in continent institutional (referring to Samuel, G., The foundations of Legal reasoning, 1994).

[241] Cooper, 1950, p.468 ff. Also, Legrand, P.1996, p.65, 68 ff.
One could claim that the relationship between numerous similar cases is horizontally reflexive. This means that the principles are not self-evidently parts of the case, but the interpretation of the principles embedded in the previous judgments is interpreted in a new factual context.

[242] Prott, L.V., 1978, p.428.

[243] Bankowski, Z., MacCormick, N., 1991, p.392.

[244] The main difference, from the point of view of the subject, can be seen in the method of justification. The free style and the affective reasoning, in the common law courts, differs from continental though (Lawson, F., 1977, p.366, quoting several authors). Naturally, the system of advocate general lessens the effect of this difference (ibid. p.369).

[245] On this, in general, see the book *Interpreting Statutes* (Dartmounth) 1991.

1.4.2. Comparative reasoning in relation to international legal obligations

European law and national legal orders. International obligations are in their formal appearance "comparative norms". They have usually been drafted on a comparative basis based on various national law conceptualizations. This is why the relationship between these "comparative norms" and the comparative interpretation and argumentation appears interesting.

Furthermore, one may speak, in connection with regional systems such as the European Human Rights system and the European Community, about a kind of practical form of subsidiarity. That is to say, the balance between the systems' superiority and autonomy is sought functionally by the institutions in these systems, mainly by the European-level institutions. This means, that the comparative material plays an extremely important role in finding the basis for these types of decisions.

Consequently, it is interesting to ask, what types of interpretative methods one could apply in state systems in the interpretation of, for example, case law related to international and regional measures, and how this relates to the question of comparative interpretation, which seems to be *a priori* a possible form of interpretation[246]. In other words, the basic question is whether one can take into account comparative law aspects in applying international and regional norms in national legal systems.

Another remark ought to be made. Comparative interpretation or the interpretation of law on the basis of international obligations may arise in cases which seem to be problematic cases. In other words, the national court may identify, for example, a conflict between its international obligations or European rules in relation to comparative generality.

Brief observation concerning the basic doctrines of the "bindingness" of the norms of these systems must be presented in this connection in order to understand the possible relevance of comparative law in realm of these systems.

The European Court has insisted on the supremacy of European Community law in its decisions. This has also been recognized by the courts of many Member States.[247] On the other hand, the idea of the use of European Community Law in national courts has its normative basis in the Treaty and the doctrines created by the European Court of Justice. The binding effect of Community law and the case-law of the European Court of Justice is based on Article 5 of the Treaty on European Union (now Article 10). There has also been a "customary" basis for the application of precedents and provisions in different Member States: principles embedded in Acts (England), constitutions (Netherlands), the Constitution and legal practice

---

[246] In this respect, the question concerning the differences between the pre-Community and the post-Community periods is also interesting

[247] See Hartley, T.C., 1994, pp.238-264, Mathijsen, P.S.R.F., 1990, pp 309-310.

of the highest courts (France), and other somewhat undefinable situation (eg. In Italy and Germany), just to mention some examples.[248]

However, the European Court of Justice, in fact on a comparative basis[249], has provided that to attain the objectives of the Treaty, the role of the executive branch cannot vary from one State to another.[250] Thus, Community measures must override national measures. Even the fundamental rights of a legal system cannot provide an exemption from this.[251] This has been contested on some occasions by certain Member States, but lately the development in Member States has confirmed the Court's opinion, as mentioned. However, the discussion concerning this is ongoing, and the latest development has revealed some difficulties[252]

There is, furthermore, the doctrine of direct effect. This can be understood in two ways: there is the obligation to apply and the obligation to abstain from acting in a particular manner and. Legal provision is are directly effective, when they grant certain rights to individuals. There rights must be recognized by national courts.[253] Directly applicable provisions in the Treaties can be said to be those provisions that do not allow addressees of an obligation a discretionary latitude. If the Article cannot create individual rights, which the national court must protect, there is no direct effect of that Article.[254] On the other hand, even if no measures are taken, by the Community, to implement such an Article (contrary to the obligation of an Article), it could still be directly applicable.[255]

The direct effect of secondary legislation of the Community law is based on the Treaty and certain case law doctrines (directives).[256] Directives can be directly applicable under certain conditions. This quality creates an obligation to directly apply the directives, and for that matter, to ask advice from the ECJ, if there is doubt on the nature of this measure.

The process of determining the direct applicability of a Community provision is covered by the new Article 234 of the Treaty on European Union (referring to the system of preliminary rulings), although courts can also ascertain this through the case-law of the European Court.

Furthermore, the European Court of Justice has created a doctrine according to which

---

[248] On this, see e.g. Mathijsen, P.S.R.F., 1990, pp.311-312.

[249] See case 9 and 58/65 *San Michele v High Authority* (1967) ECR 1.

[250] Case 6/64 *Costa v ENEL* (1964) ECR 585.

[251] Case 4/73 *Nold v Commission* (1974) ECR 491.

[252] See, Hartley, T.C., 1994, p.264.

[253] Hartley, T.C., 1994, p.195 ff., Mathijsen, P.S.R.F., 1990, p.308. According to current law, states may be penalized for not complying with Community obligations (Amsterdam Treaty). On the other hand, States may be obliged to compensate damage resulting from the failure to implement Community provisions (case 6, 9/90 *Francovich v. Italy* (1991) ECR I-5357).

[254] Case 10/71 *Ministére Public Luxembourgeois v Müller* (1971) ECR 723.

[255] Case 43/75, *Defrenne v Sabena* (1976) ECR 455.

[256] See, for example, Hartley, T.C., 1994, p.194 ff.

national courts are obliged to interpret their laws in accordance with directives.[257] This is a natural development deriving from the prohibition of the national legislative bodies to act against Community provisions.[258]

These are the basic doctrines and provisions of the Community legal system which create obligations on the national courts to take into account the Community legal system.

Regarding the European Human Rights System, Article 1 of the Convention for the protection of Human Rights and Fundamental Freedoms[259] states:

> *"The High Contracting Parties shall secure to everyone within their jurisdiction the rights and freedoms defined Section I of this Convention"*

This Article transforms the declaration of rights (in Section I) into a set of obligations for the States which have ratified the Convention.

Concerning the actual texts, some maintain that this comprises an obligation to incorporate the actual text into domestic law, while others disagree. There is, however, an agreement that States have to give full effect to these rights.[260] This has been enforced by different legal means, depending on the constitutional practices of each Party to the Convention.

The most effective method of incorporation is through national courts.[261] They have the primary role.[262] Because states are obliged *"to ensure that their domestic legislation is compatible with the Convention and, if need be, to make any necessary adjustments to this end"*, courts also play their part within this procedure.

However, court decisions alone, based on national legislation, can achieve these objectives and thereby fulfill these obligations. The Convention does not, and nor does the Court[263], oblige national courts to formally apply the Convention, its provisions, and case-law in their decisions, or to use the provision of the Convention as "comparative" or analogical material in interpretation or argumentation. The use of provisions and their interpretations performed by the European Court of Human Rights depends upon the models and practice of interpretation and argumentation in national courts. The provisions are not directly applicable law in national courts in strictly formal sense even if substantially this seems to be the case.[264]

The direct formal application of these rights takes place in the form of the enforcement of

---

[257] Case 14/83 *Colson and Kamann v Landnord Rhein Westfalen* ECR (1984) 1891. See also case 79/83 *Harz v Deutche Tradax* (1984) ECR 1921.

[258] Case 230/78 *Eridania v Minister of Agriculture and Forestry* (1979) ECR 2749.

[259] 4 November 1950 (European Convention on Human Rights).

[260] See, Jacobs, F.G., 1975, p.10.

[261] Buergenthal, T., 1965, p.215.

[262] See also, Case *Sadik v. Greece* (1997) 24 EHRR 323

[263] For the role of the European Court of Human Rights on this issue, see Martens, S.K. 1998, p.8.

[264] On the temporal and territorial scope, see Jacobs, F.G., 1975, pp.12-14.

decisions of the European Court of Human Rights, decided on the basis of a petition or a suit, by the governments and parliaments via alteration to domestic legislation.

However, our basic interest concerns the question of whether one could use comparative observations in the interpretation and application of Community law and the norms of the European Human Rights System?[265]

Basically, all disputable interpretations of Community law must be taken to the European Court of Justice on the basis of the Article 177 (the new Article 234) of the Treaty.[266] The Community system is an autonomous legal order, and only the Court of Justice is competent to interpret Community law. At first glance, one could maintain that if some comparative aspects become relevant in the interpretation of Community law, they derive only from the European level institutional interpretations.

In the European Human Rights System, national courts do interpret European Human Rights. For example, the Basic Rights of Germany which form the fundamental premisses of the legal system must be in accordance with European Human Rights. Where explicit applicable constitutional right system are not provided within the system the system must evaluate the conformity of its decisions with European human rights principles. National Courts have a relative autonomy in checking this compatibility.

Consequently, national courts are obliged to consider European Human Rights on the basis of the above-cited "conformity rule". In practice this means that in most systems, the Human Rights Court's decisions are taken into account in deciding national cases, and it is national courts which determine the practical application of human rights norms and their content in the first place. The control by the European Court of Human Rights is *a posteriori* in nature and its processes are triggered by applications to the system. Because no pending of national processes takes place automatically[267], no autonomy for the Human Rights Court exists. It is a legal order which decides always on the acceptability of material national decisions, not on any autonomous interpretation of European human rights principles.

---

[265] This idea applies, to a certain extent, also to the relationship between national systems and the European Human Rights System.

[266] The Article 177 (the new Article 234) states:

The Court of Justice shall have jurisdiction to give preliminary rulings concerning:

(a) the interpretation of this Treaty;

(b) the validity and interpretation of acts of the institutions of the Community and of the ECB;

(c) the interpretation of the statutes of bodies established by an act of the Council, where those statutes so provide

where such a question is raised before any court or tribunal of a Member States, that court or tribunal may, if it considers that a decision on the question is necessary to enable it to give a judgment, request the Court of Justice to give a preliminary ruling thereon.

Where any such question is raised in a case pending before a court or tribunal of a Member State against whose decisions there is no judicial remedy under national law, that court or tribunal shall bring the matter before the Court of Justice.

[267] However, see exceptional cases related to the pending of the internal execution processes based on the rule 38 of the Court's procedure.

Naturally, one could treat these interpretations as autonomous interpretations. However, because national courts have also the possibility of interpreting the human rights, there does not seem to exist any autonomy in the sense of the Community legal system. Furthermore, the idea of "functional subsidiarity" is embedded *a priori* in many Articles in the Convention and the European Court of Human Rights has constantly developed extensive jurisprudence on the "margin of appreciation" doctrine.

Because the application of Community law in national courts, however, demands also an interpretation of national provisions in determining the balance between national rules and Community rules or to identify and resolve possible conflicts between national rules and Community rules, the question arises as to whether one can apply comparative observations in the interpretation of national rules, when, in the same case, the matter concerns the application of Community rules? In a sense, this would make it possible to interpret the generality in national legal systems in order to "fulfil" or to "substantiate" applicable national provisions, and to integrate the national rule into the preexisting interpretation of the European rule. This would be in accordance with the "treaty friendly interpretation".

A priori national systems are considered to be in conformity with European rules. The interpretation must be determined by the principle of "Community Law friendly interpretation". In this sense, comparative material cannot justify any deviation from the Community rule, even if the national rule is be found, on a comparative basis, to be against the prevailing interpretation of the Community rule. If such a conflict existed, the national norm would be invalidated, or where the Community rule is also ambitious, it should be submitted to determination within the processes of the Community Court (Article 177 (the new Article 234)). The comparative generality in European legal systems cannot justify a deviation from the prevailing wording or interpretation at the Community level.

On the other hand, as to be seen, comparative generality, because interpreted in "qualitative" manner, is not necessarily an indication of the prevailing Community interpretation. In this sense, the role of comparative law is quite problematic in cases where the question concerns also the interpretation of Community norms[268]. At least, it does not seem to be the "same" at these two levels of legal systems. The qualifying elements are institutionally attached, and due to the superiority of the Community system, Community level comparative interpretations prevail.[269]

One may say, on the other hand, that in the case of the human rights system, national courts could interpret, by comparative means, prevailing interpretations of the European Court of

---

[268] This is quite interesting because it suggests that the "Europeanization" of national legislation actually diminishes the role of comparative law in legal adjudication. This idea seems to be contrary to prevailing opinions. For example, judges seem to consider 'Europeanization" as a possibility for the increasing use of comparative perspectives.

[269] In theoretical terms this seems to indicate that the "analogical key" or the methods of restrictive, expansive or *e contrario* interpretations can be applied only by the Community Court.

Human Rights or the decisions by the Commission. Comparative "deviancies" from these interpretations could be possible because the courts are able to regard this as an indication of the current situation within the *"evolution of European standard"*, as it is sometimes expressed in the European Court of Human Rights decisions.

Nevertheless, as maintained, the final decision is made, in the case of a petition brought by a competent person, in the European Court of Human Rights. An ongoing conflict between the European human rights principles and national provisions cannot be sustained by national courts, because in the final analysis, identification of this conflict is made only by the Court of Human Rights[270]. Basically, the application of human rights principles in national Courts is a matter of systematic interpretation based on the "human rights friendly" interpretation. In this sense, there are no obstacles to comparatively interpret law in national courts, where some European human rights aspects must be considered.

Finally, one may note that it is the idea of the *"autonomy and superiority of an order"* which is connected to the possibility of using comparative material in legal interpretation and reasoning in national courts when they are interpreting the norms of European legal systems. In the case of European Community law, there seems to be great problems surrounding the use of comparative material as interpretative material, when the norms of the Community legal system are applied in national courts. In case this material is used, there seems to be a strong assumption of the "imprecision" of the applied norm, in which case the matter would have been a matter of interpretation by the relevant European-level institution. All other sources (the case law of the European Court, general principles etc.) seem to be relevant, but in the case where comparative aspects are taken into account, the national decision-maker seems to go beyond its interpretational competence. The fascinating fact is that when the interpretation goes beyond its systematic context, a lack of clarity is assumed. This is based on the idea that the system is assumed always to apply clear rules, and that the comparative aspects raise the question of imprecision. In case of autonomous interpretation, there could be strong arguments for "non-compliance" with European procedural norms, and some doubt concerning the "correctness" surrounding the material result.

Another interesting idea relates to the fact that only the European Court seems to be able to apply qualitative comparative law. The difference between the competencies of these court-levels seems to relate to the possibility of using "complete" comparative legal method. This, on the other hand, is a question of a discourse between legal dogmatics and scientific comparative law, and determines the criteria for the evaluation of the work of the European Court.

One could claim, however, that comparative considerations may have quite a peculiar function in the relationship between European Community law and national law. First of all,

---

[270] Because of the nature of the "principled" systems, the conflicts are extremely difficult to identify a prior.

as maintained, national provisions could be interpreted by comparative means to be in confirmity with European norms. Secondly, one could imagine that comparative law considerations play a role where national courts are considering the question of the clarity of Community law provisions in relation to the the Article 234 procedure of Community law. Namely, in considering the need for a preliminary ruling, comparative law studies reveal disparity or generality (conflicting or consistent judgements) in the implementation practice, and this may give an indication - motivation and reasons to argumentation too - concerning the lack of clarity of Community law provisions. The disparity may lead to the conclusion that the Community provision is unclear, whereas the generality indicates that the Community provision has been understood in a quite uniform way. In this sense, comparative law may "systematize" the premises of the preliminary ruling procedure.

In conclusion, it can be noted that comparative law as a "complete" source of law, in general, seems to be excluded in cases where there is another "superior" and "autonomous" interpreter of the norms in question. Comparative law as a source of law is a source of law of the "superior" and "autonomous" order, but not as such for the order which applies these norms in the first instance.

If comparative material is used in the application of the norms of the Community system by national courts, it may be only a matter of "institutional or individual heuristics" by which the decision-maker may convince itself of the "good faith" application of these European norms, for example, in the realm of the Article 10 (former Article 5). In this case, as maintained, their use is instrumental because of the closed decision-making processes. This is so, because the "in-good-faith" interpretation cannot be an argument concerning the application of clear and unequivocal norms.

This does not seem to be the case when interpreting European human rights.

It is, however, a different discussion, to what extend comparative law may be taken "informally" and "unsystematically" into account, and what general function it may have in for the legal decision-maker in national courts, who is considering EC law questions. It is clear that comparative law is a critical tool in the sense that it enables evidently a judge to realize, many times, how undefined and vague the terms and provisions of the European law are. This way it certainly gives self-confidence to the national judge to construct the interpretation of the European law - as faithfully as possible (according to the Article 10, for example, in relation to Community, but also other states! (principle of loyalty)).

This function is related to the function of comparative law described in the connection to the preliminary ruling procedures. In other words, there is the function of finding obligations the second to the finding of the unclear obligations, both the function of the national judge. The function of comparative law may vary according to the hierarchical status of the legal institution.

Other types of international obligations. The relevance of comparative law in national courts can be seen particularly in the field of public international law, especially in the realm of international criminal law, procedural and extradition questions, and the questions of enforcement and recognition of foreign judgments[271].

The use of international law (legal material) as a source of law in national courts has its normative basis in each national system. It is embedded in the traditional doctrines concerning the effects of international obligations and of the sources of law in each national legal system. The implementation of international law is left to the constitutions of individual states[272].

As is well-known, in dualistic systems international law (principles, treaties, and custom) must be transformed into national legal systems by "internal" processes. Usually national courts are not able directly, in dualistic systems, to apply international law as such. In monistic, on the other hand, international obligations are directly applicable law, i.e. individuals are also able to claim rights on the basis of international provisions[273].

All the same, the application of international agreements and the material directly connected to these international measures in national courts differs from the application of international agreements effected via national legislation or a directly applicable international norm. Namely, courts might have to examine the textual and historical meaning and systematic, purposive and teleological dimensions of the international treaty and its application when using it as a legal material (traditional sources of international law). Even if implementing legislation has been enacted, in a specific dualistic state system, there might still be cases where courts, nonetheless, have to go beyond these formal sources and consider the development of practice at the international level. This may be relevant especially in cases where an international organ has been established to develop law based on an international treaty or legal procedure.

One comes to the question of the use of comparative law in national courts when interpreting and applying international norms. As in the case of *travaux preparatoires* of international treaty rules, the comparative material is also a matter for the internal doctrines concerning the sources of law. However, because no international arrangement comprises an autonomously superior interpretative order (apart from the European Community Law, as noted above) there do not seem to be problems in using comparative material as interpretative

---

[271] See, Green, L.C., 1967, pp.42-66. International element as a basis of comparative interpretation, see Schlesinger, 1980, p.29.
    For examples, see Schreuer, Ch., 1971 (supplementary text for determining lacuna and text, the normative role, pp.258-261, international law in France and the processes of interpretation, ibid., pp 260-265) In the United States, ibid., pp.265 ff. How could be used, ibid., p.272. The use may be substantiative or illustrative (Kisch, I., 1981, p.160).
[272] Screuer, Ch., 1993, p.457, Reuter, P., 1995, p.17, 21 ff.
[273] On the theories and nature of different types of systems, see Reuter, P., 1995, p.17

material. On the contrary, because international law recognizes state practices as a source of law, and because international bodies use this material, although selectively, comparative law may be particularly relevant source of law for national courts interpreting international law. However, many problems remain in the use of comparative law in international legal institutions.[274] Comparative studies related to the application of international law are always qualitatively selective, and they serve only to support certain conclusions.

In conclusion, it can be said that the nature of the normative relationship between the international and national level in general determines the possibility for the use of comparative material in the interpretation of international law in national courts. However, the basic idea could be that the use of comparative law applies the same "principles" as does to the use of comparative material in international bodies. The *"a posteriori* check" idea regulating the relationship between these levels guarantees the final word for the international legal order.

Nevertheless, one may note that some problems may appear in cases international and national levels use comparative material as a source of law. In case both have used the material in their interpretation, conflicting interpretations of comparative law may appear, which generates the idea that comparative information may be interpreted differently. This may cause problems in the international legal realm, because it introduces arguments by particularity into the international legal order. Here the question can be associated with the normative premises of the qualitative comparative interpretation. This problem may be resolved only by referring to (functional) premises of interpretation of the interpreter himself or by balancing function of comparative legal sciences in general.

1.4.3. Some examples

In the English system, there seems to be a liberal attitude towards the use of "extralegal" material in legal interpretation.[275] Although this is mainly so in cases having an international nature, there are also "national" cases, in which the courts have gone beyond traditional "internal" sources. The use of these auxiliary material has been justified basically by the uniformity of interpretation within the international legal community.

In general, it seems clear that the courts in the United Kingdom look to national systems when they are undertaking an interpretation of international law. English courts seem to refer

---

[274] See also, Kiikeri, M., 1999, pp.312-317.
[275] For detailed analysis, see Kiikeri, M., 1999, p. 264 ff.

to decisions from many countries including those from non-common law countries[276]. These sources must be, however, authoritative and they have to be studied carefully and extensively. The material does not seem to be restricted only to "authentic" comparisons, but includes also comparisons made within institutions external to the system. Furthermore, the case law considered is not necessarily restricted to the highest courts but lower court decisions can be used also.

On the basis of the analysed case law in relations to the interpretation of international law[277], one can make certain remarks. Comparative interpretation seems to be closely connected to the introduction of different ideas on interpretative techniques and methods in value-based but also in traditional way. Comparative observations have supported the use of textual sources and *travaux preparatoires* in relation to different legal (international) measures. Comparative observations have, consequently, led, in this sense, to common sense and literal interpretations and interpretations of the presumed intent of Parliament. These two methods come together in a quite interesting way.

On the other hand, the comparative approach can be used because international law has to be proved. By comparative arguments, one seems to be able to make normative statements concerning the nature of the method of interpretation of incorporated international law. Here the "generality" seems to be the main type of argument. In terms of the substance of the decision, on the other hand, example-type reasoning seems to be most commonly used.

The basic idea seems to be the harmony between domestic and international law.

Some comparative observations were made also concerning the reporting techniques in different countries so as to reinforce the comparative analysis produced.

What also seems to be remarkable is that English Courts "compare" additionally international conventions and Treaties in a quite extensive way. Some latest cases in highest courts provide also an interesting idea concerning the relationship between the role of "international law comparisons" and traditional state-law comparisons.

It is also interesting to note that the institution of *"stare decisis"* was, to a certain extent, parallelled with comparative analysis.

Some remarks can be made on the use of comparative law in some English courts in relation to European legal systems. British courts interpreted the law during the last part of the 20th century so as to ensure that the obligations of protection deriving from the protection of

---

[276] Marsh, N.S 1977, p.658.

The Judicial Committee of Privy Council decides all matters of New Zealand law as a final court of Appeal (Winterton, G., 1975, p.73, in Australian private law matters this used to be so, but the Australia has abolished the right to appeal recently). Furthermore, one can say that there is a process of internal modelling between the Commonwealth countries (idem).

The Privy Council has had a difficult role, because the judges have been obliged in Privy Council to apply for example Hindu and Islamic laws in India (Cinkalese and Tamil law in Ceylon, Chinese law in Hong Kong etc. (ibid., p.91).

[277] See, Kiikeri, M., 1999, p.264 ff.

ECHR are met[278]. The Convention Human Rights was not initially incorporated into the domestic law in England. This was changed by the recent Human Rights Bill. It has been maintained that this is a major constitutional change[279], and that it may even give horizontal effect to human rights in British legal thinking.[280] It may lead to change from the level form to that of substance.[281]

It seems, however, that the analysis of different national systems is not extensive in connection to the human rights interpretations. At least during 1996-1998, in most of the cases dealing with the European Convention of Human rights, the courts did not undertake a comparative examination of issues.

However, the method of incorporation of this type of reasoning has led in some cases to comparative interpretation and argumentation in the field of human rights and in the indirect application of the European Convention of Human Rights.

On the other hand, it looks as if comparative analysis has not had a great role in English Courts, in the quantitative sense, in the interpretation of European Community law in British Courts. However, when its role has been recognized, the question has been, as in the case of international law, about the methods of interpreting law in general. Substantially, derogations have been justified on comparative law "disparity" grounds.[282] Furthermore, it is interesting that comparative arguments have been based on European material produced in European institutions directly.

It seems that European Community cases serve also as a good starting point in the construction of arguments in general. This seems to apply also to the use of European human rights law. They do not appear as self-evident institutional standards, but assist in formulating questions, solutions, and in providing extensive and analytical reasoning.

Strictly speaking, Community law seems to be able, at this stage, to result in the suspension,

---

[278] Bankowski, Z , MacCormick, N., 1991, p.396.

[279] Lord Irvine of Lairg, 1998, p.221, for the implications of this change for adjudication and legislation, see ibid., p.225 ff.

[280] In the new Human Rights Bill in effect from 1998, interpretation of legislation should "be read and given effect to in a way which is compatible with Convention rights" (Clause 3 of the Bill). This seems to be kind of a 'choice of interpretation' rule.
See concerning New Bill, Marshall, G, 1998, pp.167-168. See historically, Lord Lester of Herne Hill, Q.C., U K. Acceptance of the Strasbourg Jurisdiction: What really went on in Whitehall in 1965. In: Public Law 1998, p.253.

[281] Lord Irvine of Lairg, 1998, p.235. On the legal and moral implications of this, see John Laws Sir, The Limitations of Human Rights. In: Public Law, 1998, p.254 ff.

[282] Interestingly, in the U. v. W. (Family Division) (Attorney-General Intervening) (1997) 3 W.L.R., 17. Oct. 1997) the contrast was seen between countries, which have organized a control system, and those who apply a liberal, "practical", and professional idea of freedom.

disapplication, or "unlawful" (nullity) declarations of legislation.[283] However, the discussion concerning spill-over effect is, nevertheless, still going on.[284]

There are some albeit few visible examples of comparative arguments deriving from the analysis of an individual state and the use of this as a source of an persuasive analogy for the interpretation of statutes in general. Reference in this regard has been made to Commonwealth precedents on statutory interpretation and occasionally to the United States[285].

Comparative observations have been used mainly so as to achieve the common interpretation of analogous bodies of statute law.[286] However, comparison does not always lead to uniform interpretation, as legal-cultural differences can lead to a refusal to follow a rule by another court.[287]

One can make some additional conclusive remarks.

Comparative law has been considered a legal source with qualification[288]. However, it seems that the role of comparative law is not systematic in the interpretation of internal rules by English superior courts, even if some examples can be seen.

One may say that there seems to be a attempt to speak to a more general audience than to the national audience only. However, the use of the comparative observations is highly value-based, illustrative, traditionally unsystematic. The analysis of different systems is strongly determined by the internal premises and ideas of sources of law prevailing in the system. One can also note that the use of comparative law is usually undertaken in relation to controversial and unstable case law.[289]

A look at the case law shows that comparative observations occur more frequently in the commonwealth context than in European context. This indicates that there are attempts to maintain a unity in this realm.[290] On the other hand, the reason for this orientation toward the common law world may be also a result of the fact that the common law cases are often more

---

[283] Lord Irvine of Lairg, 1998, p.229, and the cases mentioned therein (especially the House of Lords, *Factortame Ltd. And other v. Secretary of State for Transport* (1989) 2 All ER, p.692 ff. See also, Hartley, T.C., 1994, p.263.
Further, see *Marshall v. Southampton and South West Area health Authority* (1994) 2 WLR, 292, and *R. V. Secretary of State for Employment ex p. Equal Opportunities Commission* (1995) 1 AC, p.1 ff.

[284] Lord Irvine of Lairg, 1998, pp.230-231, also, Gordon, A., 1998.
Jolowicz, J.A. (1994, p.750) observed (1994) that comparative law has not been used in connection to European Community law. Some references, however, can be found from the contemporary case law.

[285] For American case law in England, for example see Lord Atkin, *Donoghue V Stevenson* ((1932) A.C. 562) citing *Cardoza in MacPherson v Peak Motor* ko, 217 MY, 382, 111 M.E. 1050 (1916), Cohen L.J. discussing *Cantler v Grain, Christmas & Company* [1951] 1 K.P. 164, discussing the opinion of Cardoza CJ in *Ultramares Corp. v. Touche*, 255 N.Y. 170, 1931, 970, 174 N.E. 441.

[286] Bankowski, Z., MacCormick, N., 1991, p.359 ff.

[287] Case *Temple v Mitchell* (1956) S.C. 267

[288] Jolowicz, J.A., 1994, p.753 (careful evaluation, pressing need, they should be kept separate, etc.).

[289] For some discussion on the role of comparative law, see Ward, I, 1995, 24 ff.

[290] See also, Legeais, R, 1994, p.358.

analytical that those deriving from continental Europe.[291] Naturally, the language is a decisive integrating factor too.

On the other hand, those areas of law, which have been created by English statutes seem to more likely to be interpreted by other means than comparative information. However, this does not seem to be the case in relation to the statutes which incorporate international obligations. The common law cases, on the other hand, seems to be more likely to contain comparative arguments.

One may note that the comparative arguments are usually presented by parties. The references to foreign cases can be also indirect, i.e. arguments can derive from earlier case law or even from some cases decided in the lower courts. One can also note that arguments deriving from the foreign case law are often arguments which are not directly concerning the substance of the "foreign" or the "own" case, but they are arguments which only support the analysis of the arguer. They increase considerably the analytical quality of the reasoning. Consequently, it seem to be possible to take arguments also from "analogical" foreign cases. Nevertheless, many times foreign cases are dealing with similar types of facts and this way they can be used for supporting (authoritatively) the "own" solution directly.

Direct quotations are many times extensive. This seems to assist one's own analysis of the foreign case law, and make it also accessible to the audience. In this type of approach, the "style" and subject matter of the foreign case is more visible.

On the basis of review of the interviews conducted one can make following remarks.

The use of comparative observations is in many ways "inspirational".[292] In order to explain the nature of this type of use, some comments have to be made on the procedural nature of some English courts.

In the Court of Appeal the 'skeleton" argument is prepared by the parties. If the case is justiciable case, a hearing is set. The procedure can be extremely short (lasting between 1 hour and 10 days). Each judge can produce his own reasoning, though there seems to some departure from tendency nowadays. Furthermore, there is also a tendency towards the presentation a written argument.

In theory, there seems to be a role for comparative law as a source of law, even if, in the practice, it is used infrequently. However, if there is an EC, ECHR, Hague Rules, or other international element involved, the need for comparative material may arise. German, French, and Italian decisions, for example, may be referred to. French and German courts' case law (*Counceil d'etat* and *Bundes Verwaltungsgericht*) have been discussed recently, for example,

---

[291] Jolowicz, J.A. (1994, p.753, referring to studies by Markesis, B.) Suggests that the references to continental systems, in cases where there is an international connection, is more contrasting, whereas the references to common law systems are more practical.

[292] On the fact that this use relates often to personal connections of an individual judge with his foreign colleagues, Lord Woolf, Foreword. In: Markesinis, B., Foreign Law and Comparative Methodology (Oxford) 1997..

in a case dealing with a European Community element as instances of decisions supporting a particular interpretation. Also United States law has been studied in some cases concerning the right to privacy. Furthermore, Commonwealth and Canadian case law can be considered.

The basic idea in the selection of comparative references seems to be the "importance of the court". On the other hand, the use of comparative observations depends, to a large extent, upon the lawyers having averted to it in the first place. If the barrister, for example, makes an argument that in the *Bundesgerichtshof* this matter is decided in this manner, then it will be most likely taken into account.

Generally, there is no research undertaken before the case (apart from some small notes by the administration). Furthermore, the consultation of comparative material seems to take place on an inspirational basis (*"they stimulate the discussion"*, *"...if there are books on the shelf"*). Usually the use which made of it is not extremely "academic". On the other hand, because judges rarely refer to any arguments other than those presented by the parties, the possibilities for undertaking comparative surveys are restricted. This problem is also related to time and resource constraints. The improved quality of the reasoning does not always seem to justify an the extension of time.

The main interest in wing comparative material seems to be when looking at the "philosophical' basis of a solution (*"an intellectual problem"*). On the other hand, the distinction between the 'internal' interest (interpretation of law) and the 'external' interest (integration) in using comparative observations varies according to the nature of the case. However, where international measures are involved, the external interest may be there even if the main idea is still to interpret the English law.

As in the Court of Appeal, the House of Lords undertakes practically no preliminary research of its own as such.[293] Law Lords do not have research assistance, and preliminary inquiries are made individually with the possible help of a private secretary. Administration is for the technical help. No external experts are used. Exceptionally, medical experts have been consulted[294].

The decision-makers discuss the main lines of the parties' argument. They rely, to a large extent, upon the information produced by the Counsel of the parties. Individually, they may introduce, based on academic or personal experience, information in a specific case, which is, however, connected to the arguments presented by the parties. It would be considered odd to introduce arguments which had not been introduced by the parties. Parties may make, and have made, comparative observations. The information comes also from the cross-examination of the advocates when dealing with the questions containing European elements.

---

[293] On the procedure, see Judicial work of the House of Lords, House of Lords, Session 1997-1998, internet *www.Parliament.the-statione...*, pp.4-5 of 7.

[294] In a hearing of a case in 1997.

Even where sufficient resources (library, own collections of academic literature) are available, direct comparative observations seem to be rare. Comparative influences thus seem to be indirect. It looks as if the use of comparative law as a source of argument depends on the individual law lords, and upon how beneficial the undertaking of comparative reasoning is considered to be.

Traditionally, it has been similar jurisdictions and legal systems which have been considered (also in the explicit reasoning) such as the United States and European and common law countries. Comparative aspects and experience may be influential also where law lords sit on the Privy Council as judges[295].

In conclusion, one may note that at the moment, general influences thus seem to derive from the legal systems of Germany and North America.

Some shorter observations may be presented on some other legal systems.

In <u>Swedish</u> legal thought, comparative arguments have been classified as a source of law, which may be taken into account. Comparative observations can be used according to Swedish doctrine, if they are not incompatible with Swedish law and *Ordre Public*.[296] Comparative observations can be used to support the interpretation of a domestic statute.[297]

Comparative observations can be employed so as to use a distinction made or to ask a question asked in another system. The solution can be substantiated directly by a decisions, or by a doctrine. Both empirical (or also moral) reason have been used.[298]

The influence may also be based on the perceived authority of a foreign institution. This authority may be the result of the following circumstances:[299]
- a historical relationship between systems,
- international law (eg. conventions),
- foreign law, which has influenced an international legal instrument,[300]
- uniform legislation (eg. Nordic Cooperation),
- harmonization process (eg. Nordic Council recommendations, 1974),

The authority of foreign materials (rules and interpretations) may exist even despite the harmonization of statutory rules. Here the authority is based on its ability to provide good justifications, or it is due to the fact that the court in question is highly respected.

Common Scandinavian laws have been interpreted quite similarly.[301] However, common

---

[295] Though its role has diminished in recent years.
[296] Peczenik, A., Bergholz, G., 1991, p.329.
[297] Peczenik, A., Bergholz, G , 1991, pp.329-330.
[298] Peczenik, A., Bergholz, G., 1991, pp.329-330.
[299] Peczenik, A., Bergholz, G., 1991, p.330.
[300] Case NJA, 1983, p.3, study of British system, especially the case *Sandman v Breach* [1927] concerning *International Convention on Oil Pollution* (1969).
[301] Peczenik, A., Bergholz, G., 1991, pp.330-331, referring to Eckhoff, T., <u>Rettskildalaere</u> (2 ed., Oslo) 1987, p.256.

Scandinavian case-law has not developed, except in the field of maritime law.[302]

From the interviews one can observe that comparative information is not regularly used in the Swedish Supreme Court, and that these types of studies are situationally made.

The studies in the Supreme Court is prepared by a research group. The court does not use external experts. As in Finland, the common Nordic laws may create a need to consult comparative material deriving from Nordic states. Here the interest is not only in the material law, but also in the grounding of principles. In some commercial cases, United States legislation has been consulted, otherwise these studies are concentrated on major European legal systems.

Parties may sometimes argue on a comparative basis[303].

In the realm of other types of "international" arrangements, there seems to be an interest consulting the material norms of other systems. With regard to the European Community and European human rights system, attention is paid mainly to the law of these institutions. In the field of maritime law comparative material has been used.[304]

If comparative material is used, the study includes cases and legislation and particularly international measures connected to the issue.

The use of comparative observations may be based on the need to interpret Swedish law rather than to 'harmonize" it with the law of other systems.

The obstacles for using comparative law seemed to be based mainly on practical problems (especially time and resource constraints).

As mentioned, in Nordic countries, especially in Finland and in Sweden, there are many common statutory laws (eg. family and inheritance law). The legal traditions are similar in many fields of law and legislative cooperation is (or at least was during the end of the 19th and beginning of 20th century) quite active.

In Finland, Swedish precedents and doctrinal opinions are occasionally followed in the legal argumentation and in legal science. Court practice aside from Swedish practice has not often

---

[302] Peczenik, A., Bergholz, G., 1991, p.330, referring to Sundberg, J.W.F., *Fradda Edda til Ekelöf*, Lund, Studenlite-ratur/Akademisk Förlag, 1978, p.188.

[303] An interesting case, for example, was the Sami case on property rights (HD, 1981:1, NJA I, 1981). Even though the case was decided on the basis of Swedish legislation, reference was made, by the parties, to the Canadian system of treatment of minorities etc.
The material was seen to be interesting from the sociological point of view, although the court did not see any need to use comparative elements presented by the parties.

[304] Also, Grönfors, K., The Interpretation of International Maritime Conventions by Swedish Law Courts. In: Swedish National reports to the XIIIth International congress of Comparative Law (Uppsala) 1990 (199-204). Especially English cases have been considered and even the English style of reasoning has been used, thus with some difficulties (ibid., p.202).

been followed.[305]

Finland is a dualist country. In other words, international agreements are not legal sources of law for courts as such. They have to be transformed into Finnish law before they constitute applicable law in Finland. International models have been followed by the legislator in many fields of law (particularly with regard to ILO Conventions in the labour law field, the Bern Copyright convention concerning copyright).

In Finnish courts, the use of international material in other ways is rare.[306] However, European human rights decisions, databased in the archives of the Supreme Court, are used in the context of justification constantly, and these observations appear occasionally in the justifications of Finnish Courts.[307]

One example of explicit comparative reasoning can be mentioned. In this case, the Supreme Court of Finland interpreted the doctrine of diplomatic immunity of a person working in a diplomatic mission in a case concerning contractual question.[308] The lower courts had justified the immunity based on an interpretation of international law, as set out in legal science. The Supreme Court produced the following justification:[309]

"In international law, it has been maintained... In the legal literature and in the contemporary case law of different countries, there is an established opinion that the immunity enjoyed by the state cannot be unrestricted. In the sphere of the European Council, there is an International Covenant.... Finland is not part of this agreement... However, this Treaty - and the basic principles it contains - has to be considered as a source of the prevailing international customary law. Consequently, ..."

The Court examined the provisions of this treaty. After this inquiry, the Court maintained that

"In the judicial practice of states, which legal culture resembles the legal culture of Finland, there have been cases, in which this question has been ... [the question in the case]... In these cases, states have been able to plea immunity in courts.... On the other hand, there have been cases... In these cases, state immunity has been rejected on the basis that this activity does not comprise an activity which is related to the functions normally associated with sovereignty"

---

[305] Aarnio, A., 1991, p.139.
Klami has suggested (1980) that the paradigm of comparative law in Finnish legal dogmatics seems to be that foreign law should be taken into consideration, especially Swedish material. However, clear distinctions should be made, and foreign cases and interpretative statements should not be used as primary arguments. On the other hand, when concrete interpretative recommendations are present, foreign legal writers should be used as discussion-sources (Klami, H.T., 1980, p.115).

[306] Aarnio, A., 1991, p.139.

[307] See, Scheinin, M., Human Rights in Finnish Law [Ihmisoikeudet Suomen oikeudessa] Jyväskylä, 1991.

[308] As noticed, the comparative method has been associated, also in English Courts, with the idea of state immunity. On the "comparatively" developed idea of state immunity in Western legal systems (Schreuer, C.H., State Immunity: some recent developments (Cambridge) 1988

[309] Translation author's own, Case KKO:1993 120, 30.9.1993.

The Supreme Court upheld the immunity of the person.

It is evident that uses of explicit comparative justifications are rare[310].

On the basis of interviews conducted at the Finnish Supreme Court, it can be observed that in the internal reporting comparative observations can be made. The use is situational. These reports are only for the internal use (contextual use). Experts are not used[311].These consultations of comparative material are not necessarily visible in the explicit justifications. However, comparative observations have an impact upon these interpretations.

The consultation can take place at different stages of the internal procedure, and be discussed in the decision-making realm in an informal way.

It appears as if clerks may look to other systems more extensively. It was claimed that the depth of the study depends very much on the knowledge of the clerk working on that particular question. This seems to concern also the judges.

It was claimed that the consultation of comparative legal information seems generally to be rare. However, it looks as if it may be done, if a strong link to another system is suggested, or where the domestic material is somehow lacking relevant data. This seems to be typical in relation to so called "adopted" laws[312], or where striking formal similarity exists between the legal rules within two systems[313]. On the other hand, comparative observations may be made in situations where an international measure constitutes the legal background of a measure. This is especially so in the case of Scandinavian legal cooperation. Rarely are other countries than European countries considered.

Studies of European human rights are made constantly. As mentioned, some scholars have prepared internal databases on this system[314].

Furthermore, it seems as if those functionaries who have also a academic interest in the area may follow comparative law development more. On the other hand, there are many "follow up -groups" concerning certain international conventions which result in comparative expertise in the court to be taken into account[315].

The parties rarely produce comparative law material. However, this may occur where interest in the subject is considerable. This material is taken into account by the court. Usually this type of reasoning by the parties is based upon the consultation of experts external to the

---

[310] In some legal systems, there have been explicit provisions prohibiting the use of comparative law as a source of law. (See below).

[311]The Finnish Commercial Center has been consulted in a case involving "general trade practices"

[312] Reference to Sweden (property law, trade law), Germany (especially criminal law), and Anglo-Saxon systems (especially arbitration) was made
  In the case of procedural law, an study of the United states system was mentioned.
  In the case of Sea law consultation may be made.

[313] In France, see the statute dealing with the limited housing companies [Asunto-osakeyhtiölaki].

[314] The law on the United Nations Convention on Civil and Political Rights Convention do not seem to be directly relevant.

[315] Council of Europe, Lugano Convention, Haag International Private Law, etc.

institutional system.

As maintained, the idea has been customarily to research developments in Scandinavian countries. Studies of this nature are usually not claimed to be exhaustive. However, studies of, for example, Swedish jurisprudence are not rare (cases, scholarly opinions) and, in some cases, such consultation is even expected. This may be the result of the linguistic and historical connections between the two countries. However, the conclusion of this comparative observation may be also that the legislation or the jurisprudence differs too greatly.

The interest to make comparative observations may arise also in order to find arguments for a concrete case.

There seems to be no principled objections to reasoning and justification on a comparative basis. The main obstacles for comparative consultation were resources. On the other hand, in Court, there is a lot of material (laws, commentaries) presented from other countries, and because of the databases, the available material is ever-increasing.

One could form the view that more extensive comparative studies are needed. On the other hand, the "internationalization" of law was seen a factor, which may, and which already has (Council of Europe), resulted in some comparative legal considerations.

The Court seems to address its arguments mainly to the parties, but also to the general public, and to a certain extent to the Court itself for future cases. It was emphasised that the Court is mainly searching to establish a precedent.

There has been, lately, considerable increase of quality of justifications in Finnish legal order.

In the <u>German</u> legal system, *"general principles of international law form a part of constitutional law"*, referring to the general principles of international law recognized by civilized nations[316]. The interpretations of the German Constitutional Court are much in debt to the ideas prevailing in the United States Supreme Court[317].

---

[316] Article 25 of the Constitution. See also, Doethring, 1987, p.55. For some cases, see 1 BVerfGE 332 (1952), June 13, 1952. This case dealt with the question whether one may enforce criminal law judgment, made in the Soviet occupied territories, in the Federal Republic of Germany. The Court found no obstacles to this in this particular case. The Court recognizes the constitutional provisions, according to which this type of enforcement is not possible, if the judgment is against the basic principles or constitutional provisions of the federal legal system (*"wesentliche rechtsttatliche Grunsätze... Grundrechte"*). However, in this case there were no constitutional obstacles. The Court maintained that the principle of equality is not touched upon by the judgment. Furthermore, the fact that the judgment was made in the absence of the accused did not violate basic principles. This latter observation was backed up by observation (presented by the party, *Bundesjustizieministerium)* that sentencing in absentia is allowed, in certain cases, also in other *"Kulturländer"*. A special reference was made to Austria (347). This reference was clearly made due to of the absence of existing domestic case law.

On the use in relation to general principles of international law, Drobnig, U., 1986, p 613 ff

[317] Stern, K., Der Statsrecht der Bundesrepublic Deutchland, vol 2, 1980, p.331.

In general, and for some cases on the concretization of the constitutional principles, see Mössner, J.M., 1974, p.228 ff. (for example, cases BverfG, 1, 154, BverfG, 5, 85 (135) KPD Urteil on Article 21 of the Constitution. Also Drobnig, 1986,p.630. Aubin suggests that comparisons mainly complete, confirm and control the traditional solutions (1970, p.479). Sometimes references are only to the "contextual" use of comparative law, without any trace of analysis (BverfG,

However, comparative law as a source of law has evidently a limited role. This has been also recognized by the German Supreme Court. However, comparative arguments, nevertheless, do occur sometimes.[318] The use of comparative law occurs, where there is an international connection. This connection is related to the existence of an international convention or to adoption in general or to the prevailing crossborder situation (conflict of laws, extradition, maritime law).[319]

From the interviews one can observe that the use of comparative law is basically derived from the experience of judges in both the Supreme Court and the Constitutional Court in Germany. On the other hand, in the German Supreme Court, the opinions of the professors of some faculties or institutions of law may appear in the reasoning of some parties.

In the Constitutional Court, the preliminary research differs from case to case. There are sometimes comparative studies made. Research can be undertaken in the Court by the parties, especially by the federal government (mainly in cases pertaining to the private law sphere), which may use it also in reasoning. The Court can also ask academics or an institute to produce a study by an external expert[320].

3, 225 (244) equality question).

See also BverfG, 18, 112 (117) concerning *"Kulturstaaten"* and *"demokratin der westlischen welt"*, BverfG, 20, 162 (220-221) and for comparative law considerations of the status of the press, and other issues, BverfG 1 97 (106), Bverf 1 97 (101), BverfG 7, 198 (208). BverfG 7, 377 (415), BverfG 7, 29 (40, Austria and France considered).

See also, Aubin, B., 1970, p.458. Zweigert, K., Rechtsvergleichung als universale interpretazione. In: RabelsZ 15, 1949/50, pp.5-21.

Markesinis, B (1993, pp.632-533) has suggested that the English style of judgments and handling of cases may be expected to have influence to German legal system in the future.

[318] BGHZ, 86, 240; Foreign judgments due solely to the fact that they are based on different laws are only of limited relevance for German law (Markesinis, B , 1990, p.4). On the rareness, see Drobnig, U., 1986, p.629. The court has given explicitly the preference of domestic arguments over comparative ones ("negative application"), and it has rejected foreign solutions (Aubin, B., 1970, p.471 ff. (480)). Comparative method is proposed as applicable (ibid., p.480).

BGHZ 101, 215 (223), 30 June 1987 the *Bundesgerichtshof* has used some arguments from the United States and United Kingdom (eg. rescue doctrine) in justifying a non-liability role in the medical technology (see also, Markesinis, B., 1990, p.5). In the beginning of 19th century, references were mainly to Austria (corporation law). In 30's, references were made to France, England and Switzerland. During the Nazi regime, no references can be found. After the war the US system has played an essential role (Aubin, B., 1970).

For 30 cases of jurisprudence of major trading countries and international arbitral tribunals, examined by Langen being based upon comparative law (Langen, Transnational commercial law (Leyden) 1973 pp.214-215, see Mádl, F., 1978, p.9).

The *Bundesgerichtshof* has also maintained that courts are not entitled to use the techniques employed in the interpretation of German law in interpreting international agreements (BGHst 12, (36)).

See also, Alexy, R, 1991, p.73. He refers to a following type of argumentation by the German Constitutional court: *"A look at foreign regulations shows that in the same or nearly the same version of the text of the statute the wide interpretation of the concept of dwelling predominates (compare for example for Switzerland BGE 81 I,119ff.; for Austria the constitutional Court's decisions of November 22nd, 1932, Nr.1486, March 14th, 1949, Nr. 1747, July 2nd 1955, Nr.2867, and December 16th, 1965, Nr 5182, as well as Ermacora, Handbuch der Grundfreiheiten und der Menchenrechten, 1963, 241; for Italy: Encyclopedia del diritto XIII (1964), 859 ff.; and Faso, La Libertá di domicilo, 1968, 34 ff., for the USA the Dissenting Opinion of the Justice Frankfurter in the case of Davis v United States, June 10th, 1946 - 328 US 582, 596 f - and see v City of Seattle, June 5th, 1967 - 387 US 541).*

[319] Drobnig, U., 1986, p.629.

[320] Studies has been produced for example in some family law cases. See also, Heide, H., 1994, p.732.

Comparative studies are included in the memorandum of the reporting judge. Usually comparative studies deal with the systems of European states. Considerations based upon the United States system may sometimes appear as well.

Often aspects of human rights documents (European and United Nations) are presented by the parties.

Comparative studies consist only of statutory law and case law. Sociological information derives usually only from the domestic sphere. However, it seems to be useful for the court to follow developments in other European countries. This seems to concern especially French and English law and social discourses.

There are private collections of political, legal, sociological material which may be used individually, and foreign newspapers may be looked at as well. Furthermore, active links exist with foreign courts and visits to courts in other countries may take place.

The comparative material seems to be relevant when circumstances change, and the factual events in question are unprecedented. In these cases it seems to be important to know what people may think[321]. Comparative reasoning appears when there is a need for an "*adaptation to a new situation*", a need to show that "*in other states such an idea does not exist*", to demonstrate that "*other systems have hesitated in adopting such a solution*", or merely to show that other solutions exist. Comparative interpretation seems to be aimed mainly at domestic interpretation rather than "harmonization".

The main obstacles for the consultation of comparative material seem to be procedural economic (i.e. time and resource constraints). However, unfamiliarity with comparative sources may also cause some hesitation.

The European human rights system is considered in many cases due to its similarity to the German system of basic rights.

The systems within the various "Länder" can also be compared[322].

One gets the impression that the Constitutional Court seems to address its arguments to the general public and politicians. This results in an attempt to be transparent and comprehensible.

In Italian courts, the rules of "*other legal orders*" are applied when this is necessary according to the principles of international law. The European Declaration of Human rights is also occasionally referred to when interpreting Italian statutes.

Interviews showed that the use of comparative law in the Supreme Court of Italy is not extensive. In fact, the interviews indicated strongly that systematic use of these observations does not occur at all. Neither there are explicit references to comparative observations. The

---

[321] In this context the reference was made to the question of homosexual marriage, where the Danish situation was examined, for example.

[322] Reference has been made, for instance, to a case dealing with compulsory fire protection duty for men.

possibility of making comparative observations was recognized, however, especially where the facts are new or when an legal institution is adopted from another legal system.

The main obstacles may be due to language problems and impediments may also arise due to historical factors and legal cultural considerations. If comparative influences do occur this is seen as a matter of comparative law education.

In the Italian Constitutional Court, by contrast, the use of comparative information seems to be a matter of systematic study. In 1987, there has been the Autonomous Section for comparative Constitutional Law (Sezione Autonoma di Diritto constituzionale comparato) established, consisting of foreign lawyers (two groups of eight persons). They studied constitutional systems for two years.[323] This generated 1989 the establishment of a relatively permanent department for the making of comparative studies for the Court. Even if this department appear to be extremely small, it, nevertheless, publishes comparative information for the internal use of the Court.

In the beginning of its existence this section made studies concerning questions related directly to cases before the Court, and since 1989 it began to study jurisprudence and doctrine of foreign and comparative constitutional law. It also arranged some visits to foreign institutions.

The department making comparative studies has been producing material, for example, concerning difficult cases in fields as diverse as human rights, criminal law, and family law. The studies seem to be directly related to a particular case before the court. These inquiries often contain an examination of the political context of the law in each the system (for example, a newspaper review). The material from which the information is derived is sometimes included within the internal report. Sociological or cultural aspects are not examined in more systematic way.

The information is used differently according to the preferences of each member of the court, and the attitude towards this comparative information seems to differ considerably between different members.

These studies do not necessarily have a direct impact upon the explicit justifications of the court. They usually belong to the context of justification and in this way may influence the functioning of the Court.[324]

In the argumentation of some cases before the establishment of the department (1980-1987) one has used expressions such as *"other states of the European Community..."*, *"the experience of other countries"...*, *"...the solution in European states does not differ*

---

[323] The source also the document Servizio Studi. Sezione Autonoma di diritto constituzionale comparato. Elenco dei quaderni e di lavoro della Sezione Autonomade diritoo constituzionale comparato del Servizio Studi, dalla sua instituzione - giugno 1987 - al dicembre 1992 (CORTE CONSTITUZIONALE, Segreteria generale, gennaio 1993. Prof. Sandulli, S., Consigliere preposto alla Sezione Autonoma di diritto constituzionale comparato del Servizio Studi)).

[324] See, Pegoraro, L., 1987, p.607.

substantially from the solution in Italy...", "*... the Supreme Court of the United States maintained...*", "*In most countries...*", "*... in various foreign legislations...* " etc.[325] It seems that the most interest is in the systems of France, Germany, United Kingdom, and the United States.[326] In some cases, many diverse countries have been mentioned.[327]

There are also informal channels of communication administrations of different courts in Europe, which are used for informal consultation.[328]

In the Supreme Court of <u>France</u> (*Cour de Cassasion*), the administration makes an independent study of the legal question submitted to the court. One may claim, however, that there is no considerable and systematic use of comparative law in the Supreme Court of France *(Cour de Cassasion)*.[329] These observations do not appear neither frequently in the opinions of the Advocates General of the Supreme Court (*Cour de Cassasion*).[330] However, in some administrative cases (*Counseil d'Etat*) the *commissaire du gouvernement* has given comparative consideration to certain aspects.

There seems to be some enthusiasm in the *Conseil Constitutionnel* to consider other constitutional regimes in Europe.[331]

In a particular case, the administration often examines the law of the European human rights systems. This is noticeable also in the conclusions of the *commissaire du gouvernements.*

Legal sources are mainly the texts, doctrine, precedents and fundamental decisions, and some reasoning by analogical arguments.[332] Comparative law just does not seem to have a direct role as a legal source. Influences may arrive via conferences and other types of discussions, or via some kind of internal use, which is inspirational and may be observed only indirectly.[333] This is so even if in the *travaux preparatoires* there are references to the legislation of other countries.

In private international law and some other types of cases, having an "international"

---

[325] For a list of cases and some analysis, see Pegoraro, L., 1987, pp.601-612 Apart from finding elasticity, the Court seems to search for rational and more permanent tendencies (ibid , pp.612-613). For some analysis, see de Vergotti, G., 1993, pp.12-15.

[326] Pegoraro, L., 1987, pp.609-610.

[327] Pegoraro, L., 1987, pp.603-605.

[328] No interviews were made with judges.
These observations are supported also in the light of the doctrinal discussion which exists concerning the use of comparative law in Italy, see Pizzorusso, A., 1983, pp.109-113.

[329] Also, Legeais, R., 1994, p.348, 354 ff.. This does not mean that comparative law should not be used (idem.).

[330] One may see some comparative argumentation in some opinions (such as M. Dontenwille; *L'article 1384 alinéa 1 du Code Civil: source résurgente* (Germany, Quebec, Algeria, Egypt, Japan) (*Rapport de la Cour de Cassasion, 1991* pp.82-84),

[331] Legeais, R., 1994, pp.356-357.

[332] Troper, M., Grzegorczyk, C., Gardies, J-L., 1991, p.171 ff.

[333] Legeais, R., 1994, pp.355-357.

connection, the consultation of foreign law may be, however, obligatory. This type of use is not very developed.[334] External experts are not usually used.[335]

The lack of comparative observations seems not to be the result of procedural economic obstacles, but, in general, there does not seem to be any great interest in this type of material, not even in internal discussions.[336] Nevertheless, attitudes may be changing.[337]

There has been some use of comparative observations in the Supreme Court of the Netherlands:[338]

> "In accordance with what has been accepted in that country and with what was then accepted in neighbouring countries (France, Belgium, Germany and England) under statutory judicial law", the damages for nonmaterial damage must be reasonable and just".

There was also a case in which the Court applied comparative information and based its decision (using also other interpretative methods) on uniform rule of civil law. In this case, there was extensive citation from the decisions of some other European countries (Austria, France, Germany and Switzerland)[339].

The argumentative constructions were not based on historical connections between different legal systems (i.e. combination of historical and comparative method), but, rather, they viewed foreign solutions as a model.[340]

1.4.4. Some general remarks on internal comparison, mixed courts, and private international law comparison

It is quite evident that comparative law does not have the same meaning in the practice of all

---

[334] Comparative observations may be made, to a certain extent, in cases of private international, maritime, administrative, and criminal law, having an international connection. There are however, some difficulties to observe this (also, Legeais, R., 1994, pp.353-354 ff.).

[335] On the development of the legal informatics in France, see Linant de Bellefonds, X., L'utilisation dún "systeme expert" en droit comparé. In: Rev.Int.Dr.Comp., 1994, p. 703 ff.

[336] See also, Bézard, O., 1994, pp.776-777. Reasons seem to be procedure economic and cultural. Documentation exists. European integration is conceived strictly institutionally (ibid., pp.778-779).

[337] Legeais, R., 1994.

[338] See, Kisch, I., 1981 and his analysis.

[339] For a similar case in the Supreme Court of New Jersey, see *Greensban v Slate*, 12 NJ 426, 97A.2T 390 (1953).

[340] For an example of how comparative law is used in the Netherlands (see Koopmans, T., 1996, p.545, 551). For analytical and example type of reasoning, see Advocate General Hartkamp, Hooge raad, 9 oct 1992, N.J., 1994, p.2474 ff. (ibid., p.535) referring to the Supreme Court of California, 607 P.2d 949 (Cal.1980) in the matter concerning the market shared product liability. The court rejected this reasoning. The Code Civil was used as the basis. On case law, see also Koopmans, T., 1996, p.555. See also Hoge Raad 7, Mei 1993, nr. 8152., p.1175 ff. (N.J. 1995).
See, furthermore, Kisch, I., 1981, and another example, Hooge Raad, *Van Kreuningen v Bessem*, 21 May 1943, Nederlandse Jurisprudentie N.J., 1943, 455.

countries. Furthermore, in relation to some systems, some functions could be easily considered as "comparisons", whereas in relation to other systems they do not necessarily appear to be comparisons or comparative law at all. For example, a "comparison" of English, Canadian, New Zealand, Australian experience has not been unambitiously seen as a "legal comparison" and to belong to the realm of comparative law [341]. However, these types of references would be most likely be classified by a continental lawyer as comparative law. This fact is related to different conceptions of law.

This also concerns the phenomenon referred to as internal conflict of laws.

The idea of the internal conflict of laws refers to the possibility of looking into conflicts between normative (legal) systems from within one legal system.[342] These divergences can be territorially, culturally, or personality based[343]. This type of decision-making is strongly public policy oriented, and the comparative method is used in a study of local legal systems in their own context (eg. ideologies, stages of technical development, etc.)[344]. Problems, on the other hand, occur in examining questions such as, what really is "proper law" what are the connecting factors between identified systems (of norms), and what really is the *"tertium comparationis"*.

An idea has been proposed that comparison, in this context, should proceed by examining what is compared, identifying differences and similarities, explaining differences and similarities[345]. In this sense, the whole process of comparison is an extensive comparative discourse on all problems of comparative law, and, for that matter, on the systems themselves as such (a "formative" process). This idea does not, however, explain the particular distinctiveness of this phenomenon or provide an approach to it.

The possibility of moving from ethnocentrism in this type of internal conflict of laws may be possible, if one applies a discourse principle, and lets the parties, to a certain extent, "speak for themselves" and for their legal system[346]. Here one comes, however, quite close to questions of political integrity.

Comparative law has also been of great use in so-called mixed courts[347]. In 19th century Egypt, for example, there was a mixed court interpreting Egyptian private international law and some other legal questions. The court consisted of judges from different countries and

---

[341] Hazard, J.N., 1973. In Australia, see Bates, F., 1981, p.259 ff.

[342] Sanders, A.J.G.M., 1990, p.57

[343] See, Benet T.V., 1985, p.65. The criteria for application are related to expectations, life styles, secondary agreements, nature of transactions, forms used, situation of action and property etc.

[344] Sanders, A.J.G.M., 1990, p.6.

[345] Sanders, A.J.G.M., 1990, p.62.

[346] Sanders, A.J.G.M., 1990, p.64. This could be called some kind of "functional legal multiculturalism and pluralism".

[347] Baxter, L.G., 1983.

By mixed legal systems one can understand systems derived from two or more systems generally recognized as independent of others (Mcknight, J., 1977, p.77).

they discussed legal questions with the help of comparative observations, often based on their own experiences.[348] The mixed court had an enormous role in establishing and defining the law of that system.

Contemporary private international law is, on the other hand, predominately based on the primary rule which claims that national systems have their own private international law rules and rules concerning the conflict of laws[349]. The legal basis rests, in other words, upon the private international rules of each system, though many "general" principles may also be applied.

Here the idea is not to go into details regarding this question. The main focus is in the role of comparative law in the choice of law situations[350].

In terms of choice of law, there are basically two approaches. One is the strict selection approach, and the other is the functional-instrumental approach[351]. The first seems to be based on the idea that divergences between rules are relatively few, or that it is quite difficult to establish an intelligible study of another system.[352] By contrasts, the functional-instrumental approach appears to be concerned with relevant policies and general expectations.[353]

It is evident that comparative law has a role in matters of private international law. This is due to several characteristics. Basically, because in private international law one is dealing with many laws, some kind of comparison is clearly needed[354]. Furthermore, the idea behind the application of conflict rules is clearly to evaluate whether there are material differences between systems.[355] The conflict rules do not result in clear rules which enable a solution to be found. One requires comparative processes. If comparisons are not made, the justification is a "facade" justification of the solution[356].

---

[348] Hill, E., 1978, p.299. They were abolished 1949.

[349] This seems to be so, even if one can say that private international law is a branch of law, or a legal discipline, within a system of municipal law (Kahn-Freund, O., 1976).

[350] The terms private international law and conflict of laws seem to be used interchangeably, the former in continental European, and the latter in the English speaking countries (Kahn-Freund, O., 1976, p.2).

In private international law there are three central problems: the choice of law, choice of forum, and the choices of the extent to which the substantive rules of the "foreign" law will be considered and applied (ibid., p. 3).

Some writers have envisaged a quite extensive the role for comparative law in conflict situations (*"Agreement must be reached so that one and the same international relation will everywhere be subject to the same rule in all national systems"*, David, R., Brierly, J.E.C , 1978, p.10).

[351] Von Mehren, A.M., 1975, p.751 ff.

[352] Von Mehren, A.M., 1975, p.752.

[353] Von Mehren, A.M., 1975, pp.755-756.

[354] De Boer, Th M., 1994, p.16. See, Valladão, H., 1961, p.108.

[355] De Boer, Th.M., 1994, pp.18-19. Comparative law is used in these processes for finding genuine conflicts or similarities between systems.

[356] Von Mehren, A.T., 1975, p.752.

The solution to the interpretation of the international private law may be determined by the quality of the decision, not only by the institutional authority (Mádl, F., 1978, p.9, referring to Langen, 1973). The judge can be called a mediator between systems.

On the other hand, according to some conflict of law rules, the foreign law can even be an obligatory source of law (with the exceptions of public policy).[357] In this case, foreign law has to be applied to the case. To be able to determine the applicability and content of those rules, one has to study, comparatively, foreign law in relation to the law of one's "own" system.[358]

The most favourable solution may exist in terms of the choice of law, if the comparative analysis reveals unclear, non-acceptable or otherwise problematic solutions. Within choice of law, preference is given to the national system, and this is justified in terms of national public policy. However, often the use of public policy is based on non-consideration of divergences[359]. It has been maintained that the choice of law approach, which neglects comparative law, can become unpredictable and neglect the idea of decisional harmony. This may increase the use of the public policy exception.

A approach known as non-choice, i.e. that no choice has to be made because no differences exist, is also connected to comparative observations.[360] In these cases, comparative law is a method for arriving at a solution. This leads usually to the law of the *lex fori*, but also to the so called "cumulative application of systems".[361]

The role of foreign law in private international law can be also contrasting. Although comparative law is used, the justification can be "translated" into the terms of the system.[362]

The choice of law needs comparative method in terms of substantiation of the choice of law question and justification. The choice, based on national rules, does not lead to any conclusions concerning the relationship between these systems, and in that sense the comparative analysis may be seen, to a certain extent, to be unimportant.

The comparative argumentation is institutional, unless there is a rich comparative law tradition in the national discourse. Even foreign authors can be of importance.

[357] For example, Swiss Federal International Private law Code, Article 16.

[358] Some analysis, Ereciński, C., 1978, p.208. On the relativization, Schlesinger, R.B., 1962/63, p.71.

Comparative law gains importance in the situations of *ordre public*, where the basic principles of the *lex fori* seem to conflict with the law of the foreign system.

The basic difference between comparative law as such and comparative law in private international law can be seen in their obligatoriness. Choice of law rules generate obligatory and allowed uses of comparative law, whereas comparative practice as such can practically never be obligatory, unless some internal rules of an organization so determine.

[359] Von Mehren, A.T., 1975, pp.752-753.

However, the difference between comparative law (as such) and comparative law, related to the choice of law rules, is that no prior idea of better or most favourable law exists in the realm of the choice of law. In the choice of law the national law is the premise, and even if foreign rules are applied, this takes place in the realm of national private international law rules.

There are some national rules - for example, in Swiss international private law rules, as recognized - where preference is given to the solution, which refers to the "most favourable result" (Swiss Statute on Private International, EC Contracts Convention, Article 52, 61).

An example of the restrictions upon the considerations of the foreign law (20th century, BGB Article 30):

"*Die Anwendung des ausländischen Gesetzes ist ausgeslossen, wenn die Anwendung gegen die guten Sitten oder gegen der Zweck eines deutches Gesetzes verstossen würde*".

[360] De Boer, Th.M., 1994, p.19, D'Oliveira, H U.J, 1981, p 51 ff.

[361] D'Oliveira, H.U.J., 1981.

[362] De Boer, Th.M., 1994, p.18.

The comparative method can be used also in shaping the conflict rules[363], and in their study and dissemination[364]. One can attempt to find common solutions[365].

In private international law, there seems to be two possibilities with regard to the possible approaches to foreign law: it can be considered as a question of fact or of law.[366] If it is considered as a question of fact, it does not have a "legal" status. In this case, the rules of evidence, and not only the legal analytical tools, seem to apply to the phenomena. If, on the other hand, the foreign law is seen as a "legal" feature, the legal analytical approach applies[367]. However, the distinction between pure fact and law is not so clear cut[368].

The phenomenon of the burden of proof is related to the application of the rules of evidence. Here the idea prevails that the content of law has to be shown. This recalls the comparative law principle that, should foreign law be taken into account rationally, the decision-maker has to establish a certain degree of legal analysis.[369]

Comparison within decision-making can be made explicitly. However, foreign law is often not analysed. This may be relate to the idea that when the decision not to apply foreign law is based on explicit analysis, there exists a possibility of consisting the solution on the basis that an improper analysis of the foreign law took place and that an inadequate understanding of it existed. Consequently, the use of comparative law analysis is clearly connected to the question of persuasiveness. This may also be the reason why foreign law may is treated as a fact. As the question concerns the rejection of foreign law as applicable law, this can be more easily accomplished when one can refer to the analysis and not to the substance of the foreign law as such.

On the other hand, it has been maintained that comparison in private international law must

---

[363] Loussouarn, Y., 1981, p.131.

[364] Kahn-Freund, O., 1976, p.2.

[365] Loussouarn, Y., 1981, p.133.

[366] For example, in principle, Germany as law, England as fact (Hartley, T.C., 1996, p.273, Fentiman, R., 1992, p.142, on the history since Lord Mansfield (1700) in England and United States, Schlesinger, R.B., 1962, p.56 ff.). Comparison with different approaches to proof, see ibid, p.274 ff. The question is related to *ex officio* application and to the status of the court (Hartley, T.C., 1996, p.273, Fentiman, R., 1992, p.149) or the use of statements made by (or requested from) authoritative institutes (Fentiman, R., 1992, p.145). However, in English courts, the foreign law is not, as such, treated "in equal footing" (Fentiman, R., 1992, p.143). For the process of proof (experts and judges considerations, etc), see Jolowicz, J.A., 1994, pp.748-750. For the history, practicality, and current "threats" by idea of "voluntary pleading" by Rome Convention, and on the role of already examined foreign law questions expressed in the Civil Evidence Act, see ibid, p.143 ff., and pp.155-156). The testimony of foreign law is, however, qualified by "*demeneour, clarity and persuasiveness... [and] practical experience*", and, in the end, by judges' considerations of analogy or ignorance (ibid., pp.146-148). For practical problems (solution itself, mistakes, unpredictability, costs) and policy issues (some degree of predictability, general effectiveness and time-saving, flexibility, discouraging, however, access to courts and resulting unpredictability in general) (see ibid., p. 150 ff.).

[367] Ereciński, C., 1978, pp.206-207.

[368] For some analysis of this and problem, see Kahn-Freund, O., 1976, pp.279-281. "A question of fact of a peculiar kind" (see Fentiman, R., 1992, p.145 ff. And the English cases referred).

[369] In general on the proof of foreign law, see Hartley, T.C., 1996, p.271 ff.

be extremely nominalistic. This may be associated with its strict nature based on substantive principles of civilized nations, good faith, equality and good conscience, *pacta sund servanda*, etc.[370]

It seems to be clear that in choice of law situations foreign law is treated as law more than merely as fact, even if certain ideas concerning the burden of proof may be applied. It also seems that because foreign law is treated in an "integrative manner" (eg. by considering its basic principles to be applicable) and because, consequently, the conflict really seems to be a conflict of legal principles rather than conflict of legal rules, there is also a general legal integrity principle applied (adjudicative integrity). Furthermore, it looks like the *tertium comparationis*, in this case, is the legal system itself[371].

One may claim that "comparative law" in private international law questions is not really comparative law in discursive sense. Namely, choices are usually justified on the basis of national rules concerning conflict of laws, although, sometimes, general principles are used. However, there is no attempt to justify any general principles for the international discourse, but the solution is determined not on the basis of generality or disparity in any scientific sense but on the basis of public policy disparity and institutional premises. Using the terms of the discourse analysis, national and institutional legal opinions are decisive. The audience is not any comparative law opinion or opinion of any external institution or the general legal audience.

This difference can be explained also from another point of view. In comparative law, as such, one does not have to make any choice of legal norms or rules except before the comparison is undertaken, and not always even then. Comparative considerations, in choice of law interpretation, on the other hand, aims to identify the choices of the one best interpretation. However, it is basically the internal rules of the system which are interpreted[372]. The limits come from the *"ordre public"* of each of the legal systems. In comparative law, on the other hand, there are only a few methodological instructions governing the choice of "suitable" material for the comparative survey, if any at all.

In this sense, one may say that even if the method of comparison is used, one cannot speak of a genuine comparative interpretation. Nevertheless, there are also some similarities in approach. The comparative interpreter, using comparative law as a source of law, restricts, in general, the possible considerations by reference to some subjective criteria which do not necessarily differ greatly from the *"ordre public"* considerations. However, both choice of law and the comparative interpretation have their specific practical purpose, which thoroughly

---

[370] For some analysis, Kahn-Freund, O., 1976, p.279.

[371] For example, if the acceptability of foreign rules, as applicable law, is contested, the metarule of "public policy" can apply. This concept makes it possible to maintain that the law of another country is law at the same time as it is rejected as applicable law.

[372] The comparative process is restricted to the legally regulated extent of comparison.

conditions the process. In the choice of law, there is no need, for example, to increase knowledge and understanding of legal phenomena as such.[373]

The role of comparative law, in the international commercial arbitration, on the other hand, is extremely practical and elementary[374]. In fact, it is the primary source of practice in this sphere. This applies to the drafting of the rules, to the arbitration itself, and to the choice of the place and law of the arbitration.[375] Comparative law determines the possibilities for all these elements of the arbitration, and, by determining those "strategic" choices, it has an impact to the outcome itself[376].

In international commercial arbitration one usually departs from the rules of one system, takes into account general principles, and makes a comparative evaluation of certain aspects of the laws[377].

The comparative legal aspect is connected to the international nature of the disputes, and, moreover, to the fact that the parties are often of different nationalities. On the other hand, the applicable law may not be referred to at all in the contract. In such cases, the comparative aspects are usually considered at the end of the decision-making, where the applicable law is determined.[378]

In cases of "*Lex Mercatoria*" comparative law seems to be the only source[379]. The interesting feature is that one can include all comparative aspects, comparison of the rules of international conventions, national laws, practices of different level institutions etc., within the idea of "*Lex Mercatoria*" comparison.

In the end, however, it seems that the role of comparative law in international arbitration does not differ considerably from the premises found in relation to private international law.

---

[373] Schmitthoff, M. (1941, p.107 ff.) Has maintains that "*applied comparative law begins just where the Conflict of laws end, namely in examining the contents of the different legal systems and submitting the transaction to that system which is the most appropriate to it*".

[374] Valladão, H., 1961, p.112. It has even been claimed that the interest in comparative law in commercial law is a result of the "universal" nature of the latter ibid., , referring to Jaeger, P.G., Comparazione e diritto commerciale. In: L'apporto della comparazione alla scienza giuridica (Milano), 1980 , p.303.

[375] Gaillard, E., 1988, pp.283-284, 288.

[376] Gaillard, E., 1988, pp.285-286.

[377] See, for example *SPP Middle East Limited and Southern Pacific Proprieties Limited v Arabic Republic of Egypt and the Egyptian General Company...*, ICC Arbitration Nr YD/AS nr 3493, International Commercial Code of Arbitration, 11 March 1983 (International Law reports Vol 86, 1991, Cambridge, pp.435-458). Studying the governing law, para. 49-51. See Jolowicz, J.A., 1994, p.754 ff.

[378] Gaillard, E., 1988, p.287.

[379] Gaillard, E., 1988, p.288.

2. COMPARATIVE LAW IN THE
EUROPEAN LEVEL CASE LAW

2.1. European Community law

2.1.1. General remarks

One can say that the European Court of Justice is a excellent object of study from the point of view of the subject of comparative law and comparative legal reasoning. This is so because no basic doctrine of sources really has been established. Neither are there strict rules of reasoning such as those occasionally presented in connection to the domestic legal traditions, especially within continental thinking. This feature may be related to its "self-formative" stage or nature in general.

The Community system consists of many types of legal traditions. This is one of the reasons why one can note forms of expressions and interactions of arguments which do not appear in national legal systems.

One may say that European level law is, in general, justificatory in nature, whereas in state systems, as noted, there are formal and relatively mechanical approaches to legal argumentation. Because European level systems are open in their sources, one can recognize also normative or value-based limitations upon their argumentative style. This feature is related also to a different conception of law at the European level. It is more "principle" oriented, and pure linguistic interpretation seems to be a great problem.[380]

Comparative law influences (and adoptions) in the reasoning on European Community law have been studied mainly from the "constructivist" point of view. This is the basic approach of many scholars and judges. However, certain problems exist in this type of analysis.[381]

Namely, comparative reasoning has been considered some kind of a "natural" basis for certain principles. In many legal studies, the basic idea seems to be that comparative arguments do function as basic elements for these principles. This is strongly related to the traditional "methodological" tradition of comparative law. Real "rhetorical" functions are not revealed[382]. The constructivist approach does not consider different principles and different conceptualizations together. These type of studies have not focussed on the relationship interaction of different arguments. The normative consequences remain usually, in the

---

[380] On interpretation, see Hartley, T.C., 1994, pp.85-86.

[381] See the studies of, for example, Koopmans, Pescatore etc. (judges of the European Court).

[382] In general, for the relationship between rules and principles, Bredimas, A., 1978a, p.125, principles and comparative studies (ibid., p.128). Sources (national systems, public international law and laws of non-Member States) from which principles are "drawn" (ibid., p.125 ff.). The constant integrative force (ibid., 132-133), and the idea that in the ultimate form the result is *jus commune*.

The idea is somehow "evolutionist" in the sense that comparative arguments establish something. One could claim that they interpret something rather than establish something. The principles can be also seen as "methods".

material sense, also concealed.

Consequently, a different approach would suggest a deliberation, not over questions such as "what principles are constructed", but what kind of connection these principles have to material (substantive) questions and to other arguments, i.e. in what type of situation are they used?

Furthermore, the problem of the constructivist approach is that it considers Community law somehow, in empirical sense, to be strictly subordinate to domestic legal systems. It is quite problematic, in terms of the methodological and traditional approach to comparative law, to admit that European institutions use their own powers and are autonomous as legal orders.

Consequently, one should perhaps began to consider general principles of Community law as relatively separate from general principles in the realm of comparative studies. These principles cannot be conceived only as a reproduction of the common tradition of Member States, but their application context in European law should be studied more carefully.

One of the problems of these studies is that they have not regarded the evolutive idea behind the function of the use of comparisons as such. In other words, they have not explained why comparative studies are repeated, even within the same types of situations.[383]

Consequently, this type of discursive point of view in the analysis does not exist.

Furthermore, more recent cases have not been dealt with.

On the other hand, one interesting feature in previous studies is that many of the writers are judges. This seems to be due to the fact that the use of comparative law is so deeply rooted in the institutional framework that only judges feel able to write about these issues - even if in

---

[383] The explanation for this may be as follows: states demand an examination of hard cases from different points of views. The Court protects its own case law in relation to these claims.

The constructivist approach provides very powerful explanation for the use of comparative law (See, for example, Bredimas, A., 1978a, also Pescatore, P., 1980, p.339, Jacobs, F.G., 1990, p.107). One can easily see, that the studies tend to stress the listing of the principles "constructed" by comparative law without any analysis of the phenomena.

However, one could claim that it is not necessarily so that comparative law would be "constructing" any of the principles applied. One could claim that the whole process of consideration is "princip-led" in the sense that it is the principle, which is decisive for the use of comparative law.

For a more "institutionally" oriented approach, see Demas, G., 1984. See also, Bengoetxea, J., 1993, pp.5-6. Use of comparative law as "concretization", see Mössner, J.N., 1974, p.218.

The constructivist fallacy can be associated with an "illusion" resulting in the similar "order" of arguments, and the idea of an analogy between the heuristic and the justificatory forms. If comparisons are represented before the principled arguments, it certainly looks as if the comparative arguments are somehow "constructing" the principles. The constructivist approach stresses the positive results of the uses of comparative law, but neglects the "deviations" or "non-applications" of the results of the comparative considerations as part of the systematic discourse (negative and positive "konretisierung" (Mössner, J.N., 1974, p.228), stressing of the special features of one's own system (ibid., p.240).

A more fundamental analysis can be made, if one takes into account the relationship between these arguments in a more legal-material sense, and treats them as separate methods for the question. Their uses and non-uses in comparison with other arguments might tell more about the function of comparative law in the system. The study of the constructions of argumentation is a matter of argumentative style. The idea in this study is not to explain the uses of comparative law on a constructivist basis, but its uses on the basis of the discourse theory and, in particular, by the interaction between the arguments on the functionalist basis. This way one is more able to consider also comparative arguments like "comparison by opposites" and subtle forms of uses of comparisons.

highly synthetic form. No real dogmatic analysis is made. The ideas repeated in those "institutional" analyses are quite similar, and the derived scholarly analyses, on the other hand, are often only reproductions of those.[384]

In conclusion, one should emphasize the fact that, in this study, the European level functions as one example of typical comparativist legal interpretation in contemporary legal practice. Consequently, the results of this study could be parallelled with the results obtained in the inquiry into the national legal systems in this context.

2.1.2. On interpretation in Community law

The European Court of Justice (ECJ) has used various methods of interpretation in its case law[385]. One could therefore claim that it has not bound itself to only one method. In its case-law, it has stressed the sovereignty of Member States, aspects of competition, general aspects of social security, and free movement etc. It has also spoken of the legal security of individuals.[386] From the point of view of historical interpretation, the Court has underscored future prospects rather than past and original intentions of the drafters of the Treaty.[387] In its textual interpretation, the Court has applied the principle of uniformity of Community law rather than strictly accepted the literal meaning of the words and concepts as such[388]. In these cases, one may say, it has done so in order to use an analogical interpretative method. This has been defined as "functional textual interpretation".[389] Sometimes the idea of coherence appears in the reasoning of the court.

It has been claimed that the fundamental or even the only leading principle or method in the interpretation of the Court is the pro-integrative method of interpretation. This has led to a functional approach by the Court, and the result has been that the Court can be seen as a political lawmaker in the European system.[390] It has even been claimed that the Court can never be relied upon to stay within the limits set by the commonly-acknowledged methods of

---

[384] The comparative legal studies in the realm of the European Community can be described, also in this sense, as institutionally autopoietic. This means that they are "institutionally" self-referential studies, which do not really explain legal phenomenon. They seem to form part of the self-justification of the institution.

[385] See, Schermers, G., Waelbroeck, D., 1987, p.11 ff., and Millett, T., 1988, p.163 ff., who is making a distinction between literal, schematic, teleological, [comparative] linguistic, autonomous-conceptual, general-principled, non-retroactive, restrictedly deviating, travaux preparatoires, effectiveness ("effet utile").

[386] Bredimas, A., 1978a, p.177.

[387] Bredimas, A., 1978a, p.178, and Gulmann, C., 1980, pp.198-199. Hartley, T.C., 1994, p.86.

[388] See, for example, starting from case 75/63 *Hoekstra (néeUnger)* (1964) ECR 177 (see also, Bredimas, A., 1978a).

[389] On this see Bredimas, A., 1978a, p.177.

[390] See on this, Rasmussen, H., 1986, and Blok, P., 1974, p.355.

interpretation[391]

However, if some analytical distinctions can be made in the realm of this pro-integrative approach, one may claim that the interpretative methods of the European Court of Justice are those of "institutional systematic" or contextual interpretation method, and teleological interpretation in conjunction with the idea of the "rule of effectiveness" ("*La notion d'effet utile*" "*the concept of useful effect*"[392]).

These ideas stem from the incomplete structure and the goal-oriented nature of the Treaties establishing the Community system[393], and from the constructive role played by the judges of the Court[394]. The "emptiness" of the conceptual framework of the European legal discourse has already been - and will be later - recognized. This fact has its relationship to these types of approaches.

It must be stressed that the teleological construction is different in the European system as it is within national legal systems: the aims in the interpretation of an EC rule can often be found in the objectives of the EC legislation itself and in forms part of the textual and historical interpretation. In national legal systems, on the other hand, the results of the decisions are seen at a much more pragmatic, individual level. The EC's pro-integrative approach is the decisive element in its method of the teleological interpretation, whereas in national systems one does not have to consider this feature. This does not necessarily mean that the European Court of Justice would not consider individual interests and rights.

It is the idea of levels of interpretations, nevertheless, which seems to produce this difference between the national and European systems; the ECJ does not interpret concrete cases, only EC law; in national systems one does interpret concrete cases, not European law. In this sense, the system can be defined as rather a unique type of legal order, as the Court has itself claimed.[395] Thus, the problems it addresses are also different from those faced by national courts.[396]

The Court is composed of judges coming from different legal orders with different conceptual, cultural and educational backgrounds. Thus, there are necessarily no common models, national or international, for conceptualizations. Judges personal backgrounds have a strong impact upon their opinions.[397]

Legal texts are drafted in the languages of Member States. This generates another problem,

---

[391] Blok, P., 1974, pp.355-356.

[392] Lecourt, R, 1976, p.236.

[393] Pescatore, P., 1975, p.176.

[394] Pescatore, P., 1974, p.86, Lecourt, R., 1976, p.235.
One could say that the nature of this type of method is increasing.

[395] Case 26/62 *Van Gend and Loos v Neederlandse Administratie der Belastningen* (1963) ECR 1.

[396] Gulmann, C., 1980, p.191 and 193.

[397] See Usher, J.A., 1976, p.369 and case 37/72 *Marcato v Commission* (1973) ECR 361.

the problem of the comparability of national and EC conceptualizations. Because of this, the Community rules tend to be quite weak. One may say, furthermore, that the EC conceptualization is reflected within the political consensus. The consensus is achieved sometimes by including all national systems in a Community rule.[398] This creates dynamism for the Community system.[399] It likewise makes it possible for the Court to use different methods of interpretation which have not traditionally familiar to the national legal systems and to consider broad political, economic and social developments within society. Furthermore, the interpreting institutions have to, as they fairly frequently do, refer to the "filling of gaps" in the system, for example by using a comparative approach and by accepting guidance from the national systems and their solutions, usually in a contextual form. This approach finds its normative basis also in the EC Treaties and in the case-law of the Court.[400]

2.1.3. The legal basis for the use of comparative law

The Treaty of Rome contains articles, which demand for a statement of reasons underlying the decisions reached[401]. On the other hand, one may also "comparatively" establish this kind of obligation in the context of European law. However, the rule determining the extent of justifications is not clearly established[402].

The use of comparisons is not only regulated by legal rules giving them legal status, but case law has also restricted the use of comparative observations as relevant aspects. On the other hand, the publishing of comparative studies is circumscribed by internal institutional rules such as the "principle of confidentiality".

The use of comparative observations are based, in the European Union system, on Article F.2. and Art. 215, for example. Article F sets forth the "constitutional traditions" and European human rights as a basis of the European order[403].

---

[398]In the field of tax law, see for example, Legall, J-P., Dibout, P., 1991, p.1061.

[399] Gulmann, C., 1980, p.192.

[400] For some remarks on the centrality of the teleological and comparative method, rather than the textual one, see Wilmers de, J.M., 1991, p.37.

[401]Article 190 of the Rome Treaty does not explicitly mention the Court of Justice. On the other hand, Article 33 of the Protocol on the statute of the Court of Justice of the European Community and Article 34 of the Protocol on the Statute of the Court of Justice of the European Atomic Energy Community states that *"Judgments shall state the reasons on which they are based".*
A case on this issue, see 222/86 *Heylens* (1978) ECR 4097.

[402] Naturally the European Community Court studies analytically the system which is a party to the dispute (See, Pescatore, P., 1980, p.342).

[403] Title I, Common Provisions.
The common tradition idea has been interpreted also as a legal source of inspiration (See, Pescatore, 1980, p.340. In general, Marsh, N.S., 1977 p.657). The national legal systems are *"philosophical, political and legal substratum"* to Community law (Bredimas, A., 1978a, referring to a statement by the Advocate General Delamonte).

Another article must be mentioned. The legal basis of the application of international law in the European Community system is Article 173. International treaties can be applied in the interpretation of Community law as though they are not "directly" applicable rules within the Community system[404]. All the same, because of their binding nature in the Member States, they do appear binding also upon the European institutions as long as the institutions do not challenge their validity for some reason.[405]

Different institutional actors such as Court and the Advocates General have had different ideas concerning the extent of the argumentation. There are many "institutional" structural reasons behind this, as to be seen. Sometimes the proposals presented by the Advocate Generals do not necessarily coincide with the position taken by the Court[406].

2.1.4. General remarks on the use of comparative law in the European Community legal order

The use of comparative law in European Community law has not been seen a scientific project and exact role of comparative law in general is not quite clear for its users either[407]. However, it has been seen as a method for "*lacunae* filling" as a means of revealing all possible solutions and as an extremely important part of the Community law[408]. In the practice of the European Community system, the first level of comparison is seen as useful and even neces-

---

See also, Pescatore, P., 1980, Wilmars de, J.M., 1991, p.39 ff.

[404] See, Schermers, H.G., 1979, pp.171-172, see case 21-24/72, *International Fruit Company* (1972) ECR 1226.

[405] There are references to general principles, and to the public international law, in a number of Articles of the Treaty, see also Article 234 EC. The principles at public international law have been used in filling gaps (Bredimas, A., 1978a, p.134).
   However, some scepticism has been expressed concerning the possibility of deriving principles from public international law because of the unique nature of the Community law. This has been also the approach of the European Court. The use is exceptional (ibid., pp.134-135, referring to Pescatore, P.). In the realm of the human rights openness is more visible (Bredimas, A., 1978a, p.135).
   Some analysis of the bindingness, see Hartley, T.C., 1994, p.184.

[406] The same phenomenon can be recognized in the European Court of Human Rights. Comparative analysis seem to be connected to these dissenting opinions and conflicting points of views, see below.

[407] Pescatore, P., 1980, pp.352-353. Jacobs says that it is "comparative law", which is used (Jacobs, F.G., 1990, p.99). Similarly, see Pescatore, P., 1980, p.337, Friedmann, W., 1973, p.227. Concerning the selectivity of the method, see Wilmars de, J.M., 1991, p.39.
   The emerging experiences of lawyers in the "comparative" sense explains the strengths of the European system, but also many of its weaknesses (Hunnings, H., 1996, p.52).
   Some analysis, Galmot, Y., 1990, p.255 ff.

[408] Concerning *lacunae* in the "Community system", see Wilmars de, J.M., 1991, p.38 ff.
   There have been claims that the idea that comparative law would be somehow only a European Community issue has been rejected (Koopmans, T., 1996, p.545, 549). See also Benos, G., 1984, p.247.
   See also *Note d'information sur la division recherche et documentation*, Janvier 1995.

sary.[409] It has its justificatory function, even if it appears often in a highly synthetic form.[410] European law is inter-state ("inter-etatic") law[411] not only politically, but also legally.

The use of comparative arguments and their effects are more striking in the Community order than in other international systems. This is due to the nature of Community law as a more comprehensive legal order.

One can note, as one can note in the case of general international law applied in international institutions, that "European custom" does not mean only the customary law of the Member States in comparative terms, but, for that matter, also custom in international systems. These types of norms may function as an indirect "source". Furthermore, traditional comparative legal arguments in the Community system must also be supported by additional arguments.

One could say that the system of intervening by the Member States in the processes of the Court may bring a comparative elements to legal cases. However, this type of "comparative influence" cannot be considered as a "use of comparative law". This idea does not really belong to the realm of the use of comparative law (comparative reasoning) in the context of this study[412]. Even if the process in this respect is extremely interesting, it would require a separate study. One may say that this type of process looks more like a process of political comparison. It is not based on any "systematic" approach, and is in many ways related solely to the interests of the parties. However, as to be seen, some systematic arguments, provided by parties as well as by these "additional actors" in the traditional process, can have an influence upon the court's argumentation[413].

2.1.5. Some remarks on comparative influences in Community law

It has been maintained that there are several national influences embedded in the Community system[414]. Some concepts and principles, it can be claimed, have been adopted by the Court

---

[409] Dehousse, R., 1994, p.13. Trindade, A.A.C., 1977, p.281. Ress, G., 1976.

[410] Pescatore, P., 19809, p.338, 352-355.

[411] On the concept, see Herczegh, G., 1978, p.73-76.
   Case *Lotus* (1927) PICJ Reports, p.19.

[412] How parties intervene in the procedure and its nature as a comparative process, see Koopmans, T., 1996, p.548. A good example, Case 155/79, *A.M. et S.* (1982) ECR 1575. See also, Case 67/96 *Albany*.

[413] One part of the professionalization of legal interpretation of the Community law is embedded the use of different state interventionist methods in the Community system. This "political" comparative process guarantees that political integrity can be, to a certain extent, maintained.

[414] See, Koopmans, T., 1996, p.501 (from France comes, for example, the misuse of power doctrine, the non-expression of the dissenting opinions, the role of Advocate General). See also, Schwarze, J., 1991, p.4.
   It is self-evident that European legal systems have adopted legal styles of different systems (this applies, to a certain extent, to the national systems too). The adoptions have been visible especially in the realm of the European Community

directly from national sources:[415]

- Community preferences (the external trade)[416], equality of treatment of nationals of other Member States[417], prohibition against elimination of competition[418] and the duty of "solidarity" between Member States[419],
- proportionality[420],
- legitimate expectations[421],
- legal certainty[422],
- good faith[423],
- the right to be heard[424],
- force majeure[425],
- estoppel,[426]
- unjust enrichment[427],
- legitimate self-protection[428], and

---

system, where the accession of different states has had its impact to the style of the supra-national system (For example, de Gruz, P., 1994, p.135, Koopmans, T., 1991, p.493). On this, see below in conclusions on European comparative law.

It has been maintained that the European legal institutions change their styles in result of the new legal cultures entering into it. This kind of "cultural" comparative law seems not to be based on comparative legal reasoning, but it is a kind of process of adaptation of the system to a new situation. It is quite unpredictable, and cannot included within the idea of modern law. It is rather a change in the institutional culture.

[415] See also Usher, J.A., 1976, pp 362-368 For the types of concepts have been taken, see Koopmans, T., 1996, p.547. What is its role, Markesinis, B., 1993, p.634.

[416] Case 5/67 Beus v Hauptzollamt Munich (1968) ECR 83.

[417] Case 152/73 Sotgui v Deutche Bundespost (1974) ECR 153.

[418] E.g. case 6/72 Continental Can v Commission (1973) ECR 215.

[419] Case 39/72 Commission v Italy (1973) ECR 101.

[420] "Verhältnismässigkeitsgrundsatz". See also cases 8/55 Fédération Charbonnière de Belgique v High Authority, Rec. 1955, p.199. See later case-law, 11/70 Internationale Handelsgesellschaft mbH v Einfuhr- und Vorratselle für Getreide und Futtermittel (1970) ECR, 1125, 5/73 Balkan-Import-Export v Hauptzollamt Berlin-Packhof (1973) ECR 1091, and 63-69/72 Werhahn Hansamühle and others v Council and Commission (1973) ECR 1229.

[421] "Protection de la confiance légitime" - "Vertrauenschutz". See opinion of Advocate-General Warner in case 2/75 Einfuhr- und Vorratstelle Getreide v Mackprang (1975) ECR 607. The same rule can be found in French and Belgium case law (Advocate-General Roemer (1973) ECR 723).

[422] Cases 78/74 Deuka v Einfuhr- und Vorratstelle Getreide (1975) ECR 421, and 5/75 (same) (1975) ECR 759. In other form, see Usher, J.A., 1976, p.367, and cases 48/72 Brasserie de Haecht v Wilkin-Janssen (1973) ECR 77 and 127/73 B.R.T v SABAM (1974) ECR 51.

The idea of non-retroactivity of acts of legislation has been also recognized, see Pescatore, P., 1980, p.340.

[423] Case 44/59 Fiddelaar v Commission, Rec. 1960 p.1077.

[424] Case 17/74 Transocean Marine Paint Association v Commission (1974) ECR 1063, and the opinion of the Advocate General Warner. Modifications to this, see case 136/79 National Panasonic (1980) ECR 2033. Some analysis, Schwarze, J., 1991, p.9 ff.

[425] Case 158/73 Kampffmayer v Einfuhr- und Vorratstelle Getreide (1974) ECR 110.

[426] Cases 17 and 20//61 Klöckner v High authority (1962) ECR 325.

[427] Case 36/72 Meganck v Commission (1973) ECR 527.

[428] Case 16/61 Modena v High authority (1962) ECR 289.

the idea of *non bis in idem*[429].

On the other hand, the text of the treaty is strongly influenced by French administrative law (for example, grounds for annulment (*"excès de pouvoir"*))[430], forms of judgments, organization of the judiciary, and judicial behaviour in general). German ideas on the relationship between the federal and state levels also had their influence upon the reasoning of the Court. Methods of reasoning, discussion of procedural questions, and the role of oral hearings and case law have changed gradually based on influences from common law countries.[431] One may even claim that the idea of discourse between the "bar and bench" has become emphasized[432].

All these influences derive from the fact that Community law did not emerge in a historical vacuum. Legal institutions of this kind, on the other hand, can be seen as the "hard core" of the Community legal system, but also as the "hard cores" of each individual legal system and international law too.

Next there is a look at the traditional forms of comparative observations appearing in the work of Community Court.

2.1.6. Comparative reasoning in the realm of international law in the European Court of Justice

General remarks. International law can be seen, from the point of view of the European Community legal system, as an additional source of law. It refers to law which "every court would apply"[433]. This is the traditional comparative perspective regarding the application of international norms in the European Community system.

Some examples on the use of international law in the European Court may be mentioned.

When deciding the *Stoeckel* case[434], the European Court of Justice examined only the relationship between national law and European Community Law but did not refer to the fact that France, the defendant, was a party to the ILO Convention concerning on the same matter. This reflects the typical attitude of the European Court of Justice towards the international

---

[429] Cases 18 and 35/65 *Gutmann v Commission* (1966) ECR 103.

[430] On the influences to administrative law, its development, and the problems of comparative basis of it, see Schwarze, J., 1991, p.5 ff.

[431] See, Koopmans, T., 1991, p.500.

[432] Koopmans, T., 1991, p.505.

[433] Schermers, H.G., 1979, p.169, analysis of the case 41/74 *van Duyn* (definition of state competencies, discrimination based on nationality) ECR (1974) 1351.

[434] Case 345/89, *Criminal Proceedings against Stoeckel* (1991) ECR I-4047.

legal system.[435]

On the other hand, there has been a long debate on the direct applicability of the GATT (General Agreement of Tariffs and Trade) in the European legal system. The direct applicability of that agreement could have been asserted due to the fact that the European Court of Justice has clearly stated that it has fulfilled its obligations towards the GATT agreement.[436] Later, in examining the role of GATT within the Community system, one of the Advocate Generals referred to the practices of the Member States and to the general role of GATT in the legal systems of the member states[437]. In the systems of the Member States it was considered exceptional that the GATT was *"directly invoked before the judicial institutions"*.[438]

However, despite the fact that the European Court of Justice has not explicitly mentioned the direct applicability of the GATT agreement, it has used it as source of arguments in several cases, and has recognized it as a possible source of interpretation[439]. One example is a case concerning tariff quotas from 1993[440]:

> *"As the fifth recital in the preamble to the basic regulation indicates, the aim of reallocation in the course of the year is to enable the annual quota to be fully utilized which is in the interests both of the Community operators affected and the Community partners in the GATT."*

Where the case does not derive any the rule directly from the GATT system, the Court can use the GATT as supporting material in arguing in support of its conclusion. In this case, reference was made to the interests of GATT Parties as a type of additional "comparative" observation.

Another example of this "supporting" use of the GATT agreement can be found in an interpretation dealing with anti-dumping measures:[441]

> *"In that regard the Court points out that Article 2(5) of GATT anti-dumping code provides that .. and Article 2(6)*

---

[435] The Advocate General did, however, examine the nature of the Convention.

[436] Case 21-24/72, *International Fruit Company* (1972) ECR 1219, 1227.

[437] Opinion of Advocate General Gulmann delivered on 8 June 1994, case 280/93, *Federal Republic of Germany v Council of the European Union* (bananas - common organization of the market - import regime) ECR 4973.

[438] Case 280/93, *Federal Republic of Germany v Council of the European Union* (bananas - common organization of the market - import regime) ECR 4973.
   For comparative argumentation by the Commission and counter-argumentation by the Advocate General in the field of external relations, see also Opinion of Mr Advocate General Tesauro delivered on 16 December 1993, case 327/91, *French Republic v Commission of the European Communities* (agreement between the Commission and the United States regarding the application of their competition laws - competence - statement of reasons) (1994) ECR I-3641.

[439] See case 178/87 *Minolta v Commission/Council*, 21 January 1991 (1992) ECR I-1577.

[440] Case 106/90, 317/90, 129/91, *Emerald Meats ltd v Commission*, 23 January 1990 (1993) ECR I-209.

[441] See, case 188/88 *NMB GmbH and Commission*, 10 March 1992 (1992) ECR I-1689.

provides that...

As the Commission correctly points out, the only difference between anti-dumping code and the Community regulation with respect to the construction of the export price is that, whereas the code merely lays down the principle that allowances should be made for costs incurred between importation and resale "including duties and taxes", the EC regulation specifies certain duties and other costs, including anti-dumping duties for which allowances must be made."

In this way the Court did not find any inconsistency between GATT provisions and EC legislation, which, on the other hand, confirmed the EC systems authority over the question.[442] The Court looked, in other words, into the content of the GATT agreement, although it did not grant it any superiority over EC legislation; thus, it used the GATT to support the superiority of EC legislation.[443]

This type of approach seems to apply also to the United Nations Charter[444], to certain other international treaties, and to humanitarian law in relation to the European Community system.[445] However, in the case on the Yaounde Convention of 1963, the Court has held that Article 2(1) of that Treaty was directly applicable[446]. Treaties and international agreements entered into by the Community are binding on both the Community and the Member States (Article 228, new 300 of the Treaty). The Member States are obliged to enforce international agreements as Contracting parties, but also the European Community has to do so. It is therefore the task of the Community to ensure the uniform application of the treaty in different Member States.

Furthermore, the ECJ has also used ICES (*International Council for the Exploration of the Sea*) documents and international law to gain support for its argumentation in certain cases[447]:

"...that the contested regulations are justified in so far as public international law authorizes it to decline to

---

[442] GATT assisting in the interpretation of Community norms; and on the rejection of applicants argument, see Opinion of Mr Advocate General Darmon, delivered on 7 February 1991, case 49/88, *Al-Jubail Fertilizer v Council* (1991) ECR I-3187.

[443] It is possible that the Courts attitude towards other international Treaties is based on the idea presented in Article 30 of the Vienna Convention on the Law of Treaties, which maintains, regarding on the application of successive treaties relating to the same subject matter, that
"*When all the parties to the earlier treaty are parties also to the treaty but the earlier treaty is not terminated or suspended in operation..., the earlier treaty applies only to the extent that its provisions are compatible with those of the latter treaty*".

[444] Council Regulation 2340/90 of August 1990 (*Prevention of Community Trade with Iraq and Kuwait*, OJ 1990 L 213/1.

[445] Schreuer, Ch., 1993, p.459.

[446] Case 87/75 *Bresciani* (1976) ECR 129.
However, the direct applicability of this treaty was based on the idea of non-reciprocity nature of the Treaty, and the Community in this treaty gave benefits directly upon the other party. It is hardly possible, that reciprocal treaties can be directly applicable. See, on this, Advocate General Trabucchi in this case (ECR 129 ff.), and Hartley, T.C., 1983.

[447] Case 280/89 *Ireland v Commission*, 2 December, 1992 (1992) ECR I-6185. See also, Case 279/87 *Tipp-Ex Gmbh & Co. V. Commission* (1990) ECR I-261.

*recognize the nationality of vessels which do not have a genuine link with the state whose flag they are flying...
...that under international law a vessel has the nationality of the State in which it is registered and that it is for that
state to determine the exercise of its sovereign powers the conditions for the grant of such nationality...
...and the Irish regulations cannot therefore be justified on the basis of public international law"*

In this case the examination of international law had a direct impact on the substantive
decision of the Court. However, the public international law argument was not accompanied
supported by any comparative observations in realm of national legal systems..

In general, in these types of interpretations, no traditional comparative observations seem
to be used.

The Court has also been forced to give a statement concerning the argumentative value of
practices of Member States' trading partners in this context:[448]

*"In the view of the fact that NHB's European subsidiaries have not shown that the system adopted by the Community
is unlawful, the fact that the Communities' trading partners adopt other methods does not render that system is
unlawful"*

The European Court of Justice and human rights. In the field of human rights, the situation
is somewhat different. There are normative bases which justify the use of extralegal material
as a source of EC law.

Fundamental rights have been traditionally considered as *an "integral part of the general
principles of law ... protected by the European Court of Justice"*, and the Court has stated
that *"these fundamental rights derive from the constitutional traditions of Member States".*[449]
However, the interpretation of fundamental rights has to be evaluated in the light Community
law itself.[450]

During the period before the Treaty on European Union, the Court referred constantly to the
European human rights system[451] and the rights provided in the national constitutions of its

---

[448] Case 188/88 *NMB GmbH v. Commission* (1992) ECR I-1689.
[449] In many cases, the court has examined the compatibility of Community freedoms with these fundamental rights. See
on this, cases 11/70 *Internationale Handelsgesellschaft v Einfuhr- und Vorratstelle Getreide* (1970) ECR 1125, 25/70
Einfuhr- und Vorratstelle v Köster (1970) ECR 1161, 44/79 *Hauer v Land Rheinland Pfalz* (1979) ECR 3727, and
46/87 *Hoech v Commission* (1987) ECR 1549 For some analysis, see Wilmers de, J M., 1991, p.37 ff.
The idea of fundamental rights has been seen as a program of comparative constitutional law (Pescatore, P., 1980,
p.341).
[450] Case 11/70 *Internationale Handelsgesellschaft* (1970) ECR 1125 (17 December 1970). For some analysis, see
Wilmer de, J.M., 1991, p.38 ff.
[451] Council of Europe, Rome, November 4, 1950, into force 2 September 2, 1953.
However, this reference took place only after the last Member State became a Contracting Party to this Convention (see,
Schreuer, Ch , 1993, p.459).

Member States.[452] The comparative observations have supported the interpretation of many European human rights arguments.
In one case[453] the Court asserted that

"Fundamental rights are an integral part of the general principles of law, the observance of which the court ensures. In safeguarding these rights the court is bound to draw inspiration from the constitutional traditions common to the Member States, and cannot uphold measures which are incompatible with the fundamental rights established and guaranteed by the constitutions of these states. Similarly, international treaties for the protection of human rights, on which the Member States have collaborated or of which they are signatories, can supply guidelines which should be followed within the framework of the community law"

In terms of the facts of the case, the court explained the general approach to the interpretation of these rights:

"If rights of ownership are protected by the constitutional laws of all the Member States and if similar guarantees are given in respect of their right freely to choose and practice their trade or profession, the rights thereby granted, far from constituting unfettered prerogatives, must be viewed in the light of the social function of the property and activities protected thereunder. For this reason, rights of this nature are protected by law subject always to restrictions laid down in accordance with the public interest. Within the Community legal order it likewise seems legitimate that these rights should, if necessary, be subject to certain limits justified by the overall objectives pursued by the Community, on condition that the substance of these rights is left untouched.
The above guarantees can in no respect be extended to protect mere commercial interests or opportunities, the uncertainties of which are part of the very essence of economic activity."[454]

This reasoning was based on the observations of the Advocate General[455]. There was also consideration of Joint Declarations by the European Parliament, the Council, and the Commission on fundamental rights.[456] This type of interpretation lays down the basic ideas about the value of the comparative approach in the Community system (substantive generality, derogations based on Communities' objectives).
The Treaty of European Union codified the development of the case-law and sources of law

---

[452] See cases 4/73 *Nold v Commission* (1974) ECR 491, 507, 36/75, *Rutili v Minister of the Interior* (1975) ECR 1219, 1232, 44/79, *Hauer v Rheinland-Pfalz* (1979) ECR 3727, 3745. For some analysis, see Pescatore, P., 1980, p.341
Also Commission has adopted a memorandum on the Accession of the European Community to the European human rights system (*Bulletin* of the European Communities, 4/1979, 16).
[453] Case 4/73 *Nold, Kohlen- und Bausstoffgrosshandlung v Commission* (1974) ECR 491 (14 May 1974).
[454] The judgment continued as follows (on the "substance"):
" *The disadvantages claimed by the applicant are in fact the result of economic change and not of the contested decision. It was for the applicant, confronted by the economic changes brought about by the recession in coal production, to acknowledge the situation and itself carry out the necessary adaptations."*
[455] Mr. Trabucchi. Opinion delivered on 28 March 1974 is of particular importance. This well argued opinion goes through the nature of the fundamental principles, their uses, their purposes, making comparative references to systems of the Member States - in general, and to a certain extent, in particular. On these bases he dismisses the applicants claims.
[456] OJ 1977 C-103, and *Bulletin* of the European Communities, 3-1977. See also European Council Declaration of April 8, 1978 on Democracy, *Bulletin* of the European Communities, 3-1978.

doctrine created by the European Community legal system in Article F.2.:

> "2. The Union shall respect fundamental rights, as guaranteed by the European Convention for the Protection of Human Rights and Fundamental Freedoms signed in Rome on 4 November 1950 and as they result from the constitutional traditions common to the Member States, as general principles of Community Law."

It could be claimed that this provision established some kind of normative basis and an obligation for the European Court of Justice to use comparative analysis when examining certain legal questions. One may say that this is not only a statement of the static existence of general principles common to the Member States, but that, for that matter, it imposes an obligation to follow the development of the case-law of the European Court of Human Rights and argumentation in these cases and to oversee the development of the national constitutions in this respect. In some ways, it confirms the position of comparative analysis as a dynamic part of the legal sources of the European Community legal system.

Some other changes were introduced by the Amsterdam Treaty 1997 in realm of the Article F[457]. It remains to be seen what kind of change the inclusion of fundamental rights in the Amsterdam treaty will bring into the system. One may predict, however, that comparative analysis may lose its importance due to the fact that the basic rights argument may become an independent basis of Community law claims. The Community system will define its jurisdictional relationship towards both the European human rights system and also towards the general constitutional traditions of the Member States, because for the first time, it will be able to apply the general basic rights in the context of Community law. On the other hand, there is a possibility that comparative law argumentation may become an integral part of the interpretation of the relationship between the European Community and Member State levels.

However, in general, the basic doctrine of comparative interpretation seems to be already well-established in the case law.

---

[457] "1. The Union is founded on the principles of liberty, democracy, respect of human rights and fundamental freedoms, and the rule of law, principles which are common to the Member States
2. The Union shall respect fundamental rights, as guaranteed by the European Convention for the Protection of Human Rights and Fundamental Freedoms signed in Rome on 4 November 1950 and as they result from the constitutional traditions common to the Member States, as general principles of Community law.
3. The Union shall respect the national identities of its Member States.
4. The Union shall provide itself with the means necessary to attain its objectives and carry through its policies."
(Compare the Rome Treaty and Maastricht Treaty; in them national identity is mentioned in the first paragraph.)

2.1.7. The use of state legal systems in the absence of international obligations

General remarks. As seen, Community judges are guided by the principles derived from national legal systems[458]. On the other hand, the sphere of use of such generality arguments is not restricted to any particular field of principles. It is the nature of the case in question, and the arguments made by the parties, which determines the nature of the consideration given to these general principles.

What does comparative law study mean to the European Court of Justice? This is perhaps best understood via some of its case law.

The Advocates General have stressed the fact that in the Community system there is no attempt to study concepts common to several legal systems and in this way to arrive at generalizations[459]. Furthermore, the Community legal order *"does not aim in principle to define its concepts on the basis of one or more national legal systems without express provision to that effect"*[460] The Advocate General have maintained, for example, that

> *"These minimum requirements are based on the provisions of the common customs tariff read in conjunction with regulation no 1259/72 that is to say, on provisions of Community law which <u>do not refer to legal system of the Member States in determining their meaning and scope; the Community legal order does not in fact aim in principle to define its concepts on the basis of one or more national legal systems without express provision to that effect.</u> In this case all national variations from such common requirements as to quality tend to distort the uniform effect of regulation no 1259/72 as amended and to use it for purposes other than that for which it was intended, which is the disposal of butter stock sale at a reduced price to certain processing undertakings by permitting reduction in the monetary and compensatory amounts pertaining to the market of products whose destination is not necessarily that for which a favourable rate is provided by that regulation."*

In the context of the concept of the "employee", the Court maintained the possibility of interpreting the term with reference to the term *"common to the legal systems of the Member States"*, but at the same time confirmed, with reference to the Courts interpretation of the term "worker" in another case, that there is, however, only a "Community" meaning:

> *"It is common ground that directive no 77/187 does not contain an express definition of the term' employee'. <u>In order to establish its meaning it is necessary to apply generally recognized principles of interpretation by referring in the first place to the ordinary meaning be attributed to that term in its context and by obtaining such guidance as may</u>*

---

[458] One of the first cases, Case 1/57, 14/57, *Société des Usines á Tubes de la Sarre v High Authority* (1957) ECR 105. Referred, for example, in case 137/92 *Commission of the European Communities v Basf AG* (1994) ECR I-2555 (Judgment of the Court of 15 June 1994).

[459] Opinion of Mr Advocate General Lenz delivered on 14 June 1988. Case *Weissgerber v. Finanzamt Neustadt* (reference for a preliminary ruling from the Finanzgericht Rheinland-Pfalz, effect of directives - exemption from vat - passing on of tax) (1988) ECR 4433.

[460] Case 64/81 *De Franceschi Nicolaus Corman et Fils SA v. Hauptzollamt Gronau* (1992) ECR 13 (judgment of the Court, 27 January 1982). Also Case 191/90 *Generics UK, Harris Phar LTD v So Klein and French Laborat Ltd.* (1992) ECR I-5335 (27 October 1992).

be derived from Community texts and from concepts common to the legal systems of the Member States.
It may be recalled that the court, inter alia in its judgment of 2 March 1982 (case 53/81, Levin, (1982) ECR 1035), held that the term' worker' as used in the Treaty, may not be defined by reference to the national laws of the Member States but has a Community meaning. If this were not the case, the community rules on freedom of movement for workers would be frustrated, since the meaning of the term could be decided and modified unilaterally, without a control by the community institutions, by the Member States, which would thus be able to exclude ... certain categories of persons from the benefit of the Treaty."[461]

This type of interpretative idea suggests an interaction between the ordinary (textual) meaning and the comparative method of interpretation.

Similar ideas have been expressed also in following way, based on a criticized practice:

"Moreover, the concept could not truly purport to derive from a principle common to the laws of the Member States but would be carrying too far the frequently criticized doctrine of "act of the government" whose scope is tending to be considerably narrowed in some legal systems where it was formerly most rigorously applied."[462]

This has been recognized also in the field of social security:

"...elements of particular benefit, purposes and the conditions on which it is granted, and not on whether a benefit is classified as a social security benefit by national legislation."[463]

In some cases, the Court has maintained that it is unnecessary to refer to comparative law:

"Accordingly, and without it being necessary to examine the different legal systems of Member States, the applicants are not justified in claiming that the Commission has failed to observe the above mentioned principles laid down by the Court of Justice in its judgment in the papiers peints case."[464]

The basic "doctrine" for the rejection of comparison is based on the impossibility of comparing the State's own legal system with the Community system. This may be related to the idea of the "autonomy of the Community legal order"[465]. This idea has been formulated, for example, in the following way:

---

[461] Case 105/84, *Foreningen af Arbejdsledere i Danmark v. a/s Danmols Inventar A/S* (reference for a preliminary ruling from the Vestre Landsret. - safeguarding of employees' rights in the event of transfers of undertakings) (1985) ECR 2639-2654 (Judgment of the court, fifth chamber, of 11 July 1985).
[462] Opinion of Mr Advocate General Darmon delivered on 1 June 1989 in case 241/87 *Maclaine Watson & Co. Ltd v. Council of the European Communities and Commission of the European Communities* (1990) ECR I-1797.
[463] See also, case 98/94 *Christel Schmidt v Rijksdienst voor pensioenen* (reference for a preliminary ruling: Arbeidsrechtbank Antwerpen - Belgium. Regulation (EEC) no 1408/71 - social security - national rules against) (1995) ECR I-2559 (Judgment of the court (first chamber) of 11 August 1995).
[464] Case 34/92 *Fiatagri UK Ltd and New Holland Ford Ltd v. Commission of the European Communities* (1994) ECR II-905 (Judgment of the court of first instance (second chamber) of 27 October 1994).
[465] Case 6/64 *Costa v. ENEL* (1964) ECR 585.

"Secondly, it is not open to Member States to rely on the special features of their legal systems by way of defence where they have failed to carry out their community obligations. It is well established that Member State may not rely upon provisions, practices or circumstances existing in its internal legal system in order to justify a failure to fulfil obligations arising under Community law : see, for example, case 254/83 Commission v Italy [1984] ECR 3395. In particular, a Member States may not plead administrative difficulties existing in that state in order to justify such a failure : see case 58/83 Commission v Greece [1984] 202. Moreover, to allow such a defence as that invoked by the German government here would obviously prejudice the uniform application of Community law: the application of Community law would be at the mercy of the procedural peculiarities of each national legal system".[466]

Furthermore, the "disharmony" between national and Community concepts of "legal person" (in Article 173 of the Treaty) has also been recognized by the Court[467].

The same idea has been, on some occasions, explained in a more indirect way with reference to the functioning of the Community order:

" ... finally, it should be pointed out that the Court declared in the Ferwerda judgment that no consideration whatever which under one of the legal systems of the Member States is or may be based on a principle of legal certainty can in all cases constitute a defence against a claim for the recovery of Community financial benefits wrongly granted. It must in each case be considered whether such application does not jeopardize the very basics of the rule providing for such recovery and whether it does not result in practice in frustrating such recovery".[468]

The basic rejection of comparative law has been usually based on a more extensive comparative study, which has resulted, in consequence, in some remarks on the disparity of the different systems:

"Those examples clearly emphasize that at the Community level the expression "public undertaking", which must necessarily have a uniform meaning, cannot be defined by reference to the different legal concepts of the national legal systems. For the purposes of defining the concept "undertaking" within the meaning of Community competition law and the expression public undertaking" within the meaning of directive 80/72, the greater importance must therefore be attached to function..."[469]

---

[466] Opinion of Mr Advocate General Jacobs delivered on 15 May 1990 in case 217/88 *Commission of the European Communities v Federal Republic of Germany* (Agriculture - common organization of the market in wine - national coercive measures) (1990) ECR I-2879. The same idea is expressed in the case 140/78 *Commission of the European Communities v Italian Republic* (Agricultural structure policy - submission of statements of account) (1980) ECR 3687 - 3701 (Judgment of the court of 10 December 1980), case 140/78 *Commission of the European Communities v Italian Republic* (Failure to adopt within the prescribed period the measures needed to comply with a directive - annual accounts of certain types of companies) (1986) ECR 1199-1205 (Judgment of the court of 20 March 1986).

[467] Case 135/81 *Groupement des Agences de Voyages, Asbl v Commission of the European Communities* (Application for a declaration of the nullity of a decision) (1982) ECR 3799-3811 (Judgment of the court (first chamber), 28 October 1982).

[468] Opinion of Mr Advocate General Darmon delivered on 29 November 1988. In case 94/87 *Commission of the European Communities v Federal Republic of Germany* (State aids - undertaking producing primary aluminium - recovery)(1989) ECR 175.

[469] Opinion of Mr Advocate General Mischo delivered on 4 November 1986 in case 118/85 *Commission of the European Communities v Republic of Italy* (Transparency of financial relations between Member States and public undertakings) (1987) ECR 2599.

The same idea was seen in the case concerning the equal treatment of men and women. The Advocate General rejected the references to the treatment of the principle of equality in different systems, because that would weaken the application of the "*Community principle of equal treatment*" as well as the "*uniform application of the Community rules*".[470] Surprisingly, the reference was made only to Irish, French, Italian, and Greek systems. Furthermore, in the same context, the principle of equal treatment has been seen, in general, as a "*cornerstone of contemporary legal systems*".[471]

It must be mentioned that comparative observations frequently appear in the submissions to the Court presented by the parties. These types of references have been recognized and analysed, to a certain extent, by the Court.

The Commission has pointed out, in several submissions, the "comparative" diversity of the legal systems. In a case supporting national systems´ competence, the Court recognized how

> "...as the Commission points out in its written observations, the Community legislation is largely silent on the respective interests of landlord and tenant, leaving it to the Member States to strike the necessary balance. *That this should be left to national authorities is logical, given the diversity of national legal systems and implementing legislation and the different circumstances of individual producers.*"[472]

Also "generality" arguments have been used by the Commission to support its Community law interpretation:

> "The Commission likewise contends that the termination of a contract of employment, whether by way of dismissal or automatically, is included to the concept 'conditions of employment' and does not fall within the exceptions to the principle of equality of treatment referred to in Article 2 of the directive no 76/207 or within the scope of directive... In that connection it states *that in the national systems termination of a contract of employment also falls* within the sphere of labour law rather than of social security law."[473]

However, the Advocate General was not convinced of the interpretation on these bases. Commission reports have been also used by the Court in several cases, and they may even be referred to by the Court in its justification:

---

[470] Joined opinion of Mr Advocate General Darmon delivered on 14 November 1989 in case 177/88 *Elisabeth Johanna Pacifica Dekker v Stichting Vormingscentrum voor jong volwassenen plus* (1990) ECR I-3941.

[471] Opinion of Mr Advocate General Tesauro delivered on 23 January 1991 in case 63/89 *Assurances du credit SA and Compagnie belge d'assurance credit SA v Council of the European Communities and Commission of the European Communities* (1991) ECR I-1799.
   We will discuss the comparative reasoning in this context below in this chapter and in the analysis of the Kalanke "hard" case.

[472] Opinion of Mr Advocate General Jacobs delivered on 27 April 1989 in case 5/88 *Hubert Wachauf v Federal Republic of Germany* (Reference for a preliminary ruling : Verwaltungsgericht Frankfurt am Main - Germany) (1989) ECR 2609.

[473] Case 262/84 *Vera Mia Beets-Proper v F. Van Lanschot Bankiers NV* (Reference for a preliminary ruling from the Hoge Raad der Nederlanden. Equality of treatment for men and women - conditions governing dismissal) (1986) ECR 773-793 (Judgment of the Court of 26 February 1986).

"The information provided by the Commission shows that national systems of assistance for orphans vary considerably. In the view of this variation and in order to avoid arbitrary differences according to the national systems, the term in Article 78(1) of regulation No 1408/71 must be interpreted as referring to all benefits intended under the applicable national law".[474]

In this case, the comparative study and its result (the showing of clear disparities between national legislation) had a direct impact on the result of the case.

States frequently attempt to argue on the basis of their legislation, when there is a question of interpretation of EC legislation.[475] Moreover, the parties use comparative arguments to support their views:

"In support of that submission, the applicants claim that in the legal systems of all the Member States the debtor is not entitled to profit from a delay in the payment of sums which are due. The creditor may not be deprived of interest produced by the sums which he could have used to meet his needs from the date on which they were due."[476]

There are several examples of the analysis of the rules of the directives and regulations (other than in the field of the Brussels Convention and the competition law) where, both in the institutional context of justification and in the justification itself there is the use of comparative observations.

One example can be taken up here:

"The difference in question is based on the distinction between residents' and' nonresident', which is to be found in all legal systems and is internationally accepted. It is an essential distinction in the law. It is thus also applicable in the context of Article 52 of the Treaty."[477]

Comparisons, in the Community system, can take the form of direct references, but some indirect comparisons are also made. These "indirect comparisons" can be, as noticed, derived

---

[474] Case 188/90 *Mario Donguzzi-Zordanin v Landesversicherungsanstalt Schwaben* (1992) ECR I-2039 (19 March 1992).

[475] See case 78/91 *Hughes v Chief Adjudication Officer, Belfast* (1992) ECR I-4839 (16 July 1992).

[476] Case T-16/89 *Hans Herkenrath and others v Commission of the European Communities* (Officials - remuneration - default interest and compensatory interest) (1992) ECR II-275 (Judgment of the Court of First Instance (second chamber) of 26 February 1992).

[477] Case 270/83 *Commission of the European Communities v French Republic* (Freedom of establishment in regard to insurance - corporation tax and shareholders' tax credits) (1986) ECR 273-308 (Judgment of the court of 28 January 1986).
See also, case 124/83 *Direktoratet for markedsordningerne v s. A. Nicolas Corman et fils* (Reference for a preliminary ruling from the Östre Landsret. Common organisation of the agricultural markets) (1985) ECR 3777-3794 (Judgment of the court of 5 December 1985), case T-275/94 *Groupement des Cartes Bancaires "CB" v Commission of the European Communities* (1995) II-2169 (Judgment of the court of first instance (fourth chamber, extended composition) of 14 July 1995), and case 49/84 *Leon Debaecker and Berthe Plouvier v Cornelis Gerrit Bouwman* (Reference for a preliminary ruling from the hoge raad der nederlanden. Brussels convention - Article 27.2 - service in sufficient time) (1985) 1779-1803 (Judgment of the Court (fourth chamber) of 11 June 1985).

from the material produced by the Commission or from the "comparative legal sciences":

> *"notwithstanding the preparatory work carried out at the Commission behest (Eugen Ulmer : the law on unfair competition in the Member States of the EEC, part I: comparative survey; study undertaken at the request of the Commission of the European Communities by the Max-Planck-Institut fuer auslaendisches und internationale patent, urheber - und wettbewerbsrecht, Muenchen, in particular no 432), no harmonization has been achieved with regard to designations of origin indications of provenance and so on (see written question no 250/86, 290, 17.11.1986, p. 36). Designations of origin exist in the legal system of some Member States, and to a lesser extent or not at all in that of others (see in that regard: Jean Pierre Cochet: La notion d'appell d'origine en droit communautaire, 1985, and Klaus-Juergen Kraatz: der Schutz geographischer Weinbezeichnungen im Recht der europaeischen Gemeinschaften, 1980).*[478]

The comparison of language versions is one of the "comparative" methods used by the Court. Comparisons of language versions have generated the idea of a "wide and nontechnical interpretation of concepts":

> *"Comparison of the versions in the different languages of the Community of the text of Article 2 of regulation no 1788/69 shows that these terms* must not be interpreted in the strict technical sense which the terms agent' or' concessionaire' may have in the law of one or other of the Member States *but may be interpreted* widely and in a nontechnical manner. *The terms' sole agent' and' sole concessionaire' must not be understood as referring to two quite distinct and mutually exclusive legal constructions but as intended to include the different constructions in the legal systems of the Member States refer under the one or the other of these designations to contractual relationships belonging to the category thus indicated "*[479]

In conclusion, one may maintain that the relationship between a supranational system and the national systems it "contains" is never static. The direct influence and applicability of national laws in the European Court of Justice has occasionally been discussed.

Basically, the rule is that the Court of Justice does not have the competence to apply national laws.[480] Furthermore, the Court of Justice cannot decide on the violation of a national law or interpret national provisions.[481] As recognized, the ECJ is very reluctant to look into the national legislation in the different Member States. However, claims based on the disparity between legislation in the different Member States and the absence of common rules as

---

[478] Opinion of Mr Advocate General Van Gerven delivered on 22 February 1989 in case 263/87 *Kingdom of Denmark v Commission of the European Communities* (Clearance of eaggf accounts - export refunds - Grana Padano cheese) (1989) ECR 1081.
 See also, Opinion of Mr Advocate General Van Gerven delivered on 28 January 1992 in case 104/89 *J.M. Mulder and others and Otto Heinemann v Council of the European Communities and Commission of the European Communities* (Additional levy on milk - non-contractual liability) (1992) ECR I-3061.
[479] Case 82/76 *Farbwerke Hoechst v. Hauptzollamt Frankfurt-am-Main* (Preliminary ruling requested by the Hessisches Finanzgericht. Value for customs purposes of trade-marks) (1977) ECR 335-350 (Judgment of the court of 17 February 1977). See also, opinion of the Advocate General Warner (also comparative observations in general)
[480] Case 1/58 *Stork v High Authority* (1958) ECR 17, and 36-40/59 *Geitling v High Authority* (1960) ECR 423.
[481] See, 78/70 *Deutsche* Grammophon v Metro (1971) ECR 487.

justifying discriminatory practices in Member States has been rejected by the ECJ.[482]

Nevertheless, the ECJ has to deal with and interpret national systems, at least when the Treaty makes explicit reference to the national systems (and its concepts), as in the case of human rights.[483] This also takes place in cases where there are problems with the interpretation of concepts in the European system.[484]

From the practice of the European Court of Justice it can be seen that the German, French and English legal conceptualizations have had an indirect influence on the practice of the Court.[485] However, this can be verified only indirectly, because the Court has explicitly rejected this "one-sided adaption". The use of conceptualizations foreign to the Community system derives from the fact that even if a rule is not mentioned in written law this is not proof that it does not exist.[486] On the other hand, the fact that conceptualization is used does not mean that all ingredients of particular national systems will necessarily be accepted. In fact, the use of national concepts can be extremely "analogical", and the Advocate Generals in particular have developed an extremely broad comparative approach.[487]

Because the specific rules in Member States are not directly applicable norms for the ECJ, they rather seem to be kind of "facts" of the case. In other words, they are non-normative material of the system. However, they can be used to support certain conclusions in cases, and can be used as material for the argument. The use of the results of these comparative studies is not based on the features of any one specific legal system, but rather on a set of "group" features of these systems (disparity or uniformity in an (institutionally) qualitative sense)[488].

It seems that comparative interpretation has to do with quite strict textual and literal interpretations.

---

[482] Case 191/90 *Generics UK, Harris Phar. LTD v S. Kline and French Laborat. Ltd.* (1992) ECR I-5335 (27 October 1992).

[483] Case 50/71 *Wünsche v Einfuhr- und Vorratstelle Getreide* (1972) ECR 53. See for example Article 58.

[484] This was mentioned in particular in the statement of Advocate General Roemer in the case 5/54 *Netherlands v High authority* (1954) Rec. 201. See also cases 17,20/61 *Klöckner-Werke AG and Hoesch AG v High Authority* (1962) ECR 325 ja 159/78 *Republic of Italy v. Commission* (1979) ECR 3247.

[485] Cruz, de R., 1993, Chapter 5. There have been cases, where the Court has explicitly referred to the law of other Member States as applicable law, see 7/56 and 3-7/57 *Algera and others v Assembly*, Rec. 1957, p.81,114-116. Some analysis, Schwarze, J., 1991, p 5.

However, these decisions were made before the Community system had specific provisions dealing with those questions.

[486] Case 108/63 *Merlini v High Authority* (1965) ECR 1, 10.

[487] See case 14/61 *Hoogovens v High authority* (1962) ECR 253, 280-283 and 13/61 *De Geus v Bosch* (1962) ECR 45, 58-61.

[488] One could claim that if national conceptualizations were accepted as such within the EC system, one could even claim discriminatory treatment among Member States. The idea of referring normatively only to certain systems in the EC legal system would be against the formal legal equality of the national systems. This is why the Court is unable to explicitly use direct conceptualizations of one Member State. The ECJ refers to all systems. Referring is "recognition" type of argumentation, and not argumentation by direct normative and legal-instrumental arguments.

It could be claimed, that the EC system attempts, via the adaptation of certain methods of comparative argumentation (towards national and other international systems), to achieve coherence and harmony with the other systems.

Some examples of comparative reasoning and its consequences. The Court and the Advocates General have used "qualitative" comparative analysis and argumentation in several occasions in arguing for the positive content of certain concepts, rules, and principles. The list of examples presented here is not exhaustive. Furthermore, the "legal" function of these comparisons is not analysed thoroughly in this chapter. The idea here is to present a variety of examples from different fields of law. The presentation is divided into the comparative interpretation of concepts, rules, principles, procedural rules, staff cases, and finally, some "constitutional" ideas.

In certain cases, the Advocates General, with reference to case law, have considered national conceptualizations as a source of interpretation, particularly when the matter is about the interpretation of different language versions[489]:

> *"First, the different language versions are all equally authentic and an interpretation of a provision of Community law thus involves a comparison of the various language versions (judgment of 6 October 1982 in case 283/81 Cilfit v Ministry of Health [1982] ECR at 3430, paragraph 18). Secondly, Greece joined the Community only af the adoption of that regulation. Thus, in so far as the Greek language version differs from the text as published in 1971 and since then maintained in the other languages, it can only be a translation error first question."*

and that

> *"Nothing permits the conclusion to be drawn that expression have different meaning in Community law than the one it has in the national legal systems. ."*[490]

The concept of *"minimum benefit"* occurring in a regulation[491] was, according to the Advocate General, to be interpreted with *"reference to the minimum benefits fixed by the laws of the various Member States"*. The study was based on the examination of the concept in those systems *"where the existence of it is not contested"*.[492] This study was made under the auspices of the Commission.

Moreover, the distinction between *"rights in personam"* and *"rights in rem"* was adopted by the Advocate General on the basis of the "indirect" comparative argument referred to to in the

---

[489] The question at issue was about the expression ´at the purchasers own risk´ in Article 15 (a) of Regulation no 2960/77.

[490] Opinion of Mr Advocate General Mischo delivered on 11 February 1988 in case 71/87 *Greek state v Inter-Kom AE* (Reference for a preliminary ruling from the Efeteio (court of appeal)) (1988) ECR 1979.

[491] Article 50 of regulation no 1408/71

[492] *Case 22/81 Regina v Social Security Commissioner, ex parte Norman Ivor Browning* (reference for a preliminary ruling from the High court of justice, Queen' s bench division, divisional court, London) (1981) ECR 3357-3372 (Judgment of the court (second chamber), 17 December 1981).

so-called Schlosser report.[493]

The interpretation of the concept of a *"legal person"* has been supported by observations based upon observed "tendencies in the national jurisprudence":

> *"The fact that under the second paragraph of Article 173 only legal (and natural) persons are entitled to bring actions and that only such persons are deemed to have general capacity - as distinct from the capacity to bring an action (see paragraph 8, above) - does not seem to constitute a real obstacle. There is, after all, in many legal systems, evidence of a general tendency to interpret the concept of "legal person" in a pragmatic way, allowing the courts to decide on the basis of the way in which positive law structures the legal sphere of particular organ or institution that within a specific legal relationship that organ or institution has (to a greater or lesser degree) legal personality. There is also clear evidence of that tendency in the case-law of this court."[494]*

In the realm of the Brussels Convention, which is within the jurisdiction of the Court, there is an explicit reference to the need for comparative analysis in the interpretation of certain concepts. Consequently, there have been several interpretations made on a comparative basis. Indeed, the Court has developed a doctrine of "comparative interpretation" in this field of law[495].

Comparative interpretation was expressed by the Court in cases dealing with the concept of *'civil and commercial matters'* and *'ordinary'* and *'extraordinary'* appeals (Articles 30 and 38 of the Brussels Convention). There the Court had explained that when one is interpreting the Brussels Convention clauses (*"especially title III thereof"*) the reference is to be made *"to the law of one of the states concerned but, first, to the objectives and the scheme of the Convention and, secondly, to the general principles which stem from the corpus of the national legal systems."*[496]

There the Advocate General had identified a *lacunae* in the law. The parties had been arguing on the basis of international practices. The Advocate General spoke of the different possible approaches, and referred to governmental opinions in the context of the case in addition to Commission reports and the purpose and the history of the drafting.[497] The

---

[493] Opinion of Mr Advocate General Darmon delivered on 8 February 1994 in case 294/92 *George Lawrence Webb v Lawrence Desmond Webb* (Reference for a preliminary ruling: Court of appeal (England) - United Kingdom) (1994) ECR I-1717.

[494] Opinion of Mr Advocate General Van Gerven delivered on 30 November 1989 in case 70/88 *European Parliament v Council of the European Communities* (Capacity of the European Parliament to bring an action for annulment) (1990) ECR I-2041.

[495] Brussels convention, 27 September 1968, renewed, 9 Oct 1978, OJ, 1979 LK 04, p.44. See also on the Brussels Convention cases, Pescatore, P, 1980, pp.343-344.

[496] Case 29/76 *Lufttransportunternehmen GmbH and co. Kg v Eurocontrol* (Preliminary ruling requested by the Oberlandesgericht Düsseldorf) (1976) ECR 1541-1552 (Judgment of the court of 14 October 1976).

[497] Advocates General have been referring to the absence of comparative information in the preparatory documents of the Convention, and the comparative studies produced in the so-called Generate report on the issue (OJ 1979 C 59) - including also bilateral treaties (see, for example, Opinion of the Advocate General Gulmann, 20th February 1992 in case 261/90 *Mario Reichert, Hans-Heinz Reichert and Ingeborg Klocker v Dresden Bank Ag* (reference to the preliminary ruling,

Commission had been advocating the idea of an "ideal solution" ("*independent conceptualization*"). The Advocate General, however, viewed the idea of an independent "comparative" construction as difficult and tending toward uncertainty. Consequently, he referred to the "*experience of the national courts*", and came to the conclusion that the matter should be related to the definition provided by the court (and the state), where the enforced judgment had been given.

Another good example is the case concerning the "*clause conferring jurisdiction*" in a company's statutes[498]. It shows also how the comparative law method has been developed in a "first case" dealing with the issue, and how interpretation may become somewhat dogmatic.

In case, the Advocate General made an extensive study of the idea of the "*clause conferring the jurisdiction*" in different legal systems. The Court, based on the report of the Advocate General, investigated the question as to whether the jurisdiction-conferring clause contained in the statute of the company (expressing the jurisdiction) was an agreement within the meaning of the Article 17 of the Brussels Convention.

The Court argued that there was a disparity between the legal systems concerning the relationship between a shareholder and a company limited by shares. In some systems "*the relationship is characterized as contractual, in others it is regarded as institutional, normative or sui generis.*" The Court maintained that the interpretation of this concept must be independent. This idea was explained so as to derive the "*objectives and the general scheme of the Convention*", and in order to

"*ensure the equality and uniformity of the rights and obligations arising out of the Convention. For the contracting states and the persons concerned, therefore it is important that the concept of "agreement conferring jurisdiction" should not be interpreted simply as referring to the national law of one or other of the states concerned.*"

The Court refused to interpret the concept by reference to a set of example or model, and instead used the fact that disparity existed between national laws to arrive at an independent idea concerning the concept.[499]

However, in answering to the question whether that particular clause in the statute, as it was expressed, satisfied "*the formal requirements of the Article 17*", the Court again made a reference to national legal systems. It found that there was a comparative "generality" among

---

Cour d'appel d'Aix-en-provence - France) (1992) ECR I-2149). In this case the Court went through also the different language versions of the provision in question, and made other comparative law observations.

[498] The Article 17 of the Brussels Convention. Case 214/89 *Powell Duffryn plc v Wolfgang Petereit* (Reference for the preliminary ruling: Oberlandesgericht Koblenz - Germany. Brussels convention - Jurisdiction Agreement - Clause contained in the statutes of the company limited by shares) (1992) ECR I-1745 (Judgment of the Court of 10 March 1992).

This was based on the Opinion of Mr Advocate General Tesauro delivered on 20 November 1991.

[499] In the Case 3/82 *Peters v Znav* (1983) ECR 987, the Court interpreted the concept of the '*matters relating to a contract*'.

legal systems ("*in the legal systems of all the contracting states*") regarding the fact that the statutes of a company are in written form, and that they are the basic instruments governing the relationship between the shareholder and the company. Furthermore, the way that shares are acquired does not have an effect on the fact that every shareholder ought to be informed of the binding nature of the statute.[500]

The Court's ruling has been thereafter confirmed by several cases dealing with various concepts in the Brussels Convention.[501] In certain opinions[502], detailed comparative references to the legal systems of the Member States were not even considered to be necessary, particularly where the case is "clear".[503]

Disparities were found in the idea of *lis pendens* (Article 21 of the Convention, '*first seized court'*)[504]. This resulted in *a fortiori* type of reasoning and a ruling, according to which the

"*the court 'first seized' is the one in which the requirements for proceedings to become definitely pending were first*

---

[500] This was used also in Opinion of Mr Advocate General Lenz delivered on 8 March 1994 in case *288/92 Custom made commercial Ltd v Stawa Metallbau GmbH* (Reference for a preliminary ruling: bundesgerichtshof - Germany. Brussels convention - place of performance of an obligation - uniform law) (1994) ECR I-2913.

[501] This was used as a starting point also in case 9/77 *Bavaria Fluggesellschaft Schwabe and co kg and Germanair Bedarfsluftfahrt GmbH and co kg v Eurocontrol* (Preliminary rulings requested by the Bundesgerichtshof) (1977) ECR 1517-1527 (Judgment of the court of 14 July 1977), 133/78 *Henri Gourdain v Franz Nadler* (Preliminary ruling requested by the Bundesgerichtshof. Brussels convention. Bankruptcy and proceedings relating to the winding-up) (1979) ECR 733-746 (Judgment of the court of 22 February 1979).
Furthermore, Case 150/77 *Berdhand v OTT* (1978) ECR 1432, 814/79 *Netherlands state v Reinhold Rueffer* (Preliminary ruling requested by the Hoge Raad der Nederlanden. Brussels convention of 1968) (1980) ECR 3807-3822 (Judgment of the court of 16 December 1980), 288/82 *Ferdinand M.J.J. Duijnstee in his capacity as liquidator of b.V. Schroefboutenfabriek (in liquidation) v Lodewijk Goderbauer* (Reference for a preliminary ruling from the Hoge Raad der Nederlanden) (1983) ECR 3663-3679 (Judgment of the court (fourth chamber) of 15 November 1983), *Criminal proceedings against Siegfried Ewald Rinkau* (preliminary ruling requested by the Hoge Raad of The Netherlands. Article II of the protocol annexed to the Convention on jurisdiction of 27 (for example, the distinction between 'intentionally and non-intentionally committed crimes', and the concept 'rights in property arising out of a matrimonial relationship' (1981) ECR 1391-1404 (Judgment of the court of 26 May 1981), 143-78 *Jacques de Cavel v Luise de Cavel* (Preliminary ruling requested by the Bundesgerichtshof) (1979) ECR 1055-1068 (Judgment of the court of 27 March 1979), *Martin Peters Bauunternehmung GmbH v Zuid Nederlandse Aannemers Vereniging* (Reference for a preliminary ruling from the Hoge Raad der Nederlanden) (1983) 987-1004 (Judgment of the court, 22 March 1983), Opinion of Mr Advocate General Darmon delivered on 23 November 1989 in case 220/88 *Dumez France and Tracoba v Hessische Landesbank and others* (Reference for a preliminary ruling: Cour de Cassation - France. Brussels convention - matters relating to tort, delict or quasi-delict (the concept of "ricochet"), interpretation of Article 5(3), indirect victim, injury to a parent company due to the financial losses sustained by its subsidiary) (1990) ECR I-49). In it there is really extensive and analytical analysis of the legal discourse and practice on the subject.

[502] Opinion of mr Advocate General sir Gordon Slynn delivered on 17 December 1987 in case 9/87 *S. P. R. L. Arcado v s. A. Haviland* (reference for a preliminary ruling from the Court of appeal, Brussels, referring to the detailed study in Peters case) (1988) ECR 1539.

[503] Reference to the case 14/77 *de Bloos v Bouer* (1976) ECR 1497.

[504] Case 129/83 *Siegfried Zelger v Sebastiano Salinitri* (Reference for a preliminary ruling from the Oberlandesgericht München. Brussels Convention - Article 21, court first seised) (1984) ECR 2397 (Judgment of the court (fourth chamber) of 7 June 1984).

fulfilled, such requirements to be determined in accordance with the national law of each of the courts concerned".[505]

Comparative interpretation undertaken by the Advocates General and the Court can be found in several other types of interpretations of different rules with regard to different types of legal measures.

The distinct language versions and corresponding national "contexts" have been considered by the Court in relation to the '*transfer of an undertaking*' in the realm of Article 1(1) of the Council Directive 77/187[506]. The Court noted[507], that there were discrepancies between different language versions regarding the term '*legal transfer*' and its applicability:

"A comparison of the various language versions of the provision in question shows that there are terminological divergencies between what regards the transfer of undertakings. Whilst the German ('vertragliche übertragung'), French ('cession conventionnelle', Greek ('snmssatιkh ekxvrhsh'), Italian ('cessione contrattuale') and Dutch ('overdrach krachtens overeenkomst') versions clearly refer only to transfers resulting from a contract, from which it may be concluded that other of transfers such as those resulting from an administrative measure or judicial decision are excluded, the English ('legal transfer') and Danish ('overdragelse') versions appear to indicate that the scope is wider and that, moreover, it should be noted that the concept of contractual transfer is different in the insolvency laws of the various Member States, as become apparent in these proceedings. Whilst certain Member States consider that in certain circumstances a sale effected in the context of liquidation proceedings is a normal contractual sale, even if judicial intervention is a preliminary requirement for conclusion of such a contract, under other legal systems the sale is in certain circumstances regarded as taking place by virtue of a measure adopted by a public authority. In view of those divergencies, the scope of the provision at issue cannot be appraised solely on the basis of a textual interpretation."

The analysis of these differences impelled the Court to conclude that not only textual interpretation was possible, but that one could use also the interpretative techniques such as "*in the scheme of the directive*", "*its place in the Community system*", and "*its purpose*".

Accordingly, there were differences noted also in the contexts of the interpretation of the insolvency laws in different Member States, which seemed to be essential for the

---

[505] See also, Advocate General Mancini (Opinion delivered on 11 June 1987) in case 144/86 *Gubisch Maschinenfabrik v Giulio Palumbo* (Reference for a preliminary ruling from the Corte Suprema di Cassazione. Brussels Convention - meaning of lis pendens) (1987) ECR 4861 (Judgment of the court (sixth chamber) of 8 December 1987), and Opinion of Mr Advocate General Tesauro delivered on 13 July 1994 in case 406/92 *The owners of the cargo lately laden on board the ship Tatry v the owners of the ship Maciej Rataj* (Reference for a preliminary ruling: court of appeal (England)) (1994) ECR I-5439.
  For further analysis, see Pescatore, P., 1980, pp.343-344 (case 12/76 *Tessili* (1976) ECR 1473 (6 October 1976).
[506] February 1977.
[507] Case 135/83 *HBM Abels v Bedrijfsvereniging voor de Metaalindustrie en de Elektrotechnische Industrie* [1985] ECR 469.
  See also, Opinion of Mr Advocate General Van Gerven delivered on 30 May 1991 in case 362/89 *Giuseppe d' Urso and Adriana Ventadori and others v Ercole Marelli Elettromeccanica Generale spa and others* (reference for a preliminary ruling: Pretura di Milano - Italy) (1991) ECR I-4105.

interpretation of the Article of the Directive.[508] The disparity found and the specifity of the rules on liquidation and analogous rules led the Court to conclude that the idea of *'transfer of undertakings'* does not apply in the context of current proceedings.

The provisions of the same directive have been interpreted comparatively also by the Advocate General. He referred to the "comparative *travaux preparatoirés*" of the Community system in his opinion:

> *"It is well known that in the legal systems many Member States transfer of contract is regarded as a multilateral contract and therefore requires the agreement of the third party. It should however be noted that, in drawing up the provisions of directive 77/187/EEC, the Community legislature took this fact into account."*[509]

In furthering this analysis, the Advocate General found the diversity of solutions concerning the legal status of a contract in the transfer of the undertakings in different Member States. He referred to the French, Belgian, Dutch, and Italian law.

In the same case, the parties attempted to argue on a comparative basis on behalf of the interpretation that a debt may only be transferred with the creditor's consent. This argument was based on the idea that this constituted a principle *"generally recognized in the legal systems of the Member States"* and was a general principle of obligations. The Court doubted the generality of the rule and, consequently, rejected the argument without, however, any references to comparative law.[510]

In a case dealing, once again, with the Company Law Directive, the Advocate General made a slightly more extensive comparative study concerning the question of acquisition of legal personality in the Member States. Reference was made to Dutch and Portuguese law, the laws of the parties and those prevailing in the system of the Advocate General. They served as examples for further studies concerning an acceptable model.[511]

The rule that an error in application of the Community law caused by an interpretation in good faith by the national authorities does not result in ability to recover sums paid due to that error was established by the Advocate General by a justification with reference, again, to comparative observations of the legal systems of the Member States (*"most of the Member*

---

[508] And as a general conclusion the Court stated that
"*if the directive had been intended to apply also to transfers of undertakings in the context of such proceedings, an express provision would have been included for that purpose*"

[509] Opinion of Mr Advocate General Mancini delivered on 9 February 1988 in case 144/87 *Harry Berg and J. T. M Busschers v Ivo Martin Besselsen* (Reference for a preliminary ruling from the Hoge Raad der Nederlanden. Safeguarding of employees' rights in the event of transfers of undertakings) (1988) ECR 2559.

[510] Case 144/87 *Harry Berg and j. T. M. Busschers v Ivo Martin Besselsen* (Reference for a preliminary ruling from the Hoge Raad der Nederlanden. Safeguarding of employees' rights in the event of transfers of undertakings) (1988) ECR 2559.

[511] Opinion of Mr Advocate General Vilaca delivered on 8 March 1988 in case 136/87 *Ubrink Isolatie bv v Dak- en Wandtechniek bv* (reference for a preliminary ruling from the Hoge Raad der Nederlanden. Company law - first harmonizing directive of the Council) (1988) ECR 4665.

States"). In different systems, it would have been impossible to commence administrative or judicial procedures cases such as these.[512]

In a case concerning the interpretation of the recognition of diplomas[513], there was a dispute between the Advocate General, the Government, and the defendant, as to whether the duty of recognition also existed in connection with the freedom of establishment. The "sociological" disparity presented by the parties was rejected by the Advocate General on the basis of "comparative" considerations:

> *"They take the view that a lawyer who wishes to establish himself in another Member State must acquaint himself with a wholly different legal system: the qualifications and experience acquired by him in his Member State of origin or in the host Member State are not relevant in that connection. I am not persuaded by that argument because it assumes that no significant aspects of similarity can exist between the national legal systems in the Community and the manner of legal practice in the various Member States, a supposition which I find difficult to accept in the light of the historical relationship between a number of national legal systems of the Member States (25) and the way in which justice is administered. Furthermore, and above all, it takes no account of the efforts made by a lawyer from another Member State to acquaint himself with the legal system and the legal practice of the Member State in which he also wishes to practice. That does not mean that the existing differences between the Member States would not justify an admission procedure for lawyers from other Member States; however, in my view, freedom of establishment and the exercise of a profession throughout the Community would be hindered in an unjustified manner if, upon application for admission by a lawyer from another Member State, no account at all were taken of qualifications already obtained and their correspondence with the qualifications required by the law of the host Member State."[514]*

The Court also formulated an interesting "directive" for comparative interpretation with regard to the authorities of the Member States. Namely, it maintained that there is the possibility ("*may*") for local authorities to make a comparative study when applying the principles of freedom of establishment and rules in the field of the recognition of diplomas:

> *"In the course of that examination, a Member State may, however, take into consideration objective differences relating to both the legal framework of the profession in question in the Member State of origin and to its field of activity. In the case of the profession of lawyer, a Member State may therefore carry out a comparative examination of diplomas, taking account of the differences identified between the national legal systems concerned."[515]*

---

[512] 18/76 *Government of the Federal Republic of Germany v Commission of the European Communities* (1979) ECR 343-396 (Judgment of the court of 7 February 1979), and 11/76 *Government of the Kingdom of The Netherlands v Commission of the European Communities* (1979) ECR 245-285 (Judgment of the court of 7 February 1979).

[513] Established by Council Directive 89/48/EEC

[514] Opinion of Mr Advocate General Van Gerven delivered on 28 November 1990 in case 340/98 *Irene Vlassopoulou v Ministerium für Justiz, Bundes- und Europaangelegenheiten baden-Württemberg* (Reference for a preliminary ruling: Bundesgerichtshof - Germany) (1991) ECR I-2357
    Similar types of comparative aspects played an important role also in another cases on the same subject.

[515] Case 340/98 *Irene Vlassopoulou v Ministerium für Justiz, Bundes- und Europaangelegenheiten baden-Württemberg* (Reference for a preliminary ruling: Bundesgerichtshof - Germany) (1991) ECR I-2357.
    See also Opinion of Mr Advocate General Jacobs delivered on 26 February 1992 in case 104/91 *Colegio Oficial de Agentes de la Propriedad Inmobiliaria v J. L. AguirreBorrell and others* (Reference for a preliminary ruling: Juzgado de Instruccion n. 20 de Madrid) (1992) ECR I-3003, and the judgment.

One of the general principles explicitly rejected on the basis of a comparative analysis was the principle of *"force majeure"* (in a particular context). This interpretation was based on the fact that *"its application presupposes the non-performance of an obligation upon the individual with respect to the administration"*. No general principle was discovered *"in the national legal systems where there is no such obligation"*.

The Advocate General argued that

"Reference to the national legal systems reveals that the force majeure has certain effects in criminal law, others in public law and other again in the private law.; they are for the most part governed by specific rules... the fact that there is no uniform view regarding the force majeure...".[516]

The Court agreed with this interpretation.[517]

Moreover, in the field of copyright law (concerning the right to restrain the hiring out of the video cassette) the Advocate General used a comparative "generality" argument inorder to support the rejection of the argument put by a party that the public performance should be assimilated to the hiring out of the cassette:

"In order to understand this it is useful to in keep in mind that, under many national legal systems, the pursuit of the activity of hiring-out becomes unrestricted as soon as the cassette is offered for sale or, as in Germany, entails at most an obligation to give to the author fair compensation. The determining factor, however, is that even in those states the author, following sale of the recording, retains the right to control every other form of exploitation of the hiring-out of the cassette... remains a purely commercial transaction, the risk which it carries - namely that the persons hiring the cassette may see the film several times .... the owner of the right to perform it but by the person who has hired the cassette."[518]

Furthermore, in defining the nature of copyright, the Advocate General used some comparative observations:

"In the legal systems of the Member States copyright is a typical right of exploitation in the form of the right of reproduction on the one hand and the right of public performance on the other (applying to situations where it takes place by way of a sound recording). The peculiarity of French law lies in the fact that an assignment of the reproduction may be restricted to a specific use (private use); if public use is made of the reproduction, the

---

[516] The diversity of the rule in different fields of law has been recognized by the Court in case 4/68 *Schwarzwaldmilch v Einfuhr- und Vorratstelle Fette* [1968] ECR 377.

[517] See, the Opinion of Advocate General Caporti delivered on 18 January 1978 in case 68/77 *Ifg-Intercontinentale Fleischhandelsgesellschaft Mbh and co. Kg v Commission of the European Communities (Force majeure)* (1978) ECR 353-0371 (Judgment of the Court of 14 February 1978).

[518] Opinion of Mr Advocate General Mancini delivered on 26 January 1988 in case 158/86 *Warner brothers inc. And Metronome video Aps v Erik Viuff Christiansen* (Reference for a preliminary ruling from the Östre Landsret. Copyright - action to restrain the hiring-out of video-cassettes) (1988) ECR 2605 .

supplementary mechanical reproduction fee becomes payable."[519]

Furthermore, comparative observations have also been related to the so-called *"generality of the hallmarking of valuable objects"*. In Belgium, contrary to all other Member States, silver-plated articles were also required to be hallmarked. The Court accepted the Belgian system and ruled that the obligation to stamp silver-plated articles can be regarded as necessary for the effective *"protection of consumers and promoting fair trading"*.[520]

In the context of the directive covering technical regulations[521], the Advocate General addressed to the question of whether it is accepted in Community law (in relation to the free movement of goods) that a public entity involved in the selling of equipment can also grant *"selling-permissions"* for imported equipments.[522] The Advocate General maintained that it would not be against Community law if there was a possibility for a review procedure for such decision. He noted that this would not *"lead to disruption of the legal systems of the Member States"* because

> *"While in most of them the situation regarding the approval of telephones is similar to that in Belgium [the country to which the preliminary ruling pertained] in so far as the entity holding the power of approval is not truly distinct the body holding the monopoly for operating the telecommunications network, most of them also allow for a review of the legality of refusal of approval which includes a check on reasons related to the noncompliance with technical specifications which may include the commissioning of experts' reports. New measures will have to be introduced only in Member States where review of legality does not extent to the merits of reasons relating to technical assessments, that is to say, apparently, Italy, Ireland and Luxembourg. It may be assumed that recourse to experts .. enable the national courts concerned to extent their review to technical reasons for refusal of approval which, on the face of it, should not give rise to major problems."*

In the case dealing with lotteries and the applicability of rules concerning the internal market to them, the Advocate General based his analytical argument on the regulation of the lotteries in different Member States. This report had been made by the Commission. It dealt with the functioning of lotteries, and its relationship to public control. All Member States

---

[519] Opinion of Mr Advocate General Lenz delivered on 24 February 1987 in case 402/85 *G. Basset v Societe des auteurs, compositeurs et editeurs de musique (sacem)* (Reference for a preliminary ruling from the our d' appel, Versailles) (1987) ECR 1747 .

[520] Case 220/81 *Robertson and others* (1982) ECR 2701.
See also, Opinion of Advocate General Gulmann delivered on 9 June 1994 in case 293/93 *Criminal proceedings against Ludomira Neeltje Barbara Houtwipper* (Reference for a preliminary ruling: Arrondissementsrechtbank Zutphen Netherlands) (1994) ECR I-4249.

[521] No. 83/189.

[522] Opinion of Mr Advocate General Darmon delivered on 15 March 1989 in case 18/88 *Regie des telegraphes et des telephones v Gb-Inno-bm Sa* (Reference for a preliminary ruling: tribunal de commerce de bruxelles - Belgium) (1991) ECR I-5941.

except Italy submitted their observations on the issue.[523]

The Court has also relied on comparative socio-cultural arguments in order to preserve the competence of Member States:[524]

> *"National rules restricting the opening of shops on Sundays reflected certain choices relating to particular national or regional socio-cultural characteristics. It was for the Member States to make these choices."*

In the context of competition rules, the Court has developed, on the basis of comparative considerations, the idea that the principle of the equality of the treatment of consumers is applicable in relation to economic rules. This was related to the interpretation of Article 3(b) of the Treaty on the Economic and Steel Community. The Court claimed, on comparative basis, that

> *"Pursuant to a principle generally accepted in the legal systems of the Member States, equality of treatment in the matter of economic rules did not prevent different prices being fixed in accordance with the parties situation of consumers or of categories of consumers provided that the differences in treatment correspond to the difference in the situations of such persons. If there is no objectively established basis, distinct treatment are arbitrary, discriminatory and illegal. It cannot be at all that economic rules are unfair, on the pretext that they involve different consequences or disparate disadvantages for the persons concerned when this is clearly the result of their operating conditions."[525]*

Moreover, in the context of Article 93(3) (state aid), the Advocate General maintained that the so-called *"standstill obligation"* of the Treaty should have a direct effect, and that any interested person should be able to challenge state aid in national proceedings. He made a reference to the situation in national legal systems and observed that there are

> *"differences between the various legal systems concerning the conditions and extent of judicial protection granted (for example, limitations on applications for interim measures brought before the administrative courts)"[526].*

---

[523] Opinion of Mr Advocate General Gulmann delivered on 16 December 1993 in case 275/92 *Her Majesty's customs and excise v Gerhart Schindler and Joerg Schindler* (Reference for a preliminary ruling: High Court of Justice, Queen's bench division - United Kingdom) (1994) ECR I-1039.

[524] Case 169/91 *Council of the City Norwich, Stoke-on-Trent/ B&Q plc* (1992) ECR I-6635 (20 April 1991).

[525] Case 11-57 *Societe d' electro-chimie, d' electro-metallurgie et des acieries electriques d' ugine v High Authority of the ECSC* (1958) 357 (Judgment of the Court of 26 June 1958).
See also case 13/57 *Wirtschaftsvereinigung eisen- und stahlindustrie, gussstahlwerk Carl Boennhoff, Gussstahlwerk Witten, Ruhrstahl and Eisenwerk Annahuette Alfred Zeller v High Authority of the ECSC* (1958) ECR 265 (Judgment of the court of 21 June 1958), 10/57 *Societe des anciens etablissements Aubert et Duval v High Authority of the ECSC* (1958) 401 (Judgment of the Court of 26 June 1958), 12/57 *Syndicat de la siderurgie du centre-midi v High Authority of the ECSC* (1958) 473 (Judgment of the Court of 26 June 1958).

[526] Opinion of Mr Advocate General Tesauro delivered on 19 September 1989 in case 142/87 *Kingdom of Belgium v Commission of the European Communities* (State aid - state aid for a steel tube undertaking - withdrawal by way of recovery) (1990) ECR I-959.

However, an example was found from the Italian Constitutional Court of decision that declared that *"regional laws granting aid which were approved by the regional assembly before the Community verification procedure had been completed were unconstitutional"*. Furthermore, the Advocate General took as an example a decision of the United Kingdom Court of Appeal[527], where it had been maintained that the authorities had to restrain from implementing state aid before, and on the conditions that, the Commission had approved it. The Advocate General also maintained that there is a general *"trend"* for developing procedures of such kind.

The Court has also interpreted the principles regarding the severity of the sanctions to be imposed against a company which had breached several rules of the EAEC[528]. The company had argued that the fact that the infringements notionally overlap should be a diminishing factor. The Court refused, however, to grant lesser sanctions. The Court argued that

"On the contrary, it is well established, as is apparent from the approach adopted in certain national legal systems, that in such cases it is appropriate to impose the severest sanction possible"[529].

In dealing with the effect of the Directive's provisions in the realm of the principle of the equal treatment of men and women at work and its effect upon the third parties, the Advocate General made an extensive study of the similar provisions (and their effects) in the International Convention on Civil and Political rights, the Convention on Economic, Social and Cultural Rights[530], and especially the European Convention of Human Rights, and referred to the academic writings in different Member States concerning these Conventions. He also referred to the *"constitutional traditions of the Member States"*.[531]

Furthermore, in the complex of cases dealing with the equality of treatment of men and

---

[527] 24 February 1986 *R v Attorney General ex parte Imperial Chemical Industries.*

[528] Atomic Energy Treaty.

[529] Case 308/90 *Advanced nNclear Fuels GmbH v Commission of the European Communities* (Action for annulment - Commission Decision relating to a procedure in application of article 83 of the Euratom treaty) (1993) ECR I-309 (Judgment of the court (sixth chamber) of 21 January 1993).

[530] Both 19 December 1966.

[531] Opinion of Mr Advocate General van Greven delivered on 30 January 1990 in case *262/88 Douglas Harvey Barber v Guardian Royal Exchange Assurance Group* (Reference for a preliminary ruling; Court of Appeal - United Kingdom - Social Policy - equal pay for men and women - compulsory redundancy - early payment of a retirement pension) (1990) ECR I-1889.

In the case dealing with the dismissal of a pregnant women, the applicant also referred strongly to the same international and national measures, see case T-45/90 *Alicia Speybrouck v European Parliament* (temporary staff - dismissal - protection of pregnant employees - reasons) (1992) ECR II-33 (Judgment of the court of first instance (fifth chamber) of 28 January 1992).

women and the legislative prohibition of night-work[532], the Advocate General[533] described the comparative historical and current practices at both the national and international levels with a special reference to the practices of certain states[534]. Any derogation from the principle was seen to be applied restrictively. Furthermore, the application of this principle in the context of transsexuality was also studied in the light of comparative observations of states and of a detailed study of the practice in the European system of human rights.[535]

There has also been some discussion concerning the "*protection of family life*" with the aid of comparative observations. Here one can note the way in which the interpretation of the applicable principle in Community law has been "found" within the Community system of the past, and how it has become a fundamental principle of Community law and, furthermore, how its interpretation still continues to be based on comparative observations.

One of the first cases, in which this principle was discussed was the Bergemann case[536]. The Advocate General observed, in the context of the interpretation of the concept of "*residence*", that this concept has to be interpreted in the context of the protection of family life. He observed, how

"*marriage and the family enjoy considerable protection both at international level and within the legal systems of the Member States European convention for the protection of human rights and fundamental freedoms, which all the Member States of the Community have ratified*".

He then undertook an analysis of the European human rights system and observed how even the project for establishing the family can be included within the realm of the principle. However, this did not mean that all negative consequences necessarily intervene it.

Furthermore, he analysed the provisions in the European Social charter, which have been ratified by all Member States except Belgium, Luxembourg and Portugal. It contained a provision on the social, economic, and legal protection of family life. This Charter defined also the scope of the positive measures forming part of the social security (family allowances, social benefits, tax legislation and aid to young couples, these being not, however, positive

---

[532] Directive No. 76/207.

[533] Opinion of the Advocate General Tesauro delivered on 24 January 1991 in case 345/89 *Criminal proceedings against Alfred Stoeckel* (Reference for a preliminary ruling: tribunal de police d'Illkirch - France) (1991) ECR I-4047.

[534] Italian Constitutional Court, Judgment No 210 of 9 July 1986, Gazzetta Ufficiale della Repubblica Italiana, no 38 1 August 1986.

See, similarly the case 158/91 *Ministre public and direction du travail et de l'emploi v Jean-Claude Levy* ((1993) ECR I-4287) which also took now into account a recent decision of the German Constitutional Court (28 January 1992)

[535] Opinion of Mr Advocate General Tesauro delivered on 14 December 1995 in case 13/94 *P v s and Cornwall County Council* (Reference to the preliminary ruling: industrial tribunal, Truro - United Kingdom) (1996) ECR I-2143.

[536] Opinion of Mr Advocate General Lenz delivered on 15 June 1988 in case 236/87 *Anna Bergemann v Bundesanstalt für Arbeit* (Reference for a preliminary ruling from the Landessozialgericht für das Land Nordrhein-Westfalen) (1988) ECR 5125.

rights for the individual). Nevertheless, according to him, the *"common political will"* and common values could still be recognized. Consequently, they could be used in the interpretation of the directly applicable laws.

Similarly, according to the Advocate General, the International Covenant on Civil and Political rights, ratified by all but Greece and Ireland, explicitly prohibited measures which penalized or jeopardise the right to family life. Measures obliging spouses to live apart was listed as an example of a measure which would contravene this prohibition. The family's special need for protection was recognized in this Covenant even if the actual application may differ to a certain extent between the parties due to the differences in social, economical, cultural, and political circumstances and traditions.

Furthermore, the International Convention on Economic, Social and Cultural rights, being ratified all Member States but Ireland, recognized also the *"widest possible protection"* to the family.

The Advocate General also made a traditional, albeit rather eclectic, comparative study of the laws in the Member States in this area:

"Similarly, the legal systems of the Member States make provision special protection for marriage and the family, even if the level of protection and the manner in which it is applied in practice varies. Special status accorded to the family and marriage is reflected in constitutional law in the Federal Republic of Germany, Spain, Ireland Italy and Portugal. In the Netherlands the provisions of the European Convention on Human Rights constitute directly applicable law. Under French constitutional system, the conditions necessary for the development of the individual and the family are guaranteed by the preamble to the 1946 constitution, to which the present constitution refers. In the British legal order, marriage and the family are recognized as fundamental values both by ordinary legislation and in the decisions of the court. In Belgium there is in fact no constitutional provision protecting marriage and the family. Under labour law, however, a statutory provision declares void any term in a contract of employment (19) providing for termination of the contract in the event of marriage or pregnancy. In Denmark, no express protection of the family is laid down in the constitution. On the other hand, such protection is afforded under labour law and social law. The fact that a spouse leaves his or her employment in order to follow the other spouse to the latter's place of employment does not prevent him or her from claiming unemployment benefit."

Morevover, he examined analytically the relationship between principles concerning the protection of the family and the unemployment benefits (consistency). In the end, he made the following conclusion concerning the existence of a general principle:

" A comparative examination of these provisions does not then disclose the existence of a general principle of law according to which the spouse is always entitled to unemployment benefit, where his or her unemployment is the result of a change of residence linked to family circumstances. It is to be observed, however, that the principle that an employee who giving up his employment in order to live together with his spouse or to be to continue living together should not be refused unemployment benefit is widely accepted.
The unity of the family is also a value directly recognized under legal order of the Community, as is shown by the right to families of workers (20) and self-employed workers 21) in Community legislation.
In the light of the foregoing legal assessment, the setting-up of family home in a Member State other than the previous state of residence also amounts to "residing" within the meaning of article 71 of regulation no 1408/71. The decisive factor in this respect is whether the person concerned has actually taken up residence, so that even a

relatively short period may satisfy this requirement."

The Court agreed with this argument, and decided that for unemployment benefit purposes, the relocated person should be considered as a resident in the state to which he has moved.[537]
This principle did, following this case, play a quite decisive role in the interpretation of the Court. In the case of *Reibolt*[538], the Court referred to the *Bergemann* case and to the consideration of the "circumstances" in interpreting his residence status. The same idea was repeated in the argument in the *Toosey* case[539]. In the case of *Joop van Gestel*[540] the Court explicitly justified the decision by referring to the rule in the *Bergmann* case, which expressed the idea of the possibility of receiving unemployment benefits under the most "*favourable conditions*" for those seeking new employment. This idea applied especially to persons who "*retain close ties*" in particular of a personal and vocational nature, with the country where they have settled and habitually reside:

"It is reasonable that workers that have such links with the state in which they reside should be accorded the best conditions in that state for finding a new employment."

The special case of Article 215. Article 215 of the Treaty on European Economic Community provides that the Court shall use "*general principles common to the Member States*" to decide issues of non-contractual liability and damage caused by its institutions or by its servants in the performance of their duties.[541] Furthermore, the Court shall resolve this problem, where no Treaty provisions exist, on the basis of "*reference to the rules acknowledged by the legislation, learned writings and the case law of the member countries*".[542]

---

[537] Case 236/87 *Anna Bergemann v Bundesanstalt für Arbeit* (Reference for a preliminary ruling from the Landessozialgericht für das Land Nordrhein-Westfalen) (1988) ECR 5125.

[538] Case 216/89 *Beate Reibold v Bundesanstalt für Arbeit* (Reference for a preliminary ruling Bundes socialgericht - Germany. Social Security for emigrant workers - regulation no 1408/71 (1)(b)(ii)) (1990) ECR I-4163 (Judgment of the Court (third chamber) of 13 November 1990).

[539] Opinion of Mr Advocate General Lenz delivered on 18 November 1993 in case 287/92 *Alison Maitland Toosey v Chied Adjudication Officer* (Reference for the preliminary ruling - Social Security Commissioner - United Kingdom) (1994) ECR I-279.

[540] Case 454/93 *Rijksdienst voor Arbeidsvoorziening v Joop van Gestel* (Reference for a preliminary ruling: Arbeidshof Brussel - Belgium. Social security for migrant workers - designation of the competent state) (1995) ECR I-1707 (Judgment of the Court (sixth chamber) of 29 June 1995).

[541] See case 106 and 120/87 *Asteris v Greece* (1988) ECR 5515.
     Some analysis of comparative law and Article 215, see Galmot, Y., 1990, p.256 ff.

[542] See case, 7/56 and 3-7/57 *Algera et al. v Common Assembly* (1957-1958) ECR 39.
     "In the case of contractual liability the Community shall in accordance with the common principles common to the Member States make good any damage caused by its institutions or by its civil servants in the performance of their duties" (55/71 *Zukkerfabrik Shoppenstead v Council*, (1971) ECR 975).
     For a discussion on the drafting of the liability articles in the ECSC treaty, see opinion of (acting) Advocate General Biancarelli, delivered on 30 January 1991 in case T-120/89 *Stahlwerke Peine-Salzgitter v Commission of the European Communities* (ECSC - non-contractual liability of the Community) (1991) ECR II-279. The Advocate General discussed

It can be mentioned that, for example, the general admissibility of claims for the payment of interest have been established according to comparative argument.[543] Some recent cases on the conditions of liability have included comparative observations from the systems of the Member States[544].

There are also cases in the practice of the European Court related to the question of whether Community institutions can be liable for damage caused by their legal actions. Article 215 deals with the question of this type of non-contractual liability. It has been used in examining whether the legal acts of the institution resulting in damage to an individual can be the basis of liability. These types of cases are particularly important, where communities competencies are strongly specified and attached to the legal basis. In this sense, on the other hand, a comparison to the state legislative systems based on general competence to legislate is very problematic.

Nevertheless, in the the following analysis, there is an attempt to show the role of comparative law in "new cases", and the subsequent development of the case law on the basis of comparative observations.

In one of the "first" cases, in *Zuckerfabrik Schoppenstedt*[545], the question was discussed on the basis of the admissibility of applications for damages arising from legislative measures. Reference was made also to analogous articles of the ECSC Treaty (Article 34).

The legal argumentation of the Advocate General began by scrutinizing the arguments presented in several cases of the European Court. In the context of the admissibility of the claim of liability, the Advocate General discussed firstly the question of whether a legislative act can be the basis for non-contractual liability. In this respect, he referred to comparative law. Explicit (indirect) references were made also to the conference on state liability based on wrongful conduct by its institutions held at the Max-Planck Institute in 1964, and to the publication following it.

The comparative examination showed that solutions adopted in different legal systems varied considerably. For example in Belgium and France, liability was possible. In principle,

---

the comparative "constructing" of liability Articles 34 and 40 of the ESCS treaty on the basis of the *travaux preparatoires* (*memorandum* of 28 September 1950) (p.310 ff.). At the basis of this provision were the *"general principles of law common to all developed legal systems"*. Furthermore, he discussed the interpretation of the Article on the basis of the notion of direct and special harm *"well known in all the legal systems of the Member States"* (p.336). Furthermore, comparative observations established fact, *"as is the case in all developed legal systems"*, that compensation can be granted not only for *lucrum cessans* [lost profit], but also for *damnum emergens* [future damage]), *"provided that, as in the present case, direct causality is sufficiently established"* (p.359).

[543] Joined cases 64 and 113/76, 167 and 239/78, 27, 28 and 45/79 P. *Dumortier freres sa and others v Council of the European Communities* (Maize gritz - liability) (1979) ECR 3091-3119 (Judgment of the court of 4 October 1979).

[544] Opinion of Mr Advocate General Lenz delivered on 16 June 1994 in case 23/93 Tv10 sa v commissariaat voor de media (Reference for a preliminary ruling: Raad van state - Netherlands. Freedom to provide services - national legislation (1994) ECR I-4795.

[545] See note 163.

this was ruled out in Italy and the Federal Republic of Germany. However, the differences between the various legal systems were considered to be technical in nature.

The Advocate General maintained that the expression in Article 215 *"should not be taken too literally* [*"*the general principles common to the Member States"]":

> *"For Community law the criteria is not only the rules which exist in all Member States, nor is the lowest common denominator determinative, nor does the 'rule of lowest limit' apply"*[546].

According to him, one has to likewise refer to the objectives of the Treaty and the peculiarities of the Community structure, *"and in which perhaps it is appropriate that the guideline be in the best elaborated national rules"*.[547] He made also reference to the ECSC system (Article 34) and to the fact that the individual affected can challenge regulations (Articles 177 (the new Article 234) and 184 of the EEC Treaty). Furthermore, according to him, the case law recognized a rule of non-restrictive interpretation in cases, where the protection of rights are involved[548]. The latter fact can be relevant to the control of the legality of the regulation.

These arguments prompted the outcome, according to which even if the measure, as such, is not found in all legal systems, one can, on 'incomplete' comparative basis, recognize it as a principle of liability forming part of Community law. The fact that it was widely recognized and, in some cases, even included in positive formal laws, supported this conclusion.

Secondly, the Advocate General asked whether it was possible to make the (compensation) claim before the European Court based on a measure declared valid, or does the measure have to be already declared invalid. Apart from references to the ECSC system and analogous discussion in the Courts case law[549], the comparative observations supported the latter possibility. French, Belgian and German law recognized the possibility of claiming compensation based also on valid administrative measure. In other countries this was not so because of the impossibility of the court to review the validity of administrative acts.

After having reflected upon the comparison between the different models of state systems and Community system and with the fact that the Community court had accepted a possibility to review the validity of administrative measure, he chose the alternative, according to which the question of invalidity was not relevant.

The next question was whether an act, which has not been annulled can constitute a wrongful measure. This question had been discussed on the basis of scholarly opinion

---

[546] Reference to Heldricht, Europerecht, p.349.
[547] Referring to Zweigert, K., Rabels Zeitschrift, Vol. 28, p.611.
[548] Case 6/60 *J.-E. Humblet v Belgium State* (1969) Rec. p.1189.
[549] Case 25/62 *Plaumann & Co. V Commission* (1963) ECR 96.

delivered in at the 46th conference of German lawyers.[550] These opinions had confirmed that there was no rule, in the Member States systems or in the EEC Treaty, which imposed the obligation to find a prior invalidity. On the contrary, the ECSC Treaty had claimed opposite.

Other claims of inadmissibility were rejected on other bases.

In examining the substance of the case, he did not examine the nature of the breach.[551] He discussed briefly, from the point of view of the general principles of the Member States, the idea of an "*additional qualifying factor*" which would have established the responsibility of the Community institutions. He maintained that there was no possibilities of finding

> "*sufficiently substantial evidence of the additional qualifying factor of misconduct necessary under Community law ... and which may probably also be regarded as a general principle under the legal systems of the Member States.*"

The Court, on the other hand, upheld the rule according to which there had to be a "*sufficiently flagrant violation*".

In this case, the Advocate General established a comparative approach as a basis for the evaluation of the nature of the Community rule in question.

In the case law on the subject which followed[552], the Advocate General[553] referred to the Court rule of "*sufficiently clear violation of a superior rule of law for the protection of the individual*". Furthermore, the Advocate General accepted the previous opinion of the Advocate General in the *Zuckerfabrik Schoppenstedt* case that the Community system imposes no obligation to submit an administrative complaint to the Community authorities prior to the lodging of an application to the Court for damages. He upheld the admissibility of the complaints.

In the following opinion concerning the substance of this case, the Advocate General repeated the *Zuckerfabrik* rule on the "*sufficiently clear violation*".

In the following cases, the Court also repeated the "*sufficiently flagrant violation rule*" test[554].

---

[550] Ule, Borner, Fusz, Bülow, Ganshof van der Meersch, and Goffin.

[551] Opinion of Mr. Advocate General Roemer delivered on 13 October 1971.

[552] Cases 9 and 11/71 *Compagnie d'Approvisionnement de Transport et de Crédit SA and Grands Moulins de Paris SA v Commission of the European Communities (1972)* ECR 391 (Judgment of the Court 13 June 1972).

[553] Opinion of the Mr Advocate General Dutheillet de Lamothe delivered on 14 July 1971 ((1972) ECR 409) on admissibility, and opinion of the Mr Advocate General Mayras delivered on 24 May 1972 ((1972) ECR 415) on the substance of the violation.

[554] Case 23/72 *Mercur Aussenhandels GmbH v Commission of the European Communities* (1973) ECR 1055 (Judgment of the Court 24 October 1973)/ Opinion of Mr Advocate General Mayras delivered on 27 June 1972 (1973) ECR 1076, 153/73 *Holtz & Willemsen GmbH v Council and Commission of the European Communities* (1974) ECR 675 (Judgment of the Court of 2 July 1974)/ Opinion of Mr Advocate General Reischl delivered on 8 May 1974, (1974) ECR 697, 74/74 *Comptoir National Technique Agricole (CNTA) SA v Commission of the European Communities* (1975) ECR 533 (Judgment of the Court of 14 May 1975)/ Opinion of Mr Advocate General Trabucchi, delivered on 23 April 1975 (1975) ECR 543, cases 54 and 60/76 *Compagnie Industrielle et Agricole Comte de Loheac and Others v Council*

Subsequently, the question was dealt with, for example, in the case *Bayerische HNL*[555], where the applicants claimed compensation for damage which they had suffered through the effects of a Council Regulation[556]. That regulation had been declared null and void by the Court in its decision[557].

The Advocate General reaffirmed at the outset [558] the rule that the legislative nature of the regulation does not *a priori* prevent the examination of the Communities' liability. Furthermore, a specific examination was needed because the declaration of nullity was not an automatic basis for compensation.

In connection to the first question, the Advocate General undertook a brief comparative analysis of the different solutions existing in the Member States. Special attention was paid to the differences between the systems making no clear distinction between constitutional rules and legislative rules (England) and, on the other hand, the systems which clearly establish such difference (Italy and Germany). In the context of comparative observations, he remarked that in general the liability of the state for damage caused by unlawful regulations or orders is accepted "*even if the conditions vary from one system to another*".

Non-contractual liability, based on Article 215, was to be decided on the basis of the general principles found in the laws of the Member States. However, first it was to be decided what kind of measure the regulation was in relation to the measures existing in the national systems. Only that way could one identify, from the national systems, the general principles applicable.

Even if it was clear that structural and political differences existed, and that the analogy was not perfect, regulation was seen more as a legislative act, as a statute, than an administrative act. In this connection, the Advocate General referred to a comparative study produced by the Advocates General in previous case law.[559] He claimed, however, that

---

and Commisision of the European Communities (1977) ECR 645 (Judgment of the Court of 31 March 1977)/ Opinion of the Mr Advocate General Reischl delivered on 10 March 1977 (1977) ECR 655.

[555] Case 83/76 *Bayerische hnl Vermehrungsbetriebe Gmbh and co. Kg and others v Council and Commission of the European Communities* (Skimmed-milk powder - liability) (1978) ECR 1209-1226 (Judgment of the court of 25 May 1978).

[556] No 563/76 of 15 March 1976. On compulsory purchase of skimmedmilk powder held by intervention agencies for use in feeding stuffs.

[557] In case 114/76 *Bela-Mühle v Grows-Farm* (1977) ECR 1211 (Judgment of the Court of 5 July 1977), 116/76 *Granaria Hoofdproduktschap voor Akkerbouwproducten* (1977) ECR 1247 Judgment of the Court 5 July 1977), 119 and 120/76 *Öhmühle Hamburg and Hauptzollamt Hamburg and Hauptzollamt Bremen-Nord* (1977) ECR 1269 (Judgment of the Court of 5 July 1977).

[558] Opinion of Mr Advocate General Capotorti delivered on 1 March 1978 in case 83/76 *Bayerische hnl Vermehrungsbetriebe Gmbh and co. Kg and others v Council and Commission of the European Communities (1978)* ECR 1226.

[559] Opinion of the Advocate General Roemer on 13 July 1971 in case 5/71 *Zuckerfabrik Schoppenstedt* (1971) ECR 975 (Judgment of the Court 2 December 1971) (opinion (1971) ECR 986).
  In order to see the role of the comparative examination, one has to observe the evolution of this case law.

"In my opinion, in view of the extreme difficulty of making the hierarchy of the Community legislative measures coincide with that of the national legislative measures, it is logical that more rigorous solution concerning the liability of the public authorities should be adopted with regard to the Council of the European Communities., which has the twofold capacity of legislature and administration without having the democratic mandate and the power to express the sovereignty of the people which may justify exempting the legislature from the general rules on liability."

On the other hand, in discussing the idea of "sufficiently serious breach", the Advocate General maintained that

"... It seems that since there is no possibility of eliciting any other guidance from the general principles common to the laws of the Member States, Community law accepts, for the purposes of the non-contractual liability of the Community, that the undoubtedly voluntary nature of the acts adopted by the institutions is sufficient and that nature gives rise to a presumption of blame when an unlawful measure is enacted. This moreover is the solution accepted with regard to unlawful administrative measures in the legal systems of certain Member States, including Italy, the Netherlands, Belgium, and Luxembourg (see in this connection the article entitled "Zur Reform des Staatshaftungsrechts" by the Max-Planck-Institut für Öffentliches recht und Völkerrecht, 1975, p.8)".

On this basis he came to the conclusions that the "unjustifiable" nature of the Community conduct had been already established.

Related to the seriousness of the breach, the Advocate General referred also to the decisions of the *Conseil d'État* contained in a Max-Planck-Institute study. However, he proposed some elements for interpretation, but maintained at the same time that his interpretation was, nevertheless, autonomous of tendencies in national systems which seemed to assert, on the contrary, that the compensation is not dependent upon the extent of damage. Furthermore, in discussing the categories of persons to be compensated, he referred also to German legal theory, but wished to avoid these types of analogies. In the end, some distinctions made by the Bundesgerichtshof were discussed with a view of extending these principles also to Community law. According to this rationale, a wide category of persons should be considered to be able to claim compensation.

Finally, the Advocate General came to the conclusion that

"Council regulation..., which has been already declared null and void ... was in serious breach both of the superior rules on non-discrimination and proportionality conferring rights on individuals and of the second subparagraph of Article 40(3) and Article 39 of the Treaty."

The Court restated, on the other hand, the idea of "sufficiently serious breach" prevailing in case law. It regarded the principles applicable in different Member States and maintained that liability is a relatively exceptional phenomenon and is incurred only in special circumstances. It followed from this that

"Individuals may be required, in the sectors coming within the economic policy of the Community, to accept within a reasonable limits certain harmful effects on their economic interests as a result of a legislative measure without

being able to obtain compensation from public funds, even if that measure has been declared null and void".

and that

"In legislative field such as the one in question... the Community does not therefor incur liability unless the institution concerned has manifestly and gravely disregarded the limits on the exercise of its powers"

Furthermore,

"In these circumstances the fact that the regulation is null and void is insufficient for the Community to incur liable... "

In conclusion, one may ask why was the principle of "serious breach" discussed more thoroughly, on comparative basis, in the *Bayerische HNL*, a subsequent case to quite similar cases. One can say that this was related to the fact that only in this case the claim of compensation was based on a Council regulation which had already been declared null and void. In the earlier case law, the issues had been concerned compensation claims on the basis of regulations, which had not been previously declared invalid, or which were issued by other Community Institutions. On the basis of comparative observations, the Advocate General tried to apply the previous case law in a new situation. Furthermore, it seems clear that the Advocate General tried to reach a solution regarding the opinions of two different Advocates Generals concerning the issue of *"seriousness of the breach"* basing his reasoning on comparative observations.

However, one may observe that for the Court, which opposed the Advocate General's conclusion, the idea of a *'sufficiently serious breach'* no longer neither provided a clear basis of justification. The question was more pressing and concrete than in the previous cases, for, in this case, one could quite convincingly claim that a *"serious breach"* had occurred. The declaration of nullity was a strong basis for that argument. Accordingly, the Court seemed to establish a new rule concerning the obligation of an individual to *"accept in reasonable limits certain harmful effects on their economic interests"*, and that liability is *"exceptional and incurs only in special circumstances"*. It reached this conclusion on the basis of comparative observations.[560]

Comparative observations related to some procedural, staff, and "constitutional" questions. There are several interpretations of the procedural traditions of the European Community order which have been accomplished by means of comparative analysis.

---

[560] For some analysis of Article 215 and comparative law, see Pescatore, P., 1980, p.342. He maintains that comparative law defines, not the basis of Community principles, but rather the limits of the Community legislature's responsibility.

The Advocates General have recognized national discussions concerning distinction between issues of fact and questions of law, concerning ideas on errors of fact and of law.[561] Furthermore, the characterization of certain official documents as proof has also taken place by reference to national traditions.[562] Procedural rules concerning the *"right to fair hearing"* and the *"confidentiality of certain information"* have been discussed with a help of comparative references by the Advocate General:[563]

"Most commentators on European and American anti-dumping law..."

The idea was to "harmonize" rules via some comparative remarks:

"...However, the Commission and Court should be invited to consider the feasibility of such rules, and hence of introducing in the Community measures similar to those that exists in the United States".

Some remarks were made also on European Human Rights.[564]
However, the main argument was justified with reference to comparative law *de lege ferenda* by means of an extensive reference to scholarly writings and cases, particularly to the American law:

"I am of course aware of the difficulties inherent in having to reconcile the observance of the right to a fair hearing with the protection of the confidentiality of certain information. However, I will point out that, in other legal systems, solutions to those difficulties have apparently been found.
Under American law, since the trade agreements act 1979..."

Further analysis was taken along the following lines:

---

[561] Opinion of Mr Advocate General Jacobs delivered on 10 November 1993 in case 53/92 *Hilti v Commission of the European Communities* (Appeal - competition - abuse of a dominant position - concept of relevant market) (1994) ECR I-667.
[562] Opinion of Mr Advocate General darmon delivered on 7 February 1991 in case 49/88 *Al-Jubail fertilizer company (Samad) and Saudi Arabian fertilizer company (Safco) v Council of the European Communities* (Application for a declaration that Council Regulation (EEC) no. 3339/87) (1991) ECR I-3187.
[563] Opinion of Mr Advocate General darmon delivered on 7 February 1991 in case 49/88 *Al-Jubail*. The interpretation related also to the interpretation of the GATT rules.
[564] The remarks is interesting, if one wants to understand, for example, the recent proposed changes to the European Human Rights system (Commission merged to the Court) in relation to the introduction of Basic Rights to the jurisdiction of the Community Court:
"Furthermore, the situation is not really satisfactory in the terms of fundamental rights. If the European Commission of Human Rights declares inadmissible applications directed against national decisions enacted pursuant to Community Act [reference: Application No 13258/87 M. & Co. V Federal republic of Germany: Decision of 9 February 1990] the main reason is that, through its successive judgments, the Court has established the principle that it reviews the Community institutions' observance of fundamental rights. It is therefore far from important to avoid conspicuous discrepancies between the construction of this Court puts on the rights to a fair trial and the requirements already laid down by the European Court of Human Rights".

"... The last point has been the subject of much discussion in academic legal texts and American case-law. Until 1983 the Court of International Trade had refused disclosure to "in-house counsels" or "corporate counsels" on the ground that it did not wish to place them "under the unnatural an unremitting strain of having to exercise constant self-censorship in normal working relations (86). That line of decisions was terminated judgment of the Court of Appeals of the Federal Circuit, establishing that granting disclosure was a matter to be examined... The Court of Appeals proceeded largely on the basis that "in-house counsels" and "retained counsels" are officers of the court and are bound by the same Code of Professional Responsibility, and are subject to the same sanctions. In-house counsels provide the same services and are subject to the same types of pressures as retained counsels...".

The question of "modelling" was raised and the answer given affirmed its role:

"Can such a system be transposed to Community law? As noted above academic legal texts seem broadly favourable, and the European Parliament hopes that this avenue will be explored. The American experience has been declared satisfactory. Canada also uses a similar system. As the president, Mr Due, stated: "there may be justification in aligning even the procedural rules on those of the other partners" of GATT...."

Are the legal difficulties insuperable? Advocates, solicitors and barristers are required to observe the rules of professional ethics in all the Member States, no matter whether those rules are imposed by the legislature or by the profession by itself. A breach of confidentiality is, in principle, punished under the domestic legal order in every Member State.... It is difficult to see what arguments could support the view that, even given the same guarantees, European lawyers are not in a position to perform the same function as officers of the court as their American counterpartners "

The Court maintained the conclusion arrived at by the Advocate General that the regulation is void in so far as it affects the applicant.[565] It maintained that the role of confidentiality is more important in Community law because of the lack of such procedural guarantees that exist in certain national systems. No other comparative law references were expressed.

The Court has also made an extensive study of the legislation and case-law of different Member States in order to resolve problems in certain staff cases.

According to *"generally accepted principle in the national legal systems*" the applicant's claim was well founded *"if he had suffered loss corresponding to the alleged enrichment of the other party".*[566] Furthermore, the exclusion of suicide from compensation refers only to voluntary suicide *"in accordance with a general tendency in the legal systems of the Member States both regard to accident insurance and social security".*[567] The disciplinary procedure and the principles of *"audi alteram partem"* were to be interpreted *"in the light of the rule in*

---

[565] Case 49/88 *Al-Jubail fertilizer company (Samad) and Saudi Arabian fertilizer company (Safco) v Council of the European Communities* (Application for a declaration that Council Regulation (EEC) no. 3339/87) (1991) ECR I-3187.
[566] Case 26/67 *Henri Danvin v Commission of the European Communities* (1968) ECR 315 (Judgment of the Court (second chamber) of 11 July 1968).
[567] Case 18/70 *X v Council of the European Communities* (1972) ECR 1205 (Judgment of the court (first chamber) of 6 December 1972).

the most legal systems of the Member States".[568]

The rules for calculating time limits for bringing actions were considered to be in accordance with this *"survey of comparative law...except in France and Ireland".*[569] Furthermore, the Advocate General did not agree with the claim that there is no possibility to challenge a decision rejecting a complaint, where the decision merely confirms the contested act. This was supported by reference to the Italian and French system.[570]

The Court has also explicitly noted certain concepts embodied the Staff Regulations as being derived directly from the legal systems of the Member States[571],

"which, under their laws, impose a mutual obligation to provide maintenance on relatives by blood and/or marriage of a greater or lesser degree of proximity. That concept must therefore be understood as referring exclusively to an obligation of maintenance imposed on an official by a source of law independent of the will of the parties' end as excluding maintenance obligations of a contractual, moral or compensatory nature. Since neither Community law nor the staff regulations provide the Community Court with any guide as to how it should define, by way of independent interpretation, the meaning and scope of the concept of a legal responsibility to maintain entitling an official to receive a dependent child allowance under Article 2(4) of annex vii to the Staff Regulations, it is necessary to determine whether the national legal system to which the official in question is subject imposes such a responsibility on the official."

In this case, the Court formulated some ideas on a new doctrine of comparative interpretation, by which it tried to maintain the autonomous character of Community concepts[572]:

---

[568] Case 141/85 *Henri de Compte v European Parliament* (Official - disciplinary measures) (1985) ECR 1951-1968 (Judgment of the court (third chamber) of 20 June 1985).
Concerning the statement of reasons (referring to the situation in Member States), see Opinion of Mr Advocate General Mancini delivered on 19 January 1988 in case 319/85 *Misset v Council of the European Communities* (officials - disciplinary measures) (1988) ECR 1861. On time limits for bringing actions, see also the opinion of Mancini in case 152/85 *Misset* (1987) ECR 223 He maintains, for example, that "*even two exceptions to which I have referred prove to be more apparent than real; that is to say in substance they are in conformity with the rationale of the calculation prevailing in the Community...*" (the reasoning based on analysing and justification on Latin terms).
On comparative basis, limiting the responsibility to give reasons, see case T-160/89 *Gregoris Evangelos Kalavros v Court of Justice of the European Communities* (1990) ECR II-871 (Judgment of the court of first instance (fifth chamber) of 13 December 1990).
[569] For this in detail, see Opinion of Mr Advocate General Mancini delivered on 18 November 1986 in case 152/85 *Rudolf Misset v Council of the European Communities* (Official - admissibility - period for commencing proceedings) (1987) ECR 223.
[570] Opinion of Mr Advocate General Tesauro delivered on 30 November 1988 in case 224/87 *Jean Koutchoumoff v Commission of the European Communities* (Official - assistance pursuant to article 24 of the staff regulations - damages) (1989) ECR 99.
[571] For a concept of "legal responsibility", see Article 67; annex vii, art. 2(4).
[572] Often comparative arguments are related to the justification of the autonomy of the European interpretation. The idea that no generality can be found in legal systems justifies the possibility of the European Court of Justice to coming to an autonomous interpretation, see also, Pescatore, P., 1980, p.344.
See also, Wilmers de, J.M., 1991, p.38. The autonomous interpretation does not means, however, that the interpretation would be absolutely contrary to some interpretation in member States.

"The terms of a provision of Community law which makes no express reference to the laws of the Member States for the purpose of determining its meaning and scope must normally be given an independent interpretation which must take into account the context of the provision and the purpose of the relevant rules.... in the absence of an express reference to the laws of the Member States, the application of Community law may sometimes necessitate reference to the laws of the Member States where the Community court cannot identify in Community law or in the general principles of Community law criteria enabling it to define the meaning and scope of such a provision by way of independent interpretation "[573]

Likewise, rules governing pre-recruitment medical examinations have been approved with reference both to the European system of human rights and to the legal systems of the Member States.[574] The confidentiality of medical findings was also confirmed by a comparative study, which asked by the Court from the Commission. This study had a direct impact upon the outcome of the case[575].

Various parties have also presented comparative rationales in these type of cases. Retrospective appointment, for instance, was alleged to be unlawful as *"generally regarded in legal systems"* unless there were urgent and compelling reasons for it.[576] The Advocate General accepted this reasoning as decisive.

Furthermore, one applicant referred to the *"German and Luxemburgian law"* in order to support the idea of a *"tax abatement for taxable persons with a child doing military service"*. The Parliament, as a defendant, sought to reject the argument on the basis of the nature of the Community tax system as "autonomous". The Court ultimately upheld the European Parliaments argument on the basis of its own case law[577].

The court has also used *"general principles of labour law"* to examine the right of staff to engage in trade union activities.[578]

One can also speak of comparative reasoning in relation to the fundamental "constitutional" aspects of the European order. The Court has used comparative legal observations, for

---

[573] Case *85/91 Lilian r. Khouri v Commission of the European Communities* (Official - dependent child allowance - person treated as a dependent child) (1992) ECR II-2637 (Judgment of the court of first instance (fourth chamber) of 18 December 1992). Reference made to the Case 327/82 *Ekro v produktschap voor Vee en Vlees* (1984) ECR 107.

[574] Case T-10/93 *A. V. Commission of the European Communities* (Official - recruitment - person who is HIV positive - refusal to appoint - physical unfitness - legality of article 33 of the staff regulations) (1994) ECR II-179 (Judgment of the court of first instance (third chamber) of 14 April 1994).

[575] Case 155/78 *Mlle M. v Commission of the European Communities* (1980) ECR 1797 (Judgment of the Court of 10 June 1980).

[576] Opinion of Mr Advocate General Jacobs delivered on 24 January 1989 in case 341/85 *Erik van der Stijl and Geoffrey Cullington v Commission of the European Communities* (Officials - implementation of a judgment annulling an appointment) (1989) ECR 511.

[577] Case T-41/89 *Georg Schwedler v European Parliament* (Officials - tax abatement - dependent child) (1990) ECR II-79 (Judgment of the court of first instance (fifth chamber) of 8 March 1990)
See also, for example, Case 90/74 *Deboeck v Commission* (1975) ECR 1123.

[578] Case 175/73 *Union Syndicale v Council* (1974) ECR 917 and 18/74 *Syndicat Général v Commission* (1974) ECR 933.
For some analysis of staff cases, see Pescatore, P., 1980, pp.344-345.

instance, in justifying decisions concerning the external and internal relationships of its institutions.

The idea of the separation of powers has been discussed by the Advocates General.[579] This notion was connected to the discussion of the Article 178 powers of the Court. According to the "*principle common to all legal systems requiring clear separation of judicial function and lawmaking*", the courts only decide cases, but do not interfere within the legislative choices of the competent institutions. [580]

The relationship between different institutions has been also discussed [581] by the Advocate General on a comparative basis. One question was related to the Council's argument, in a case against the Commission, that the matter is not really a "dispute". The comparison took place between the countries "*having the constitutional court*" (Federal Republic of Germany, Spain, France, and Italy). In this way the Advocate General came to the conclusion that conflicts between the institutions are legal disputes concerning the rights and duties of the institutions. Such disputes are not merely political, but are also legal.

Of particular interest was the comparative observations made in the case adopting the idea of the "*continuity of a legal system*". The Court observed that

"*in accordance with the principle common to the legal systems of the Member States, the origins of which may be traced back to Roman law, legislation is amended, unless the legislature expresses a contrary intention.*" [582]

In a case concerning the idea of public access to documentation, on the other hand, the Advocate General extensively discussed the context of the legislative acts enacted by the Council. The principle discussed was seen as fundamental for "*any democratic system*".[583] This included a recognition that citizens have a "*broad rights to be informed*", which "*all*

---

[579] Opinion of Mr Advocate General Tesauro delivered on 23 January 1991 in case 63/89 *Assurances du Crédit sa and Compagnie Belge d'Assurance Crédit sa v Council of the European Communities and Commission of the European Communities* (1991) ECR I-1799.

[580] The Court, on the other hand, in its judgment on that case, did not consider the question put forward by the Council, see case 45/86 *Commission of the European Communities v Council of the European Communities* (generalized tariff preferences, application for the annulment of an act, legal basis, obligation to give reasons for Community acts) (1987) ECR 1493 (Judgment of the Court of 26 March 1987).

[581] Opinion of Mr Advocate General Lenz delivered on 29 January 1987 in case 45/86 *Commission of the European Communities v Council of the European Communities* (Generalised tariff preferences - application for the annulment of an act) (1987) ECR 1493.

[582] Case 23/68 *Johannes Gerhardus Klomp v Inspektie der Belastingen* (Preliminary ruling requested by the Gerechtshof, the Hague) (1969) ECR 43 (Judgment of the court of 25 February 1969).
A similar type of case with comparative observations, see Opinion of Mr Advocate General Gulmann delivered on 24 June 1992 in case 187/91 *Belgian state v Société Cooperative Belovo* (Reference for a preliminary ruling: tribunal de premiere instance de Neufchateau - Belgium) (1992) ECR I-4937.

[583] Opinion of Mr Advocate General Tesauro delivered on 28 November 1995 in case 58/94 *Kingdom of The Netherlands v Council of the European Union* (Action for annulment - rules on public access to Council documents) (1996) ECR I-2169.

national systems" maintain. Certain variation between member states were, nevertheless, observed. The Advocate General analysed different types of documents, and undertook a short historical survey.[584] Furthermore, he referred to the measures adopted by the Council of Europe.[585] Consequently, certain "tendencies" were identified. On this basis, the Advocate General concluded that certain legislative acts at the Community level were "*desirable*". However, "self-regulation" by the institutions was seen to be the rule, and the Council act on "the code of conduct" was not considered to be a legislative act. Consequently, it was not able to form the subject of a process of annulment.[586]

The principle of the right to effective protection by a court[587] and *interim* protection[588], as well as the generalities and disparities concerning the application of the principle of protection of written communications between lawyer and client have also been examined on comparative basis.[589]

With regard to the laws governing the budget of the European Community, the concept of "*commitment*" has been based on comparative observations, which have enabled the prevailing interpretation to emerge. In this case the Advocate General[590] asked whether Community concepts in this matter are different from those prevailing in national legal systems. After providing a negative answer to this question, the concept was given a comparative interpretation mainly by referring to French budgetary law. Some references to other national systems were also made (particularly with regard to Belgium, Italian, Greek, and Spanish systems). Overall, it was claimed that under most of the legal systems of the Member States, "*commitment*" goes beyond a strictly financial or accounting operation. It

---

[584] The Advocate General explicitly mentioned that the comparative survey was produced by the court's own documentation service.

[585] Recommendation no 854 (1979) of the Assembly of 1 February 1979, and Recommendation no r (81) 19 of the Committee of Ministers of 25 November 1981

[586] Council decision 93/731/EC of 20 December 1993, and 93/662/EC of 6 December 1993, and the "code of conduct", 93/730/EC, restricting in certain cases the access to documentation.

[587] Opinion of Mr Advocate General Darmon delivered on 27 October 1993 in case 228/92 *Roquette freres sa v Hauptzollamt Geldern* (Reference for a preliminary ruling: Finanzgericht Düsseldorf, Germany. Monetary compensatory amounts on derived products of maize, declaration of invalidity, temporal effect) (1994) ECR 1445.

[588] Opinion of Mr Advocate General Tesauro delivered on 17 May 1990 in case 213/89 *The Queen v Secretary of state for transport, ex parte Factortame Ltd and others* (Reference for a preliminary ruling: House of lords - United Kingdom) (1990) ECR I-2433.
   The Advocate General discussed the idea of interim protection (suspending of the application) as a general phenomenon in the legal systems of Member States (except the Danish system). He undertook relatively analytical study of the French, German and the Italian system, and the doctrinal writings.
   On the Courts case, see Judgment of the Court of 19 June 1990.

[589] Case 155/79 *Am and S Europe limited v Commission of the European Communities* (Legal privilege) (1982) ECR 1575-1616 (Judgment of the court, 18 May 1982). Some analysis, Galmot, Y., 1982, p.256 ff, and Schwarze, J., 1991, p.10 ff.

[590] Opinion of Mr Advocate General Darmon delivered on 30 June 1989 in case 16/88 *Commission of the European Communities v Council of the European Communities* (Authorisation conferred on the Commission under article 145) (1989) ECR 3457.

encompassed substantive decisions as well. Accordingly, he maintained that the Court should refer to the comparative generality of the conceptualizations of the legal systems of the Member States when interpreting the Community concept.[591]

Many other cases could be mentioned. However, analysis of them is not presented here.[592]

---

[591] On the control of "legality" relating to the balance of interest, proportionality, respect of confidence etc., see Wilmer de, J.M., 1991, p.37. He speaks also about reverse development, where Belgian procedural law seemed to have been modelled, in the course of federalisation, upon European Community law (Article 177 (the new Article 234) system). However, one should note that a similar system has existed also in Italian constitutional law.

[592] Case 222/86 *Heylens* (1987) ECR 4097

Case 81/87 (*The Queen v H.M. Treasury and Commissioners of Inland Revenue, ex parte Daily Mail and General trust plc.* (1988) ECR 5483) deals with freedom of establishment.

The Advocate General recognizes disparity *"at the point where the company law meets the tax law"* has resulted interpretation of Community law *"as it stands"* (Opinion of Advocate General Darmon on 7 June 1988 in case 81/87 *The Queen v H.M. Treasury and Commissioners of Inland Revenue, ex parte Daily Mail and General trust plc.* (1988) ECR 5483). However, he uses comparative generality in order to establish the Community interpretation (*"Generally, in most Member States...")*. The interpretation left quite extensive powers for the Member States to determine the tax treatment of companies transferring the central management and control of a company to another Member State.

The Court referred to the Comparative observations presented by the Commission, and it maintains that the Treaty recognizes this difference a prior (Article 220 to be used as a basis for further acts). Further measures were to be taken to include such a cases into the realm of freedom of establishment (Judgment of the Court 27 September 1988, ECR 1988, 5483).

Some cases also: fundamental rights, see Bredimas, A., 1978b, pp.330-331. First cases, 5,11,13, 15/62 *Fer.Ro., Erba, ALMA, & co.* (1962) ECR pp.449 ff. See 16/61 Ferriere di Modena (1962) ECR 289 (Articles 85,86 EEC 60 ECSC modelled, Anti trust law in USA, 71, Sherman Act, Robinson Act, US case law) (pp.313-315) Also Opinion of Advocate General Mayras in case 48/69 *ICI Ltd v Commission* (1972) ECR 619. Opinion of Advocate General Lagrange in case 14/61 *Koninklijke Ned. Hoogovens* (1962) ECR 277. He takes into account the aims of the treaty, and interprets the comparative material based on these assumptions. One can also check the economic and political climate in accordance with the objectives (see, Bredimas, A., 1978a). Opinion of Advocate General La Grange in case 3/55 *Assider* (1954/1956) ECR 72 (misuse of power, Article 33, ECSC, judicial review of administrative action). That comparative examination is necessary, ibid. and case 28/67 *Molgereit-Zentrale* (1968) ECR 143 (different tax systems).

Also Opinion of Advocate General Lenz 21 September 1995 in case 415/90 *Union Royal Belgie de Sociétés de Fotbal association ASVLM others v J-M- Bosman and others* (1995) ECR I-4921 (Judgment of the Court 15 December 1995) compares different rules of different social subsystems (UEFA, FIFA rules, Member States, mainly produced by the UEFA, points, UEFA published: can be national emphasis etc.).

With regard to abortion case 159/90 *The Society for the Protection of Unborn Children Ireland Ltd v Steven Grogan et others* (1991) ECR 4685 (Judgment of the Court of 4 October 1995) Court maintained:

"Termination of pregnancy lawfully practised in several Member States is a medical activity, which is normally provided for remuneration and may be carried out as part of professional activity"

and it concluded that

"it is not for the Court to substitute its assessment for that of the legislator in those Member States where the activities in question are practised legally"

Jurisdictional questions and Convention of Human Rights Article 10(1), opinion of Advocate General Van Gerven delivered on 11 June 1991 in case 159/90 *The Society for the protection of unborn children Ireland Ltd v Steven Grogan et others* (1991) ECR 4685 (Judgment of the Court of 4 October 1995) (1991) ECR I-4685:

"Indeed, in those Member States where the abortion is permitted under certain conditions there are frequently requirements laid down regard to advice and counselling, which are designated to prevent abortion become routine and commercialized, or to ensure that the information is provided only by authorized persons, and that the decision to carry out an abortion is taken with knowledge of the facts that is to say, with the necessary advice and counselling".

He goes through German, France, Belgium laws. The norm (restriction on the distribution of information valid) follows directly from this analysis. Interpretation of Community law is in accordance with Article 10 of the European Convention

2.1.8. Conclusions

On the basis of the case law. Comparative argumentation has had different results. Comparative studies have supported a relatively wide interpretation of EC-legislation. If comparative observations are rejected, it appears as if no wide interpretation is applied, but the Court examines the question textual-functionally. The disparity between systems has supported independent argument solely on the basis of EC legislation and general principles (equality).

The use of the conceptualizations and definitions of one legal system have been rejected in defining the content of EC legislation, and the Court has preferred an independent "EC" interpretation for concepts. However, it is clear that in some cases certain national conceptualizations have had a direct impact upon the Courts interpretation[593]. In fact, there seems to be a tendency toward a non-autonomy of comparative interpretation.

An extensive study of different systems has resulted in the adoption of certain models which have been found to be common to most of the Member States[594]. There have been some "generality" based interpretations even based on the analysis of "tendencies". Furthermore, US influences are quite strong.[595] The US systems are studied usually extremely thoroughly, and clear "modelling" has even taken place. The "extra-Community" comparison appears especially in cases where there is a general international agreement involved. In general, there is a strong interaction between the international rules and national rules in comparative

---

of Human Rights etc. Analysis is assisted by a "moral" argument; the objective is justified under Community law, if it relates to the policy choice of a moral and philosophical nature, the assessment of which is a matter for the Member States and in respect of which they are entitled to be involved on ground of public policy, (Article 56, 66, 36 of the EC Treaty, *"grounds, which can justify discriminatory measures"*, *"A genuine and sufficiently serious threat to the requirements of public policy effecting one of the fundamental interests of the society"*).

For the review of how the internal principles determine the extension and nature of the comparative adoption, in staff regulations, Opinion of Advocate General Warner delivered in March 1973 in case 81/72 *Commission v Council* (1973) ECR 588:

> *"The Council, which is responsible for the organization of staff, may, as part of the means implementing Article 65, incorporate procedures of collective bargaining similar to those practised in Member States according to their various methods, and devide up the decision making process in the successive phases in accordance with the practice usually in the Community".*

For various "comparative" cases, see Bredimas, A., 1978a, pp.128-134, Jacobs, F.G., 1990, p.109 ff., Pescatore, P., 1980.

[593] See also, Schermers, G., Waelbroeck, D., 1987, p.13.

[594] See Unger, J.A., 1976, pp.370-373, a case-study of the extensive comparative analysis by Advocate General Warner and a rule introduction by the Court in the case 17/74 *Transocean Marine Paint Association v Commission* (1974) ECR 1963. *"The right to be heard"* was found to be part of the Article 164 of the Rome Treaty.

[595] Interest in US law can be also result of the fact that German and English law have been strongly influenced by it, Bredimas, A., 1978a, pp.132-133.

studies. These two spheres are often linked together in justification.

Socio-legal and cultural arguments and the "coherence" demands of one national legal system[596] (which obviously requires study and an understanding of that particular legal system) have supported the independence of a Member State to decide on the issue. This could be described as some kind of functional subsidiarity. On the other hand, the demand for this special treatment has usually been made by many, if not all, Member States in one particular case which means, on the other hand, that the case has been strongly influenced by the demands or objections of Member States and the cultural and coherence arguments are function as legitimating constructions.

The Court also uses comparative private law analogies in establishing principles having a clearly public nature.[597] Legal fields are not necessarily kept separate in constructing analogies. More traditional comparisons are clearly effected in the field of the Brussels Convention.

Some systems are sometimes studied more thoroughly, while others remaining in the referential context. This is connected to the value-based nature of comparative reasoning and interpretations. Sometimes this type of reasoning appears quite incomprehensible from the legal point of view. The choices of the compared are made in accordance with the "main" or "most important" systems. One may speak about strongly "institutional" qualitative comparative law studies. On the other hand, systems which have constitutional courts are frequently examined more thoroughly.

Often the peculiarities of the system of the party to the dispute are examined in the light of other systems.

Roman law serves often as a *tertium comparationis* but also some systems, such as the French system, functions like this. Much depends upon the Advocate General in question and his background.[598]

Interestingly, sometimes the Court has given a directive to national systems to interpret certain provisions based on comparative interpretations. Furthermore, a reference to the comparative nature of Community rules is also found.

In general, one may say that the nature of the comparison differs depending on the legal basis which makes it possible. However, no really systematic structure of analytical reasoning can be identified. Furthermore, the institutional actors' influences in relation to each other are not very self-evident. However, there is a strong idea of cooperation between different Community institutions. On the other hand, comparative studies are many times seen as "frustrating" the main interpretation.

---

[596] See cases 204/90 and 300/90 *Hans Martin Bachmann v Etat Belge, Commission v Etat Belge* (1992) ECR I-249 (28 January 1992). Coherence arguments were put forward by most of the Member States.
[597] On this type of exercise, see Gutteridge, H.C., 1944, pp.5-7.
[598] For some indications of this type of approach, Pescatore, P., 1980, p.350.

In conclusion, it seems that the comparative generality arguments seem to interact with common sense textual interpretation. This seems to apply also to the rejection of comparative observations. However, in the latter case the question is about the common sense textual meaning of the Community provisions. On the other hand, any disparity identified seems to interact with "practical" interpretation attached to ideas of purpose, intention, scheme and a more systematic interpretation of Community system.

It also seems that whenever there is a new situation, the comparative situation has to be studied again.

On the basis of the interviews. The interviews which were undertaken can be used in defining the scope of comparative reasoning in Community law and to explain the context of the justificatory uses.

One can make distinctions between three levels of informal use of comparative law in Community adjudication. Namely, comparative law can be instrumentalized in connection with the special knowledge of the staff, special knowledge of the judge himself, or by the special knowledge of other judges represented in the internal discourses in the court. The special knowledge of each national lawyer functions as a basis of the comparative information.[599]

Usually, in the European court's research division, there is one lawyers from each country doing this national report. However, from some countries like France, there has been four persons doing this. Each judge has also his or her own assistant making studies, for example, on a specific field of law the judge is rapporteur to.

In 1995, for example, there were at least 20 extensive comparative surveys made in the preliminary preparation of a case.[600] The studies seem to have had a tremendous use and impact. The studies are not necessarily reflected in the explicit judgments, and they were for internal use.[601] Comparative studies, were, however, not routine.

The Court initiates these studies. However, there is also a coordinator of the study, who designs the framework for the study.[602] The research made during the proceedings is usually only comparative in nature. The reporting judge can ask the research division to make a comparative study on a specific legal question. Advocate Generals and judges have their own staff, which may be asked to make a study, especially when there are problems in finding a consensus.

---

[599] See also, Pescatore, P., 1980, p.349.

[600] However, Pescatore, P., 1980, p.358, speaks about "daily use".
   On preparation, see European Courts, Hunnings, H., 1996

[601] Also *Note d'information sur la division recherche et documentation* (Janvier 1995), and Pescatore, P., 1980, p.338. These explicit references were made until 1980 in 15-20 judgments (25 years of functioning), see Pescatore, P., 1980, p.338.

[602] *Note...*, 1995, p.2.

All states are alleged to be considered. In competition cases, consideration has been given also to the Japanese legal system, and some remarks have been made on legal systems of other European countries than the Member States[603]. In some cases the jurisprudence of the Supreme Court of the United States has been looked over (5-6 studies).[604]

The papers produced are usually 50-60 pages in length. The studies produced are usually given to the Court in a shortened version, 10-15 pages[605]. They contain a description of the situation in each Member State. On the other hand, there are usually remarks made on the extent to which the systems differ from each other. One of the main interests arises also from the need to know, what results the decision will have in different Member States.

Studies are usually only "legal". Databases are available in the Court. This means a description of the law in force, and an evaluation of legislation and precedents, cases from supreme and the constitutional courts. However (for example in competition cases) there can also be an economic analysis of the consequences. Sometimes the comparative studies include a description of a system which is common to all Member States (eg. The European Human Rights System). There may also be sociological and political remarks in the conclusions.

Historical descriptions are rare. This was explained to be due to the fact that "the Court is already near to the solution". However, some historical "evolution" may be taken into account. However, the Court usually takes into account only the minimum common denominator[606]. Advocates General can take into account more features deriving from these studies.

It is not rare that the parties produce comparative studies. The basic argument seems to be that some states have a system such as the system in question. Moreover, the exceptions are sometimes described. All the same, it is rare that states make extensive studies. The studies produced by the parties are taken into account. Mainly the states' studies are considered, less so other parties' studies. The basis is, however, the internal studies of the institution. It was claimed that the Commissions' studies are not used as such[607]. It seems as if the Court's own investigations are independent, at least from the legislative preparatory work of the Commission. On the other hand, the Commission's reports are considered valuable, and they

---

[603] This was so especially in relation to EFTA states. Most of them were not yet Member States of the European Community. There may have been also studies of the Israelian system.

In most recent cases (316/95 *Generics v. Smith, Kline & French Laboratories Ltd.* ((1997) ECR I-3929) dealing with medical patents. In his opinion Advocate General Jacobs studied also the system of New Zealand, because its *"case-law is of persuasive value in the United Kingdom and in Ireland"* (in addition to German, Italian, United States, and the United Kingdom case law).

[604] For some judges the selection of countries seems to be Latin centred. Pescatore claims that the original Community was based on some kind of a "bipolarity" between Latin and Germanic systems, Germanic systems were seen as containing "Roman heritage". The extension took place after accession of new countries. This "continentalist" nature is, however, still stressed. (Pescatore, P., 1980, pp.350-351)

[605] A case mentioned, publicity of documents.

[606] For some analysis, de Wilmars, J.M., 1991, p.39.

[607] The role of the Commissions studies in the work of the Court is quite unclear. The Court refers in many cases to the Commission's studies.

are often used also in decision-making[608]. The Commission is clearly considered sometimes a specialist on comparative law by the Court.[609]

It was claimed that Advocates General make more extensive studies. At least they argue more analytically. Their role is to discuss different possibilities, and to make a synthesis. The Court's reasoning is more formal. From the interviews one gets the impression that usually no special studies are presented to the Advocates General, but the same studies prepared by the research division may be used by both instances. The division is working for both of them.

In oral proceedings, comparative studies are not usually discussed. However, as mentioned before, in the preliminary ruling procedures, Member States have possibility to make oral or written statements (*amicus curiae*). In general, the function of this seems to be to inform the Court about the importance of the case in relation to a particular system. These remarks are not "comparative" in nature, though acknowledged by the Court. Each Member State may present some conclusions concerning the features of their legal systems.

In general, comparative studies seem to have a clear and even a decisive role. The substantive impact of the study depends on its content. If the systems seem to differ greatly, there is a different impact than when the systems seem to be relatively similar. Then the solutions have to be "created". The comparative studies play a role in cases, where there is no case law on that legal question, no clear text is available, or where the Court wants to decide as a matter of principle, or if the case is, for example, economically important[610]. The role of comparative law is seen as "filling the *lacunae*". Comparative studies can have an effect upon the final decision in many ways. However, it can be also of minor importance for the substance of the decision.

It is probable that comparative law studies play a decisive role in considering the European standard in general, but that they have a function in evaluating the nature of the Member States' actions, that is, whether the Member State has implemented the Community provisions in good faith etc. Here the matter concerns, of course, the Article 10, but, for that matter, also the possibility to apply different types of punitative and compensating measures of the Community law on the basis of the breach.[611]

The main obstacles to making extensive studies and examinations, and to using them, were seen in the work load etc. No principled obstacles were seen to prevent the disclosure of comparative material in justification. The fact that studies are made in a strict relation to a concrete case must have an effect on their analytical quality.

Some documents such as comparative law studies produced by an institution are not,

---

[608] Pescatore, P., 1980, p.348, also Lando, O., 1977, p.656

[609] Pescatore, P., 1980, p.348. Pescatore sees this to be due to its connections with permanent representations and also because of the material it has due to its law-proposing function.

[610] Reference was made to VAT calculation

[611] À la *Francovich* case, different provisions of Amsterdam Treaty etc.

nevertheless, available for external observers such as researchers. This is due to the principle of confidentiality. This feature may be related, on the other hand, to the unofficial and draft nature of these studies. However, the studies are produced in a quite complete report form within the internal circulation of the institution, even if there seemed to be also more unsystematic material produced.

It was claimed that the Court directs its arguments to the parties and the institutions of the Member States, but also to the wider institutions in some difficult cases, where their social or economic impact seems to be enormous.

The inclusion of new states within the European Community and European Union has led to a greater "comparative" input into the internal functioning of the Court.[612]

In conclusion, it appear as if the use of comparative law in the European Court of Justice is extremely instrumental from the point of view of the legal discourse.

---

[612] See also, Pescatore, P., 1980, p.350. The need of comparative studies has been explicitly mentioned in the Commissions new communications (2000) on the development in the Mediterranean area (cooperation and enlargement).

2.2.   The European System of Human Rights

2.2.1. General remarks

In this chapter, there are few examples and an analysis of comparative reasoning in the European human rights system in different fields of law[613]. The list is not exhaustive. The case law studied is restricted mainly to the freedom of expression principle. However, some interesting examples in the realm of other principles are analysed too.

The interpretation methods of the human rights systems vary. The report of the Commission of the European system of human rights in the *Golder* case[614] examined the normative principles of interpretation of the European Convention of Human rights. In this system, the Vienna Convention of the Law of Treaties can be applied to the interpretation of the Convention. In this sense, the interpretation methods can be seen as the method embodying the principles of interpretation like *"good faith"*, *"ordinary meaning in context"*, *"in the light of its object and purpose"*, and the *"intention of the Contracting Parties"*[615]. This has been expressed by the Court in certain cases.[616]

These features lead to certain dynamics within interpretation. For example, social and political attitudes have to be taken into consideration.[617] Thus, preparatory material is used very cautiously[618]. This also means that the "comparative context" has to be ascertained all over again.

In the earlier case law, the Commission has used also material connected to other international Conventions (eg. From the International Labour Organization) mainly in order

---

[613] For some other cases: *Wemhoff* ECHR (1968) A/7 and some other cases 1968-1978, see analysis by van der Meersch W.J.G., 1980, pp.323-324. On the use of the decisions of the supreme courts of some Member States of the Council of Europe, and the diplomatic protection of companies by International Court of Justice, European Court of Human Rights, *Agrotexim and others v Greece*, A/330 (1995) EHRR 250 (25 Oct 1995), *Bryan v United Kingdom*, A/335 (1995) EHRR 290 (22 Nov. 1995) concerning systems of judicial control of administrative decisions, In international law, the legitimacy of collective bargaining, *Gustafsson* (1996) EHRR, Freedom of association, negative right not to enter into collective agreements with trade unions, use of different international instruments (European Social Charter, International Covenant of Economic, Social and Cultural Rights, Conventions of International Labour Organizations). *Sunday times* (1979-1980) EHRR 2:245, how contempt of court seems to be only a British speciality.
  For some "hard cases" dealing with the concept of family, see the analysis by van der Meersch W.J.G., 1980, pp.332-333.
  On international treaties, see Jennings, R.Y., 1996, p.5
  It looks as if some parts of the legal provisions of the system, such as the idea of *"necessary in the democratic society"* (ECHR) do demand comparative observations in deciding the extension of these definitions (Doetring, K., 1987, p.54).
[614] Case *Golder* (1975) EHRR 1:524.
[615] Article 31(1) of the Vienna Convention. Compare also Article 30 of the Vienna Convention and Article 60 of the Human Rights Convention.
[616] Case *Wemhoff* (1968) EHRR.
[617] Jacobs, F.G., 1975, p.18.
[618] *Golder* (1975) EHRR 1:524, Commission, para. 46., and *Lawless* (1979-80) EHRR 1:1, para. 14.

to avoid inconsistent outcomes of similar instruments in the international field.[619]

Comparative observations appear throughout the systemic interpretation and argumentation, and comparative reasoning has been the basic feature in the history of the European system of human rights - even it has been seen "dangerous" field of inquiry from the point of view of the system[620]. Comparative analysis has had an effect upon the interpretation of the Convention in the Commission, in the Court, and in dissenting opinions.[621] This way the Court has been able to find a strike between the international and national traditions. The European Convention is based on the common traditions of constitutional law and on the common legal tradition of the Member States of the Council of Europe.[622]

Next there is the presentation of some cases including comparative reasoning. First observations are general observations relating to various subject fields of law. Subsequently, There is a more thorough analysis of cases in the realm of the freedom of expression.

2.2.2. Some examples of comparative reasoning.

Trial within a reasonable time or release pending trial ("English system and those derived from it"). In *Kemmance v France*[623] the question at issue concerned the duration of pre-trial detention (Article 5(1)(c), Right to liberty and security of person). The criminal proceedings in question had lasted more than eight and half years. This detention had been prolonged on four occasions. The Commission argued comparatively that

> "With regard to the pre-trial detention provided for in Article 5(l)(c) it is true that in certain legal systems, particularly the English system and those derived from it, the opening of a criminal investigation is very closely associated with arrest. The Court's case law takes account of this in accepting that the persistence of reasonable suspicion "after a certain lapse of time ... no longer suffices" to justify detention [referring to the case LETELLIER v FRANCE (A/207), 1992) 14 E.H.R.R. 83, para 35.].
> In the present case the "certain lapse of time" had no doubt been exceeded by several years. In order to justify further detention, therefore, the Government should prove its necessity for recognised reasons, such as the risk of absconding, collusion or repetition of an offence.
> The Commission has shown that in this case the applicant's detention was not necessary on any of these grounds."

Corporal punishment in private schools: "Western European States", "developments Throughout Europe". In *Costello-Roberts v United Kingdom*[624] the question concerned

---

[619] Jacobs, F G., 1975, p.19.
[620] Van der Meersch, W.J.G., 1980, p.317.
[621] Scheuner, Ch, 1968, p.214.
[622] Concerning this and the legal basis in general, see van der Meersch, W.J.G., 1980, pp.319-320.
[623] A/218 (1995) EHRR 349.
[624] 25 March 1993, A/247-C (1995) EHRR 112.

corporal punishment in schools in relation to Article 3 (*"No one shall be subjected to torture or to inhuman or degrading treatment or punishment"*) and Article 8 of the ECHR.

The Commission justified the alleged infringement of Article 8 (right to private life) with reference to the purposes mentioned in Article 8(2). In his dissenting opinion, a member[625] of the Commission rejected this idea on the following comparative basis:

> *"I find it difficult to accept that corporal punishment could ever be necessary in a democratic society for any of the purposes enumerated in Article 8(2), as no other Western European State practices it, most schools in Britain now reject it and the House of Lords supported its total abandonment since this case corporal punishment has been abolished in State schools. Now that State schools are no longer permitted to use corporal punishment any proposition that corporal punishment might be necessary in a private school will be even more difficult to defend."*

The Court's argument made reference to Article 28 of the United Nations Convention on the Rights of the Child[626], which explicitly refers to the maintenance of school discipline related to the child's human dignity. It found, with the help of this reasoning, that corporal punishment falls within jurisdiction of the European Convention. In the end, however, the conduct was found not to breach the Articles in question.

In their partly dissenting opinions, four of the judges[627] found that a breach of Article 3 had occurred on the basis of comparative considerations:

> *"At the relevant time the law relating to corporal punishment applied to all pupils in both State and independent schools in the United Kingdom. However, reflecting developments throughout Europe, such punishment was made unlawful for pupils in State and certain, independent schools. Given that such punishment was being progressively outlawed elsewhere, it must have appeared all the more degrading to those remaining pupils in independent schools whose disciplinary regimes persisted in punishing their pupils in this way."*

Non-enforcement of access and custody rights ("situations in Member States"). In the case of *Hokkanen*[628], the question concerned claims of infringement of Articles 6, 8, and 13 of the Convention, and Article 5 of Protocol 7. The reasons given were that when the applicant had given the child to the custody of her grandparents, they refused to give her back, and also the police chief officer refused to execute the custody order. Furthermore, the Appeal Court had permanently transferred custody to the grandparents, and declined to enforce access against the child's wishes.

The Government had referred to Article 3 of the 1989 United Nations Convention on the Rights of the Child, Article 19(1)(b) of the 1980 European Convention on the Enforcement of Decisions Concerning Custody of Children and on Restoration of Custody of Children, and

---

[625] Mr. Schermers.

[626] 20 November 1989.

[627] Mr. Ryssdal, Vilhjalmsson, Matscher, and Wildhaber.

[628] (23 September 1994) A/299-A (1995) EHRR 139.

Articles 1 and 12(3) of the 1980 Convention on the Civil Aspects of International Child Abduction.

In arguing about the infringement of Article 8 (respect for family life), the Commission interpreted the concept of ´respect´ according to the Convention:

> *"The Commission recalls in this connection that the notion of "respect" enshrined in Article 8 is not clear-cut. This is the case especially where the positive obligations implicit in that concept are concerned. It requirements will vary considerably from case to case according to the practices followed and situations obtaining in the Contracting States. When determining whether or not such an obligation exists regard must be had to fair balance that has to be struck between the general interest and the interest of the individual as well as to the margin of the appreciation afforded to the contracting States."*

The Court noted the Commission´s observations, but maintained that even if the boundaries between the State's positive and negative obligations do not lend themselves to precise definition, the *"applicable principles are similar"*. However, it came to the conclusion that the non-enforcement of the applicants right to access had violated the Article 8 of the Convention.

Non-recognition of paternity (no clear European notion of respect, differing court practices in European countries, reform tendencies and their results, a historical comparison). In *Kroon and others against The Netherlands[629]*, the biological father had claimed the right to paternity in a court, but his application was rejected, because, according to Dutch law, child's father is the married husband of the mother, and because the legal husband refused to deny the paternity. The claim brought was the breach of Article 8 (right to family life) in conjunction with Article 14 (discrimination).

The Commission justified its opinion by referring to the comparative observations made by the Court in the *Rasmussen* case[630]. There the Court had remarked that

> *"in the Contracting States' legislation regarding paternity proceedings there is no common ground, and that in most of these States the position of the mother and that of her husband is regulated in different ways".*

On this basis, the Court had found that the difference in time-limits, applicable to the institution of paternity proceedings in different states, was not an argument justifying a discriminatory treatment.

The Court in this case, on the other hand, found a violation of Article 8.

In his dissenting opinion, where no violation of Article 8 was found - on the basis that the

---

[629] 27 October 1994, A/297-C (1995) EHRR 263
[630] *Rasmussen v Denmark,A /87* (1985) EHRR 371, para 40

rejection by the court was justified interference - one of the judges[631] analysed the Court's case from the standpoint of the ideas of "evolutive interpretation" and "living instrument"ideas. The Court had previously proposed such an method of interpretation on several occasions.

This judge remarked that the dilemma of the creative interpretation is more serious in the cases on "*marriage, divorce, filiation or adoption, because they bring the existing religious, ideological or traditional conceptions of the family in each community*". He referred to the Court's comparative argumentation in the case of *Johnson and Others v Ireland*[632] dealing with the question:

"*... especially as far as those positive obligations are concerned, the European notion of 'respect' is not clear-cut: having regard to the diversity of the Court of practices followed and the situations obtaining in the Contracting States, the notion's requirements will vary considerably from case to case. Accordingly, this is an area in which the Contracting Parties enjoy a wide margin of appreciation in determining the steps to be taken to ensure compliance with the Convention with due regard to the needs and resources of the community and of individuals ...*"

On the same occasion, the judge referred to other instruments produced by the Council of Europe to harmonize family laws:

"*This has led to reforms in family law in many countries of Europe, from the 1970's onwards. These reforms have achieved a certain approximation of national laws but not their uniformity, particularly in regard to the regulation of procedures for denying legal paternity, which still take many different forms. On the other hand, there is a tendency in the regulation of the use of new techniques of human reproduction towards prohibiting challenges to legal paternity by anonymous sperm donors.*
Account should also be taken of the importance of the family in many Contracting States, of the persistence in these countries of a social rejection of adultery and of the common belief that a united family facilitates the healthy development of the child."

Furthermore, another judge[633] presented his dissenting opinion on comparative and historical (Roman law) basis, finding no violation:

"*2. Netherlands law, like the legislation of some other Contracting States, in given circumstances "presumes" the paternity of a child, in conformity with the maxim of Roman Law pater is est quem nuptiae demonstrant [L.5 De in jus voc.] thereby establishing and ensuring inter alia the rights of the child. In matters of this type, I believe that it is a principle of good law to hold that the interests of the child are paramount.*"

"*4. In conclusion therefore, I cannot agree with the majority of my colleagues because, (a) in the legislation of a substantial number of Contracting States rules similar to those of the impugned Netherlands law are principally concerned with the protection of the rights and interests of the child (even against the "opportunist" wishes of the*

[631] Mr. Morenilla.
[632] A/112 (1987) EHRR 203, para 55.
[633] Mr. Bonnici.

parents) and this vital and important factor has not been given sufficient consideration in a matter which may have a substantial impact as to where exactly the margin of appreciation lies which each one of the Contracting States enjoys in this matter; and (b) there is no "family life" in the instant case, even if there are biological reasons for holding that there are "family ties". Moreover, in paragraph 40 of the judgment, reference is made to "social reality' as one of the factors which should prevail over the legal presumption of paternity. In my opinion, ever mindful of the frequent appeals avocations made to "social reality" in justification of certain notorious laws enacted in Soviet Russia [1920-1989] and in Nazi Germany [1933-1945], it is dangerous and unsafe to bring such criteria into the field of family rights. The approach to those rights should be made from steadier and more stable platforms.
5. It follows from the above that I am against granting any financial relief to the applicants under Article 50."

Transsexuality: ("Changing attitudes", but differences between "Member States of the Council of Europe", developments of legislation and case law, "no consensus between Council of Europe Member States"). In the case *B v France*, dealing with the refusal of the government to recognize a changed sexual identity and the change of civil status based on this change, the Court supported its argumentation with a relatively extensive examination of the legislation in Member States of the Convention.[634] When examining the notion of "respect" the Court noted, as before, that *"its requirements vary considerably from case to case according to the practices followed and situations obtained in the Contracting States"*.

When dealing with the former case law on the same subject against another Contracting State (England)[635], the Court examined the differences in the legislation of these two countries (France and England) and the consequences of these differences from the point of view of the Convention.

When examining scientific, legal and social developments in this area, the Court considered (also on the basis of an examination of former cases) that

"attitudes have changed but there are still differences in the attitudes between the Member States of the Council of Europe"

This was, however,

"counterbalanced to an increasing extent by developments in the legislation and the case law of many of those States".

The Court also considered the applicants' references to the resolutions and recommendations of the European Parliament.[636] However, the Court foresaw problems in uniformity related to many issues: in definitions, in the conditions under which a change of sexual identity could be authorized, in international aspects, in the legal consequences of such a change, in

---

[634] 25 March 1992, A/232-C (1993) EHRR 1.
[635] Case *Rees v United Kingdom* (1987) EHRR 56, para. 35, and *Cossey v United Kingdom* (1991) EHRR 622, para.36.
[636] These were mainly the arguments put forward by the applicant based on the dissenting opinion of judge Martens in *Cossey v United Kingdom* (1991) EHRR 660-661.

opportunities for choosing a different forename, in the confidentiality of documents, in information mentioning that change, and finally, in the effects on the family-dimensions of this change (legal consequences). The Court found that

"*there is no sufficiently broad consensus between the Member States of the Council of Europe to convince the court to reach opposite conclusion to those in the former cases.*"

The extensive comparative argumentation was not, therefore, a decisive element in the argumentation as a whole. The final conclusions of the Court related mainly to the factual differences between the previous cases and to the daily situations of the applicant and the balance between general and individual interests. It found a violation of Article 8 of the Convention (right to respect for his private and family life... and the exercise of this right).

Pre-trial detention (average length of pretrial detention, comparative scholarly opinion, legislation and case law in other countries, comparative law as a source of law). In the case of *W v Switzerland* concerning pre-trial detention and its length, the dissenting opinion of a judge[637] devoted extensive attention to the comparative analysis, supported by the opinions of scholars in various States. When referring to comparative criminal law, he found that the

"*average length of pre-trial detention is less than two or three months and that with respect to economic offences and bankcrupties the average length is less than one year*".

Furthermore, he took as a

"*typical example of the official statistic of the French Ministry of Justice, which could be transposed with similar results of other European States with similar population, the list of serious and less serious crimes by category for 1989...shows: for bankcrupties, an average length of two months (seven cases of three months, one only in excess of 18 months); for fraud; extortion and blackmail, an average length of four to eight months. Yet in France parliament has often deplored the excessive length of pre-trial detention and has attempted to remedy this by reforming the Code of Criminal Procedure*"

Furthermore, he referred to legal writings on criminal law and criminal policy in different countries and found that

"*no academic specialist or practitioner in Europe justifies pre-trial detention lasting four years for economic offences, even multiple ones...*"

and that "*authors regret the excessive length of pre-trial detention*". Reference was made to writers and law in Belgium, England, France and Italy.

---

[637] 26 January 1993, A/254 (1994) EHRR 60 The dissenting opinion of Mr. Pettiti.

A historical comparative analysis supported the observation, that a

> "*number of States have enacted legislation* laying down a maximum length of pretrial detention (six months or one year, for example in Czechoslovakia)

and that

> "the *case law of the other States*" [than Switzerland] limits the length of pre-trial detention to about six months to two years" Furthermore, the "*comparative law shows that no country (other than Switzerland) practices detention for four years in the field of bankruptcy and fraud, even for criminal cases which are more serious than economic offences*".

Finally, he noted that

> "*in the Member States of the Council of Europe which have investigative proceedings*, practitioners have noted that certain judges have a propensity to anticipate the sentence sometimes by pre-trial detention, or to press the accused to make admissions by postponing appearances for months while dismissing requests for release"

With reference to philosophical, teleological, and case law-arguments, he came to the conclusion that the length and the manner in which pre-trial detention was executed violated Article 5 of the Convention (the "preassumption of innocence").

2.2.3. Comparative reasoning related to Article 10(1 and 2) ("freedom of expression" and the "necessity in a democratic society") in the European system of human rights

Case Handyside (Practice at the international level, interpretation methods, practice in the majority of the Member States of the Council of Europe, analogical legislation in other Contracting States). The *Handyside* case[638] dealt with a situation where a publisher had been charged and convicted under the law by having in his possession obscene books. Books were seized, forfeited and destroyed. The book was circulated also everywhere else in Europe, and in some other parts of the country of the parties to the dispute. Both the Court and the Commission did not find any breach of Article 10, or rather, the Court declared it justified under the Article 10(2) of the Convention.

The *Handyside* case has been one of the most influential cases in the European system of human rights. In this case the Court established the basis for the idea of the *"absence of the general concept of European morals"*.[639] Furthermore, the Court also developed its idea on the *"marginal appreciation"* doctrine, and the idea of *"European level supervision"* combined

---

[638] 7 December 1976, A/24. See for some analysis also, van der Meersch, W.J.G., 1980,pp.328-331.

[639] This idea will be observed closely in connection to the hard case in chapter 3.1.1. *(Otto Preminger Institute)*

with this national supervision.

The Court defined the nature of the European system of human rights in its relation to the national systems[640]. The Court also made explicit its method of interpretation, which is related to the idea of "comparative interpretation":

> "It follows from this that it is in no way the Court's task to take the place of the competent national courts but rather to review under Article 10 the decisions they delivered in the exercise of their power of appreciation. However, the Court's supervision would generally prove illusory if it did no more than examine these decision in isolation; it must view them in the light of the case as a whole, including the publication in question and the arguments and evidence adduced by the applicant, in the domestic legal system and then at the international level. The Court must decide, on the different data available to it whether the reasons given by the national authorities to justify the actual measures of interference they take are relevant and sufficient under Article 10(2)."

The Court had to take a comparative standpoint mainly because the book had been circulated also in other states parties to the Convention:

> "The applicant and the minority of the Commission laid stress on the further point that, in addition to the original Danish edition, translations of the Little Book appeared and circulated freely in the majority of the Member States of the Council of Europe. Here again, the national margin of appreciation and the optional nature of the ' restrictions ' and ' penalties ' referred to in Article 10 (2) prevent the Court from accepting the argument The Contracting States have each fashioned their approach in the light of the situation obtaining in their respective territories; they have had regard, inter alia, to the different views prevailing there about the demands of the protection of morals in a democratic society. The fact that most of them decided to allow the work to be distributed does not mean that the contrary decision of the Inner London Quarter Sessions was a breach of Article 10. Besides, some of the editions published outside the United Kingdom do not include the passages, or at least not all the passages, cited in the judgment of 29 October 1971 as striking examples of a tendency to 'deprave and corrupt'."

Here the Court explicitly rejected the decisiveness of these types of comparative observations, which, nevertheless, seemed to indicate a generality of practices.

However, the applicants claim that the seizure was not 'necessary' in a democratic society was dismissed on the basis of comparative observations:

> ".... If the applicant is right, their object should have been at the most one or few copies of the book to be used as exhibits in the criminal proceedings. The Court does not share this view since the police had good reasons for trying to lay their hands on all the stock as a temporary means of protecting the young against the danger to morals on whose existence it was for the trial court to decide. The legislation of many Contracting States provides for a seizure analogous to that envisaged by section 3 of the English 1959/1964 Act."

---

[640] Referring to the cases (for Art. 5(3)) *Wemhoff* (1968) EHRR 55, 76, para. 12; *Neumeister v Austria* (NO. 1) (1968), I E.H.R.R. 91, 126, para. 5; *Stög-Müller v Austria* (1969), 1 E.H.R.R. 155, 190, para 3 *Matznette v Austria* (1969), 1 E.H.R.R. 198, 224, para 3,; and *Ringeisen v Austria* (1971), 1 E.H.R.R. 493, para 104.

Case Engel ("the common denominator" conception, "traditions of the Contracting States"). The case of *Engel and Others v The Netherlands*[641] dealt with the relationship between the publication and distribution of certain prohibited writings by some soldiers in the Netherlands armed forces and the Article 19 (freedom of expression) and Article 5 (right to liberty)[642]. The applicants had been sentenced and arrested on the basis of the writings' publication and distribution, which was covered by the laws of military discipline.

Although the Court found that the Article applied to servicemen as well as to ordinary persons, it was not breached by the penalties which had been imposed because the interference was legitimate and justified by the desire to protect the military discipline.

The Court argued comparatively to show that the action taken by the state belonged to the sphere of the Convention's Article 6. It also undertook a comparative examination of whether the action by the state belonged to the realm of criminal law or that of disciplinary law, or to both. The Court defined it as an inquiry *"in the light of the common denominator of the respective legislation of the various Contracting States"*.

The Court maintained that

"The seriousness of what is at stake, <u>the traditions of the Contracting States</u>, and the importance attached by the Convention to respect for the physical liberty of the person all require that this should be so [powers of the supervision by the Court of Human Rights].

It is on the basis of these criteria that the court will ascertain whether some or all of the applicants were a subject of a "criminal charge" within the meaning of the Article 6."

However, the Court refused to undertake an extensive interpretation of the provision.

Case X v Germany (similar legislation in most European countries). In the case of *X v Federal Republic of Germany*[643] dealing with freedom of speech and its *"necessary restrictions in the democratic society"*, the Commission stated that

"Moreover, the Commission has had regard the fact that <u>most European countries</u> that have ratified the Convention have legislation which restricts the free flow of commercial "ideas" in the interest of protecting consumers from misleading or deceptive practices"...

Taking both these observations into account[644] the Commission considers that the test of "necessity" in the second paragraph of the Article 10 should therefore be a less strict one when one applied to restraints imposed on commercial ideas."

---

[641] 8 June 1976, A/22 (1978).
[642] Article 11 on the freedom of association was also involved.
[643] Appl. 8410/78, 13 December 1979. The case dealt with the advertising activities of religious communities and its misleading character.
[644] The other observation concerned the jurisprudence of the Court (*Handyside*, A/24, 7. December 1977).

On this basis the Commission came to the conclusion that the injunction granted by the Market Court of the Federal Republic of Germany was necessary in a democratic society for the protection of the rights of others (i.e. consumers).

Case Arrowsmith (The United States Supreme Court's doctrine, "Unusual in a democratic country of our time"). In the case *Arrowsmith v United Kingdom*[645], the applicant had been delivering pacifist leaflets in front of an army camp directed to soldiers persuading them to seduce from their duty or allegiance in relation to service in Northern Ireland. She was convicted to imprisonment. The question in the Commission was about the "*necessity of the interference*" in relation to the right guaranteed in the Article 10, where the act aimed at protecting national security and the prevention of disorder within the army.

Before the Commission, the applicant wanted the case to be examined comparatively:

" *It remains to be examined whether the applicant's prosecution and conviction, and the sentence imposed [seven months' imprisonment] were necessary in order to secure this aim [protection of national security and the prevention of disorder within the army].*
The applicant has suggested that the ' clear and present danger doctrine', as developed by the United States Supreme Court, be applied.
The notion 'necessary' implies a 'pressing social need' which may include the clear and present danger test and must be assessed in the light of the circumstances of a given case."

The Commission decided that the justification for restrictions, penalties etc. upon the freedom of expression (and the concept of necessity in Article 10(2)) "*implies a pressing social need which many be include the 'clear and present danger' test, and must be assessed in the light of the particular circumstances of the case*".

One of the members of the Commission, in his dissenting opinion, made a general comparative observations to support his argument that long imprisonment was out of proportion to the legitimate aim pursued[646]:

"*Finally, I consider that the interference by a way of a long imprisonment, even as it was reduced upon appeal, was out of proportion to the legitimate aim pursued as required by the European Court of Human Rights in the HANDYSIDE case. It is to my knowledge, quite unusual in a democratic country in our time to punish anyone in this way for non-violent political offences such as those committed by applicant, and I cannot reconcile it with the requirement of necessary in the present case it leaves me with the unfortunate impression that in this case, because of the serious and violent conflict in Northern Ireland, the authorities have over-reacted.*
That tolerance for the views of dissidents which we expect of other countries should not be abandoned in Western Europe even in times of crisis. Although the applicant's action remotely threatened public policy, this is not in my opinion a sufficient justification for interference under the system of the European Convention whose claim to credibility it is very important to preserve in the world-wide debate on human rights."

---

[645] 12 October 1978, Application 7050/75(1981) EHRR 218.
[646] Mr. Opsahl.

Case Glimmerveen (other international measures). The case of *Glimmerveen v Hagenbeek v Netherlands*[647] dealt with the question, whether the possession of leaflets inciting racial hatred was to be protected by Article 10 of the Convention.

In this case, the Commission, concluding that Article 10 of the Convention was inapplicable, made reference to the other international systems presented (as an argument by the Government Party):

> "*Indeed, the Government have drawn the attention of the Commission in particular in the light of Article 60 of the Convention, to the Netherlands' international obligations under the <u>International Convention on the Elimination of all Forms of Racial Discrimination of 1965, to which the Netherlands acceded in 1971.</u>*
>
> [20] *The Netherlands' authorities, in allowing the applicants to proclaim freely and without penalty their ideas would certainly encourage the discrimination prohibited by the provisions of the European Convention on Human Rights referred to above and the above Convention of New York of 1965.*
>
> [21] *The Commission holds the view that the expression of the political ideas of the applicants clearly constitutes an activity within the meaning of Article 17 of the Convention.*
>
> [22] *The applicants are essentially seeking to use Article 10 to provide a basis under the Convention for a right to engage in these activities which are, as shown above, contrary to the text and spirit of the Convention and which right, if granted, would contribute to the destruction- of the rights and freedoms referred to above.*
>
> *Consequently, the Commission finds that the applicants cannot by reason of the provisions of Article 17 of the Convention, rely on Article 10 of the Convention.*"

Liberal Party (similarities between the systems in some countries, examples of legal decisions). In the case of *Liberal Party v United Kingdom*[648] the Commission found that Article 10 does not guarantee the right to vote as such, nor does it guarantee the right to stand for election or any other right already provided by Article 3 of the First Protocol. In this manner the Commission found that Article 10 alone was inapplicable also when it was read in conjunction with Article 14. In its reasoning, the Commission made an extensive reasoning on comparative basis:

> "*Article 3 requires that elections are being held under conditions which will ensure the free expression of the opinion of the people in the choice of the legislature. The applicants seem to suggest that the disadvantage existing for the Liberal Party, as for any smaller party, does not really assure the free expression of the opinion the people. Although the Commission agrees that this disadvantage exists and may be of considerable political impact it cannot find a violation of Article 3 of the First Protocol alone or in conjunction with Article 14 of the Convention on that basis. The simple majority system is one of the two basic electoral systems It is or <u>has been used in many democratic countries</u>. It has always been accepted as allowing for the free expression of the opinion of the people even if it operates to the detriment of small parties.*
>
> 10. *This reasoning is supported by the fact that even countries which know of a fundamental right to equality of voting still admit the simple majority system as complying with the requirement. The <u>Federal Constitutional Court</u>*

---

[647] 11 October 1979, appl. 8348/78 and 8406/78 (1982) EHRR 260.

[648] Appl. No. 8765/79 (1982) EHRR 106, 18 December

of the Federal Republic of Germany [Bundesverfassungsgericht, Decision, Vol. 34, 81, 100 with references] has held that both electoral systems, proportionate representation and simple majority vote, are constitutional and in line with the requirement of equality of voting. The United States Supreme Court controls election laws on the basis of the equal protection clause of the 14th Amendment to the US Constitution [WHITCOMB v. CHAVIS 403, U.S. 124, 156 (1971)- WHITE V. REGESTER, 412 U.S. 755, 766 (1973)]. It accepts the prevailing system with simple majority electoral districts, including, under specific circumstances, multimember districts although these may be very much to the disadvantage of smaller groups."

Case Barthold (no comparable provisions in other states and in international instruments, similarities between the legislation of the state parties, no general practice, evolution in Europe and in North America, Supreme Court of United States). In the case of *Barthold v Germany*[649] the question concerned the alleged breaking of professional rules by a veterinary surgeon, who had advertised and published in a manner which contravened the law.

He had also been critical in a newspaper article of the lack of emergency services available at night. Interim and final injunctions required him to refrain from repeating statements on the basis of the *"non-objective nature"* of the statements. The Court found there to have been a violation of Article 10.

In the course of its argument the Government attempted to justify its conduct on the basis of comparative similarity of competition rules in different national and international instruments:

> " .. *Finally; in the submission of the Government, in the field of the "policing" of unfair competition the Contracting States enjoyed a wide margin of appreciation and the legal traditions of the Contracting States had to be respected by the Convention institutions. In this connection, provisions comparable to those of the relevant German legislation were to be found in other States of the Council of Europe, in international instruments and in the law of the European Communities. "*

The Court refused to accept this argumentation because of the subsidiarity nature of the powers[650], and maintained that the margin of appreciation *"enjoyed by the Contracting States has to go hand in hand with the European supervision, which is more or less extensive depending on circumstances"*[651].

However, two members of the Court[652], who also found that violation of Article 10 had not taken place responded directly to the comparative argument put forward by the Government:

---

[649] A/90 (1985) EHRR 383, 25 March 1985.

[650] Some analysis of the idea of "subsidiarity" in the European Human Rights system is provided by van der Meersch, W.J.G., 1980, p.328 (Belgian linguistic and Handyside cases).

[651] This refers to an idea of coherence of a national system and to a teleological derogation.
  However, to maintain the integrity of the general human rights system, the future observation is explained ("*together with the European surveillance .... "at this stage...*")

[652] Mr. Vilhjalmsson and Mr. Bindschedler-Robert.

> *"Although restrictions on advertising and publicity by members of the liberal professions are <u>well known in the</u> <u>States Parties to the Convention</u>, the combined application of rules from these two categories ["professional conduct and unfair competition"] are not general practice."*

Another member of the Court[653] put forward an interesting "comparative legal development" argument in his dissenting opinion. He came also to the conclusion that there had been a violation of Article 10, but he stressed the importance of a wider scope for the argumentation:

> *"As of now, however, one cannot ignore the considerable <u>evolution that has occurred, in Europe as well as in North</u> <u>America</u>, within the professional bodies representing the liberal professions in opening themselves up to certain forms of collective advertising about their activities and even to certain forms of individual advertising, in particular so as to indicate practitioners' specialities. Standards of professional conduct are thereby undergoing development and, for members of the liberal professions, it is not possible to divorce assessment of professional conduct from the degree of liberty afforded in relation to advertising, which is what happened in Dr. Barthold's case. Freedom of expression in its true dimension is the right to receive and to impart information and ideas. Commercial speech is directly connected with that freedom."*

He motivated the inclusion of "*commercial speech*" within the realm of freedom of expression with a direct reference to the case law of the United States Supreme Court:

> *"Such was the import of a decision by the Commission; such is the case law of the <u>Supreme Court of the United</u> <u>States</u> under the First Amendment [VIRGINIA STATE BOARD OF PHARMACY V. VIRGINIA CONSUMER COUNCIL 425 U.S. 748 (1976); BATES V BAR OF ARIZONA 433 U S 350 (1977), CENTRAL HUDSON GAS & ELECTRIC CORP V PUBLIC SERVICE COMMISSION 447 U.S. 557 (1980)] albeit that the commercial communications are afforded a different degree of protection to that granted in respect of the press."*

Case Glasenapp (sources of law doctrines compared; other international measures (The Declaration of Human Rights and International Covenant on Civil and Political Rights), geographical position compared). In the *Glasenapp* case[654] the question concerned the revocation of an appointment of a school teacher on the basis of her unsuitability. It was claimed, by the German responsible authority, that she was not prepared to approve or uphold the principles of a free and democratic society. Legal proceedings in Germany had upheld this conclusion.

In its opinion, the European Commission of Human Rights argued by the comparative generality of doctrines of sources of law. That established the basis for an interpretation of the "*lawfulness of the restriction*" in the following way:

> *"Since judicial precedent is relied upon by the Government as an additional source of law which added the required precision to the statutory texts, it is relevant to refer also to the further dictum in the SUNDAY TIMES judgment*

---

[653] Mr Pettiti.
[654] A/104, (1987) EHRR 25, 28 August 1986.

according to which the word law in the expression 'prescribed by law' covers not only statute but also unwritten law. The Commission regards this consideration as valid not only in respect of the common law but also in respect of other legal systems where the legislation deliberately leaves room for judicial precedent. Accordingly the judicial principles established by precedent must be regarded as "law" within the meaning of Article 10(2), provided that they are adhered to by the courts in a consistent manner."

On this basis the Commission found that the application of judicial principles comprise valid basis as "law" in this case.

In studying the nature of the European human rights system, the nature of the rights included within it, and the aims of the Convention, the Court agreed with the government's argumentation:[655]

"48. The Universal Declaration of Human Rights of 10 December 1948 and the International Covenant on Civil and Political Rights of 16 December 1966 provide, respectively, that everyone has the right of equal access to public service in his country and that every citizen shall have the right and the opportunity to have access, on general terms of equality, to public service in his country'. In contrast, neither the European Convention nor any of its Protocols sets forth any such right. Moreover as the Government rightly pointed out the signatory states deliberately did not include such a right; drafting history of the Protocols 4 and 7 shows this unequivocally. In particular, the initial versions of Protocol 7 contained a provision similar to Article 21(2) of the Universal Declaration and Article 25 of the International Covenant; this clause was subsequently deleted. This is not therefore a chance omission from the European instruments; as the Preamble to the Convention states, they are designed to ensure the collective enforcement of 'certain' of the rights stated in the Universal Declaration."

The Court discovered, in other words, that the Convention was in conflict with other international instrument. It seemed to find it impossible to interpret the Convention in the light of these other instruments, but related the *travaux preparatoires* and the intention of the parties with this contrastive use of other international instruments.

Consequently, the Court did not find a breach of Article 10 by the national authorities.

Comparative reasoning was used likewise by the dissenting judges in finding the inapplicability of Article 10 to the case.

In his dissenting opinion, in finding a violation of Article 10, another judge pointed out comparatively (in general terms) that,

"While the contracting states did not wish to commit themselves to recognizing a right of access to the Civil Service in the convention or its protocols, the High contracting Parties nonetheless undertook in Article 1 of the Convention to secure to everyone within their jurisdiction the rights and freedoms guaranteed in the in the Convention. It follows that access to the Civil Service must not be impeded on grounds protected by the Convention (for example, freedom of opinion, freedom of expression).

21. Taken to its extreme, the reasoning of the majority of the Court could authorise a State to refuse to admit to the Civil Service candidates who, while fulfilling all the requirements of nationality, age, health and professional

---

[655] Similar type of case, see *Kosiek v. Germany (A/105 (1987) EHRR 328, 28 August 1986)* where also the concurring opinion of judge Bindschedler-Robert, Pinheiro, Farinha, Pettiti, Walsch, Russo, Bernardt stressed the importance of *"national tradition and the system governing the Civil Service".*

qualifications, did not satisfy certain criteria of race, colour or religion. Obviously such a situation is unthinkable for all the Member States of the Council of Europe."

The government's comparative argument was rejected by this judge in following manner:

"A second argument expounded by the Agent of the Government to justify current legislation in the Federal Republic of Germany was the following (translation from the German): ... Germany is a divided nation whose position bordering on the Communist States of the Warsaw Pact exposes it to special dangers. This requires us to take additional precautions to safeguard our free democracy and makes us different from other Council of Europe States."

In other words, the government had presented a comparative argument based on that country's peculiar national, geographic, and political circumstances to legitimate an exception from European human rights. The judge refused to uphold this type of comparative argument:[656]

"Without wishing to enter into a debate on that argument, I consider nonetheless that the Federal Republic of Germany is not the only country in such a geographical position. Yet it is the only country to have the legislation complained of."

Case Markt Intern (the practice in other Member States of the Council of Europe, hypothetical "non-reaction"). In *Markt Intern and Beermann v Germany*[657], the question concerned right to publish claims of a dissatisfied client of a company in a newspaper. In the specific context, this was found, by the German court, to involve *"acts contrary to honest practices".* The European Court accepted this finding of the German Court. The restriction was found to be legitimate on the basis of its aims.

In his dissenting opinion, however, one of the members of the European Court of Human Rights[658] analysed comparatively the general discourse in European States:

"The problem is all the more serious because often the States which seek to restrict the freedom use the pretext of economic infringements or breaches of economic legislation such as anti-competitive or antitrust provisions to institute proceedings for political motives or to protect 'mixed' interests (State-industrial) in order to erect a barrier to the freedom of expression.
The economic pressure which groups or laboratories can exert should not be underestimated. In certain cases this pressure has been such that it has delayed the establishment of the truth and therefore put back the prohibition of a medicine or substance dangerous for the public health.
The economic press of numerous Member States publishes each day articles, millions of copies of which are circulated, containing criticism of products in terms a hundred times stronger than those in question in the Markt Intern case. It is this freedom accorded to that press which ensures the protection of the public at large."

---

[656] Exactly same argument in *Kosiek* case.
[657] A/164 (1990) EHRR 161, 20 November 1989, The case must be distinguished from the case Markt Intern and Beerman v. Germany, 18 December 1987.
[658] Mr. Pettiti.

Another member of the Court expressed his dissenting opinion based on the generality of "non-existing" law in Europe (the party's laws constituting an exception to this)[659]:

"...It should therefore be asked whether it can be necessary in a democratic society to restrict the rights and fundamental freedoms of an organ of the press in this way solely because that organ has espoused the cause of specific economic interests, namely those of a particular sector of a specialised trade. I am in no doubt that this question must be answered in the negative. This is clear from the fact that, as far as I know, such a rule extending the scope of the law on unfair competition to the detriment of freedom of the press is unknown in the other Member States of the Council of Europe, and rightly so because, in certain respects, all newspapers may be regarded as partisan, having espoused the cause of certain specific interests."

On this basis he came to the conclusion that such acts by the state were not necessary in a democratic society, and consequently, that there had been a violation of Article 10 of the Convention.

Case Groppera (rejection of the analogy derived from another international measures, the European Community as example, tendencies towards democracy in Eastern Europe, scholarly opinions in Europe and the United States, the United States constitution and its interpretation, the factual situation in European countries, other international conventions). In *Groppera radio Advocate General v Switzerland*[660], a company was obliged to terminate its transmissions by cable. The Swiss authorities imposing this obligation referred to a new law prohibiting transmissions by those stations, which did not comply with international treaties and agreements.

Two members of the Court stated in their dissenting opinion that

"I cannot accept paragraph 61 of the judgment [of this Court]. In my opinion, it is unacceptable to reason on the basis of drafting history of a later instrument drawn up in a different community (the United Nations), not within the Council of Europe...
"...the fact that the sentence was not included in the International Covenant of Civil and Political rights is of no importance when interpreting paragraph (1) of the Article 10 of the European Convention of Human Rights, in which it does occur."

The members rejected also the "implicit" adaption of the European Community doctrine on *"precision and clarity"* of the publication in the reasoning of the Court.[661] They claimed that

"There was no publication in the Swiss official gazette. I honestly doubt whether what may be acceptable in respect of European Community legislation included in Community's Official Journal, which is regarded as an official gazette in the Member States too, can be acceptable in respect of other international instruments."

---

[659] Mr. Martens.
[660] A/173 (1990) EHRR 321, 28 March 1990, Mr Matscher, Mr Bindschedler-Robert.
[661] Argumentation in para 68 of the judgment (*Groppera* case).

However, the members came to the same conclusion as did the Court.

The same case also inspired other judges[662] to present detailed example type of comparisons of case law in their strong dissenting opinion:

"Recent European cases concerning jurisdiction, copyright (author's rights), and tort damages have examined and classified the rules and systems which are applicable and are brought out the distinctions to be made by reference to different situations:

(a) the transmission itself, or the reception, is contrary to national law [Paris Court in case Potasses, "referring to the European Court of Justice"] ..."

In stressing the importance of the freedom of expression (including the freedom to receive information) especially in connection to telecommunications they maintained in rather value-based form:

"The countries of Eastern Europe have been encouraged towards democracy thanks to the transborder broadcasts and wish to join the European Convention on Transborder Communication Satellites. Case law and academic lawyers in this field, both American and European, agree that this freedom should be extended to the field of telecommunications.

The European Court should uphold this safeguard and promotion of the freedom of expression in the same spirit as that of the first amendment to the Constitution of the United States and the work of United nations (16th session). It should be remembered what Helvetius said, "it is necessary to think and to be able to say everything"- and the Declaration of Virginia (1776), "freedom of press is one of the most powerful bastions of liberty".

In justifying the decision, the Court examined the general tendencies in Europe[663]:

"Since then [signing of the Convention], changed views and technical progress, particularly the appearance of cable transmissions, have resulted in the abolition of State monopolies in many European countries and the establishment of private radio stations, often local ones, in addition to the public services. Furthermore, the national licencing systems are required not only for the orderly regulation of broadcasting enterprises at the national level but also in large part to give effect to international rules, including in particular number 2020 of the Radio Regulations"

Furthermore, the Court, in dealing with the interpretation of the broadcasting licencing system in Switzerland, also compared Article 19 of the 1966 International Covenant on Civil and Political Rights, and maintained[664] that

"It does not include a provision corresponding to the third sentence of Article 10(1) of the Convention [of Human rights]. The negotiating history of the Article 19 shows that the inclusion of such a provision in an Article had been proposed with a view to the licensing not of the information imparted but rather of the technical means of broadcasting in order to prevent chaos in the use of frequencies. However in inclusion was opposed on the ground that it might be utilized to hamper free expression, and it was decided that such a provision was not necessary because licencing in a sense intended was deemed to be covered by the reference to 'public order' in paragraph (3)

---

[662] Mr. Pettiti.

[663] With regard to tendencies approach, see Schreuer, C.H., 1971, pp.275-277 (*Otto Preminger Institute*).

[664] Reference to UN doc. A/500, 16th session of the United Nations General Assembly, 5 December 1961, para 23.

of the Article.

This supports the conclusion that the purpose of the third sentence of the Article 19(1) of the Convention [on the Human Rights] is to make it clear that states are permitted to control by a licencing system the way in which broad casting is organized in their territories, particularly in its technical aspects. It does not , however, provide that licencing measures shall not otherwise be subject to the requirements of paragraph (2) [of the Convention], for that would lead to a result contrary to the object and purpose of Article taken as a whole. "

The Court used, in other words, another international agreement as a comparative reference. It analysed the legislative history of this convention, and on this basis interpreted the content of the European Convention by analogy.

On this basis, it came to the conclusion that the third sentence of Article 10(1) was applicable to this case (*"This Article does not prevent states from requiring the licencing of broadcasting, television or cinema enterprises"*).

However, the scope of its applicability needed also to be interpreted. Accordingly, the Court came to the conclusion that the interference by the Swiss authorities was in accordance with the Article. The question thus concerned only whether the interference was "prescribed by law", and had legitimate aims, and "was necessary in a democratic society". In the end, the interference was found to be in accordance with Convention's Article 10.

Case Autronic (the practice of states, some states particularly, Council of Europe as tertium comparationis, international developments, international measures and their interpretation; implementation by parties, questionnaires answered by authorities: no general practice, international measures and their objectives). In the case of *Autronic v Switzerland*[665] concerning the applicability of the Article on freedom of expression to the receiving of uncoded television programs (an application by a party to get a permission from the state to do so), the Court referred to the Commissions report, which included comparative observations:[666]

"The practice of several Council of Europe member States, including France and United Kingdom, suggested that the International Telecommunication Convention and the Radio Regulations did not preclude direct reception of signals retransmitted by telecommunication satellite where they were intended for the general public."[667]

Furthermore, in looking into the necessity of restrictions in a democratic society, the Court observed, that

"In the legal field, developments have included, at international level, the signature within the Council of Europe on 5 May 1989 of the European Convention on Transfrontier television and, at national level, the fact that several

---

[665] A/178 (1990) EHRR 485, 22 May 1990.

[666] Commission report, 8th March 1989

[667] The applicant company had suggested in its argumentation, comparatively, that other Contracting States had more liberal rules.

Member States allow reception of uncoded television broadcasts from telecommunication satellites without requiring the consent of the authorities of the country in which the station transmitting to the satellite is situated.

The latter circumstance is not without relevance, since the other states signatories to the International telecommunication Convention and the international authorities do not appear to have protested at the interpretation of Article 22 of this Convention and the provisions of the Radio Regulations that it implies. The contrary interpretation of these provisions, which was relied by the Swiss Government by the support of the interference, is consequently not convincing. This is also apparent from paragraphs 19 and 20 of the International telecommunication Union's reply to the Governments questions."

On this basis, the Court did find that the Article 10 can be applied to the case. Consequently, after examining the facts of the case, the Court concluded that the Swiss authorities, in refusing an application to receive the programs, violated Article 10 of the Convention.

In their dissenting opinions two members of the Court[668] referred to an interesting comparative study made by the Swiss authorities, which was a basis for some kind of a *bona fide* argumentation, and argued on the basis of diversity existing between states:

"According to the interpretation prevailing at the time (ad also quite recently), Switzerland accepted that this undertaking obliged it to make authorisation for reception subject to the consent of the transmitting State, in the instant case the Soviet Union, as is clear from the replies by several foreign administrations to which Switzerland had sent a request for information (The Soviet Union of 7 February 1981, the Netherlands of July 1985, Finland of 8 July 1985, Germany of 29 August 1989). It was also in accordance with the recommendation adopted in 1982 by the European Conference of Postal and Telecommunication Administrations. Therefore Switzerland legitimately believed that it was not only authorised but obliged to make the authorisation sought by Autronic Advocate General subject to the consent of the competent Soviet authority, in order to meet its international obligations by fulfilling them as they were understood by the appropriate international organisations and the other States, particularly the State interested in the present case, the Soviet Union. In other words, as the consent of the Soviet authorities was not obtained, the refusal of authorisation which is the subject of the complaint by Autronic Advocate General could be regarded at that time as a measure necessary to prevent disorder in international telecommunications.

Even though in recent years some national administrations seem to have waived the condition of obtaining the prior consent of the transmitting State, it appears from the replies received in 1989 that this is not yet the general practice. This is proved by the international agreements signed for the creation of Entersat and Intelsat, which permit transmissions from satellites to be picked up only by specially authorised earth stations. Even if this were not the case and although ideas have changed, it cannot be used as a criterion for deciding whether there is a violation of the Convention in this case and whether the State is liable, because this question must be assessed in the light of the legal rules in force (and as understood) at the time of the relevant facts.

The fact that the ITU considers that it is for the administration of each member of the Union itself to take the 'necessary measures to prohibit and prevent the unauthorised interception of radiocommunications not intended for the general use of the public' and that every national administration is empowered 'to lay down the terms and conditions on which it grants such authorisation' means only that, in the framework of the International Telecommunication Convention and the Radio Regulations, States have some degree of discretion in deciding on suitable measures for attaining the objectives of those international rules. The grant of such discretion cannot lead to the conclusion that a measure which is taken on this basis ad appears to be perfectly suited and proportionate to the legitimate objective, viz. in casu the prevention of disorder in international telecommunications, is not necessary. Furthermore, the contested measure was not an absolute, unqualified prohibition, but a reasonable

---

[668] Mr. Binschedler-Robert and Mr. Matscher.

response to the international undertakings of the State in question and a response which took account of the legal interests of the transmitting State.
On those grounds we consider that there was no violation of Article 10".

The comparative observations refer to many different types of comparative observations. The government had produced a comparative study in order to discover a "general tendency" in different states, and this provided a grounding for good faith implementation.

However, this type of comparative argument by the other judges did not seem to persuade the Court. It found a violation of the Article. In fact, the Court rejected this argument by relying on the recent study made by the Commission, referring explicitly to different states (France and United Kingdom) from those which the party had examined (the Netherlands, Germany, Finland and the Soviet Union). The Commissions study was more recent.

The judges presenting the dissenting opinion, on the other hand, referred to this same study, and connected it to the fulfilment of international obligations. However, they refused to consider the Commission's comparative arguments to be valid, because the practice in international treaty law proved contrary to the claimed "general practice". Furthermore, the claimed generality would not be a persuasive argument, because, according to them, the breach should be examined on the basis of the "historical context". They also referred to the "subsidiary" nature of the provisions in certain international treaties in order to uphold the competence of the Swiss authorities to decide the case.

Case Müller (common principle of law in Contracting States). In *Müller and others v Switzerland*[669], the question concerned confiscation of a painting on the grounds the protection of morals. Legally it delt with the necessary restrictions of freedom of speech (artistic freedom) in a democratic society and the "*margin of appreciation*"doctrine. The Court argued comparatively concerning the rule of confiscation[670]:

"A principle of law which is common to the Contracting States *allows confiscation of items whose use has been lawfully adjudged illicit and dangerous to the general interest In the instant case, the purpose was to protect the public from any repetition of the offence."*

This comparative observation was one of the main arguments by which the Court came to its conclusion, that the Article 10 had not been infringed by the Swiss Court.

Case Observer (the European Court of Justice and constitutional traditions, international treaties, analysis of case law in the United States (concurring opinions)). In *Observer*[671] case

---

[669] A/133 (1991) EHRR 212, 24 May 1988
[670] Reference to the *Handyside* case.
[671] *Observer and the Guardian v United Kingdom*, A/216 (1991) EHRR 150, 26 November, 1991.

the question concerned the legitimacy of the action by the British Court in imposing interlocutory injunctions. The applicants, two newspapers, claimed that these restrictions upon publishing articles concerning the book "spycatcher" (which included according to the government, confidential information) contravened the freedom of expression.

A member of the European Court of Human Rights[672] referred to the decision of the European Court of Justice[673], which had held that

"as regards Article 10 of the European Convention of Human Rights...its should be noted in the first place that, as the Court has consistently held, fundamental rights form an integral part of the general principles of law, the observance of which it ensures. In so doing, the Court draws inspiration from constitutional traditions common to the Member States and from indications provided by the international treaties for the protection of human rights on which the Member States have collaborated or of which they are signatories[674]. In this connection the European Convention of Human Rights is of particular significance. It follows that, as the Court affirmed in the judgment of 13 July 1989, Wachauf, measures incompatible with the respect for the human rights their in recognized and secured are not permissible in the Community".

This member of the Court explicitly referred to another international system (the European Community and European Court of Justice), which refers, on the other hand, to the European human rights system itself and the effect of international conventions in general, and, furthermore, to the constitutional traditions of the Member States of the European Economic Community. The argument clearly attempted to establish coherence among all these systems.

This was one of the methods by which the member, unlike the Court, concluded that there had in fact been a violation of Article 10 of the European Convention of Human Rights.

In the same case, a member of the Court[675], in his dissenting opinion, referred to the case law of the Supreme Court of the United States:

"I firmly believe that "the press must be left free to publish news, what the source, without censorship, injunctions, prior restraint". In a free and democratic society there can be no room, in times of peace, for restrictions of that kind, and particularly not if these are resorted to, as they were in the present case, for 'governmental suppression of embarrassing information or ideas. (Judges Black, J , Douglas, J., In the case about the Pentagon papers, New York Times v US and US v Washington Post, 403 US 713 (1971).

On this basis this member (and the joining members) came to the conclusion, contrary to the opinion of the Court, that there had been a violation of Article 10 of the Convention during the whole period, not only during a part of the period.

In the same way, another member of the Court[676] justified his dissenting opinion with

---

[672] Mr. Petiti.
[673] Case 260/89 *Elliniki* (1991) ECR I-2925 (18 June 1991).
[674] Expressed also in the case 4/73 *Nold v EC Commission* (1974) ECR 491.
[675] Mr de Meyer, joined by Pettiti, Russo, Foighel, Bigi.
[676] Mr. Morenilla.

reference to an extensive study of US law:

"The United States case law cited by Article 19, the International Centre against Censorship has consistently held that the principal purpose of the First amendment's guarantee is to prevent prior restraints. With regard to the national security aim the US supreme court declared in Near v Minnesota (285 US 718) that: "The fact for approximately 150 years there has been almost an entire absence of attempts to impose previous restraints upon publications relating to the malfeasance of public officers is significant and deep-seated conviction that such restraints would violate constitutional right'
The other leading decisions of that Court, such as those in NEW YORK TIMES CO. LIMITED V. US (403 US 713 [1971]), LANDMARK COMMUNICATIONS INC. V. VIRGINIA (425 US 829 [1978]), NEBRASKA ASSOCIATION V. STUART (427 US 593 [1976]) and US v. THE PROGRESSIVE (486 F. Supp. 990 [1979]) have consistently required that very strict conditions ('all but totally absolute') must be satisfied before prior restraints can be imposed on the publication of information on matters related to national security. In the words of the NEBRASCA judgment, 'the thread running through all these cases is that prior restraints on speech or publication are the most serious and least tolerable infringement of the First Amendment rights. . . A prior restraint, by contrast and by definition, has an immediate and irreversible sanction. If it can be said that a threat of criminal or civil sanctions after publication "chills" speech, prior restraints "freeze" it, at least for a time.' Brennan J., concurring with the judgment, stated 'although variously expressed it was evident that even the exception was to be construed very, very narrowly: when disclosure "will surely result in direct, immediate and irreparable damage to our nation or its people".'

Case Castels v Spain (the European Parliament as a democratic body). There are many examples of references to activities of other European systems and international systems, in the form of *a fortiori* argumentation.

The question in *Castels* case concerned a withdrawal of parliamentary immunity from one member of the Spanish parliament by the Parliament, because he had written an article to press, which contained accusations against the government.[677] This resulted in a criminal prosecution and a suspended prison sentence.

A member of the Commission of the European system of Human Rights claimed in his dissenting opinion[678]:

"I think that the measure with which we are concerned comes within the margin of appreciation granted to States by the Convention. In addition, this measure does not prove to be contrary to what is necessary in a democratic society. The European parliament, which embodies 12 well established democracies, withdrew his immunity of one of the members for having expressed his views in less dangerous terms and circumstances."

Case Colman (general tendencies and developments; similarities with legislations of the past). In the case of *Colman v United Kingdom*[679] the question concerned the restrictions upon a medical professional's advertising by the General Medical Council, and the acceptance by

---

[677] A/236 (1992) EHRR 445.
[678] Mr. Martinez, L.F
[679] A/258-D (1994) EHRR 119, 28 June 1993.

the Court of the restriction.

In finding no violation of Article 10, the Commission referred to comparative law development, and to general remarks made by the Court of Appeal in its judgment of which the complaint concerned:

> *"The Commission has regard to the particular facts of the present case: the applicant was seeking to attract patients. His concern was therefore one of advertisement of his professional activity, a clearly commercial matter. There was not a blanket restriction on doctors' advertising at the material time. He was affected only by the prohibition on advertising in newspapers. From 1987 the matter was under actual review by the Government, the MMC and subsequently the GMC As the Court of Appeal observed in this case, the question of advertising in the liberal professions has undergone significant <u>developments recently</u>: Only a few years ago any form of advertising, even if only informative in content, would have been unthinkable. <u>Today it is widely accepted</u>, although still subject to some restrictions. Moreover, at the material time, <u>other High Contracting Parties to the Convention maintained similar restrictions over such advertising.</u>*
> *In the light of these considerations, and having regard to the duties and responsibilities attaching to the freedoms guaranteed by Article 10 of the Convention, the Commission finds that it cannot be said that the advertising policy of the GMC went beyond the margin of appreciation left to national authorities."*

Case Chorherr (the use of individual state system as an argument by an applicant). In the case of *Chorherr v Austria*[680] the question which arose concerned the fact that the applicant had been arrested, placed under police custody, and called to administrative criminal proceedings after he had demonstrated against the purchase of fighter aircrafts by the respondent state during a military ceremony. He had not ceased the demonstration after a request to do so.

The Court found that there was breach neither of Article 10 and Article 5.

In his reasoning, the applicant referred to the practice of the German Constitutional Court to support the idea that the arrest contravened his rights under Article 10 of the Convention:

> *"[The applicant refers] to a judgment of the German Federal Administrative Court (Bundesverwaltungsgericht) of January 1990 (Entscheidungen des Bundeswervaltungsgerichts, Vol. 84, p.297) in which the Federal Administrative Court found that a plaintiff who distributed leaflets and held up posters should not have been refused access to the Rathausmarkt in Lübeck where a military ceremony was taking place. The Court considered that if the Army uses a public place to obtain maximum publicity for itself, it must accept that critics of the army use the event as an opportunity to express their criticism."*

The Commission did not deal, as such, with the argument put forward by the applicant. However, it found that there had been a disproportionate involvement by the authorities, and that there had been a violation of Article 10 of the Convention not based on 'necessity in a democratic society'.

---

[680] A/266-B (1994) EHRR 358 (25 August 1993).

Case Informationsverein Lentia (similar factual situations, differences in laws, no genuine European model, comparable experiences, rejection of generality). In the case of *Informationsverein Lentia v Austria[681]* the applicant had been refused broadcasting licences, by the competent national authorities for the establishment of radio and television stations. This refusal was based on monopolistic legislation. The Court found a violation of Article 10.

The government had attempted to argue that a monopoly is not, as such, incompatible with Article 10. This interpretation was based on the "comparative fact" that at the time of the drafting of the Convention, monopolies were allowed in most of the states. Even if the development had been, since then, towards liberalization, no general European standard existed.

The Commission declared, in its opinion, that there had been an interference with the applicant's rights. The Commission referred to the *Groppera* case and the "comparative" observations presented therein. It maintained that monopolies still existed in many states. However, according to the Commission, the real question was not the permissibility of the system of monopolies, but rather the existing system of licencing. Because Austria had no functioning system of licencing, it infringed Article 10 of the Convention.

However, the question arose whether the state had legitimately infringed the right. The Commission made some comparative observations in order to reject the "economic difficulties" argument put forward by the Government, by which the government attempted to maintain the ´necessity´ nature of the restriction:

> *"The Government has also referred to possible economic difficulties and the emergence of new monopolies. In this respect the Commission is aware of the different solutions adopted in Convention States with regard to broadcasting in general. These solutions include systems whereby private broadcasting licences are granted within a system of public broadcasting, for instance by limiting them to special times. The possibility to obtain licences may also vary as to local, regional or nationwide broadcasting The Commission cannot therefore assume that private broadcasting would necessarily bring about the difficulties indicated by the Government."*

In his dissenting opinion, and although agreeing with the conclusion regarding breach of the Convention, one of the members of the Commission[682] explained the change in the Commission doctrine. In the present case the Commission, more or less, established a requirement of licencing system contrary to its former opinions:

> *"That [earlier] view was based in part on the fact that systems of monopolies then existed in most Member States. It is true that there has since then been a great increase in the access of individuals and organisation in particular of commercial enterprises to broadcasting facilities this has been achieved in various ways. A licensing of private broadcasters is one. Another is the making of contractual arrangements for the sake of air time to programme makers, who recoup the cost by in turn selling space to advertisers Yet another is by conferring a right of reply.*

---

[681] A/276 (1994) EHRR 93, 24 November 1993.
[682] Mr. Hall.

Though this is so, the situation remains that in some states and in some regions, monopolies still exist.
The Convention must be applied against the background of existing conditions, but it does not seem to me that the time has yet arrived when it can be held that the right to freedom of expression given by Article 10 requires Member States to provide a system under which individuals and organisations can apply for permission to establish broadcasting stations, or that an individual or body can claim that there has been a violation of Article 10 because such a system has not been introduced."

This partly dissenting opinion gives an interesting glimpse at the evolution of system of the European Human Rights and its relation to the use of the comparative method[683].

The Court referred in its reasoning to the Government´s argument, however, not being persuaded by it, and it made its own comparative observations in maintaining that a breach of Article 10 had occurred:

"In opting to keep the present system, the State had in any case merely acted within its margin of appreciation, which had remained unchanged since the adoption of the Convention; very few of the Contracting States had different systems at the time. In view of the diversity of the structures which now exist in their field, it could not seriously be maintained that a genuine European model had come into being in the meantime....
The Court is not persuaded by the Government's argument. Their assertions are contradicted by the experience of several European States of a comparable size to Austria in which the coexistence of private and public stations, according to rules which vary from country to country and accompanied by measures preventing the development of private monopolies, shows the fears expressed to be groundless."

Case Casado Coca (similar laws, international measures, liberal and general tendencies at the international level, disparity of rules in states in relation to cultural tradition, The Council of Europe as tertium comparationis). In the case of *Casado Coca*[684] the Court did not find a violation of the freedom of expression. In this case, a lawyer had been advertising his legal practice in local newspapers. This had resulted in warnings and notices to him from the competent local authorities. His complaints concerning these warnings and notices had been unsuccessful at all stages of the legal procedure. The complexity of the case inspired the parties to make comparative observations on many levels.

The government party to the dispute relied directly upon comparative observations in order to justify the 'necessity' of its action in the context of a 'democratic society':

"The Government observes that many of the States party to the Convention have restrictions on advertising by lawyers similar to those which in Spain led to the imposition of a penalty on the applicant. Moreover, the Deontological Code of the lawyers of the European Community adopted on 28 October 1988 in Strasbourg by the representatives of the 12 Bar Councils of the European Community and the Conference of European Bar Councils held on 24 May 1991 in Crakow maintained the principle of prohibiting advertising while introducing more flexible rules concerning lawyers' freedom to express themselves in the media to make a name for themselves and to participate in public debate. In line with this more liberal tendency, the Regional Council of the Catalonia Bar adopted new rules on the question leaving only certain forms of publicity still prohibited, including classified advertisements in the press,

---

[683] See also case *Marckx v Belgium* (1979-80)EHRR 2:330. (Wildhaber, Mahoney/Prebensen).
[684] A/285 (1994) EHRR 1, 24 February 1994.

advertising on radio and television. etc. "

The Commission itself did not take a standpoint regarding these comparative arguments, but maintained that the restrictions were not necessary in a democratic society, and that the infringement of Article 10 had taken place.

In their dissenting opinion, three members of the Commission[685] found no violation. They referred comparatively to the fact that "*in many of the Contracting states special restrictions have often been applied to the liberal professions, such as the legal profession*". This is why there should be a "*wide margin of appreciation*" applied. The same idea was expressed by five other members[686] who also found that no violation had occurred. They added that these practices were made "*with the aim of protecting both lawyers who do not have sufficient means to use such methods and the public as a whole*".

The Court looked into, and even accepted, the comparative argumentation made by the Government in finding that no violation of Article 10 had occurred:

> "... *Nevertheless, the rules governing the profession, particularly in the sphere of advertising, vary from one country to another according to cultural tradition. Moreover, in most of the States parties to the Convention, including Spain, there has for some time been a tendency to relax rules as a result of the changes in their respective societies and in particular the growing role of the media in them. The Government cited the examples of the Code of Conduct for Lawyers' in the European Community [Strasbourg, 28 October 1988] and the conclusions of the Conference of the European Bars [Cracow, 24 May 1991]; while upholding the principle of banning advertising, these documents authorise members of the Bar to express their views to the media, to make themselves known and to take part in public debate. In accordance with these guidelines, the new rules on advertising issued by the Council of the Catalonia Bars allow the publication of circulars or articles, including in the press. More recently, the Government have begun to study the draft of the new Statute of the Spanish Bar, which permits somewhat greater freedom in this sphere.*
> *The wide range of regulations and the different rates of change in the Council of Europe's Member States indicate the complexity of the issue. Because of their direct, continuous contact with their members, the Bar authorities and the country's courts are in a better position than an international court to determine how, at a given time, the right balance can be struck between the various interests involved, namely the requirements of the proper administration of justice, the dignity of the profession, the right of everyone to receive information about legal assistance and affording members of the Bar the possibility of advertising their practices.*"

It is interesting, how the Court fell in with the comparative argumentation produced by the Government. On this basis, the Court developed a new doctrine of a margin of appreciation of the Bar authorities. The doctrine of the margin of appreciation was no longer the doctrine to be applied only to autonomous national authorities such as courts, but, for that matter the lawyers' association as well, and perhaps also other autonomous associations.

---

[685] Mr. Danelius, Mr Frowein, and Mrs Liddy.
[686] Mr. Geus, Mr. Jörundson, Mr, Soyer, Mr. Hall, and Mr Baxter.

Case Oberschlick (conditioned by the traditions of the community, political fields of established democracies, in legal and social orders of contracting states no uniform conception of morals, general discourses). In *Oberschlick v Austria*[687], which dealt with the restriction of freedom of expression of a journalist publishing a text "containing criminal information", one of the members of the Commission of human rights[688] made a rather abstract "disparity" comparison of legal and social orders in order to arrive to a type of "subsidiarity" of systems:

> *"The borderline between the freedom of information and libel depends largely on the traditions of the community concerned. In some communities it is quite customary to use harsh language, in others one is more polite. In the political field many established democracies consider it an achievement that one can say almost anything about politicians, in other countries libellous attacks against those who perform democratic functions are seen as attacks democracy itself. To decide what expressions are defamatory and what are not we have to take into account that it is not possible to find in the legal and social orders of the Contracting States a uniform conception of morals.*

He continued with the words of the Court of human rights:

> *"The view taken of the requirements of morals varies from time to time and from place to place, especially in our area, characterized as it is by a fa-reaching evolution of opinions on the subject. By the reason of their direct and continuous contact with the vital forces of their countries, State authorities are in principle in a better position than the international judge to give an opinion on the exact content of these requirements as well as on the 'necessity' of a 'restriction' or 'penalty' intended to meet them"[689]*

Commission's member dealt in his comparison with the disparity of the legal and moral concept of *"libel"*, traditions of the social discourse, ideas of *"democratic discourse"*, *"defamation"* etc.. On this basis, he considered the idea of the *"margin of appreciation"* to be applicable to the case, and he transferred the jurisdictional competence to the national system, in particular to its judge. By reference to some other arguments, he did not ultimately find a breach of Article 10 of the Convention.

The European Court of Human Rights, in arguing for the acceptability of the journalists publication, stated:

> *"The Court agrees with the Commission that the insertion of the text of the said information in Forum (the magazine) contributed to the public debate on a political question of general importance. In particular, the issue of different treatment of nationals and foreigners in the social field has given rise to considerable discussion not only in Austria but also in other Member States of the Council of Europe."*
> *... A politician who expresses himself in such terms exposes himself to a strong reaction on the part of journalists and the public".*

---

[687] A/204 (1995) EHRR 389, 23 May 1991.

[688] Mr Schermers.

[689] Referred to by the Courts in *Müller and others v. Switzerland,* A/133 (1991) EHRR 212, and also, *Handyside v United Kingdom* (A/24) 1 EHHR 737, and the *Sunday times v United Kingdom* (No.1)A/30, 2 EHRR 245.

This argument was one of the basis for the conclusion that

"...the interference with Mr Oberschlick's exercise of his freedom of expression was not "necessary in a democratic society... for the protection of the reputation... of others".
There has, accordingly, been a violation of Article 10 of the Convention".

Case Jersild (general societal experience, general trends at the national and international levels, other international measures and their travaux preparatoires). In the case of *Jersild v Denmark[690]*, the question concerned decisions of Danish courts maintaining restrictions against the screening of a television program containing racist remarks. Both the Commission and the Court found a violation of freedom of expression.

The Government argued that there had been no infringement on the basis of comparative observations:

"The Government submits in particular that present-day actions against racist activities are based on the inter-national community's bitter experience of the dire' consequences of such acts which have led to great suffering. This phenomenon is not only something which belongs to the past but is a reality of today as recent trends in various European countries show. This had led to the adoption of declarations within the United Nations and the European Communities against racism as well as motions in the Danish Parliament condemning all forms of discrimination. The Government agree that it is desirable to give the media as free conditions as possible in order to enable them to report on what is happening in society, but this is not tantamount to giving them a free rein."

In looking over the necessity of the sentencing of the applicant, the Commission, on the other hand, took into account other international convention, which the Government had ratified and which it had referred:

"When examining the necessity of convicting the applicant for having aided and abetted the dissemination of racist remarks the Commission cannot confine itself to considering those remarks alone. As they were not made by the applicant himself, there is a particular need to look at these remarks in the light of the context of the programme and all the circumstances of the case. In this respect the Commission has taken into consideration that the Government have ratified the International Convention on the Elimination of All Forms of Racial Discrimination of 1965 whereby they are obliged to "condemn racial discrimination and undertake to pursue by all appropriate means and without delay a policy of eliminating racial discrimination in all its forms and promoting understanding among all races. ... Nevertheless, although the television programme affected the reputation or rights of others due to its discriminatory contents, a fair balance between their rights and the applicant's right to impart information must be struck. The limits of what can be accepted may vary depending on the circumstances of the case."

After analysing the relationship between the proportionality of the measures compared to the legitimate aim, the Commission found that they were not 'necessary in a democratic society', and concluded that there had been a violation of Article 10.

---

[690] A/298 (1995) EHRR 1, 23 September 1994.

In their dissenting opinion, four of the members[691] stressed comparative developments in Europe, analysed the contents of the measures subsequently adopted and focussed on developments in relation to other international measures including the European Convention:

"There can hardly be much disagreement about the seriousness of the <u>threat of racial persecution in Europe</u>. Racially motivated violence poses a <u>constant threat to the lives and security of many groups of people in the European countries</u>. At an international level, States have found it necessary to act against this threat by inter alia introducing the United Nations Convention of 21 December 1965 on the Elimination of All Forms of Racial Discrimination. In Article 4(a) of this <u>Convention</u> the States Parties have undertaken to "declare as an offence punishable by law all dissemination of ideas based on racial superiority or hatred, incitement to racial discrimination ... against any race or group of persons of another colour or ethnic origin ...". The <u>Convention was ratified by Denmark on 8 September 1971.</u>

They continued with the drafting history of the international measures and the European Convention:

"It is interesting to note, that <u>during the drafting</u> of this Convention the relationship between Article 4 and the fundamental right of freedom of speech was discussed at length. The opening paragraph of Article 4 provides that the measures the State Parties have to adopt must always have due regard to the <u>principles embodied in the Universal Declaration of Human Rights</u>. This so-called "due regard" clause was introduced by the Third Committee in order to meet objections of those who maintained that Article 4 would violate the principles of freedom of speech and freedom of association. <u>It was interpreted as</u> giving State Parties the right to understand Article 4 as <u>imposing no obligation on any party to take measures which were not fully consistent with their constitutional guarantees of freedom, including freedom of speech and association.</u>

In examining the conflicting interests of freedom of speech and the security of special groups of people, they referred again to other international measures:

"These conflicting interests were first considered during the <u>drafting of the Convention</u> on the Elimination of All Forms of Racial Discrimination and again during the preparation of Bill introducing the amendment of the Danish Penal Code and later when it was dealt with by the Danish Parliament."

Furthermore, in the course of the argument of the Danish Courts, where it discussed the lack of the balancing statements in the film, the members compared the situation to that which prevails under another pertinent international measure:

"This is very much <u>in line with the interpretation indicated in the preparatory work of the Convention on the Elimination of All Forms of Racial Discrimination and of the following amendment of the Danish Penal Code</u> which clearly were not intended to restrict scientific or otherwise serious discussion of problems of public concern."

The comparative development in Europe was ultimately taken, in the end of the reasoning, as an argument against the interpretation that the applicants would have been sole reasons

---

[691] Mr. Gaukur, Jörundsson, Sir Hall, and Geus.

for anyone experiencing racist actions:

"The assumption that the sole effect of the programme was to ridicule the persons behind the propaganda appears as purely theoretical. The fact that racism and xenophobia are <u>wide-spread in important sections of the European population</u> shows on the contrary that addresses of a clearly primitive character may be experienced as convincing, despite the lessons of the past."

Another member[692] stressed the importance of the obligation of the state to take measures:

"Article 4 of the <u>International Convention</u> on the Elimination of All Denmark Forms of Racial Discrimination, adopted by the General Assembly of the United Nations on 21 December 1965, <u>makes it obligatory for States party</u> to "declare as an offence punishable by law all dissemination of ideas based on racial superiority or hatred". <u>At international level, therefore, there has been for decades a perceived need to provide a grave sanction</u> against dissemination of racist comments, whatever the motivation of their proponents. The <u>wisdom and experience of the drafters and adopters of that Convention deserve respect.</u>"

However, she came to the conclusion that there had been no violation of Article 10, because the act of the state was proportionate to the aim pursued and it answered a pressing need in a democratic society.

In their dissenting opinions four judges[693], on the other hand, considered the value of the international convention in the interpretation of the European Convention in a different sense:

"The <u>International Convention on the Elimination of All Forms of Racial Discrimination probably does not require</u> the punishment of journalists responsible for a television spot of this kinds. On the other hand, it <u>supports</u> the opinion that the media too can be obliged to take a clear stand in the area of racial discrimination and hatred."

Furthermore, two of the judges[694] came to the same conclusion by specifying the role of the international convention in relation to the interpretation (independent from the national implementation laws):

"... in particular the 1965 Convention on the Elimination of All Forms of Racial Discrimination. That Convention manifestly cannot be ignored when the European Convention is being implemented. It is, moreover, <u>binding on Denmark</u>. It must also guide the European Court of Human Rights in its decisions, in particular as regards the scope it <u>confers on the terms</u> of the European Convention and on the exceptions which the Convention lays down in general terms."

Both groups of judges came to the conclusion that there had not been a violation of Article 10.

The Court remarked upon the applicants' and the Commission's comparative reference. Furthermore, it took a standpoint upon the use of these "comparative" analyses, when

---

[692] Mrs Liddy.

[693] Mr Ryssdal, Bernhardt, Spielman, and Loizou.

[694] Mr. Gölcüklü, Russo, Valticos.

examining the importance of the question of racial discrimination and of acting in "good faith":

> "... Nevertheless, the issue was already then of general importance, as is illustrated for instance by the fact that the UN Convention dates from 1965. Consequently, the <u>object and purpose pursued by the UN Convention</u> are of great weight in determining whether the applicant's conviction, which, as the Government have stressed, was based on a provision enacted in order to ensure Denmark's compliance with the UN Convention, was "necessary" within the meaning of Article 10(2).
> In the second place, <u>Denmark's obligations under Article 10 must be interpreted, to the extent possible, so as to be reconcilable with its obligations under the UN Convention</u>[695]. In this respect it is not for the Court to interpret the "due regard" clause in Article 4 of the UN Convention, which is open to various constructions. The Court is however of the opinion that its interpretation of Article 10 of the European Convention in the present case is compatible with Denmark's obligations under the UN Convention."

Furthermore, it maintained, in general, that

> "Bearing in mind the <u>obligations on States under the UN Convention and other international instruments</u> to take effective measures to eliminate all forms of racial discrimination and to prevent and combat racist doctrines and practices, an important factor in the Court's evaluation will be whether the item in question, when considered as a whole, appeared from an objective point of view to have had as its purpose the propagation of racist views and ideas."

On this basis, the Court came to the conclusion that there had been a violation of Article 10 of the Convention.

2.2.4. Conclusions on the European System of Human rights

On the basis of the case law. The following types of arguments related to comparative arguments in the work of the European System of Human Rights can be recognized:
– arguments pertaining the general discourse on human rights
– general societal experience
– general principles
– more general conventions
    - as illustrations
    - conventions' *travaux preparatoires* and context
– tendencies in treaty law
– participation in conventions (in general and in particular)

---

[695] This is clearly an interpretation of national law in relation to international law. The phenomenon could be called an interpretation of internationalized national law (the interpretation of national law is not allowed, but it can be done, when the national law is internationalized).

— comparable experiences
— constitutional comparisons
— tendencies in legislation
— generalities in legislations (or in example systems)
  - at the time of the examined act or in the past or in general
  - at the time when the act is examined
  - general systems
  - general norms
— the system of the party to the dispute[696]
— case law in general or in a particularly influential country
— comparative studies made by scholars
— comparative studies made by the state
— American case law and scholars
— scientific discussion
— traditions, societal experience, tendencies
— socio-phenomenological observations
— morality and functionality (national judge in better place -argument)

One could claim that the comparative reasoning in the European system of human rights seems to be, in general, an extremely value-based and rather open form of reasoning. The main form seems to be the legislative tendency and traditional legislative comparison, and observations upon the socio-political discourse. However, the United States case law seems to be valuable in problematic cases. It is usually looked into quite thoroughly. However, the existence of formal comparative observations does not necessarily indicate that an systematic study had been undertaken.

When the United States system is viewed analytically, it seems to support more progressive interpretations.

On the other hand, comparative observations do not seem to function as a context for any change. On the contrary. Comparative arguments usually support quite conservative solutions. However, occasionally, when the comparative generalities seem to "change" (develop, i.e. the system become more alike), also the doctrine of the European institution changes (interpretation by *"background of existing conditions"*, *"stages of development"*[697]), at least some opinions in the Court and Commission.

Moreover, the degree in the comparative generality seems to be related to the degree in the

---

[696] For a very good illustration of this type of analytical approach by the Court in case *Delcourt*, see van der Meersch, W.J.G., 1980, pp.325-327.

[697] On this latter point, see van der Meersch, W.J.G., 1980, p 319.

"margin of appreciation" ("*wide margin of appreciation*", "*margin of appreciation*"). On the other hand, the extreme divergencies ("*moral*") usually result in an argument "*the national judge is in better situation to decide*". In other words, the generality is usually the main argument used, though the qualitative generality plays some role. If there are differences, and these differences can be accepted, the outcome is that of "no common concept in Europe" and the "margin of appreciation".

The justification of a legal particularity due to economic necessity, related to the ´margin of appreciation' or to 'necessity in democratic society', has been breached by introducing legal disparity argument combined with argument by similar economic situation with differences in methods of legislating.[698]

It seems also that comparative reasoning may be used for and against a particular interpretation. In these types of cases, there are differences in the choices of countries (even absolutely contrary examples have been used), or a comparison may even be rejected by changing the object of comparison.

The Court seems to rely also on previous comparisons in its case law. Furthermore, cooperation between different institutional actors (the Commission, Court, and governments) in the matter of comparative studies is visible. However, as it has been noted, explicit comparative analysis rarely takes place in the Court´s justification. And if it does, the reference is highly synthetic.[699]

Compared, for example, to the European Court of Justice, the comparative discourse in the European Court of Human Rights is much more pluralistic. It demonstrates[700] how many different types of comparative interpretations it is possible with regard to the same subject matter. This brings some kind of clarity also to the substantive issue discussed, and seems to lead to an discursive type of evolution within the case law. However, it has also been claimed that the role of comparative law in the work of the Court is systematically less important in the work of this Court.

"International comparison" (comparison of international measures) is often made as well. A special feature, related to this, can be noted. It looks as if the relationship between Human Rights Convention and other international instruments relates to the extension of legal sources in interpretation. *E contrario* argumentation by another international measure has supported the inclusion of the travaux preparatoires within the practical legal sources of the

---

[698] Some analysis of the margin of appreciation, see van der Meersch, W.J.G., 1980, pp.330-331. On possible changes in this respect (toward a more universalistic approach) via institutional changes and the obligatory nature of the jurisdiction, see Martens, K.S., 1998, p.10.
  Brems, E. (1996, p.240 ff.) has analysed well the common elements and patterns of the margin of appreciation in Court's case law. She has isolated nine factors relevant for the doctrines application (ibid., p.293 ff.).
  One may say that the margin of appreciation is an extremely effective way of avoiding inter-European criticism.
[699] Also, van der Meersch, W.J.G., 1980, pp.321-323.
[700] Van der Meersch, W.J.G., 1980, p.321.

European human rights system.

From the normative point of view, one can make following conclusions.

As mentioned, it seems that comparative observations function, in general, quite conservatively. Both disparity and generality support usually the existing case law and the existing stage of legal development in national systems. The only arguments are breaking this feature are the arguments by "European supervision", some kinds of generality in more liberal attitudes, or a liberal tendencies. Furthermore, the balancing of general and individual interests may also support a progressive interpretation of human rights. Moreover, observations concerning the nonexistence of comparable law, or an observation on some kind of general sociological tendency also seem to have less conservative effect.

On the basis of interviews. Basically, the material for the comparative studies may be found in the institutions' archives.

The legal basis for in depth consultation of comparative material could be found in the rules 7:3 and 54:3 of the General Rules of Procedure of the system. The obligation to explicitly state reasons can be based on the Convention (*"judgments shall be pronounced publicly"*).

Usually systematic comparisons are not made, because if the case is in accordance with the "pattern" of the Courts case law, it is resolved on this basis. This means, basically, that where there are some differences in European practices, or there is no old case law, comparative studies are made.

External experts are not really used in this system. Sometimes statements have been requested from the UNHCR (United Nations High Commissioner for Refugees), and observations have been made concerning reports of some non-governmental organizations such as Amnesty International. They have given sociological and political perspectives to the systems studied.

The use of comparative law in the European Commission of Human Rights seems to depend on the nature of the case. The basic idea seems to be the finding of the common European standard. If there have been similar types of cases, the comparative material may be already there. However, in these types of situations the information may be checked again. In a "new" case, comparison is usually made.

Comparative observations can arise likewise in a very informal way in the internal workings of the Commission (internal consulting). This is connected to the information deriving directly from the people in the administration. In some difficult cases, the secretary and the members of the Commission can discuss comparative aspects. There is a possibility to make more thorough studies.

The comparative aspects referred to in the assembly meetings also arise spontaneously and in fragmentary form as members seek to explain certain characteristics of a system. This is often based on the personal knowledge of the member.[701]

If some studies are made, these are included in the report of the rapporteur, which makes it in collaboration with the secretary[702]. This is basically confidential material. No official reports are published on these studies, unless there is a separate reporting system established. However, these latter types of studies are not connected to any particular case in question. They are provided by the Legal department of the Council of Europe. They are used mainly to prepare recommendations and so on. There is a separate research Unit in the General Secretary. Extensive comparative studies by the Secretary have been made only couple of times during 90's.

The rapporteurs and members of the Commission do not usually undertake systematic studies themselves. However, sometimes they have made such studies individually. In the discussions in the Commission there might be comparative aspects taken up based on the information provided by each member.

The comparative information seems to be restricted to legislation and case law. The comparisons are not politically or sociologically oriented. The idea is to find the general legal situation in various states. Other information, such as that concerning the circumstances which prevail in the country, may be included, especially with regard to difficult case. This, it was mentioned, has been the case, for example, in questions dealing with the protection of private property.

The comparative information is usually related to the countries of the Council of Europe, but there have been cases, where, for example, aspects of Chinese law have been observed. European Community law is not directly consulted, though states may often use it in the course of reasoning.

Basically, there is no rule as to the extension of the study. The real constraint seems to be that of time and resources.[703]

It was claimed that parties very rarely present comparative observations in their preliminary arguments. There can be references to Courts cases, where comparative information is mentioned. However, independent studies are not usually presented. Occasionally, states present such studies, claiming mainly the generality of their system.

One could claim that the comparative studies, presented in dissenting opinions, are also part of the internal discourse of the Commission and the Court, and that comparative aspects have an important role in these internal discussions. On the other hand, the fact that the comparative observations are made in dissenting opinions is due to the fact that a member of

---

[701] See in this respect, van der Meersch, W.J.G., 1980, p.318.

[702] The rapporteur is one member of the Committee. Linguistic abilities often determine the choice of the rapporteur. The level of cooperation between the secretary and the members varies.

[703] Usually the case is dealt within 4-5 years. There is a priority system. 11 months is usually the minimum delay.

a Committee is more free to express his opinion[704]. The main opinion is usually a compromise, and the decisions follow a particular form. It is difficult to produce common comparative statements and conclusions.

Sometimes, even if the comparative study is made or comparative material discussed, it is not reflected in the justifications[705]. It was maintained that sometimes they are revealed, especially when very new interpretations are involved[706]. The reasons for the absence of comparative analysis in the justifications may be found in the general comparative nature of the system. Even if the comparative observations are there always as a background element, they are not seen the central to the justification.

As to the use of comparative observations in the justifications there seem to be no principled obstacles. The main reasons for the lack of open justification seems to be in the lack of time and in work pressures. Even if extensive studies in depth might be interesting and illuminating, there are no resources available to make them. On the other hand, parties could produce such a form, if they see in it a possibility for a convincing.

It seems that comparative perspective is necessary. This information reveals the practices of the systems, and changes in societies. This way one can achieve a certain "objective' standpoint with respect to the changes. Difficult cases are often resolved taking into account comparative aspects[707]. However, it seems to be difficult for the person working in the system to say how the comparative studies determine the results of the case.

It seems that the Committee's main task is to address arguments to the parties, and consequently, states are the audience of the decision. The formulation of the decisions seems to be based on consistency. The principles of interpretation in general derive from the Vienna Convention.

It must be also mentioned that there is a possibility for "intervening" (Article 37 of the Working procedures). Furthermore, the Secretary of the Council of Europe can request reports from the Parties to the Convention on the situation in their legislation[708].

The Court, on the other hand, seems to follow social and legal development in Europe. Comparative research ought to be undertaken but the resources are not available for this scale of analysis. The comparative reasoning in the Court seems to be often based on the members' personal knowledge on the legal system, usually with respect to his own system, apart from the information provided by the parties and the Committee and its Secretary.[709]

It was maintained that comparative aspects come into play when there seems to be a need

---

[704] This seems to apply also to the Court.

[705] eg. Criminal processes against a juvenile, Article 6, comparative study made, but not reflected in the decision.

[706] Mentioned, case on the negative right to unite, the Article 1.

[707] Case on Article 10 (source of the newspaperman).

[708] Article 57 of the Convention.

[709] See also, van der Meersch, W.J.G., 1980, pp.321-323.

to change the previous case law. This takes place in very rare cases due to the fact that case law is extensive and developments are slow[710]. The members of the Court have an occasion followed closely development in the United States. However, no systematic studies are produced on a continuous basis.

Other Treaties can also provide the context for a comparative study. Usually no external systems other than United States system are studied.

The comparative material concerning specific matter would be used if it existed. Indeed, some judges have been already expressed the need for comparative information[711].

The Court seems to argue mainly to the parties of the case, whereas dissenting opinions seem to be directed more toward the general public.

2.3. Some general conclusions

2.3.1. General remarks.

It has been observed, that comparative studies made in relation to systematic preparatory work are strictly legal in all legal orders[712]. No analysis of sociological or other material of this type was used in any of the courts. However, in the Italian Constitutional Court, the systematic studies seemed to be also connected to the contemporary political discussion of the issue. This was evidently so also with regard to the "inspirational" consultation of other systems. This type of information on the context is based on the individual knowledge possessed by the person in the administration.

On the other hand, in national systems, the use of comparative law information seems to be rare. Especially for the Italian and French [713] Supreme Courts, the idea of comparative studies seemed to be fairly alien.[714]In contrast, in Nordic systems comparative law was used and studies occasionally made. In the English Appeal Courts the use of comparative law is seen to be quite inspirational. However, due to the characteristics of the English system, the comparative observations are provided usually by the parties, and they are considered often

---

[710] Mentioning a case dealing with the problems of transsexual persons.

[711] Pekkanen, R., On the evolutive interpretation of the European Human Rights Convention [Euroopan ihmisoikeussopimuksen evolutiivisesta tulkinnasta]. In: Lakimies, 1991, p.360.

[712] It has been claimed, in the context of Community law, that the studies in each case are very concrete (Pescatore, P., 1980, p.345).

[713] The Cour Constitutionel was not studied, but from the information before the Italian constitutional court, one may assume that there is some use of comparative observations also there

[714] However, it must be noted that the extreme brevity of the justifications can give a misleading impression about the internal considerations. No indications are found either in the French scholarship (See, Interpreting Statutes, 1991).

explicitly by the judges.[715] As mentioned, in the Italian Constitutional Court the study of comparative law was quite systematic, though the system was at the developing stage.

Furthermore, the use of comparative law does not seem to be strictly systematic, and it is not based on any generalizable characteristics. There seems to be no general "European" standard for the use of comparative observations in different national courts. It is highly dependant upon the discursive forms internal to each system. In regional organizations, especially in the European Court of Justice, the use of comparative law is more systematic than in national systems. This will be discussed in detail below.

One can note that comparative information is consulted, where an 'international" or more general element is embedded within the case. In this sense, one could claim that national courts use comparative law in cases, where there is a practical institutional or legal connection to the regional or international organizations. However, this is not necessarily so. The interpretative processes build into the regional systems and the direct applicability of the decision in these systems may reduce, on a contrary, the use of comparative law information, even if the claim was by many interviewed that the internationalization and integration of law may increase the need for comparative law. This does not, however, seem to be the case in the English courts. They tend to compare both international and national solutions in the course of their argumentation.

On the other hand, the fact that the use of comparative observations was quite *ad hoc* supports the argument that they are used in situations where there are certain fundamentally problematic issues at stake.

It is nearly impossible to make observations on the issue of the extent to which comparative material is used inspirationally in order to find arguments for internal or external justifications. Furthermore, the true extent of the use of the comparative law in internal discussions is also behind the scenes. However, many interviewed persons stressed the fact (likewise in the European systems) that those, who have personal experience and knowledge from their "external" work, use these comparative aspects at times, both within internal discourse of the court and in "coffee-table" discussions. This use seems to be connected to their studies, visits to conferences, personal reading etc.[716]

The fact that the comparative observations were strongly based on the personal endeavour of the individual actors supports the idea that comparative observations are used as instruments to find arguments for different types of institutional discourses.

---

[715] The reason for the use of comparative observations in English courts in relation to application of European Community Law may be also due to the fact that in the Common Market Law Reports, starting from the first number, there has occasionally been translations of a body of case law from other European Countries (mainly from Germany and France). At least in the beginning, they were translated quite literally in order to stress the distinctiveness of the foreign decisions, the peculiarities of that foreign system, and the characteristics of its methods of interpretation of Community Law. (I owe thanks to Mr. Neville Hunnings for the discussion in the F.I.D.E. congress in Helsinki, where these points came up.)

[716] On this, see Markesinis, B., 1993, p.622 ff.

One key difference in terms of personal orientation was found between those judges who were professional researches and those who were not. The role of comparative aspects are - thought of more frequently by the judges who are engaged with academic tasks and have academic interest in the subject. Furthermore, those who worked on the preparatory stages of the case had considered more carefully the role of comparative observations.

In certain systems there are tendencies to look toward certain systems. The judges in the major European countries are oriented towards other major European legal systems (eg. England toward France and Germany, Germany toward France etc.). The "minor" European legal systems do not seem to really appear as sources for the considerations.

However, in some cases the observation depends on the substance of the matter.[717] This means that there is some *a priori* knowledge of the rules of another system, which has been discussed in public.

In regional systems, studies seemed, at least formally, to take into account all systems of the Member States. However, this idea is not really supported by the analysis of the justifications in these systems. Restrictions in argumentation seem to be ultimately extremely value-based and selective. The orientation may depend on many things. One thing their particular cultural point of view[718]. Another aspect is the systems' specific legal-historical connection.

However, the obstacles for the orientation, in national legal systems, do not seem to differ greatly from each other. The basic problems were seen to be concerned with linguistic competencies. The existence of resources (and time) seemed also to be a major obstacle.[719]

There seems to be always some kind of legal cultural sphere of operation, which is not abandoned. No *a priori* obstacles seemed to exist for the examination of more distant legal systems. Still, these systems were not studied. The main concern seemed be related to the

---

[717] There were some cases, in which abortion cases from the Danish system were considered as a source of inspiration. This seemed to be based on the extensiveness of the discourse on the subject in Denmark.

[718] Also Bredimas, A., 1978a, 1978b.

[719] There exists, for example, a Convention by the Council of Europe on Information on Foreign law (1968, Eur.T.S. no. 62, Council of Europe, European Conventions and Agreements II (Strasbourg 1972), Additional Protocol No. 97 (1978). It is a convention on the "horizontal" *ad hoc* information-providing.
The Convention applies to civil and commercial law and to the law of judicial organization. The request can be made by judicial authority, and only where proceedings have been instituted. This is limiting the scope of its application. The Additional Protocol has extended it to apply also to criminal, criminal procedure, and legal aid and advice. The Additional protocol extents the right to request information also to authority or person acting on behalf of a person within official systems of legal aid or advice. Furthermore, the request can be made also where the institution of proceedings is envisaged.
The application can be extented by the parties The Convention has been ratified also by other states than by European Council states.
Similar types of provisions on information-providing can be found in many European Council Conventions in the field of tax law, penal law, public and international law.
Furthermore, the application of the norms in this Convention has possibly changed due to the internet and databases. In fact, a convention on the database-keeping would be needed.
Regarding the idea that these type of Conventions do not have an effective application, David, R., 1981, p.196, Legeais, R., 1994, p.353. David maintains that basic knowledge have to exist in order to be able to send questionnaires, for example (ibid.). On different information sources, ibid. p.197 ff.

legal development of in European states and the United States. Japan was mentioned, especially with respect to competition law. This may be also due to the extent of the commercial relationships (argumentation based on attempt to justify persuasively those cases involving interests of a party coming from a distant country).

The premises in English law, most likely because of its commonwealth connections, differs considerably from other European systems.

2.3.2. Some analysis

Different types of formulations of comparative reasoning can be identified. There has been argumentation, for instance, by *"neighbouring states"*, *"leading legal systems"*, *"culturally similar"* states, *"surrounding states"*, *"over a large area"*, *"tendencies"* etc., and many more types listed in the conclusive chapter on the European human rights system.

Different types of restrictions make different approaches possible. A more ideological-functional approach makes larger adoptions possible. On the other hand, a more historical approach restricts the adoptions only to those features which derive from purely historical unity[720].

Why is it so that in state systems comparisons are not generally used as arguments?

A major factor could be that national courts try to maintain their internal political "formal" integrity. National law is the main feature of this formal political integrity. Another law cannot be used openly, for fear it would jeopardise the nature of the law as a basic element of this political integrity ("constitutionalism", etc. (the legal-political aspect). On the other hand, one could claim that this is simply based on the fact that the national discourse, even if sometimes analytically restricted, is linguistically the only sensible approach to law (the legal-cultural aspect).

Consequently, could one say that in those systems where the comparative arguments are used, the political integrity of the system is not based on the formality of law? Or, is political integrity through law somehow something different, and consequently, the idea of formality thus also differs?

In the English system, there seems to be a tradition of using "foreign law" in justifications, whereas in many "constitutionalist" systems this type of use does not appear, at least not openly. The concept of law, in functional sense, seems to be different. One could claim, for example, that in the English system the institutional and historical interpretation functions in guaranteeing legal-political integrity. This is not only based on the positive form of law. This type of national system can be called "discursive" and not legally political in a strictly

---

[720] Kisch, I., 1981, pp.165-166.

formal sense. The argumentation is not necessarily restricted on the basis of some national systematic "legalistic" premise. At the same time, it seems to stress the discursively autonomous nature of the adjudication (i.e. autonomy from other autonomous institutions within the system). This seems to be the feature of the European system of human rights too probably also because of the discursive character of its procedure.[721]

Finally, one may observe that in systems where comparative law has been defined explicitly as a source of law and its bindingness is *a priori* defined, this seem to result in its non-analytical use. Namely, the fact that the comparative generality has been legally accepted as a legal premise makes it possible to approach legal justification by referring directly to the general principles without making any contextual analysis in a given situation.

Next there is some discussion on "hard cases" within European level systems. These cases chosen deal with the forms of political and economic sovereignty from the point of view of European law.

3. "HARD CASES" AND THE COMPARATIVE LIMITS OF EUROPEAN LAW

3.1. Introduction

It has been already noted that traditional horizontal comparisons are related to the basic legal constructions and principles at the supra-national level and that they are frequently connected to the tradition in international and regional systems. However, these comparisons are based on some traditional conceptions of legal sources of legal arguments. Traditional comparison includes only the traditional structures of the legal systems' sources such as rules, cases and limited interpretations of that society according to the traditional standards of reasoning.

The alternative approach, perhaps more profound and more "hard case" related comparison is involved when one arrives at the frontiers of the modern European legal order, in social, philosophical, practical, and legal terms. Here the comparative argument extends towards concrete sociological, moral and philosophical-practical argumentation, which tends to deviate from traditional comparative argument.

The following cases are concerning, it seems, with the internal problems but also the

---

[721] This may change, to a certain extent, when the establishment of the new single Court of Human Rights is practically actualized. Changes discussed in the Human rights information bulletin, No.41, an update on human rights activities within the Council of Europe, July-October 1997, Council of Europe, p.76 on the action Plan and the Protocol No. 11 to the European Convention of Human Rights. These changes came into force at the end of 1998.

"structure" of developing European law. The question is about the issue of respective competences between the supranational, national, and other types of traditional forms of organization, as decided on a legal basis by a supranational body. The question no longer seem to be about the "easy" case of comparative "construction", a confirmation of the existence of a traditional legal norm and on the need to convince an international, regional, and national legal audience on this fact. The question seems to be instead about the competence of an institution and a legal system as such, a choice of "law", or rather a "legal system". In this sense, one is confronted with legal cultural questions.

3.2. Value based comparative reasoning

3.2.1. Hard case I (The Otto Preminger Institute in the European system of human rights) (blasphemy, no general conception of blasphemy, "no uniform conception of morals", morals as tertium comparationis, integrity of the legal system, the argument of comparison by opposites, acceptance of the "margin of appreciation", "common supervision", "common understanding of images", "no general functionality of religion")

General remarks. The *Otto Preminger Institute* case[722] in the European system of human rights dealt with freedom of expression. An Austrian association had been announcing a series of public showings of a satirical film of an Austrian artist, with a religious subject matter. Criminal proceedings were instituted, and the film was seized and later forfeited. The criminal proceedings were, however, ultimately dropped. On the other hand, although the forfeiture and seizure were originally effected in the Tyrol area, their application was extended, permanently, to Austria in general.

The applicants argued that the seizure and the forfeiture of the film contravened Article 10 (freedom of expression) of the European Convention of Human Rights.

Context of justification. The Commission found a violation of the principle of freedom of expression[723] based mainly on the ideas of "artistic" methodology, limited publicity, and the general applicability of the restrictions in Austria.

In finding no violation of freedom of expression in relation to the forfeiture (but not the seizure of the film) and in defining the scope of the *"margin of appreciation"*, three members of the Commission argued with the words of the European Court of Human Rights in the case

---

[722] A 295-A (1995) EHRR 34, 20 September 1994

[723] Seizure: nine to five, forfeiture: 13 to one. Similar suggestions in relation to the announcement were made by the Austrian Advocate General.

of *Müller*[724]:

> *"With regard to "morals" the Court noted that there was no uniform European conception: the view taken of the requirements of morals varies from time to time and from place to place, especially in our area, characterized as it is by a far-reaching evolution of opinions on the subject. By the reason of their direct and continuous contact with the vital forces of their countries, State authorities are in principle in a better position than the international judge to give an opinion on the exact content of these requirements as well as on the 'necessity' of a 'restriction' or 'penalty' intended to meet them".*

What the Court in *Müller* and the members of the Commission in *Otto Preminger* analysed was the "common morality of Europe" in comparative terms. However, they found that no such uniform concept exists.

This "disparity" of "European morality" was based on differences in *"time and place"* (geographical and historical perspectives), which, according to the Court, is typical to *"our area"* (socio-philosophical argument).

On the other hand, the *"margin of appreciation"* granted to the Austrian Courts was based on the idea that the Austrian Court, or rather <u>judges</u>, function or work in that particular culture where the *"forces"* (environment or culture) of the society are seen or experienced more "authentically" (phenomenological argument). This seemed to be based on the fact that the contact with these *"forces"* was *"continuous and direct"* unlike the contacts with international judges. There was a premiss that the factuality surrounding the normative decision-making can better be analysed by a person living in direct contact with that cultural sphere.

The members of the Commission continued:

> *"It is out of any proportion as an attack against religious feelings and <u>the common understanding of the image</u> of Jesus Christ prevailing in countries, where the majority of people belong, at least formally, to the Christian religion, an image which has prevailed over centuries in objects of art and in the public life of the society in the Tyrol. The presentation of the Jesus Christ in the film as announced would have violated the rights of others who believed in Jesus".*

The following argument was, in other words, based on the comparison of religions (comparative religion argument). This was backed up by the idea of the historical continuity of religious ideas and historical religious culture. This represented kind of integrity of religion as a cultural image, and the role of integrity of religion as a social phenomenon. Furthermore, this was backed up by sociological statistical argumentation. Finally, it involved the assertion of the right to the inviolability of the religious sphere.

The same ideas appeared in the "phenomenological" and value-based argument of another

---

[724] See dissenting opinion of Mr Ercamora, F., Weitzel, MM.A., Loucaides, L., case *Müller and others v Switzerland*, A/133 (1991) EHRR 212.

member of the Commission[725]:

"Religion does not play the same role in every society in Europe. The protection, which a State may, or must, grant to a religion therefore varies from place to place. Much should be left to the discretion of the national, or even the local authorities."

In both these opinions, the idea of "disparity of morality", and the authority deriving from it is connected to the disparities of geography and history, which, on the other hand, is a legitimation of the authority of a "social-systemic" national judge to make authoritative decisions.

Surprisingly enough, at the same time, the comparative generality of religious understanding was found in the countries having, *"at least formally"*, a common Christian religion. According to them, there was comparatively common understanding of this matter in European institutions, which gave to them the possibility of granting competences to the national judge in this sphere and approve the actions taken by them.

It seems that the value-based phenomenological understanding of this common religion, according to the Commission members, made it possible for European institutions to understand the affront to religious feelings and to maintain that action by national authorities was acceptable. On the other hand, the lack of any common morality resulted in the *"incompetence"* of the European institutions to make such decisions, and this forced them to leave the decision-making regarding the collision of various religious, moral and legal ideas to the national judge. According to these members of the Commission, the work of the artists and the publisher of the work would have disregarded the others religious rights in that area. From this perspective it appears as if the members established another right, namely, the right to the protection of religious feelings. This collided fundamentally with the freedom of expression.[726]

On this basis, the members of the Commission thus came to a conclusion to allow a *"margin of appreciation"*.

The comparison undertaken by the members was relatively extensive in sociological and philosophical terms. They strived to take into account every possible aspect of society in their decision-making, all the possible ingredients of comparative law. They presented different levels of social life in analysing the situation comparatively. However, their analysis was

---

[725] Mr Schermers, H.G.

[726] This become explicit in the dissenting opinion of Mrs. Liddy:
"...led me to the conclusion that the seizure answered a pressing social need for the "prevention of disorder" in a locality at the relevant time, rather than being necessary for the protection of the "rights of others"".
Similar ideas can be seen in the dissenting opinion of some judges of the Court (Pekkanen, Palm, Makaczyk):
"The need for repressive action amounting to complete prevention of the exercise of freedom of expression can only be accepted if the behaviour concerned reaches so high a level of abuse, and comes so close to the denial of the freedom of religion of others, as to forfeit for itself the right to be tolerated by the society."

strongly value-based. They did not attempt to really analyse the situation in strictly legal terms, but relied, instead, on the phenomenological and holistic observations which derived from their own cultural background. This way they arrived at the appropriate level of restriction upon the freedom of expression against religious feelings and established their "European" authority of the case.

Another type of analysis was related to the analysis presented by one of the same members of the Commission:[727]

> *"I find it difficult to accept a general European notion of blasphemy. Like many other words this word should be read in the context of the cultural tradition of the community concerned. It may well be that the same expression is blasphemous in one community, and not so in the other. I agree with the majority of the Commission, that Article 10 is applicable to the case, but in my opinion Article 10(2) justifies the interference. It was prescribed by law and it served the legitimate aim. As to the question whether it was necessary in democratic society opinions may differ... In my opinion the circumstances of this case sufficiently justify them to so conclude."*

This type of comparative argument studies only the legal generality of the concept of blasphemy, which was seen, consequently, to be differently understood throughout Europe. In these circumstances, the competence to decide the case rested on national authorities (a type of subsidiarity), and thus no violation was found. This argumentation also remains situational, and does not rely on any holistic societal analysis.

Justification. In analysing the forfeiture and seizure of the film and what constitutes a necessary restriction in a democratic society, the Court of Human Rights used a comparative argument in the following way in determining the content of the principle of *"margin of appreciation"*:

> *"As in the case of "morals", a concept linked to "rights of others", it is <u>not possible to discern throughout Europe a uniform conception</u> of the significance of religion in society[728]; even within a single country such conceptions may vary. For that reason it is not possible to arrive at a comprehensive definition of what constitutes a permissible interference with the exercise of the right to freedom of expression, where such expression is directed against the religion of others. A certain margin of appreciation is therefore to be left to the national authorities in assessing the existence and extent of the necessity of such interference."*

The Court's argumentation was also phenomenological. It took for granted, without any real analysis, the idea of the disparity of morals and religious feelings.

However, one may say that the Court, to a certain extent, defined more clearly the content of the idea of "morals". It maintained that in the case of morals, one is speaking about a relationship of two rights. In other words, in case where morals are involved, the right has to be examined in relation to this other right. This supported the idea presented by three of

---

[727] Mr. Schermers, H.G..

[728] The Court referred to the *Müller* case (1991) EHRR 212.

the Commission members.

On the other hand, the extension of the "*margin of appreciation*" was to be related to the evaluation of the "*circumstances*". This seemed to relativize strongly the norm underlying the decision. It seemed as if the importance of the freedom in question would demand that the solution be different.[729] In the end, the substantive solution was based also on the idea that the *national judge was better position to decide than the international judge*".

According to the Court, the forfeiture and the seizure were legitimate, and no violation of the freedom of expression had taken place.[730]

Some further analysis. In this case, the European Institutions argued by reference to "circumstantial" arguments (cultural, social, and phenomenological). By introducing these "circumstantial" arguments, the Court confirmed that the "meaning" of the same forms of human rights principles may be different throughout Europe.

This case could be analysed in many ways. One could claim that the fact of the statistical Catholic "majority" (*"in the Tyrol 87%, in Austria 78%"*) and the desire to protect the religious and social subsystem, with the help of a "*right to religion*" argument, were simply means of maintaining the subsystem as a functionally accepted subsystem in the society. As the Court maintained, the question is only a "*social need for the preservation of the religious peace*". In this way there was an attempt to maintain the general functionality of the social system.[731] In this sense, the analysis, at first sight, reveals deep historical, philosophical and social understanding of the roots of the cultural conflicts in that particular area.[732]

However, one may make another type of legal-functional analysis of the situation.

It looks as if the criticism of the artist was directed against a social institution in general. This critique was not based on any factual (at least not explicit) violation of anyone's rights in any concrete sense (whatever had happened in the past). Consequently, one may see the critique of the individual as a functionalist critique against the prevailing institutionalized religion and the church. As it was claimed in the description of the work in the announcement, religion (and the church) may have an oppressive function in society. Concerning the distributor of the film, no intentions other than commercial and discursive ones can be discerned.

Because the critique seemed to be directed against this religious "system" in society and was not related to any "real" oppression, the artist did not produce any indication or examples of the oppressive functions and acts directed against him or against any other person in any

---

[729] This referred, in this regard, to the case of *Informationsverein Lentia and others v Austria* A/276 (1994) EHRR 93.
[730] The Court voted six to three.
[731] Mrs. Liddy.
[732] The statistical argument was, naturally, very persuasive - especially in relation to the Austrian audience.

concrete sense. If there were some illustrations of this nature, the examples remained unclear. The functionalist critique in the work seems to remain "abstract" as in all artistic production. The critique is directed against the social institution rather than any of its concrete functions.

The normative idea in the case seemed to be that if the individual does not recognize the functionalist traditionality of the prevailing religion, and if this traditionality seems to have a rationale in this society, the functions of this religious entity and community are protected in the abstract. Furthermore, it looks like as if the national judge saw the function of this religious group as a main element in the functioning of the society, as some members seemed to view it in the European institutions. These types of religious ideas were considered to be essential in maintaining the coherence of the society. This is why the integrity of the person seemed to be defendable also in the terms of individual religious rights.

However, the abstract nature of the critique could have resulted also in an idea that no individuals were really harmed. In this sense, the involvement of individual rights of expression, which evidently were at stake, seemed simply to constitute a protection of the institutionally prevailing religion and the "symbolic" system.

Nor does the idea of a functionalist abstract critique fit well with the ideas of the European Court, according to which the state judge is in a better position than the national judge to evaluate the situation (because being "*better placed*").[733] Namely, it is likely that national judges may be more sensitive to the discursive integrity of the system, but in this case the discourse is, in many ways, restricted. The question is not necessarily about any "*vital forces*" of the society in any dynamic and discursive sense.

Furthermore, against this background, it is difficult to understand, why the Austrian courts, and some members of the Commission, seemed to maintain that the functionalist critique oppresses also the religious rights of some individuals in that particular religious society, namely, a "*right to freedom of religion and conscience*". On the other hand, the "*religious feelings*" argument reduced the question to the subjective level without any societal analytical aspects.

Consequently, it could be maintained that the Court seemed to compare two functional systems, the Austrian and European human rights one. It recognized the extension of the religious functional system ("in the Tyrol area", and Austria in general), and concluded that religion has a function in that particular system. However, the problem is that the basic principle of the European Court seemed to be the idea that a functionalist critique against a culturally institutionalized social group cannot be made in such an abstract way, and nor can it be made empirically. In other words, the protection of this form of social grouping and religious feelings was granted on a quite abstract basis. There was a strong idea of this type of religious institution as an historical "fact", as some members of the Commission suggested.

---

[733] However, the prevailing forces are, in terms of this idea, connected directly to the legal institution.

The idea comes close to the protection of a religion as such, and to the protection of a social grouping and its social functionality in general. This functionality of that particular religion was seen to be rational within society. The abstract criticism of this prevailing form of functionality was seen as "weaker".

The decision seems to establish a very obscure religious right based on the historical-rational functionality of a grouping in society. This right seems to override the individual right of expression. It seems to move in some meta-level of European legal culture.

"Morality" and procedural polycentrism. In the context of this case, there seems to be some kind of moral autonomy of a national legal system. What is remarkable is also the national-religious connection established in this case. Reasoning based on legal coherence is not applied, but the normative system is contrasted and compared based on the non-comparability of its social autonomy. The national system is analysed with respect to highly extensive philosophical and quantitative sociological terms. The analyses go through a variety of socio-philosophical questions. The comparison constructed and maintained, in a way, some static and permanent systemic identities based on certain societal functions. It confirmed also the cultural particularities.

One of the central explicit arguments appearing in this case is the idea of '*societal peace*'.

It is quite extraordinary that societal peace is used as an argument in this case. The conflict between societal actions evaluated in the case may cause, according to the European judges a breach of the societal *"religious peace"*. Furthermore, even if the international judges do not seem to be competent to decide the case, they seem to be well aware of the conditions of the society in question.

The claim based upon the disparities which exist between legal and social systems based on morality argumentation has certain characteristics.

First of all, the claim of moral non-comparability establishes morality as a valid legal argument. Secondly, the claim of "moral" disparity between social systems, as a form of "comparison by opposites", is an extremely instrumentalist type of argumentation. The law, in this latter sense, is seen as an instrument of morality, which, nevertheless, is divergent. The problem is, naturally, who's morality one is speaking of ?

The non-comparability of morality is a form of argumentation, which refers to the basic "social life -formative" values of the system, but for that matter also to its recognition. It appears as if there is an establishment of the logic that as no common morals exits, particular morals prevail. To a certain extent, the case recognizes a polycentric form of European law, where the intensity of the national legal system, in representing certain normative standpoints, seems to define the scope of "European law".

In theoretical terms this phenomenon looks interesting. The argumentation seems to be based on some kind of a "saving operation" of the state paradigm of law prevailing. Namely, when the supranational institutional system maintains that the particular state legal system can keep its method of regulation without regarding that type of regulation universalizable norm (or "Europeanizable" norm),[734] it looks as if the Court similarly maintains that the national system is not universalizable (or "Europeanizable") as a legal system. This, theoretically, is a step out from the paradigm of (European) law! This would put the constitutional traditions under a heavy pressure.

This problem is solved by the Court (or by the majority of judges) by explaining the deviance as to be based on particular nature of European morality. Here the question of universalizability of a state paradigm is maintained by associating the universalizability of a state system to the moral evaluation. The conflict between the state paradigm of law and the particular state system, in abstract, is solved by moral argumentation.

Moreover, because this morality seems to be particular in Europe, it does not mean that morality as such would be particular. Consequently, here it is European institutional argument.[735]

The strategy of some other judges was to analyse the problem as a question of correct interpretation of a legal form, while some others considered it to be a matter of policy. I think this gives a quite interesting example of the difference conceptions of law in Europe.

Finally, one cannot avoid making the observation that the approach by the Court appears quite absurd[736]. However, it does seem to be well adaptable to the postmodern and polycentric idea of international and regional law, where the decision-makers in adjudicative processes seem to be the representatives of legal discourses. By this polycentrism any political "burden" of the international, regional, and more particular community is avoided. The international community is institutionally and legally declared disparate. Consequently, with these types of reasoning, any criticism from the point of view of another particular state, for example, is avoided[737].

---

[734] This concerns also the dissenting opinions.

[735] In the context of legal theory, this operation transfers the question to be about a conflict between the universalizability of a legal system and universalizability of morals (in legal context). In other words, this European institution is transforming the legal discussion to be a moral discussion by making the distinction between particularity of the European morals vs. morals in general. This way one maintains the universalizability of the state-paradigm of law and the morality as the basis of this paradigm.

This strategy defines one idea of the state paradigm of law.

[736] A question may come up concerning the moral disparity within the European system. The problem is, however, that a moral disparity arises in a philosophical sense. If one have to speak about morality in some legal-institutional sense, one could perhaps refer to ethics or custom.

[737] It looks as if it is exactly in this "turn" from the generality to particularity, where the "morals" seems to "be" in this case. It seems that morally the generality is seen to be absurd from the point of view of the particular. One goes from the general traditionality to particular traditionality (in human rights).

Politically, this seems very communitarian idea. One can legitimately ask, is there a turn here, which is typical to European Human Rights thinking at the moment. Furthermore, legal philosophically the idea seems to be related to some kind of postmodern polycentrism. As a normative idea, it is characterized by universal particularity. One may wonder how this philosophy suits to the idea of Human Rights.

In legal terms, the question seems to be, in the end, a matter of recognition of the coherence of the Austrian (legal) system. Namely, the fact that three stages of court procedures maintain the solution, where the public authority actions are declared compatible with Austrian law seems to suggest that the European Court was influenced by this type of unanimity. This seems to be the empirical basis for the idea of "*a national judge being better placed to make a legal decision*". The case seems to be based on a functional, legally institutional "will theory" of state law. This functionality is related to the fact that the consensus appeared in adjudicative form.

Consequently, what is really the "*margin of appreciation*"? In these terms, the "*margin of appreciation*" seems based on the fact that several levels of Court procedure agree on a certain question. Consequently, one can ask legitimately, what comes first in the European Court of Human Rights in a case; the idea of moral incomparability or the "will of the state" established in the intensity of the national courts in defending the breach of the right? Is the first determined by the second, or vice versa? Or, does one speak about absolute disagreement internal to the European institution. In the latter case at least, the reference to morality go too far. Institutional disagreement does not seem to be a question of morals.

Because the question seems to be about the lack of general moral standards, as expressed by the Court, one may perhaps assume the prevailing idea of particular morals as being determining factors, related to the intent of national legal solutions. Empirically, the problem seems to be related to the idea of the integrity of the legal system as morality, at least in the European Court of Human Rights.

One may also wonder when looking into the substance of the case, how this type of protection of "religious feelings", granted in this case is possible at the same time European society full of many forms of oppression in many other social sectors. Moreover, one can ask, whether, because of the particular nature of the case, the application of this case should be, as has been done, restricted only to that particular society. One should refrain from extending any of the analysis, presented in the case, to other social systems. In this sense, the cases of "*marginal appreciation*" related to the "*national judge being better qualified to adjudicate*" and that fact that "*no uniform European conception of morals exists*" seem to take on some kind of normative (even strongly disintegrative) value in European law.[738]

---

[738] Some analysis of the case may be found also in Grabenwarter, C., 1995, pp.128-165. He maintains that the Court does not discuss in detail the content and the purpose of the film. Furthermore, the emphasis of the regional circumstances by the Court is remarkable, especially in terms of the use of statistical information. Basically his criticism is related to the extension of the justification.

3.2.2. Hard case II (Bachmann in the European Court of Justice) (the discrimination on the basis of nationality, maintenance of the disparity of national legal systems because of the "cohesion of a legal system")

Introduction. This case dealt with the question of the compatibility of the Belgian tax provisions with Community law.[739]

The basic question, presented by the Belgian Court to the European Court in the realm of the Article 177 (the new Article 234, preliminary ruling), was the following:[740]

> *"Are the provisions of Belgian revenue law relating to income tax pursuant to which the deductibility of sickness and invalidity insurance contributions or pension and life insurance contributions is made conditional upon the contributions being paid 'in Belgium' compatible with Articles 48, 59 (in particular the first paragraph thereof), 67 and 106 of the Treaty of Rome?"[741]*

Even if the main task of the Court was not to

> *"make any declarations as to the compatibility of the rules of national law with Community law, ... it may provide the national court with all relevant guidance as to the interpretation of Community law, with the view to enabling that court to assess the compatibility of those rules with the provisions of Community law mentioned."*

The Advocate General based his argument mainly on the previous case law of the Court[742]. However, certain interesting comparative observations were presented which had a direct connection to the results of the case. Also some premisses concerning the use of comparative law, which had been expressed in the previous case law, were restated[743].

Context of justification. The basic "comparative law" starting point for the Advocate General, in his opinion, was that the comparative disparity of the laws in question in different legal systems is an irrelevant argument in the case. He maintained that the problems in this case related to free movements

> *"...does not arise, strictly speaking, from any disparities between national laws.[744]*

---

[739] Case C-204/90 *Hanns-Martin Bachmann v. Belgian State* (1992) ECR I-249, Opinion of Mr Advocate General Mischo delivered on 17 September 1991.

[740] As in other cases, I will not go into the details of the facts of the case.

[741] Free movement of persons workers, equal treatment, freedom to provide services, restrictions, deductibility from taxable income of certain contributions relating to the insurance of individuals, deductibility conditional on payment to an organization established in the territory where the tax is levied, possible justification of the restriction by reason of the need to safeguard the cohesion of the tax system.

[742] Joined opinions of Advocate General Mischo delivered on 17 September 1991 on case 204/90 *Hans-Martin Bachmann v Belgium State* (1992) ECR I-249, and 300/90 *Commission v Kingdom of Belgium* (1992) ECR I-305.

[743] For example 120/78 *Cassis de Dijon* (1979) ECR 649.

[744] This was related to the *Cassis de Dijon* case.

The question became a matter of vertical comparison between Community law and Belgian law.

However, the Advocate General made some comparative remarks, but based his observations on the remarks presented by Denmark and the Netherlands in the course of proceedings. He maintained that

"... in those countries the tax exemption of insurance contributions was inextricably linked to the taxation of the capital created at the time when the capital is paid out. That system is regarded in those countries as a carrying over of liability to tax. The insurance companies are obliged to retain the tax at source and to pay it over to the state, to which they are liable to make such payments. Consequently, the legislation has been brought into force requiring such tax to be paid even where the policy-holder no longer resides in the country at the time when the capital is paid out'.

and he concluded after this remark that

"There is thus a strong temptation to conclude that the Belgian legislation is objectively justified by the need to prevent tax evasion."

Furthermore, remarks were made on the fact that

"In the Netherlands, where similar legislation exits, a person finding himself in the [similar] situation would be able to deduct his insurance contributions from his income tax."

This argument was combined with the argument presented by the Belgium government on the existence of the bilateral tax treaties between Belgium and some other countries, which would make it possible to deduct the contributions in question. Furthermore, the relationship between countries with certain types of systems would have resolved the tax evasion problem. However, the tax evasion argument by the government was rejected.

Consequently, for the Advocate General, the question seemed to become a question of the vertical relationship between this comparative generality and the general provisions of Community law. However, the Advocate General found an unconditional violation of the central provisions of the Treaty.

Justification. The Court agreed explicitly with the argument, which presented comparative information regarding the bilateral tax treaties. Unlike the Advocate General, it found a justification for the derogation from the Treaty:

"It is true that bilateral treaties exist between certain Member States, allowing the deduction for tax purposes of contributions paid in a Contracting state other than that in which the advantage is granted, and recognizing of the power of a single state to tax sums payable by insurers under the contracts concluded with them. However, such a solution is possible only by means of such conventions or by the adoptions by the Council of the necessary coordination or harmonization measures".

The fact that the bilateral conventions seemed to be aiming at ensuring the cohesion of the tax systems led the Court to observe that the provisions of the Belgian type

> "*are justified by the need to ensure the cohesion of the tax system of which they form part, and that such provisions are not, therefore, contrary to the Article 48 of the Treaty.*"

Some analysis. Basically, the problem in the case was related to the different treatment of Community actors according to their nationality (whether legal or natural persons). This may not even be, according to Court case law, indirect[745]. The basic rule is that discrimination on the basis of nationality is not permissible.

Consequently, the problem in the case was that national provisions examined in the case may lead to the "*detriment of those workers who are, as a general rule, nationals of other Member States*". This was related to the idea that usually the persons who move maintain insurance which they have had in their country of origin, especially life insurance. On the other hand, the Court concluded that provisions of this kind "*operate to deter those seeking insurance from approaching insurers established in another Member State, and thus constitute a restriction of the latter's freedom to provide services.*" In this sense, the legislation discriminates also against legal persons of this type.

The idea of the Belgian government was that there is no "factual discrimination", because, first of all, the question is about non-taxable income, and secondly, the idea of non-deductibility could be based on the public interest (monitoring interest, cohesion of the system). These arguments were not fully accepted by the Advocate General and the Community Court.

The Court maintained, however, that even if the basic rule was non-discrimination, in some circumstances the decisions can indirectly discriminate against nationals from different countries, especially in the field of tax law[746]. However, this type of argument cannot be the basis of the decision as such, but the distinction between different nationals must be related to the cohesion of the legal system.[747]

The introduction of the idea of the cohesion of the tax system meant essentially that there is "*a connection under the Belgian rules between the deductibility of contributions and the liability to tax of sums payable by insurers pursuant to pension or life insurance contracts*". In other words, the payments paid on the basis of the contract are taxable and the tax deductibility of the contributions paid on the basis of the contract are balanced by the taxation

---

[745] i.e. "*Lead to the same result*", Case 152/73 *Sotgiu v Deutsche Bundespost* [1974] ECR 153.

[746] The Advocate General considered the case "Avoir fiscal" (case 270/83 *Commission v France* (1986) ECR 273, para 19 (28 January 1986).

[747] In the cases dealing with cohesion, the supranational system relativizes (and compares) itself with a subsystem, and gives, consequently, relative autonomy of regulation for the legal subsystem. In this case, however, the capacity for regulation is determined by the *ad hoc* nature of the situation. Any permanent conclusions are neglected.

of the payments by the insurer.

Consequently, there is a strict "legal-economic" relationship between these two provisions. This "relativity" was confirmed by the idea that the payments, on the basis of these contracts, are not taxed, if the contributions on the basis of the contracts have not been tax exempted. On the other hand, the main objective is to guarantee the revenue of the state. In general, it seems that a legal and logical relationship between two provisions of the legal system instituted a basis for an exception from the general rule of the non-discrimination between nationals.

On the other hand, the case was established as well on the fact that a state cannot tax a company situated in another Member States. This would mean an enforcement of the tax law of one state by another state, which may generate problems (for example, the enforcement could be contested on the basis of public policy).

On the other hand, even if - or, in fact, because - the bilateral conventions exist[748], the Community Court considered itself unable to establish the illegality of the provisions of the Belgium law. This was likewise based on the absence of the general Community legislation.

The Court maintained that it cannot guarantee the cohesion of individual tax systems, and that the competence remains the matter of the Member States.

Conclusions. What is interesting in this case is that the cohesion of the tax system can be interpreted as a feature of the legal system, which enables persons to move freely. The cohesion of the state tax system guarantees, in other words, the effectiveness of the Community provisions. The state provisions seem to, to a certain extent, complement Community law. They guarantee the free movement of natural persons, and their return to their country of origin.

However, the case also confirmed the possibility that life insurance etc. is contract with companies of one´s home country. It does not encourage the taking of insurance of this kind from the country, where the work is done.

In this sense, it also encourages national corporate structures, which are based on long -term financing.

To conclude, the comparative argumentation undertaken by both Advocate General and the Court, was strongly influenced by the "tax cohesion" argumentation provided by the states taking part in the procedure. These arguments were "legal" in the sense that they concentrated strongly on the maintenance of the internal balance between different provisions of the revenue laws. The state parties presented both observations on their own systems, and also comparative information.

On the other hand, the Court used - as a direct justification of the "cohesion" principle - the

---

[748] i.e comparison by opposites.

system of international bilateral treaties. It seemed to be possible to use a comparison of international level treaties in interpreting the extension of Community competence.

3.3. Traditional comparative reasoning:

3.2.1. Hard case III (Hoechst in the European Court of Justice) (confirmation of the interpretation by comparative analysis, the inviolability of home, individual protection?)

General remarks. This analysis concentrates on the opinion of the Advocate General and the joined cases of the Court.[749]

The (European Community) Commission had used its powers by giving some decisions, based on the Article 14(3) of Regulation no. 17 of the Council of 6 February 1962, ordering various undertakings to submit to investigation, where their possible participation in agreements or concerted practices which fixed prices and quotas or sales objectives for PVC and polyethylene in the Community was investigated.

Five of the undertakings applied to the Court *"for a declaration that the decision addressed to them was void"*. In support of their application they referred to the infringement of the fundamental right to the inviolability of the home, to the lack of reasons on which decision is based, and to formal and procedural defects. The refusal to submit to investigations had caused the imposition of fines upon the undertakings.

This complex of cases presented a type of 'hard case', where the question related to the relationship between the economic actors and the legal authority, the latter attempting to find out the premisses of the former´s economic activity.

The question is fundamental. Economic strategic activity is based on relatively closed system of information, and secrecy regarding some internal functions. Furthermore, private interests and undertakings' interests might coincide. The actions taken by private actors can be based on premisses, which are not accepted by the authority. The task of the authority is to secure the interest of the individuals (customers) and the economic community as a whole. There is a fundamental collision of interests.

The interesting point comes up, in other words, where these interests coincide in the form of Commission investigations of the fundamental documents of the economic actor or in the order to submit oneself to these investigations. The principles, law, and their interpretation concerning this collision are put in a discursive manner, which includes all possible

---

[749] Joined cases of 46/87 and 227/87, *Hoechst AG v Commission,* (1989) ECR 2859, 85/87 *Dow Benelux nv v Commission* (1989) ECR 3137, and 97, 98 and 99/87 *Dow Iberica sa, Alcudia sa and Empresa Nac el Petro eo sa v Commission of the European Communities* (1989) ECR 3165, and the opinion of the Advocate General Mischo delivered on the 21 February 1989 (1989) ECR 2875.

arguments supporting the correctness of the decision. From this analysis one can note, how the various comparative aspects are taken into account, and how they function in the process of justification. The hard case nature of these types of cases can be seen also in the way the competencies to use power is divided between Community actors and the national authorities. The national authorities have the exclusive competence to physically use power against individuals.

The "easiness" of the case, however, relates to the fact that Community clearly has autonomy to interpret Community competition rules, and the national authorities, on the other hand, have the exclusive competence to use force and regulate on this use.

Furthermore, the difficult nature of the case derives also from the fact that the case is a "first" of a kind, a case on the inviolability of home claimed by a legal person. No analogous cases have arisen in the history of the Community. For that reason, to be able to establish "doctrine" or a "precedent" the Community institutions have to establish reason its decision firmly on the basis of strong and general arguments[750].

Context of justification. The Advocate General begun the explanation of his opinion by explaining his comparative approach:

> *"After establishing on the basis of a study of the national laws of the Member States, the European Convention on Human Rights and the Court's case-law that undertakings have a fundamental right to the inviolability of their premises, I shall consider whether that right is infringed by investigations carried out on the basis of the abovementioned provisions."*

The Advocate General explicitly maintained that his approach had to be systematically comparative.

The party to the dispute, the company *Hoescht*, relied on the fact that

> *"even voluntary submission of business documents in order give effect to a decision ordering an investigation constitutes a search where the Commission knows neither the precise nature nor the detailed contents of the documents submitted"[751]*

It claimed that the nature of the investigation was a "search" rather than an investigation. This argument of the party was neglected by the Advocate General on the basis of a value-based comparative argument:

> *"I cannot accept that reasoning because, as the Court will see later, in all the national legal systems there are*

---

[750] One of the striking features connected to this case is the fact that corporations really claim to be subjects to the same protection as the individuals. In previous cases, on the same subject (cases concerning such Commission intervention), no such claim has ever appeared. At the moment it seems that the corporations seem to employ such arguments in European Community law.

[751] Minutes of the investigation of April 1987, cited at p. 7 of the reply in case 46/87 (see supra n 132).

investigation procedures which presuppose the cooperation of undertakings, in the context of which the competent administrative authority does not know in advance whether it will find information which will lead to the conclusion that the undertaking has committed an offence and, a fortiori, it is not aware of the nature of that information. Such operations cannot on that ground be regarded as searches."

The comparative argument was overall in generality form. The interpretation of the nature of the Commissions action was based on the analogy between the generality of the state practices and the Community level.

The use of such an argument was quite natural, because the term, used by the party to the dispute, had to be interpreted according to the traditional legal vocabulary or even by the "common language" found in the practices of the states. A term *"search"* in the legal context was not seen to be strongly different in the national legal systems than in the *"Community language"*. This way the generality of the legal-linguistic practice resulted in an *a fortiori* form of emphasis within the argumentation.

The Advocate General continued his argumentation by examining the way the characterization of the documents was to be made in different systems and in different fields of law. Certain differences were recognized:

"The duties of the Commission's officials are in no way comparable to those of officials of the national authorities carrying out an investigation in a tax or labour law matter. In regard to taxation, the inspectors consider very specific categories of documents, namely accounting ledgers and invoices for purchases or sales whereas, in relation to labour law, it is essentially pay-slips and personal files which are relevant."

This comparison made it possible to consider the differences between the definitions connected to the different fields of laws, labour laws, tax laws and competition laws, and to discover that the *a priori* preciseness of the definition is dependent on the type of information one is searching for. In the field of competition law, as he explains, the information can be hidden within different types of documents and files. An *a priori* definition is difficult to make. If it would be casuistically defined:

"they would probably never be able to find indications of unlawful agreement. Such indications are more likely to be found on pieces of paper", often hand-written, such as notes containing cryptical coded references made at secret meetings held outside the undertaking sometimes in a hotel situated in a country outside the Community."

It is quite easy to recognize, why the Advocate General decided to make comparisons with the tax and labour law procedures of the Member States. There are no analogous functions in the field of Community law. This is why the comparisons had to be taken from the national legal systems. On the other hand, the different functions of search in different fields of law supported the autonomous interpretation of competition law in this respect.

The wide power of examination, also conferred by the Court in several cases, was seen as antecedent even to the principle of confidentiality. This was, on the other hand, explained by the Advocate General, on a comparative basis, to be a common principle applying in Member

States:

"In no circumstances, therefore, it is for the undertaking itself select the documents which it is prepared to submit even if it considered that certain are protected under the general principle of confidentiality common to the legal systems of all the Member States.
... it is for the Commission to assess whether or not a particular document contains business secrets the confidentiality of which is protected by a general principle which apply during the course of the administrative procedure."[752]

It is not difficult to see why the issue of the *"principle of the inviolability of home"* arose in this connection. After a brief description of the manner of making "secret" deals and to document them, the Advocate General explains that this

"... is why I consider that the Commission's officials were also entitled to look into the briefcases of the undertakings' managers and even into their diaries to see if they contain documents indications relating to their business activities."

In the beginning of the examination of the possible breach of the fundamental right to the inviolability of home, the Advocate General relied, in general terms, upon the national implementation laws. He regarded that

"In any event, no Member State have adopted, on the basis of article 14(6), measures incompatible with its own concept of the protection due to the fundamental right to the inviolability of the premises of undertakings. Therefore, in all cases in which the Commission calls upon the national authorities to overcome an undertaking's opposition, the protection of that fundamental right will be automatically guaranteed to the full extent provided for in the national legal orders."

Therefore the question arose, whether the actions by the Commission, where it concerned *"merely ... handed files... without themselves searching the cabinets"* (including the threats of a fine etc.), violates the fundamental right to the protection of the home. The comparative studies formed a basic supporting approach to this inspection:

"In order to decide that question it is necessary to consider the <u>situation</u> existing in the national legal systems and the <u>guidance</u> which may be drawn from the European Convention on Human Rights and the case law of the Court of Justice."

The inquiry into the Member States' systems. In the realm of the national legal systems, the Advocate General went through all the national legal systems in the European Community. Here are presented only the essential features of the "traditional" inquiry. The presentation of this inquiry gives a good example of the way the traditional comparative reasoning takes

---

[752] For the latter part, case 53/85 *Akzo chemie v Commission* (1986) ECR 1965 (24 June 1986). Some analysis of this case, see Schwarze, J., 1991, p.12 ff.

place in Community legal order.

Concerning Belgium, he studied the inviolability of home (Article 10) in the Constitution, its interpretation, and in terms of the laws in force. He found it to be disputable as to whether the provision refers also to corporate and legal persons. The Constitution itself did not give any indication. The laws required, on the other hand, a prior court order for inspections and searches of premises used as private dwellings. However, this did not apply in the field of commercial matters. Competition laws provided powers to search without prior orders. Similar provisions were in force in the laws implementing Article 87 of the EEC Treaty and Regulation no. 17. The latter laws made it possible to even use criminal sanctions in the case of refusal, and to use powers through warrants issued by the head of the general economic inspector.

The Danish system was also studied from the point of view of its Constitution, laws, and Supreme Court practice. The Constitution demanded a prior court order, except according to the exceptions provided by a separate law. In the implementation laws, no derogations to that basic principle had been permitted. However, consent by the undertaking may justify a search without a court order. In the context of the case law, the rule seemed to be that the court only scans the existence of the Commission decision without examining the material content of it. Furthermore, it was possible, in the case of refusal, according to the case law impose fines, even where a court order was not issued.

The German law was studied from the point of view of the constitution, laws, the case law of the Federal Constitutional Court, and legal dogmatics. *A priori* permission was to be given by a court, or, in the case of "urgency", by another body authorized by the law. The dogmatics was, according to the Advocate General, quite unanimous on the interpretation that business premisses also included within of these interpretations.

The study of the case law was more specific. The Federal Constitutional Court had made a distinction between the search and the investigation. The Advocate General made an explicit reference to these definitions in English and in German. He interpreted the definitions so that the main rule was that the *"cooperative"* investigation was allowed, but that it could be *"enforced"* by periodic penalties or fines based on an *"administrative"* offence. A steadfast refusal demanded a search warrant by the court with in certain restrictions. On the other hand, the implementation laws of the EEC regulations authorized the president of the *"bundeskartellamt"* to issue such permission.

Concerning the Greek system, the study was devoted to the inspection of the constitutional and statutory laws, and Greek Council's opinions. According to the unspecified general opinion, the protection applied also to legal persons. However, legislative practice, in general, interpreted *"home"* restrictively by excluding business premisses. According to opinion of the Council of Ministers in the realm of environmental law and in competition laws, a search of industrial or undertaking premisses does not constitute a search of the "home" within the meaning of the constitution.

According to the Spanish constitution and constitutional practice, business premises enjoyed protection. The situation seemed to be quite similar to Denmark. However, the powers in the realm of competition laws were related to the tax authorities' powers, which meant that only the consent of the corresponding state authorities was needed in order to search and enter places where economic activity took place. However, a court order was needed for entrance into the homes of natural or legal persons[753].

In France, constitutional protection was based on individual liberty and human dignity. The degree of legal protection varied. The trend in legislation seemed to be towards greater protection of business premises. The analysis of the ordinances by the Advocate General was quite thorough and included direct references. The active searches had been made conditioned upon court orders, and the substance of the application had to be checked in the proceedings. This interpretation was supported also by the recent decision of the Conseil Constitutionnel.

The Irish constitutional protection was interpreted textually by the Advocate General. It included legal persons and business premises. In the field of taxation and customs, the powers for an investigation seemed to be quite extensive and without the need for judicial authorization. The same idea applied to competition matters. It is the searched person who has to make a petition the court in order to avoid criminal sanctions in the case of refusal.

The Italian constitutional protection of the inviolability of home covered also business premises. According to several laws in different fields, a prior court order was not necessary unless the case involved a search rather than *"verifications"* or *"inspections"*. In competition law, it was decreed that the power to investigate does not include opening of suitcases, safes and doors, which are locked and which the *"tax payer refuses to open"*. A priori judicial authorization is needed if there is to be a use of force.

In the analysis of the Advocate General, the Luxembourgian system was assimilated with the system in Belgium. The powers of inspections were to be determined by individual laws. The protection of legal persons was still open in the jurisprudence of the courts. Inspections were relatively openly regulated in many fields of administrative law (taxation etc.). In the field of competition law, powers were extensive being based on the authorization of the Ministry. The laws implementing Community decisions, directives and regulations, in many fields of law, granted extensive powers of access to authorities unless the question concerned private dwellings.

The Netherlands Constitution recognized such protection, unless the law decreed otherwise. The legislature delegated powers to confer the power of entry upon different authorities. The provisions which did not contain the obligation to have *a priori* judicial control did not apply to legal persons or to places other than the dwellings of natural persons. Furthermore, it

---

[753] The idea of the home of a legal person is quite interesting in this connection. This analysis, nevertheless, remain unclear.

presupposed that the occupier had not given his consent.[754] On the other hand, there was a distinction between private dwellings and other places. The entering of private dwellings was more strictly regulated. There was *a posteriori* judicial control for the entry to business premises. Competition law, on the other hand, restricted only dwellings from the scope of the right to unrestricted entry.

The Portuguese constitutional protection was viewed quite strictly. This was based on a literal interpretation of the relevant constitutional provision.[755] However, the situation concerning business premises was seen to be unsettled. However, there were ideas expressed in Portuguese law that consent authorizes the entry.[756] The implementation of Community competition law authorized fines in the case of refusal of entry by the company.

The Advocate General tried to interpret the system in the United Kingdom in the context of the peculiarities of that legal system. He started by referring to the principle of the absolute sovereignty of the Parliament, and to the absence of any positive constitutional system of rights. However, the common law courts had a tradition of ensuring them. Furthermore, the interpretation of the Advocate General was that there is a similar tendency as well in the legislative practice.[757]

The applicability of the inviolability principle was considered first in the sphere of other fields of law than in the field of competition law. Prior judicial control was lacking in all other cases than in a case calling for the use of force. In the field of competition laws, no implementation measures of the EEC regulations had been taken. However, entry was to be authorized by a High Court order. A continuous refusal could justify for the action by the police authorities.

In conclusion, the Advocate General stated that the independent study undertaken by him confirms the Commission's argument that the principle is generally applicable in the *"constitutional traditions of the Member States"*. The answer to the question as to whether the principle was applicable in the systems of the Member States in the context of this particular case was negative. In context of business premises, there was a disparity in state

---

[754] This extremely difficult construction has been interpreted weakly by the Advocate General The actual argument made was the following:
"The legislature May therefore leave to the executive the power to determine itself, in the abstract, within the framework of the law, cases in which dwellings May be entered. Furthermore, that provision, which contains no obligation of prior judicial supervision, does not apply to legal persons or to places other than the dwellings of natural person and presupposes that the occupier has not given his consent."

[755] This referred in particular to Article 34(2):
"Entry into homes of citizens against their will may be ordered only the competent court in cases provided for by law and in the forms prescribed by law. Under article 34(3), there is a total prohibition of entry during the night."

[756] Here he referred to the decision of the Constitutional Court of Portugal

[757] For discussion and references, see "Commission's powers of investigation and inspection", House of Lords, session 1983-84, 18th report, Hmso.

practices, or, in the Advocate General's words, the *"situation was not identical"*[758]. The Advocate General saw the situation in some countries as being indefinite and unclear, and in certain countries negative (mentioning especially the Netherlands and Ireland)[759]. There he found a general trend of assimilation of home and business premises, although conditioned by procedural prerequisites.

In the light of this conclusion, there was a difference between the applicability of the principle to the private dwellings and business premises:

"In the economic, fiscal and social spheres, there are, in the various national legal systems, many measures providing for inspections of various kinds from a mere request for information to a search for documents with the help of the police. The terms used to describe such measures vary (inspection, check, inquiry, search...) and do not correspond in all legal systems.

On the other hand, even in Germany, Denmark, Spain, France, Italy Portugal, where prior judicial supervision is required by constitutional law, that requirement is not absolute. In Denmark, exceptions may provided for by law. In Spain and Portugal, by virtue of the constitution itself, judicial authorization is not required if the person concerned consents to the search. In Italy, investigations and inspections particularly for economic and fiscal purposes, are governed by special laws.

Finally, in the field of competition law, even in Germany and in France, no prior court order is required to enter premises or inspect documents which the undertakings themselves submit. It is only in so far as the inspectors wish to carry out a search themselves for documents which have not been submitted to them voluntarily that such an order is necessary.

It should further be noted that, also in regard to competition laws in Spain and Greece, notwithstanding the constitutional requirements, prior court order is required for inspections in business premises, even if they have to be carried out by force.

Finally, in the Member States which, like Germany, Denmark and France, make the use of force conditional on the issue of a prior court order, undertakings may be ordered to submit to inspections and to cooperate in investigations under pain of sanctions such as fines or periodic penalty payments without any prior judicial intervention being necessary.

The inquiry into the European system of human rights. In the realm of the European

---

[758] This view appears disputable. Why should it be identical? Is it not sufficient that the principle could apply, to a certain extent, or, that the solution in some systems was more persuasive.

The absence of this type of idea could be due to the relatively superficial treatment of the subject. There was no normative comparative analysis, where the different solutions were related to each other. On the contrary, the comparative aspects were studied with the same source-dogmatical measure, which seemed to result in a quite mechanical conclusion concerning the disparity.

Another possibility could have been that different arguments were taken from the different justifications (from cases or *travaux preparatoires*). On those basis, one could have decided, whether the principle had a role in the Community system as modified by this analytical study.

The study stressing the "generality"/ disparity" aspects, as *a priori* method, is somehow unconventional. It treats the legal situation as generality (or generally disparate), and is not designed to persuade anybody to adopt or not adopt the principle. The comparative study, in a certain sense, produces directly conclusion concerning the existence of the principle or non-existence of it. The intention seems to be making a comparative study, and of deriving from that general-comparative argument, and not to produce a legal argument (with the help of the comparative study).

[759] *"In which the concepts of "dwelling" and "woning" are defined in such a way that the legal protection of the home is regarded as applying only to the private dwellings of persons living there."*

Convention, the Advocate General referred to Article 8(1) of the Convention, which stated that

"everyone has the right to respect for his private and family life, his home and his correspondence"

However, he maintained that

"The European Convention on Human Rights, for its part, expressly provides for the right of the legislature to derogate under certain decisions from the principle of the inviolability of the home. Article 8(2) of that Convention reads as follows :
  "2. There shall be no interference by a public authority with the exercise of this right except such as is in accordance with the law and is necessary in a democratic society in the interests of national security public safety or the economic well-being of the country, for the prevention of disorder or crime, for the protection of health or morals or for the protection of the rights and freedom of others". "

A study of the case law of this system was absent[760]. There was no study of the jurisprudence or the interpretation of the principle in the case-law of the Court in the European human rights system. Some dogmatic writings were used, however[761].
The Advocate General studied the case law of the European Court of Justice[762], where the

---

[760] The ECJ does not study the dogmatic systematization of another system, and try to develop it. An extensive argumentation, on comparative basis, could "problematize" the systems "own" interpretation (of its own rules). A "foreign" system could become a source of law of a system, which rules it is not able to interpret, in principle.
This idea may apply also to the relationship between the state systems and the international systems. The study of dogmatics has to be extremely conventional and open, if it is to be able to maintain the autonomy of the interpreted system. This explains also, why the comparative studies are made, many times, in the realm of the principle of the organizational "confidentiality". The "closing" of the systems interpretations by the Community interpreter undermines the complexity and the political nature of the interpretation of the rules. This will be discussed below.
The supra-system has to also remain within an extremely "traditional" sphere of reasoning.
[761] Reference was made in this regard to the book of Mr Frowein on the European Convention of Human Rights (*"Europäischen Menschenrechtskonvention, Emrk-kommentar", Article 8, no 27, 1985*).
[762] Case 136/79 *National Panasonic ltd v Commission* (1980) ECR 2033 (26 June 1980), and Case 5/85 *Akzo Chemie v Commission* (1986) ECR 2585 (23 September 1986). Also, case 155/79 *A.M. & S. Europe* (1982) ECR 1575. See analysis of the latter, in Koopmans, T., 1991, pp.498-500. In this case companies faced with similar kind of investigation had appealed to the protection of the correspondence between client and a lawyer. By asking comparative material from the parties, and by using this comparative material (legislation, academic opinion, and case law), the court did find common principle of confidentiality applicable. Because of the differences, it made an autonomous interpretation.
In the *National Panasonic* case it was the applicant, which used the arguments deriving from the System of the European Human Rights. The Advocate General Warner analysed, on this basis, the Convention (Opinion, 30 April 1980), and the laws of the Member States, comparatively. According to him *"in general, but not always, the laws of the Member States required a warrant before the entering to the private premises"*. Mr Warner came to the conclusion that a warrant is not part of the system, and that the application should be dismissed.
The Court came to the same conclusion, but not, however, quoting Mr Warners comparative findings, although it did mention the idea, that the Community observance in accordance with the constitutional traditions of the Member States (as in 4/73 *Nold, Kohlen-, und Baustoffgrosshandlung v Commission of the European Communities* (1974) ECR 491, for example).
Mr. Advocate General Roemer had produced , in case 31/59 *Acciaieria e Tubificio di Brescia v High Authority of the European Coal and Steel Community* ((1960) ECR 71 (84)), a comparative study of the powers of inspection available under national systems of taxation. This was based on the demand of Article 86 of the Treaty on Coal and Steel

compatibility of the Community competition rules with the European Convention of Human Rights had been "implicitly" studied.[763]

Conclusions. These comparative studies resulted in the interpretation of principles and the legal basis of the Community legal order. The Advocate General concluded that the right to the inviolability of the home is one of the fundamental rights, which the *"institutions of the Community must respect"*. On the other hand, he proposed, agreeing with the Commission, that the principle of the protection of business premises should be considered to exist at the Community level. He also referred to the Court's own case law[764].

However, the harmony between the European system of human rights and the European Community system, already expressed by the Court, and the way the business premises are generally protected in different Member States, made the Advocate General to conclude that:

"the exercise of the powers conferred on the Commission by article 14(3) of regulation no 17 cannot pose any problem in regard to the principle of the inviolability of the home as applied to undertakings notwithstanding the fact that those powers are exercised under threat of a periodic penalty payment or a fine."

This meant that the principle of inviolability, proposed by the applicants, was not applicable to this case as a valid argument. However, he applied a "principle of cooperation" to the investigation procedures, and, on this basis, concluded that

"it does not give those officials themselves the right to search cabinets and remove the document from them."

Furthermore, the "legal protection" of the undertaking was found to be sufficient, if the applicant is able, as it was in this case, to contest the investigation in the European Court of

---

Community, where the powers of the High authority officials, to make inspections, were determined by reference to the *"rights and powers as are granted by the laws of a Member State to its own revenue officials"*. The analytical study was devoted to the provisions in the German *Adgebenordnung* (Code of Taxation) and its commentary (Kühn), French *Code Général des Impôts'* and the commentaries in its context (Laroque, P.), articles in Italian Law and the Netherland's's's law. The examination of the formal conditions, which should be applied, when requesting information (formality), was concluded by quotation of the German administrative and competition law and its commentaries.

The claim of the undertaking was held to be well founded and admissible. The Court, on the other hand, dismissed the application on a different basis without reference to the comparative material

[763] *"Even though in national Panasonic, it was the absence of any communication prior to the investigation which was the subject of the dispute, I consider that it May be deduced from that judgment that in court's view, the powers of investigation provided for in article 14 regulation no 17 fulfilled the conditions laid down in article 8(2) of the European Convention on Human Rights.*

That conclusion is supported by the case Akzo Chemie v Commission."

It must be mentioned that the Advocate General, in interpreting the counter arguments, made also an analogical statement, internal to the system, introducing safety inspections, the idea existing in the European Atomic Energy Community (Article 81 of that Treaty)

[764] Cases 136/79 *National Panasonic ltd v Commission* (1980) ECR 2033 (26 June 1980), 31/59 *Acciaier Tubificio de Brescia v High Authority* (1960) ECR 71, and the opinion of the Advocate General Warner delivered on 30 April 1980 in the 136 *National Panasonic Ltd* v Commission.

Justice *a posteriori*. On the other hand, if the refusal by the undertaking results in the use of force in effecting the search, the "national provisions" must be applied and, consequently, prior judicial orders can be obtained.

In the application of these principles it was found that Commission decisions ordering investigations were not unlawful, and that the claims of violation of one's home, in addition to the claims of breach of essential principles of procedure (the principle of collegiality and formality), the use of unlawfully obtained information, the breach of the presumption of innocence, the principle of proportionality, the principle of non-discrimination, the principle of non-retroactivity *(nulla poena sine lege)*, and the right to a hearing were dismissed.[765] Furthermore, the imposition of periodical payment was considered lawful, and the demand for its reduction was also dismissed.

In examining the claim that the principle of proportionality, applied in the Spanish system, was infringed, the Advocate General based his dismissal on the rejection of any "reflexivity" of the Community system towards one particular national legal system:

> *"That submission must also be rejected. On the one hand, the validity of Community measures may be assessed only in regard to Community law not in regard to any provision of national law, even a constitutional provision. Similarly, compliance with a general principle of community <u>cannot be made to depend on concepts and rules drawn from national law.</u>"*

Justification. In the decision of *Hoechst*[766], the Court maintained that the Articles (of the regulations) in question must be interpret in the light of general principles and the fundamental rights of Community law (as part of the generally applicable principles) and that these Articles cannot be incompatible with those principles. They are *a priori* in accordance with the *"constitutional traditions common to the Member States and the international treaties, on which the Member States have collaborated or of which they are signatories"*[767]. The European Convention of Human Rights was seen as particularly relevant.[768] The Court put emphasis on the right of defence.[769]

Concerning the principle of the *"inviolability of home"*, the Court maintained that even if it is a fundamental principle in the Community legal order *"common to the laws of the Member States in regard to private dwellings of natural persons"*, the same was not true with

---

[765] In the examination, the Advocate General used various "internal" arguments of the Community system and different general conceptual evaluations.

[766] Case 46/87 and 227/87 *Hoechst AG v Commission*, (1989) ECR 2859 (21 September 1989).

[767] Referring to case 4/73 *Nold v Commission* (1974) ECR (Judgment 14 May 1974).

[768] Referring to case 222/84 *Johnston v Chief Constable of the Royal Ulster Constabulary* (1986) ECR 1651 (judgment 15 May 1986). Some analysis, Galmot, Y., 1990, p.257 ff. This case dealt with the equality between men and women and the interpretation on the basis of general principle.

[769] Referring to case 322/81 *Michelin v Commission* (1983) ECR 3461 (9 November 1983) para 7, and 155/79 *S v Commission*, (1982) ECR 1575 (18 may 1982).

regard to undertakings. This is so because (referring directly to the comparative outcomes by Advocate General) there were *"inconsiderable divergences between the legal systems in regard to the nature and degree of protection afforded to business premises against intervention by the public authorities"*.

Similar conclusions were drawn in relation to Article 8 of the European Convention on Human Rights. The Court maintained that

> *"the protective scope of that <u>Article is concerned with the development of man's personal freedom and may not therefore be extended to business premises.</u> Furthermore, it should be noted that there is <u>no case-law of the European Court of Human Rights on that subject.</u>"[770]*

However, there was, in all the systems of the Member States (generality), a 'minimum protection'. In all the systems, there was a demand for a legal basis for the interference, and the intervention was not to be arbitrary and disproportionate. This was considered to be a *"general principle of Community Law"*. Furthermore, the rights of the undertakings were to be ensured by the obligation of the authorities to specify the purpose and the subject-matter of the investigation.

These general principles were to be applied in the case. Furthermore, there was also an argument to this effect put forward in the case law.[771] Moreover, the idea, expressed in competition provisions, was to ensure competition in the market, to prevent violations of the public interest, interests of individual undertakings, and consumers, and the maintenance of the general system.

After the examination of the facts and claims, the Court dismissed the applications, and found that the Commission had not violated these principles.

Similar observations were made in two other cases, decided on the same day, which dealt with the same subject matter.[772]

Some analysis; a principle of individual protection vs. protection of business premises?
Underpinning the argumentation of the Advocate General, there was a systematic study of the laws of the Members States and the European human rights system. This was reflected also in the Court decision. There was a quite careful and extensive study undertaken of different laws, not only in relation to analogies with competition matters. The study was independent

The extension of the explicit analysis was remarkable. Constitutions were explicitly cited,

---

[770] The Court thus mentions the non-existence of the case law.

[771] Case 136/79 *National Panasonic* (1980) ECR 2033 (26 June 1980).

[772] Joined cases 97/87, 98/87 and 99/87 *Dow Chemical Iberica SA and Alcudia, Empresa para La Industria Quimic and Empresa Nacional del Petroleo SA v Commission of the European Communities* (1989) ECR 3165 (17 October 1989), and case 85/87 *Dow Benelux nv, formerly Dow Chemical (Nederland) bv v Commission of European Communities* (1989) ECR 3137 (17 October 1989).

and all countries were studied. Furthermore, the source structure consisted of laws, case law, dogmatic observations, and even some systematic connections (eg. to UK). Furthermore, some "grouping" was proposed. Furthermore, direct references were taken from certain systems.

On the other hand, no contextual interpretation was applied, and there was a use of a fairly "weak" doctrine of legal sources. No *travaux preparatoires* were used. The quality of the analysis was based on the institutional approach. A type of idea of legal sources was applied. In this sense, the analysis was restrictively traditional.

Consequently, it was not really a surprise that the analysis resulted in a "disparity" conclusions.

The connection between the comparative observations and the general argumentation is, however, interesting.

The argumentation departed from the analysis of the rule and norms existing in the regulation by the Council, which explicitly gave authority to the Commission to investigate. Because there was a dispute as to the extension of this investigating power, the Court had to look into the principle and conceptual context of the case. The Court thus studied the conceptual context.

The Court seemed to examine the principled context in a following way. First of all, it maintained that there is no "common principle of inviolability of the home" which could apply also in the case concerning companies within Member States. It is noteworthy that the principle was not interpreted to be part of the Community legal system as such. The principle common to Member States system was to be respected. It was, in this sense, "external" to the Community legal order.

The Court noted that there are no objections of having the principle of inviolability of home as part of the Community legal order. However, for the above-mentioned reasons the Court found it necessary to limit its applicability in connection to company activities in the Community context. Instead, companies receive other types of protection against illegal interference.

It is interesting to note that the Court maintains that the inviolability of home belongs to the protection of the fundamental rights of the individual within states, and that it refused to grant similar protection for companies.[773] It is evident that if application of the principle could be done, the system would arrive at problems concerning the relationship between companies and the individuals in future cases and in legal protection in general.

This idea can be backed up also by the idea of the objectives of competition law as whole. Namely, the objectives and aims of the Community system, by and large, can be interpreted

---

[773] *"The protective scope of that Article is concerned with the development of man's personal freedom and may not therefore be extented to business premises. Furthermore, it should be noted that there is no case-law of the European Court of Human Rights on that subject."*

as dealing primarily with the protection of the individuals against the misuses of different types of dominance in the market. For this reason, there is no room for the similar protection of individuals and companies. This interpretation can be maintained, although the Court argues, on a comparative basis, that protection cannot be analogized to companies, because *"there are no inconsiderable divergences between the legal systems of the Member States in regard to the nature and degree of protection afforded to business premises against intervention by the public authorities"* and that the interpretation *"is not incompatible with the interpretation of the Article 8 of the Human Rights Convention"*. These comparative observations seem to support the objectives of Community competition law.

Consequently, one could claim that the comparative arguments presented in this case support a principle, that a company cannot be given the same protection of information as an individual is granted. This seems to be the "rule by comparison", to which the acceptability of the comparative arguments are reflected. This is the implicit principle embedded in the case. One may say that, in this case, the comparative observations are interacting with a kind of a general principle of individual protection. This principle is embedded in the argumentation on the aims of the European system and competition law. This principle confirms that the individual is considered legally to be the basic object of protection by Community law. Corporations cannot be interpreted as being in the same situation as the individual in the protection of the private sphere. The analogy between the company and the individuals cannot be made because then the Community would equalize the individual and the company. That would generate an unbearable conflict between legal interests. It would be impossible to interpret the "protectionist" measures with this kind of analogy. There would be a fundamental collision embedded within the situation.

Furthermore, as the Advocate General notes, the protection of individuals by reference to basic principles must be respected by the Community. The principles of individual protection are superior principles at the Community order. In this sense, the legal protection of undertakings must be accomplished by other means.

It appears as if the comparative reasoning, in this case, is a form of 'contrastive' reasoning. Through comparative observations it was possible to justify the decision of the "applicability" of the principle of inviolability of home. Legally it would be problematic only to refer to the principle of individual protection and to an abstract "possible conflict" between the two spheres of actors in the Community system. This way it was possible to maintain the balance between the different spheres of interests and, at the same time, implicitly the superiority of individual protection in principle. This idea cannot follow solely from the aims of competition law, but it must be derived from the general aims of the Community system as a whole, because the interpretation is dealing with very fundamental principles of the Community law, based on the traditions of Member States.

Here one may recognize some kind of a structuration and hierarchization of the norms of the Community system[774].The idea that the inviolability of home does not apply to the companies is an indication of "the internal structural principles" of the Community system.

3.3.2. Hard case IV(Albany in the European Court of Justice) (value based and traditional comparative analysis vs. systematic analysis, consistent interpretation of the Treaty and the Treaty as a whole, relationship between competition and collective agreements, right to collective bargaining as a basic right)

General remarks. Case *Albany*[775] and related cases[776] represent definitely the basic hard cases for the European Community legal order. Previous case law does not exist and the support for the solution is found in the legal systems of some Member States and some other states. Furthermore, the Court solves the interpretational problem by introducing somewhat "new" method of interpretation into the Community law.

The general problems relate to the relationship between law of collective agreements and competition and, furthermore, to the relationship between the fundamental rights of the individual as individual, consumer, worker, and citizen. The question is also about the possibility to have a right to collective bargaining and who's right that could be.

This analysis is an illustration of the value-based and the traditional of comparative legal reasoning. There is a comparison between more value-based and institutional and traditional comparative law inquiry, the first presented by the institutional actor (Advocate General) and the second by dogmatic specialists produced after the case had been decided.

The hardness of the case may be associated also with the novelty of thinking of collective agreeing from the point of view of the competition law. As the comparative studies and the reasoning by the European Court of Justice and the Advocate General Jacobs indicates, it is very labourious to find clear answer to the question what is the European standard.

The case is fascinating also from other viewpoint. Namely, the argumentation by the Advocate General Jacobs differs considerably from the argumentation of the Court, even if the normative results are not altogether conflicting. There are several explanations to this, as

---

[774] For some remarks on the aims of European Community competition policy, compared with the United States approach, on the social and human demands and, recognition also a non-economic values at stake, see Hawk, P.E., United States and Common Market anti-trust, A comparative guide, 1990, p.7, 10.

These are, for example, political and sociological concerns for individual traders, fairness in the market place, equality of opportunity for all commercial operators, legitimate interests of users, workers and consumers (in general the consequences for national social systems), see Commission Ninth Report on Competition Policy (ibid., 1980, pp.9-11).

[775] C-67/96, Judgement of the Court 21 September 1999 (Compulsory affiliation to a sectoral pension scheme-Compatibility with competition rules. Classification of a sectoral pension fund as an undertaking) (1999) ECR.

[776] Joined cases C-115/97, 116/97, 117/97 *Brentjens 'Handelsonderneming BV*, and C-219/97, *D. Bokken*. (Interesting case in this context is also the case *van der Woude* (21.9.2000).)

we will see later in this chapter. These differences may derive from the legal cultural sphere.

Furthermore, as it is common in very difficult cases, the roles of these two institutional actors differs remarkably. The reasoning of the Advocate General is captivating from the point of view of the comparative law, and the Court's reasoning, on the other hand, from the "deductive" point of view.

Also the progression of the process is discursively tempting. The distance between the Advocate General's opinion and the Court's decision provided time for the parties (governments) and the general legal (comparative) discourse to give its opinion on the Advocate General's opinion before the final rulings. The discussion after the case has been active too, due to the fact that there are cases to be decided on the same subject-matter and due to the expected effects of the *Albany* case in the national legal systems.

The case uncovers, moreover, the social aspects prevailing in European competition law and legal culture in contrast to the more economic oriented approach dominating, for example, in the United States.[777]

The facts of the case. The case dealt with a single sectoral pension fund established, by collective agreement, to administer the supplementary sectorial pension system. The system had been declared to be binding all workers in the sector, unless exempted (*erga omnes*).

The Dutch law and some other rules given based on that law regulated the representation in the fund, investing activities, exemption procedure, and the ministerial competencies related to the system.

The plaintiff of the case, company *Albany,* had its main activity on the textile industry sector. It complained that the European competition law norms had been violated because it had not been granted the possibility to leave the fund and because it was not able legally to appeal the decision made by the fund's decision-making body. Originally, the case had been triggered by the fact that *Albany* had refused to make the regular payments to the fund, and the fund recovered these fees in a customary Dutch legal procedure. The European preliminary ruling procedure, on the other hand, was prompted by the Dutch court (*Kantoonrecht Arnheim*) because of the unclearness of the European Law in relation to the questions about the relationship between the competition law and collective agreeing.

Consequently, Albany claimed that the Dutch Law and the decision of the fund violated the 3g (new 3:1g), 52 and 59 (43, 49) and 85, 86, and 90 (81, 82, 86) of the Treaty.

In the preliminary ruling procedure, the interpretation questions asked by the national court from the European Court were following[778]:

---

[777] See the analysis of the case *Hoescht,* and especially the footnote 162.

[778] These are the questions in Albany. The *Brentjens* case includes a preliminary question on the nature of the agreements as such.

—   is the sectoral pension fund - established in accordance of the Dutch Law -
         undertaking in the sense of the European competition law provisions?
—   does the compulsory nature of the membership of the industrial
         undertaking in the sectorial fund undermine the effectiveness of the
         European competition law?
—   could the compulsory membership be against the state monopoly provisions
         of the European competition law?

As noted, the basic difficulty of the case was associated with the status and nature of the
collective agreement in the legal system. This analysis will concentrate mainly to the second
question.

Some procedural arguments were presented too. Some parties claimed that the information
given by the national court was insufficient. This argument was rejected both by the Advocate
General and the Court based on the observation that other cases had been lodged too and that
the information all together was enough for the parties to formulate their opinion and
reasoning. Also the Court could give an useful answer to the national court on the basis of the
delivered information.

Albany claimed that the collective agreement establishing the pension system and the fund
was an agreement prescribed in the competition law provisions. The effects to the competition
were noticeable. Indeed, the effects were cumulatively seen in the trade between the Member
States. Furthermore, the acts of the Dutch administration were claimed to be illegal from the
point of view of the competition law rules.

The Commission, Sweden, the Netherlands, and France claimed that the Article 85 does not
apply materially to the case. The argumentation was based on the social aims contained in the
Treaties and on the idea that there is a basic right to collective bargaining and agreeing
recognized by the international and European legal instruments. Furthermore, they claimed
that the application of the Article 85 would be against the encouragement to the collective
processes, the agreements were not made between undertakings, the competition is not
effected, and that there are no cross-border effects or at least the influence is in the realm of
the "*de minimis*" rule.

The governments claimed that the ministerial decision does not give any monopoly and that
there is no dominant position involved in this case.

Albany claimed, moreover, that in the end the pension system does not satisfy the needs of
undertakings and that a new system is needed. The operative system, it was declared, was
ineffective and administratively expensive. Other comparable "new" types of systems already
existed. *Albany* stated also that method of granting exemption by fund was unjust in nature.

The context of justification (the Advocate General's opinion). The comparative study of the
Advocate General, made evidently on the basis of the study conducted in the Court's

administration, gives ground to several observations[779]. Indeed, one could be critical about the comparative study and reasoning devised. This is confirmed by some latest special reports.[780]

In this connection there is no reason to go through in detail the whole comparative argumentation presented by Mr. Jacobs. However, one can maintain that the use of comparative law by the Advocate General is more or less traditional in the sense that he quite carefully refers to the main legal instruments in countries studied. The reasoning is narrow[781], but, however, relatively analytical. The use of the legal sources is quite successful. Advocate General Jacobs' analysis on the law in different countries is more or less based on the corresponding doctrines of legal sources in these countries[782].

The legal cultural background of Advocate General comes clearly up in his strong attachment to the case law type of analysis. This may apply also to the use the distinctions *ratione materiae/ratione personae,* not used by the Court at all and to his attachment to the case law deriving from the United States. Furthermore, the Advocate General speaks also about the *"established principles of interpretation"* but, on the same time, suggests that the interpretation of the collective agreements can be made on the basis of the general principle of freedom of contract. These remarks must be interpreted in the context of the common law legal culture where analogical approach is common.[783]

The utility of this comparative study does not really come up clearly in his opinion. It may be asked, why was it used in the reasoning considering the discernible differences and disparities of the systems. Moreover, one can notice that his analysis of the relevant sources moves quite restrictively in the basic description of the norms.[784]Furthermore, it can be asked, whether the interpretation of the national systems really transferrable to the Community law, where the interpretation by the Community Court must be somewhat more extensive and the nature of "social rules" is very different. The "social rules" in Community law are just on

---

[779] It is *""a goldmine of references and ideas in itself"* (Gyselen, L., 2000, p.430).

[780] COLCOM Final Report. Collective Agreements on the Competitive Common Market. A Study of Competition Rules and Their Impact on Collective Labour Agreements (Niklas Bruun, Jari Hellsten) 3.7.2000. Reporters: Christian Felber (Austria), Humblet, P., Rigaux, M. (Belgium), Nielsen, R (Denmark), Hellsten, J. (Finland), Vigneau, Ch. (France), Blanke, T. (Germany), Veneziani, B., Ieone, G. (Italy), Fransen, E., Jacobs, A.T.J.M. (The Netherlands), Ojeda Avilés, A. (Spain)Malmberg, J. (Sweden), Bercusson, B. (the United Kingdom). Members of the steering group were: Bercussion, B., Blanke, T., Jacobs, A., Ojeda Avilés, A., Veneziani, B., Vigneau, Ch., Clauwaert, S.

[781] Sulkunen, O., 2000, p.150.

[782] See below, however.

[783] See also the footnotes 19, 21, and 56. On the common law "analogical method of interpretation", see Legrand, P., 1996, p.65, referring to Samuel, G., The foundations of legal reasoning, 1994). Also page 72 in this book.
The Court seems to take this aspect seriously, and gives its own method of interpretation, see footnote 19, 21 and 56.

[784] Mr. Jacobs explains that *"In view of its relative novelty and the far-reaching implications of the Court's answer it may be helpful to examine how the antitrust systems of different Member states and of the United states deal with the problem"*, and once again *"It will be helpful to examine briefly three major decisions of the United States Supreme Court on the non-statutory labour exemption"* (underlining authors).

developmental stage.

The choice of countries to the comparative analysis and argumentation gives raise to certain enigmas (included were France, Finland, Denmark, Germany, the United Kingdom, the United States). On what basis they were really selected, when most of the European Union Member States were excluded? The selection was not really motivated by the Advocate General. Apparently he focuses to the legal systems were some relevant case law material can be found. This may be associated with the legal cultural background of the Advocate General.

The analysis of the United States law was quite central to the reasoning and argumentation. Several interesting "comparable" aspects came up. Nevertheless, the differences in the nature of these systems was not discussed.

In the end, the Advocate General makes summary on the scope of the shelter granted and the unlimited nature of the immunity. He classifies different systems of legal sources associated with the question of immunity, and differentiates the legal mechanisms through which the immunity is reached. The variation is affirmed to be considerable. The questions national courts ask frequently are summarized.

This all functioned as a background for him in the analysis of the Article 85(1) of the Treaty.[785]

According to Mr. Jacobs, the comparative study supports the conclusion, that the collective agreements are protected to a certain extend. However, there is no absolute protection. Different sources of protection can be discovered in the legal measures like basic rights, law, case-law, some general and particular criteria established, and there is also a "tradition" not to examine the relationship between these two spheres of law (collective agreeing and competition law). This gives an indication about the difficulties to arrive at any comprehensive results on the basis of the comparative study. The situation is, furthermore, fairly unclear also in some national legal systems. According to the Advocate General, no general exemption for collective agreements exists. However, there is a special status for collective agreements.

The basic problems (recognized by the national courts) relate to the notion of terms of the collective agreements enjoying the immunity from competition law provisions. Furthermore, according to him the effects of the terms of the collective agreements to third parties, the idea of the intention to distort competition, and the nature of the national decisions as "rule-creative" or "situationally balancing" decisions are problematic.[786]

Mr. Jacobs asks the question: is there a basic right to collective bargaining? There seems to

---

[785] Vousden, S. (2000, p.183) maintains that *"the inconclusiveness of his comparative review threw him back to the wording of the Article 85(1)"*. Nevertheless, it is clear that the his interpretation was no textual in nature.

[786] *"Is it more appropriate to apply hard and fast rules or to engage in a case by case balancing process of the conflicting interests involved?"*.

be the right of an individual to associate and act collectively. There can be a right to collective bargaining and negotiation, which is not, however, explicitly recognized by the Treaty. This right, the Advocate General finds, is prevailing in Sweden. This last detail can be detected only indirectly in his argumentation dealing with the decisions of the European Court of Human Rights.

Mr. Jacobs notices that there are, moreover, other international instruments dealing with this theme; the European Charter of Social Rights and Rights of Workers, the European Convention of Human Rights, the instruments created by International Labour Organization. Nevertheless, according to Mr. Jacobs, they do not support any categorical conclusion as to the existence of the basic right, even if they may support the idea.[787]

Also the Court's case-law, deriving inspiration from the constitutional traditions of the Member States, and the general principles of labour law, could support the prevalence of the above mentioned right in general. However, Mr. Jacobs declares that the general freedom of contract protects this right enough. Nevertheless, even in this form the right is not absolute for it is restricted by the Community law and general principles.

This seems to leave open the possibility of interpreting the collective agreements on the basis of the free movement principles and the principle of non-discrimination by nationality. The Advocate General is, surprisingly, prepared to solve the *"politically and socially sensitive question"* (as he describes their nature)[788] by these quite open principles and constructions.

The final conclusions by the Advocate General suggest that collective agreements are immune as far as they have been made in the general framework of the collective bargaining, are built on good faith (*bona fide*), remain in the hard core of the traditional subject-matter of collective agreeing, and there is no immediate effect to third parties[789].

Finally, the Advocate General goes through the nature of the entities (parties of the collective agreeing) and deals with the question of dominant position. He comes to the conclusion that European competition law provisions concerning monopolies apply in cases where the demand in the market cannot be satisfied or where there is no general right to appeal the decision by the monopolized instance.[790]

The Court's reasoning. The argumentation of the Court is deductive in nature. It relies on the basic instruments of the Treaty. The Court departs from the basic Articles of 3g and 3i (competition policy and social policy), examines the aims in the Article 2 (economic, employment, and social protection), it refers to the obligations of the Commission to promote

---

[787] Some discussion, COLCOM, pp.46-47, and Sulkunen, O. (2000).

[788] Opinion, paragraph 162.

[789] Some analysis, Sulkunen, O. 2000, p.149 ff.

[790] See also, Gyselen, L. (2000) p.433.

the collective bargaining and negotiating, and the right to associate (Article 118). The Court takes up the European agreement on social policy, which characterizes the commitment by the Community and the Member States to achieve certain objectives and establishes procedures giving effect to these measures. Nevertheless, the Court does not apply the Amsterdam Treaty retroactively.[791]

The Court does not give any direct value to the comparative reasoning, except in relation to the idea of *erga omnes* (*"being a system established in a number of Member States"*).[792] The use of international measures is also absent.

It maintains that collective agreements have by nature competition law restrictive effects, and when interpretation of the Treaty

"as a whole which[793] is <u>both effective</u> and <u>consistent</u>[794] [effet utile et cohérent] ... agreements concluded in the context of collective negotiations between management and labour in pursuit of such objectives [social policy objectives][795] must, by <u>virtue of their nature and purpose,</u> be regarded as falling outside the scope of Article 85(1) of the Treaty"[796]

---

[791] Vousden (2000, p.188) maintains, however, that the Court is selective in reading the Treaty.

[792] See also, COLCOM, p.37, 57-58. Nevertheless, not in Italy, the United Kingdom, Denmark, Sweden.

[793] Linguistically this sentence is peculiar. The *"which"* refers to the interpretation, but misunderstanding can easily follow. Namely, this *"which"* (in the English version) could be easily seen referring to the *"Treaty as a whole"* (and, consequently, the Treaty would be consistent and effective, not the interpretation). However, the French version confirms, for example, that the reference is to the interpretation (*"which is both consistent and effective"*):
"*Il résulte ainsi d'une interprétation utile et cohérente des dispositions du traité, dans leur ensemble, que des accords conclus dans le cadre de négociations collectives entre partenaires sociaux en vue de tels objectifs doivent être considérés, en raison de leur nature et de leur objet, comme ne relevant pas de l'article 85, paragraphe 1, du traité.*"
This idea related to the method of interpretation is very interesting. However, the examination of this aspect must be made in another study. However, see below, footnotes 20, 22, 57.

[794] See also, Advocate General's "systematic" interpretation (later, footnote 15). It is interesting to note that the term *"consistent"* is used as a decisive argument also in the *Bachmann* case analysed in this book in chapter 3.2.2. In that case too, a strong margin of discretion was granted to Member States because of the systematic reasons. In this case, on the other hand, the systematic reasons are social-political in nature, whereas in *Bachmann* the idea was motivated by the argument of the interdependence of several relatively technical norms of the national system. In this case, the margin of discretion of the Member States was achieved by the argument related to the consistence of the European system, or rather, to the *autopoietically interpreted consistency European institutional interpretation*. This is very interesting method. See also, footnote 20.

[795] Discussion on this, see COLCOM, p.36 on *Bretjens* case (C-115-117/97). It is maintained that it is also possible to interpret the "such objectives" refer to "conditions of work and employment". The conclusion is, however, that *"such objectives"* means wider objectives than "conditions of work and employment". Sulkunen, O. (2000, p.150 ff.) maintains that the conditions of employing (hiring) and employment security have been included since the beginning of the collective agreeing to protect for example, the "dumping" of employment *[Schmutzkonkurrenz]*. See, however, *van der Woude*.

[796] Sulkunen maintains that this interpretation is finalistic, not teleological. It can also be seen, however, as "systematic" ("coherent, consistent").
Also Mr Jacobs applies an interesting "systematic" interpretation (paragraph 177 ff.) based on the *"established principles of interpretation"*. In this construction, he sees the *"tension between two sets of rules"* of *"same rank"* (Article 85 and the encouragement to collective bargaining), and he maintains that one set should not take precedence over another, and they should be not empted their entire content by this interpretation, and comes to the conclusion of automatic immunity of the collective agreements. Some comments on this, see below.

In applying this rule, the Court finds that these agreements in question do not belong to the scope of the Article 85, and that the Member States may regulate on the obligatory nature of these arrangements. Neither does the Netherlands favour arrangements which would be against the Article 85. The legal order does not make ineffective the Articles 3g, 5 and 85.

After the analysis of its own case law and the criteria established, the Court comes to the conclusion that the fund is an undertaking characterized in the establishing Treaty.[797] However, based on its preceding case law and the analysis of the list of the criteria established in it, the Court does find that if the monopoly of the fund would be abolished, its function would be endangered. This way the monopoly of the fund is justified.[798]

Referring to the *GB-Inno* case[799], the Court rejects the unjustness argument put forward by *Albany* and it maintains that it is essentially the task of the national courts, facing the appeal, to examine the arbitrariness, legality, and the accordance with the equality principle of the decisions taken by the fund.[800] The legality of the fund's decision can be controlled, effectively, by the national courts dealing with cases relating to the refusal to pay contributions to the fund.

Furthermore, in the Court's opinion, the competence to create any "alternative" and "new" types of systems which could replace the pension system in question (idea proposed by *Albany)* is in the hands of the national authorities regulating on the social security systems in general.[801]

In conclusion, the norms established were following:
–   the compulsory nature of the membership in the fund, established by the authorities on the basis of the application by the collective parties in question, is not against the provisions of the Treaty
–   the fund in question is an undertaking

---

[797] Criteria: (*Poucet, Pistre* C-159/91, 160/91 (1993) ECR I-637): economic activity despite the form and method of financing, exceptions: administration of solidarity based obligatory social security systems; benefits same for all, benefits not relative to payments, surplus to the financing of systems with structural problems, single organization responsible. However, an undertaking competing with other undertakings *(Federation Francaise,* C-244/94 (1995) ECR I-4013): does not aim to profits, supplementary pension system, optional, capitalization principle, financial results determine the benefits (even if: social objective, non-profit-making, requirement of solidarity, restrictions in the administration of the fund).
    It can be asked, whether the classification of a fund as an undertaking is logical where, on the same time, its function remains social, and it is established on the basis of the collective barganing process.

[798] Monopoly, but not essential, if not abuse or there are circumstances, where has to abuse. In this case can be justified, because: an instrument of economic and social policy, cannot manage the tasks without monopoly, division between "good" and "bad" customers (workers and companies), solidarity principle would not apply anymore (now no risks management, all insured, ability to work not criterion, bankruptcy situations managed etc.). Economic balance would be endangered.

[799] C-18/88 (1991) ECR I-5941.

[800] A question of legality. Exemption must be granted in some circumstances (fund's rules determine), do not have to be granted, if results danger of economic unbalance.

[801] Also, Gyselen, L. (2000) p.433.

–   the monopoly established by the state authorities is not against the Treaty

Some analysis of the reasoning. There are clearly two types of reasoning related to this case. The reasoning of the Advocate General is "dynamic" in nature with its far reaching analysis and because the strong attachment to the comparative legal observations. It is distinctively directed to the national legal audience. The reasoning of the Court, on the other hand, is deductive in nature. It clearly gives a "general" rule-creating opinion on the nature of collective agreements. In this sense, the case obviously has a precedent value. It is noteworthy that the deductiveness in Court's reasoning is indubitably attached to the analysis of the social aims as basic objectives of the Treaty.[802]
It must also be noted, that the Court does discuss neither the limits of the immunity of collective agreements nor the limitation of the immunity by good faith consideration or by "core subject" -evaluation or any reference to the affects resulting to any third parties (unlike the Advocate General did).[803] Indeed, the Courts silence is understandable, because the application of the complex criteria, developed by the Advocate General, would have perhaps meant eventuality the scrutiny of collective agreements under the competition law.[804]

Some other studies. This case has triggered several comments[805] in the field of labour and competition law. One of these is the substantive study proposed to the Commission by certain European labour-lawyers, who tried to answer to the question, what really is the status of the collective agreements in EC-law and in national law.[806]
The comparative law study, included to this project, was extensive and very analytical. It applied the comparative reporting system. The questionnaire was send to specialist in the field in most of the Member States.[807] Their reports were independently published in the report. No real "models" were used, but the questions were invented on the basis of careful

---

[802] Sulkunen maintains that if the social aspects in this fundamental way had not been taken up, the new norms on the social policy in the European level would have incomprehensible.
[803] Also, COLCOM, p.35, 56-57. Vousden, S (2000), who clearly mises this point, and his reading of the Courts argumentation seems to be essentially wrong in this respect (2000) p.182.
    On some problems related to the Article 137(6) (new) and the European Social Agreement, see Sulkunen, O. (2000) p.153. Also, Vousden, S. (2000) p.188.
[804] Mr. Jacob's opinion, paragraph 190 ff. The idea that the agreement should have been made in the framework of collective bargaining, in good faith, it deals with the core subject, and can be *"fully justified"*[?]. Mr. Jacobs sees it possible to evaluate the "social objectives" of these collective agreements. He proposes also that the Court and the Commission could be able to evaluate the scope of these agreements made in the national context. This would be quite problematic (paragraph 193).
[805] Some analysis, Vousden, S. (2000) and Gyselen, L (2000).
[806] COLCOM Final Report.
[807] Greece, Ireland, Luxembourg and Portugal were excluded.

considerations of the subject-matter.[808] The choice of the systems included was based on the idea that

> *"the essential differences both in the position or status of collective agreements vis-à-vis national competition rules, including different methods applied in the legal definitions of that relationship, could be covered by a group of eleven Member States."*[809]

The methodology of this study is relatively well established. The study is not really a comprehensive and independent comparative law study, but it is related predominately to the latest development and it is subject-matter based. The research-economic restriction seems to be the main restriction.[810]

The general reporter of the study makes first an overview of the relevant rules (competition), concepts and case law in the context of European law. The reason for the current judgements in the field (including *Albany*) is recognized:

> *"[there is a] wide acceptance of the principle of freedom of association and the right to collective bargaining... part of the constitutional traditions of most Member states."*

However, it is affirmed that the original drafters of the Treaty did not really pay attention to the labour agreements in the context of competition law, and no case law really existed before these new cases in the end of 90's.[811]

The conclusions of this study propose that on the basis of this recent case law, the negotiating social partners are not subject to competition rules and that sectoral agreements are *a priori* excluded from the scope of the competition rules.[812] Furthermore, it suggests that because 1) the reasoning in the case is based on balancing the Treaty provisions on social policy and collective agreements with the EC competition regime, 2) it is related to the basic objectives of the Treaty, 3) the expression of the judgement is *"interpretation of the treaty as a whole, which is both effective and consistent"*, 4) the decision is fulfilling a gap of 40 years , and 5) because it gives Member States competence to appreciate the *erga omnes* effect of collective agreements, it follows that the immunity is now a fundamental rule of the European Community law.[813] It is also suggested that national authorities and courts could not apply to collective agreements stricter national laws where the agreements do not fall under

---

[808] Jari Hellsten, 20 7.2000.

[809] COLCOM, p.50.

[810] COLCOM, p.50.

[811] COLCOM, pp.24-25.

[812] COLCOM, p.42, 56-57..

[813] On the victorious nature of the decision to the role of Member States and social partners, see Vousden, S. (2000) p.181

CHAPTER 3

Community law (based on the inter-state criterion).[814]

This comparative study gives background to the inquiry and conclusions of the Advocate General in *Albany*. It suggests, in general, that no uniform regulatory framework really exists in Europe in relation to the liaison competition law/collection labour law, even if the activity in this field is growing.

The study advocates that in some countries there are expressed, derived or right-to-strike - anchored constitutional guarantees to the collective bargaining (Austria, Belgium, France, Germany, Italy, Spain, Sweden). In this sense, it is conceptually more sophisticated than the study of Mr. Jacobs and the administration of the Court.

Some relevancy of constitutional law can found also in the systems of Greece and Portugal.[815] These last systems were excluded from the scope of the reporting, also by the Advocate General (who, nevertheless, obviously had in his use the material produced in the administration[816]).

In these systems with some type of constitutional guarantees, the international obligations do not have to be necessarily employed. In the countries with a constitutional court, the scope of this guarantee can be better observed (Germany). Free competition, on the other hand, does not enjoy the status of constitutional right.[817] One could claim, furthermore, that this last observation can be backed up also by the decision of *Albany*, where the margin of discretion is strongly attached to the national level. Namely, if the EC competition law would override the national guarantees, this would mean an opposite evaluation of the legal interests involved.

Basically, however, there are systems, where the relationship between competition law and labour law is not regulated (Austria, Belgium, France, Germany, Italy, the Netherlands, Spain and the United Kingdom), and countries, where there is the recognition of the position of social partners/collective agreements in the competition law. However, even if no explicit legal provisions exist, it has not prevented the courts to take the floor in this matter in many countries (except in Italy and Austria).[818] The Spanish system provides procedure against certain types of terms *("ill will")* behind the agreement. In the United Kingdom, changes have taken place obviously due to the EC law, which could imply the applicability of

---

[814] COLCOM, p.48, 62.

[815] COLCOM, p.51.

[816] However, it is clear that the studies exist in the Courts administration It is unlikely that comparative reports from these countries would have been excluded.

[817] COLCOM, p.51.

[818] This is interesting, because it clearly shows that where the political bargaining process does not achieve results, the court system has to solve the up-coming problems. This seems to suggest that the problem could be a constitutional in nature, but neither of the collective parties are ready to establish a constitutional solution. The matter remains a matter of legal dispute. Where such a question, however, appears - as it now has - in the European level with all its possible "constitutional" (supremacy) implications, the legal discourse is even more vigorous.

competition law to collective agreements. Community law is to be followed also in the reforms of the Netherlands. The situation is, however, quite anomalous, especially now after these European level decisions.[819]

In all Nordic countries, the recently enacted laws exclude *a priori* the applicability of the competition law rules to collective agreements[820]. One could interpret this as a sign of a consensus in the political level. However, contents and the effects can be examined in relation to the competition aspects. The application of this kind is still very uncertain[821].

The report does not really draw any tangible conclusions from the comparative study regarding the differences and similarities. According to the report, the differences could be technical in nature.[822] However, a classification of regulatory models is proposed: the Nordic model with explicit exemption, the Continental model with constitutional emphasis, and the Anglo-Saxon model with kind of a situational regulation. This conclusion is one of the advanced details of this report.

The specialist report gives very different impression about the situation in comparison to the one designed by the Advocate General. For example, the specialist report seems to support a somewhat different conclusion on the German situation. The report clearly takes more seriously the judgements and the analysis of the German Constitutional Court and the Federal Labour Court.

This difference can be explained by the fact that the uncertainty is greater in the institutional reporting system of the Court than in the discourse by the labour law specialists. The conclusions by the Advocate General are rather confusing. On the other hand, the lack of a more historical approach[823] and the strong attachment to the case law by the Advocate General is apparently one reason to the differences. Nevertheless, it must be noted that the argumentation in the specialists report on case law is a bit more quantitative in nature.[824] Perhaps the Advocate General's background as an experienced Anglo-Saxon judge qualifies him higher in the analysis of the cases.

The specialist report explicitly recognizes some of these differences.

One cannot find a counterpart to Mr. Jacobs' analysis of the United States in the specialists' report. This exclusion is not motivated. The report only gives impression that the differences in the conclusions may be due to that. The exclusion may be motivated by idea that the focus is on the European law and that there are deep and obvious differences between the United

---

[819] COLCOM, pp.52-53.

[820] COLCOM, p.53.

[821] COLCOM, p.53.

[822] COLCOM, p.54.

[823] See also, COLCOM, p.55, Sulkunen, O (2000) p.148.

[824] See, COLCOM, p.52.

States and European philosophy in relation to these questions.

The criticism in the report is focussing also on the Advocate General's treatment of the French system. The use of doctrinal discussion (as a source of law) was absent. This could have been a basis for more critical analysis of the French cases. This fallacy is clearly a problem of the institutional reporting system of the European Court. Last-mentioned applies also, to certain extend, to the analysis of the Finnish case law, in which all implications of the case (effects to the terms of employment and working conditions) were not covered in the Mr. Jacob's analysis[825]. The Labour Court decisions were neither considered[826]. This shows some systematic problems in the Advocate General's approach. This is already a more serious problem, because the opinion of the Advocate General is meant to be an independent advice to the Court dealing with the facts of the case.

Despite these latter aspects the report, however, does not show any fundamental mistakes in the Advocate General's traditional type of comparative legal reasoning. Many problems in the opinion seem to be due to the methodological problems of the opinion and, consequently, the advising of the Court can be criticized on those basis. The sensitivity in the methodology is not really developed. The specialists' report seems to be more susceptible to the national legal discourse as a whole. Also the emphasis is a bit different in these two comparative studies. They coincide in many points, but clearly the conclusions are drawn in different ways and for different reasons.[827]

Some conclusions. This case has provoked some confusion in Member States' legal discourses - not only because of its comparative law observations. The discussion is still pending on the relationship between collective agreements and competition law rules.[828] It is unquestionable that all these decisions have to be considered seriously in national legal systems[829] - also from the point of view of fundamental rights.[830]

In Finland the decision of the Highest Administrative Court has been reexamined by some labour lawyers. In this Finnish case - also referred by the Advocate General in his comparative law inquiry - the terms of the collective agreement affirmed a right for the employee party to do exclusively the work in certain field of industrial sector (cleaning inside the paper mills). Consequently, the hiring of any external labour to do this work would have

---

[825] COLCOM, p.56.

[826] Sulkunen, O., 2000, p.151.

[827] The comparison of these two studies is interesting from the point of view of comparative law. Is it so that the basic differences lay in the level of the use of legal sources, comparative law methodology, and the aims of the study, and the basic conceptions of law?

[828] COLCOM, p.50.

[829] See also, COLCOM, p.44 ff., for Spain, Finland, Sweden, see COLCOM, p.57. Gyselen, L. (2000) p.448.

[830] COLCOM, p.46.

been against this agreement. The general problem in the interpretation of the case from the point of view of competition law was the concept of "terms of employment". As mentioned before, the Finnish Administrative Court came to the conclusion that because these terms did not have a direct impact to the terms of employment in the sector, those terms were not in the scope of labour-market in the sense of the exemption clause embraced in the competition law and, consequently, the competition law provisions applied to them with restrictive results.[831]

The distance between the collective parties in the public discussion seems to be prominent. The main argument has been that the decision of the KHO should be reconsidered or at least that the *Albany* decision has far reaching implications to the consideration of similar types of cases.

The tendency to apply competition rules in the sphere of collective agreements seems to be a fashionable phenomenon, especially in Nordic countries.[832] In general, the interest to this type of operation arises clearly from the general economic situation characterized by high employment, traditionally low labour mobility. These economic-legal systems have historically been more closed and foreign trade dependent. One could say that the accession of these systems (countries) to the just accomplished liberalized economic market has had stronger effects to these systems than to the traditionally more liberal economies. How much the increasing consideration of labour measures from the point of view of competition law is related to the finalization of the European market in general and to abolishing of the all kinds of obstacles to the free movements is a question to be studied.

Consequently, the relationship between these two spheres of law must be made clearer. Moreover, this seems to be, undoubtedly, a matter of analysis of the subject from the point of view of basic rights.

The following analysis may provide some arguments to this discussion. This review is

---

[831] The idea presented in this case is disputable, and one could say that it represents a hasty and even untraditional consideration by the Supreme Administrative Court. The untraditional nature of this decision can be traced also from the comparative study between the Nordic countries (Swedish report by Malmberg, J., COLCOM, p.160 ff.).

It seems to be clear that no anchoring of collective agreements to the constitutional sphere exists in Finland (Finnish report, COLCOM, Jari Hellsten, p.93). However, the doctrine has been telling another story for some time. The semi-constitutional nature of these arrangements can be derived from international instruments, and the Appeal Court case law supports this idea too (also, Hellsten, J, p.93)

Another critical argument is "systematic", and it is supported by the reasoning of the Advocate General in the *Albany* case: because these two sets of rules, *"in same rank"*, should not - according to the well established principles of interpretation - *"take precedence over another, and they should be not empted their entire content by this interpretation"*. As noted, he came to the conclusion that there exists the automatic immunity of the collective agreements. On the other hand, the criteria developed by the Advocate General for defining the limits of the immunity do not seem to coincide with the evaluation criteria of the Finnish Supreme Administrative Court (in the paper mill case), even if the results, on many points, seem to concur.

The Court clearly takes seriously the challenge presented by Mr. Jacobs in relation to the methods of interpretation, where it explains its own method of interpretation in the case as interpretation based on "consistency" and "efficiency" and more holistic approach (*"Treaty as a whole"*).

[832] See also, COLCOM, pp.50-51.

motivated by the fact that the observations of the Advocate General in *Albany* case contains both ideological and realistic reasoning.

Collective agreements and competition law; basic rights, market rights, and the hierarchy of these rights based on the idea of functional interpretation. The basic problem in the Finnish case, as in the European cases, is that it is fairly strange to apply a set of norms designed to protect consumer - and the functioning of the selling and retailing market - to activity, which is designed, on the other hand, to protect the interests of the individual as worker, especially where the individual interests are agreed in an agreement between the collective parties (employees and employers) having, in this respect, rather different aims.

Furthermore, the criteria of examining the validity of "normal" contracts seems to be also foreign to the evaluation of collective agreements. This is so because the bargaining power in the collective societal (contractual) discourse is obviously political and social in nature. Consequently, it appears that the limits of the collective agreeing cannot be interpreted (normally) based, for example, on ideas like direct threat of physical nature, fraud, insanity, mistake, "*non est factum*" or other that type of plea prevailing in most of the legal systems.

It is intelligible that there are limits to what collective agreements can regulate. These limits are associated with the rights of an individual in a very fundamental sense. Namely, collective agreements may be, in "wicked" systems, part of the system suppressing individuals. In such cases, the basic principles of discrimination apply.

Nevertheless, if the matter is interpreted predominately based on a fear of "conspiracy in every corner", a serious mistake is made.[833]

Is the relationship between collective agreeing and competition law ultimately a basic right question? Could there be a right to collective bargaining?[834] What relevance has the basic rights dimension in the interpretation of the relationship between collective agreeing and competition law?

Some answers to these questions may be found by examining the basic right dimensions of competition law and free competition.

The competition law norms regulate the way competition must be exercised. This economic activity must take place in the interests of the market (society?) as a whole, of course, but also in the interest of others' economic rights and in the interest of consumers' rights as consumers. These aspects can undoubtedly be reduced to the property of rights of those functioning in an active market. Furthermore, the rights of companies must be guaranteed,

---

[833] We come to this fundamental question concerning individual rights and collective agreeing later.

[834] Sulkunen, O. (2000, p.152, referring in p.152 also to opinions of Blanke, Aur, 1/2000). He maintains that the right to collective bargaining is a basic right in the light of the Court's decisions. He motivates this observation by the fact that the Court took distance from the Advocate General's idea that the right to collective bargaining is already sufficiently protected by the general principle of freedom of contract.

for example, in the case of a thorough investigation or search (as noted in the analysis of the *Hoescht* case above).

The collective agreements and the system of collective agreeing, on the other hand, are designed to protect social rights of a worker.

One could claim that the relationship between the scope of collective agreeing - and the norms created thereby - and the competition law norms is, from the point of view of basic rights, not so interesting in this sense that these both types of fields of activity are functional. Furthermore, the regulative framework regulating this activity is designed to protect different types of individual rights (liberal and social) in the economic and social market. The collective agreements protect individuals in their role as workers and individuals in relation to their basic social rights, whereas the competition law protects individuals in their role as active users of their property rights as well as consumers rights. When thinking about the role of an individual as a possessor of these two types of rights, any conflict between these two sets of law must be due to individual's social role and function in the market, and not so much as a owner of basic rights as an individual in the society as a whole.

Accordingly, the point of departure to the interpretation of this question - relating to the conflict between legal interests - appears to be in the conflict between collective agreements and competition law and not so much in the realm of basic rights. The relationship must be interpreted in the functional sphere of a market. The conflict is between these two spheres of functional regulation. The basic starting point is the functional nature of these two sets of norms, even if it is certainly unquestionable that, in the end, these market roles must be subordinate to the individuals basic rights in the legal system.

Consequently, the balancing of these two sets of rights takes place in a functional interpretation regarding the market and social elements involved in these rights (worker/consumer/undertaking), and no really "hard" basic right conflict does really exist.

The solution to this problem concerning a conflict between these two sets of functional norms must be found - as the Advocate General in the Albany case maintains too - from the general principles of interpretation.[835]

First of all, there can be no question as to the existence of the basic rights to collective association and action. The protection of these rights is evident, as was concluded also by the institutional actors in the cases under examination.

However, the autonomous basic right to bargain collectively would mean, ideally, a right for the collective entity to bargain on any types of terms related to their function, which right would be in the same category as the rights of individuals whose rights these collective activities are designed to protect (social objectives). This does not seem to be possible from the point of view of constitutional law and the system of basic rights.

---

[835] Mr. Jacob's opinion, para. 179, see above

There is also another problem. Namely, the restrictions to the use of this basic right would have to be interpreted quite materially, for the interpretation of the "intention" of the collective entity making these agreements is already a great problem. This resembles the problem of interpreting "contracts" in the realm of competition law and the intention of parties (the intention to distort competition). The nature of these contracts, even as presumed contracts, is occasionally times interpreted in the light of the economic analysis. Furthermore, the methods of investigation of the factual context of these arrangements - falling into the competence of the competition law authorities - are very wide and may even demand the use of force. As Advocate General notices, the scrutiny of these collective agreements would entail an introduction of a notification system and the possibility for the court to evaluate these collective agreements. This would be rather problematic.

However, the idea that collective entities have a "right" to bargain collectively has been, to a certain extend, accomplished indirectly by giving constitutionally or constitutionally "anchored" way some collective entities an assignment to achieve social objectives in a transparent and politically functional process.[836] This process is a system's measure to protect social rights and achieve social aims, a way to delegate the state function of guaranteeing rights to a collective entity. However, this does not mean that in accomplishing these social objectives, the collective entity would have a basic right to bargain collectively in any more general sense. The "right" is strongly tied to the function of achieving social objectives.

From the legal systematic point of view the analysis above is essential. The system of collective agreeing seems to have *a priori* a distinctive status in the legal system, because the agreements made in this sphere are designed to achieve social objectives and to actualize the social rights guaranteed also by the state to an individual (rights recognized in one form or another in most of the legal systems in the western world). This appears to be so from the systemic and policy point of view. From the point of view of the civil society and "natural" rights, it is clear that this type of function has to be in a strong control. Furthermore, if the transparency of the political collective bargaining process cannot satisfy this need, the question must be seen from the point of view of the basic constitutional and institutionalized system of rights. Nevertheless, even here the question is a matter of protecting the equal possibility and a right of a person to be involved in political and contractual relationships of any kind whenever their interest so determines. Thus, the ultimate aim of this control has to be the protection of discursive processes, actions and autonomy, which are the basis of the

---

[836] The main idea behind the basic right to collective bargaining is that only by having a basic right to collective bargaining individuals part of a collective can protect their legal interests. However, this is quite odd idea from the point of view of an institutionalized legal system. Namely, this type of construction prevails "basic" only in a non-functional liberal democracy where the institutionalized forms of protection of social and liberal rights (politically functional) cannot be maintained. Naturally, one may establish basic rights for a collective, but then it means legal balancing of the rights of individuals and collectives. This is not very desirable.

democratic system.

Consequently, competition law provisions seem to be, from the systematic point of view in the end a lower rank set of norms, and the right to free competition lower than the right to collective bargaining. Namely, a right to free competition is a right (especially for companies) guaranteed by the system in order to accomplish the functioning of the market and consumers rights, and against this idea the achievement of the social rights seems to be more fundamental.

On the other hand, if the right to collective bargaining is, for example, contrasted with the employers' right not to get involved in the bargaining process[837] and the second one is preferred, the assumption that collective processes aim at "social objectives" is lost. This would also mean the possibility to interpret collective agreements in a functional way, which results unbearable problems to the system as a whole, as maintained above.

This issue can be seen also purely from the legal interpretational point of view - from the point of view of the methods of interpretation of collective agreements *vis-á-vis* the normal market agreements between undertakings.

The methods of interpreting these two types of contracts (commercial and collective bargaining based) differs greatly and is essential in answering to the question about their status and hierarchy in the legal system.[838] Namely, the interpretation of commercial contracts in the realm of competition law is highly functional because of the expected strategic acting (covered agreements) whereas the functionality of the collective agreements is related to the general economic and social policy of a state and a policy-making institution. The meaning of collective agreements must be interpreted in the light of the open and transparent policy ("social objectives"), and this sense the interpretation must be more "positivistic", legalistic, and restrictive. Namely, where there is, in a contract itself, embedded the notion of "social objectives", the provisions of that contract cannot be seen *a priori* in instrumental and strategic terms from the point of view of the parties of the contract - and neither from the systematic point of view. They must be observed from the point of view of the general social policy -maker (whether it is a Member State or the Community, for example). The terms of the contract are assumed to be in their positive form an expression of the "social objectives" without any contextual strategy (as "distortion of competition") because they are accomplished in a transparent process and because they already are controlled by several societal actors during this process. This makes their status in comparison to "normal" market contracts (belonging to the scope of competition law) very strong.

If needed, these types of collective contracts may be invalidated on very general basis as not

---

[837] See Mr. Jacobs' analysis of the *Gustafsson* case (25 April 1996 R.J.D 1996 - II No 9)in the European Court of Human Rights.

[838] Advocate General Jacob's reasoning related to this, see Opinion, paragraph 183 ff.

belonging to the category of collective agreements at all. We come to this question later. As one may note, this issue is related also to the basic rights question.

Consequently, the provisions of competition law - measures for the invalidation of normal market contracts and their terms - are highly instrumental and interpreted in an instrumental way. It is very problematic to use them in invalidating collective agreements and their terms. The interpretation on the basis of these provisions assumes an analysis of the aims and objectives, but competition distorting aims are only one extremely narrow category of aims. In practice, in the collective agreeing the intention is strongly presumed to be social and the scope of the terms of these contracts which qualify the definition of "social objectives" is quite far-reaching. The definition is very broad and it includes, as mentioned in the specialists report, terms related not only to physical protection but also the terms associated with economic protection of the worker in the sense that the wages and all pension benefits must be assured.

Finally, it is no wonder why in this problem, the distinctions like *"bona fide"* and *"ill will"* have been employed both in the material produced in the national legal systems as well as in the context of Community Law.[839] Namely, the presumption of collective agreeing having a social objective is so strong that where the involvement to the collective agreeing and to the scrutinizing of these agreements takes place, we are speaking about total failure of this presumption of "social objectives". The "bad faith" causes the collapse of the whole system of collective agreeing when they these contracts are noticed to be only a facade for some other types of aims - in this context, the aim to distort competition.

This is the reason why the good faith idea comes up in the connection of interpreting collective agreements stronger than in the interpretation of normal market agreements. But also here the good faith is relatively meaningless conception. How can the intentions of the collective agreements be interpreted, where the parties to these agreements are collectives and where the assumption is the achievement of social objectives?

Some words may be said about the potentiality of collective agreements to breach other collective and individual rights which may be, in some very exceptional cases, the reason to invalidate their terms or them as a whole.

Where the breach in the presumption of the realization of the social objectives takes place, we are not speaking about protection of the individuals' social rights and rights as a worker anymore, but assumably "protection" of some interests of an collective entity, which clearly cannot be identified with any "social" and predefined collective as such, but is conspiratory in nature - even if other types of claims would be presented by the agreeing parties in these types of cases. The new "collective" in this type of conspiratory agreement is another type of economic - not legal - entity.

---

[839] Some analysis, Gyselen, L. (2000) p.443. He claims that such collective agreements are not exceptional at all.

Against the background of some historical examples, one may say that this type of economic thinking relates to totalitarian economies and fits neither to the liberal markets nor to the constitutional basic rights thinking including the protection of liberal or social rights. Thus, it is also against any type of competition law norm designed for any type of liberal market (however, this latter aspect being a minor question in those kind of cases).

These last comments must be obviously associated with the ideological background of the system of basic rights, and they are not related directly to any legal analysis.[840] Nevertheless, it must be stressed that the collective agreements are, can, and must be under strong constitutional control from the point of view of individual rights in both national legal systems and in European legal orders complementing each other.

In conclusion - more or less summarizing the aspects taken up in this analysis - it can be affirmed that collective bargaining and agreeing have social objectives which are many ways defined in the context of the democratic constitutional system. What is a social objective in this sense is a matter of a political and fundamental legal system to define positively. Furthermore, the collective bargaining and agreeing is qualified by such elements, which restrict their scope in relation to the "normal political rights". They are socially and politically defined functions and their scope, as it regards the social objectives, is defined in a constitutionally valid process. In this sense, it is problematic - but not absolutely impossible - to consider the right to bargain collectively as a fundamental right belonging to the same category as fundamental political and social rights. Thus, it seems to be a subordinate "right" implementing the social rights.

How much the explicit right to collective bargaining (prevailing, for example, in the Swedish system) promotes social peace and is "realistically" beneficial, and how much there could be differences in considering the "culture of right" in general is a matter of further discussion. The Advocate General maintains that the question is basically about the choice between systems of "encouragement or right". He recognizes[841] the benefits of the realistic model in *"[preventing] the costly labour conflicts.. [reducing] the transaction costs... [promoting] the predictability and transparency..."* and in creating the equilibrium in micro and macro levels *("society as a whole")*.

General conclusions. The material conclusion of this analysis is that no real support from Community law can be indeed found for a general examination of collective agreements by the competition law rules.

---

[840] However, one could interpret the reasoning of the United States Supreme Court on these basis, and explain the existence of the *Clayton Act* 1914 in the United States. In Europe, the relationship between collective agreeing and competition law is regulated on the level of competition law - if at all (on this, Sulkunen, O., (2000) pp.146-147).

[841] Opinion of Mr. Jacobs, paragraph 181.

Concerning the study of comparative reasoning, it is interesting to note that some kind of balancing by "comparative law dogmatics" may be developing currently in the context of European law because of the more critical attitude towards the institutionally conducted comparative law decision-making. Moreover, the *Albany* case and the reasoning it and the specialists' report contains shows the dangers of the institutionalist comparative law and restrictive approach to legal sources and legal discourse - applied too easily in the European legal discourse.

3.4. Functional comparative reasoning: Hard case V (Kalanke in the European Court of Justice) (culture, the use of third law, constitutional generality, rejection of legislative generality, comparison by opposites, comparability, substantive equality)

3.4.1. General remarks

The *Kalanke* case dealt with the quota regulation adopted by a German federal state (Bundesland) and its compatibility with EC law[842]. The question was about the possibility for national legislation to give priority to women in recruitment based on a quota system[843].

The German Court asking for a preliminary ruling was, on the other hand, considering a case, where a female person (with the same qualifications as the male applicant) had been appointed to the post in the administrative department of Bremen City on the basis of the quota provisions[844].

The EC law interpretation related to the Directive on Equal Treatment, which provided the derogation from the strict equality principle. This possibility for a derogation was expressed so that they could be allowed, where they are *"removing existing equalities which affect women's opportunities in the areas referred in the Article 1(1)"*. Article 1(1), on the other hand, refers to employment policy. The problem was, basically, how one should interpret the idea of *"measures to promote equal opportunities for women"*[845].

---

[842] Case 450/93 *Eckhard Kalanke v Freie Hansestadt Bremen* (1995) ECR I-3051, and the opinion of the Advocate general Tesauro delivered on 6 April 1995.
   The law applicable was the Bremen *Landesgleichstellungsgesetz*.
[843] In case women were underpresented, they were to be promoted or appointed instead of male applicant, if the applicants had same qualifications.
[844] The case had been taken to the *Arbeitsgericht* (the Labour Court), to *Landesarbeitsgericht* (the State Labour Court), and to the *Bundesarbeitsgericht* (the Federal Labour Court), which asked for a preliminary ruling in realm of the Article 177 (the new Article 234) of the Rome Treaty.
[845] The question was asked because of the interpretation of the Equal Treatment Directive (Council Directive 76/207/EEC of 9 February 1976 on the implementation of the principle of equal treatment for men and women as regards access to employment, vocational training and promotion, and working conditions, OJ 1976 L 39/40).

The Council recommendations[846], concerning affirmative action in equality cases, also recognized the Article in question and the need for action where attitudes, behaviour and structures in society are oppressing women.

The main legal question was, consequently, what type of derogation the national legislation can have from the strict rule of equality based on the Article 2(4) of the directive[847].

3.4.2. Comparative law as an acceptable and non-acceptable legal source

The Advocate General rejected some comparative law observations in his analysis of the case:

"I am also conscious that a position different from the one which I regard as the correct one would be supported, not only by the legislation which is the subject of the main proceedings, but also by a number of measures adopted in Member States of the Community and in non-member countries in order to guarantee, for their part too, not equal opportunities but an equal share of jobs"

Nevertheless, I consider that I can and I must resist the temptation to follow the trend, convinced as I am, and firmly so, that I would have to follow it, and propose that the Court should follow it, only if I agree that were the right direction to take".

At the time of the case, these affirmative measures were in force, in one form or another at least in France, Denmark, England, Germany and in some of its states, and apart from countries such as Finland, Sweden, Norway. The last three had applied for the membership of the European Union, and had an extensive and constitutionally coherent systems of equality laws with provisions on positive discrimination[848].

On the other hand, the justification of the Advocate General had, as its basic comparative

---

[846] 84/635/EEC of 13 December 1984

[847] There are cases dealing with the question of equality between men and women. Although in different contexts they still include strong comparative reasoning by the parties (case 248/83 *Commission v Federal Republic of Germany* (1985) ECR 1459 (Judgment of the Court of 21 May 1985)). See also, Galmot, Y., 1990, analysing *Razzouk et Beydoun* (1984) Rec 1526, *F.N.V.* (1986) Rec. 3853, *Mac Dermott et Cotter* (1987) Rec. 1468.

[848] See, for some recent studies, Schiek, D., Buhr, K., Dieball, H., Fritsche, U., Klein-Schonnefeld, S., Malzahn, M., Wankel, S., Frauengleichstellungsgesetze des Bundes und der Länder. Kommentar für die Praxis zum Frauenfördergesetz für den Bundesdienst und zu den Frauenfördergesetzen, Gleichstellungsgesetzen und Gleichrechtigunggesetzen der länder, mit Beschäftigtenschutzgesetz, Köln, 1996, McCrudden, C., Equality in Law between Men and Women in the European Community, United Kingdom. Commission 1994, Bertelsmann, K., Rust, U L'égalité juridique entre femmes et hommes dans la Communauté européenne, Allemagne. Commission of the European Community, 1994, Callender, R., Meenan, F., Equality in Law between Men and Women in the European Community, Ireland. Commission 1994, Asscher-Vonk, I., Equality in Law between Men and Women in the European Community, The Netherlands, Commission of the European Community, 1995, Martins de Oliveira, T., Equality in Law between Men and Women in the European Community, Portugal, Commission of the European Community, 1995, Nielsen, R., Equality in Law between Men and Women in the European Community, Denmark, Commission of the European Community, 1995.

In countries like Ireland, Italy, Spain, Greece, the Netherlands (where the discussion has been positive, however, and no obstacles has been seen constitutionally), no such provisions existed.

On this subject, see also Peters, A., Women Quota and Constitution. A Comparative study of Affirmative Action for Women under American, German, EC and International Law (The Hague) 1999

premise, the general constitutional principle of equality (and the idea of comparative constitutional law). He notes:

"... it is also true that it is one which most affects the principle of equality as between individuals, a principle, which is safeguarded constitutionally in most of the Member States legal systems."

Both types of comparisons were extremely superficial and formal, and they were supported by subjective arguments.[849] Any deeper analysis was lacking.[850]

The quota norm was seen, by the Advocate General, as a positive and affirmative action. Consequently, he concentrated on the analysis of the affirmative action by taking into account the *"country of its origin"*[851], In comparative terms he explained that

"Affirmative action received its name in the United States from the Democratic administrations of the 1960's, which utilized a typical judicial measure (until then affirmative action had been imposed by the courts of employers responsible for discriminatory conduct) and made it into an administrative instrument....
In fact, quotas and goals are the two systems which have been used in the United States since the late 1960's to pursue the objective of eliminating existing inequalities. ... The case law of the Supreme Court has consistently been hostile to the criterion of strict quotas (see Regents of the University of California v Bakke 483 US 265 1978)... must be transitional (see United States Steelworkers of America, AFL-CIO-CLC v Webster 443 US 193 1979)...
In Europe, positive action has begun to take hold or, at any event, to become the object of attention at the very time when affirmative action seems to be a state of crisis in its country of origin. Indeed, in the United States, recourse is now had to the criterion of strict scrutiny, whereby rules affecting a fundamental right can be justified only if they satisfy a compelling governmental interest (see, for example City of Richmond v Croson 488 US 469 1989"

The analysis of the United States relied on the political historical context and tendencies in law, in the light of the case law of the United States Supreme Court. The reasoning was strongly value-based and teleological, and even ironic in style.[852]

Furthermore, the Advocate General had an idea of 'perfection' of the formal equality principle found in the constitutions of the Member States. This takes place by introducing the idea of substantive equality[853].

---

[849] *"I am conscious...", "I must resist temptation...", "convinced as I am, and firmly so... ", "..right direction to take".*

[850] In this sense, he does not consider constitutions from the point of view of discursive integrity.

[851] It must be remembered that this analysis seems to have a general importance from the point of view of social policy considerations.

[852] *"Democratic government...", "...administrative instrument", "hostile", "typical", "on the same time ... it is .. in crisis in the country of its origin".*

[853] This is the doctrine behind the Italian constitution, for example, see Biscaretti di Ruffia, P., 1989, pp.829-834. This means that (Second paragraph of the article 3 of the constitutution *"è compito della Repubblica rimuovere gli ostacoli di ordine economico e sociale, che, limitando di fatto la libertà e l'eguaglianza dei cittadini, impediscono il pieno sviluppo della persona humana e l'effettiva partecipazione di tutti i lavoratori all'organizzazione politica, economica e sociale del Paese".* This article is meant to guarantee equality of participation, which would be a guarantee for example, a minimum level of social security. All remarkable social disparity is recognized to mean difficulties for the democratic functioning of state (ibid. p.832).
See also, Martines, T., 1981, pp.239-240.

3.4.3. "Substantive equality"

In the argumentation of the Advocate General, the basic idea, related to the question of equality, seemed to be the idea of "*elimination of existing obstacles*". This way one could achieve equal opportunities. Affirmative action was designed to abolish obstacles usually by "*granting preferential treatment*". According to him, here a shift towards a "*collective vision of equality*" takes place.

Positive action had, according to the Advocate General, several forms. In the first type, the conditions of <u>disadvantages are abolished</u> with positive action. Causes of "*less employment or opportunities*" are eradicated. These types of measures can be associated with vocational training and guidance. A second model aims more at <u>the effective sharing of responsibilities</u> (such as arrangement for working hours, fiscal measures etc).

These two types of approaches strive at achieving equal opportunities, and they lead to substantive equality. Substantive equality is not an immediate outcome, but requires a period of transition.

A third model analysed by the advocate General is the remedy <u>compensating the inequality</u> ("*punitive*"), which, according to the Advocate General, may be related to preferential treatment. This includes the systems of quotas etc. The idea is to achieve equal results. This seems to be problematic constitutionally from the point of view of the general principle of equality.

In all types of "positive action", as the Advocate General describes them, the general principle of formal equality is affected. The question becomes whether the preferential treatment is acceptable from the point of view of the formal equality principle, and, for that matter, whether the concrete system of quotas is acceptable according to the directive's derogation clause. The Advocate General assumes, in this sense, that the directives' derogation clause is in accordance with the principle of equality.

The Advocate General departs from the strict formal equality idea, and goes on to discuss what is really meant by the concept of "equal opportunities". The problem is whether "*it means equality with respect of starting points or with respect to points of arrival*". Here the constitutional equality question and the positive action itself in its preferential treatment form (the third type of positive action in the analysis of the Advocate General) are intertwined.

The Advocate General claims that the idea of equal opportunities means putting people in

---

It seems that substantive equality in its Italian form is strongly related to the guaranteeing of an abstract "political potentiality" of a person in a pluralistic liberal society (ibid., pp.240-241).
Crosa, E., speaks (1951) about this article 3.ii as "*l'uguaglianza di fatto*" (p.158).
          It is notable that Finnish btranslation of the Kalanke case speaks about "real" (todellinen) equality instead of "substantive" (sisällöllinen). Same in Swedish (verklig).

"*a position to be able to attain equal results... and restoring the conditions of equality ... as regards starting points*" ("equal opportunities" means, in this sense, equal starting points). This relates, on the other hand, to the removal of existing barriers standing in a way of the attainment of equal opportunities.

The construction presented by the Advocate General appears like the following:

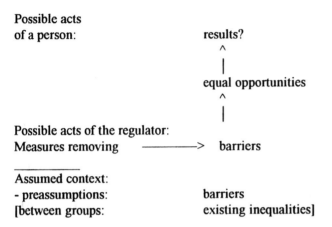

Possible acts
of a person: results?
                                                 ∧
                                                 |
                                         equal opportunities
                                                 ∧
                                                 |
Possible acts of the regulator:
Measures removing   ————>   barriers

Assumed context:
- preassumptions: barriers
[between groups: existing inequalities]

One notices that a regulative action requires two operations: identification of the barriers and their removal with suitable measures. This will be deal with below.

On the other hand, the Advocate General refers also to a previous case of the Court[854], which ruled that special rights for women are not allowed because despite the measures *are "discriminatory in appearance they are in point of fact intended to eliminate or reduce actual instances of inequality, which may exist in reality of social life"*. This case ruled out, from the scope of the derogation and the Community law,

"*shortening of working hours, advancement of the retirement age, obtaining leave when the child is ill, granting additional days of annual leave in respect of each child, payment of an allowance to mothers who have meet cost of nurseries and the like and so on*"[!?]

Consequently, the Advocate General argued that only those measures, which attempt to remove the obstacles from equal opportunities can be complied with. This is the idea of "*real and effective substantive equality*", and the achievement of "*actual equality*"[855]. Only discrimination in "*appearance*" is allowed

---

[854] Case 312/86 *Commission v France* (1988) ECR 6315.

[855] He remarks that "*the ultimate objective is therefore the same: securing equality as between persons*".

"in so far as it authorizes or requires different treatment in favour of women and in order to protect them with a view to attaining substantive and not formal equality, which would in contrast be the negation of equality"[856].

Furthermore, the Advocate General defines, in concrete terms, the available measures. First of all, measures related to eliminating the unfavourable biological conditions are allowed[857]. Here the Advocate General confirms the idea that preferential treatment cannot be allowed only by considering *"to all women as such"*, but only *"specific conditions of women"*[858]. Quotas are seen *"irrelevant"* from the point of view of the *"substantive equality"*. Furthermore, the Advocate General maintains, referring to the previous case law, that measures of organizing working hours, structures for small children, and other measures, which enable women to reconcile the *"family and work commitments... with each other"*[859] are allowed[860].

The Advocate General sees the problems mainly in the fields of historical, cultural and social conditions, where one identifies disparity in educational and vocational training[861]. Furthermore, the Advocate General considers the types of preferential measures as *"compensations for the historical discrimination"*.[862]

---

[856]This idea assumes a kind of a automatic realization of the norm. One could ask, why, then, does this matter seems to be structural, and why such strong measures are produced?

It appears as if Advocate General does not want to look at the political development behind all these achievements. He concentrates only to the women/men perspective in an isolated sphere. However, this is not the context of these declarations and provisions of Community and national law. The question is also about a political balance and integrity, not about some kind of a philosophical balance and coherence. The Advocate General does not concentrate on the legal provisions as socio-political norms, but treats them as cultural norms, which, I think, is not the point here.

Furthermore, one could claim that the question cannot be compared so easily with the question of the general equality of persons. The general equality question cannot be analogized with the gender question. This problematic feature is, as well, connected to the idea of using the positive discrimination analogy deriving from the United States practice.

The considerations of the general principle of equality is highly problematic. In connecting the gender question to general equality one actually politicizes the question again. The repolitization can be seen rational, but not from the point of view of the Community system and law.

The strict distinction between law and politics presented here by the Advocate General is very interesting.

[857] One is faced with the definition of biological conditions. The Advocate General speaks about *"pregnancy"*. That remains the only definition. The question about results of the pregnancy in social life is not treated here by the Advocate General. In general, his conception of the" biological" allows an extremely restricted scope of derogations.

[858] Interestingly, "women's conditions" can be separated from "all women as such". Is it not so that "women's conditions" are somehow connected to "all women as such"?

Advocate General continues: *"The rationale for the preferential treatment given to women lies in the general situation of disadvantage caused by past discrimination and the existing difficulties connected with playing a dual role".* (*A dual role of women?*).

[859] This would seem to suggest, wrongly, that men are not doing also. This seems to relate to differences in social contexts.

[860] *"Measures relating to the organization of work, in particular working hours, and structures for small children and other measures which will enable family and work commitments to be reconciled with each other"*

[861] One interesting question related to education is; could it be possible that these educational measures actually reproduce the structural inequalities in the society?

[862] The problem is at this point in terms of what society reference is made to.

Consequently, the measures allowed in derogation from the directive were those which remove actual obstacles. One of their characters is that they are temporary. The assumption in the quota system seems to be a long-term perspective.

The Recommendations of the Council seemed not to be a clear basis for another type of interpretation. The Advocate General uses also the doctrine of *"strict interpretation of derogation from an equal right"* and the *"principle of proportionality"*. Furthermore, the opinions of the Parliament and literature, which would support another type of conclusion, were not considered clear enough[863]. He referred also to the agreement on social policy[864].

Accordingly, the Advocate General came to the conclusion that the measures adopted by the federal state were not in accordance with Community Law.[865]

---

[863] Court's reasoning emphasised the strict interpretation of derogations, which was only one of the questions dealt with Advocate General's reasoning. However, it is quite difficult to claim that the Advocate General's reasoning did not have an impact upon the Court's decision.

Furthermore, the influence is more visible from the discursive point of view. "European" dogmatics has a tendency to look the decisions based on the argumentation by the Advocate General.

[864] Maastricht Treaty, Protocol No. 14.

[865] The Court does not seem to have a clear idea of the extension of the derogation. The Court's judgment is very short. It states, basically, that quota regulation treats men and women differently. Consequently, it *"involves discrimination on grounds of sex"* (Article 2(1) of the directive). The derogation provided in Article 2(4) of the directive is *"specifically and exclusively designed to allow measures which, although discriminatory in appearance, are in point of fact intended to eliminate or etc ... actual instances of inequality which may exist in the reality of social life. It thus permits national measures relating to access to employment, including promotion, which give a specific advantage to women with a view to improving their ability to compete on the labour market and to pursue a career on an equal ... with men."*

Consequently, the derogation, according to the Court, must be interpreted strictly. National rules which guarantee absolute and unconditional priority for appointment or promotion go beyond promoting equal opportunities.

It must be noted that the Court came to the same conclusion as the Advocate General without referring to his analysis, Case Judgment of the Court of 17 October 1995. Case C-450/93, ECR 1995 p.I-3051.

How strong is the case law on substantive equality? It appears as if the doctrine of the substantive equality has entered permanently to the work of the European Court. The doctrine has been referred by the Advocate General Tesauro again in the case 13/94 *P v S and Cornwall County Council* (opinion on 14 December 1995, ECR 1996 2143), referring also to the case of (West) German Constitutional Court (BvefG, 11 October 1978, in NJW 1979, p.595 et seq.), and in the case 32/93 *Carole Louise Webb v Emo Air Cargo (UK) ltd* (opinion on 1 June 1994, ECR I-3567). Lately, referring directly to the idea of substantive equality defined in the previous cases, 400/95 *Handels, og Kontorfunktionaerernes Forbund i Denmark, acting on behalf of Helle Elisabeth Larsson v Dansk Handel & Service, acting on behalf of Fotex Supermarked A/S* and opinion of Mr Advocate General Ruiz-Jarabo Colomer delivered on 18 February (Reference for a preliminary ruling: So- og Haldelsretten, Equal Treatment of men and women, Directive 76/207/EEC, conditions governing dismissal, Absence due to an illness attributable to pregnancy or confinement, Absence during pregnancy and after confinement) (1997) ECR I-2757.

Moreover, parties (case T-368/94 *Pierre Blanchard v Commission* (1996) ECR II-41 (Judgment of the Court of First Instance of 9 January 1996)), and Commission (case 132/92 *Birds Eye Walls ltd v Friedel M. Roberts* (1993) ECR I-5579 (Judgment of the Court of 9 November 1993)) have been using it as an argument.

It may have to be used in the case dealing with the reference for the preliminary ruling (case1154/96 *Louis Wolfs v Office National des pensions* (reference for the preliminary ruling from the 11th Chamber of the Tribunal du travail, Brussels) OJ No C-197, 1996-07-06, p.12 (pending).

3.4.4. Some analysis

The Advocate General claims, in this case, that the candidates (the man and the woman) had equal opportunities. In fact, the Advocate General claims that the candidates had equal opportunities merely because they were qualified, explicitly, as equal in the employment situation[866]. On the other hand, he seems to suggest that therefore the measures were designed for aiming at an outcome, not to abolish barriers.[867]

Here one recognizes some problems. The Advocate General claims that, in this case, equal opportunities already existed, and that there were no barriers. This may be the reason, why he is able to claim that the legislator has thought of men and women as groups and concentrated on to ensure "*numerical terms*" an equal distribution of jobs as an outcome.

It is true that this appears to have occurred, if one starts from the fact that the candidates had been qualitatively evaluated as equal and that the decision was backed up by the quota requirements. Furthermore, it is also true that the result of the case was that the number of women increased in the organization. Against this background it is understandable, for example, why the Advocate General sees the measures related to education and vocational training more suitable to eliminate unequal opportunities.

However, the problem of the case does not lie in the individual case only. Here the question is about the acceptability of this types of measures in general. One can easily fail to see the single case in question actually as a consequence of some more general measures of equality law previously enacted in order to abolish the structural inequalities in society between groups.

One could claim that the analysis should have been, instead, based on the assumption that the legislator had in mind the general features of the relationship between the groups and their employment in the design of the general legal measures[868], and that these measures had their political and socio-cultural background. One could claim, for example, that if no preferential treatment provisions (based on political conflict resolution) had been available, there could have been no consideration, like in the employment situation there was, of any right to equal treatment. Then the case would have been only a matter of choosing between two candidates. However, in this type of situation, if structural inequalities exist and they could prevail, the man would have been chosen without any further consideration.

The Advocate General seems to suggest that the aim of the legislator, in establishing quotas and preferential treatment, is only to fulfill the quota, and not to balance the structural

---

[866] The Advocate General states that having the same qualifications *"implies in fact by definition that the two candidates have had and continue to have equal opportunities: they are therefore on an equal footing at the starting block"*.
[867] Note the transfer from the general analysis to the individual case!
[868] It seems that the Advocate General does not consider important the democratic political bargaining processes and the contextual thinking of the legislator.

inequalities (*"numerical terms"*, *"punitive measures"*). However, one has to note that the quota in this type of regulatory measure, in general, is not the main aim itself, but a criterion of evaluating the outcomes of the appointment and promotion policy in an organization and in society in general.

Consequently, one could claim that the Advocate General, consciously or unconsciously, interprets the situation himself in numerical terms (which is quite formal approach), and fails to see the aim of the legislator in removing, in group terms, existing and identified inequalities. On the other hand, he may consider that the cultural and contextual structural inequalities recognized by the legislator are illusory in nature. Advocate General also considers the employment as an aim or result as such, but fails to consider the aims beyond (economic status of women in society etc.).

However, the real formal problem in his reasoning seems to be the fact that he moves the individual case to the interpretation of more general legislative measures and their intentions.

The Advocate General, nevertheless, notes that also the results have to be taken into account to a certain extent. The substantive consequences could not always be attained only by a "equal footing" approach. The Advocate General finds, in his analysis, that it may be the social structure which results in unequal treatment. Relating this to the case he maintains that woman could have been set aside because of "social" (informal) reasons, even if she has similar qualifications. Then he seems to pose the question as to whether this consideration of the results would be in accordance with Community law? In other words, the Advocate General seems to ask himself whether informal social reasons can be valid in considering the outcome.

Here he seems to make the inductive fallacy again. The Advocate General seems to think that the informal reasons are the informal reasons of the case, not the informal reasons of the legislation in general. One could claim, for example, that, in the legislation, the reasons are not informal (as the political discourse in general), but they can be also formal, where, for example, the *"travaux preparatoires"* may be used as a source of legal reasoning.

In conclusion, from the argumentative point of view, the recurrence of the idea of *"substantive"* in the Advocate General's argumentation seems to lose its persuasiveness. The constant repetition seems to indicate that no real idea of the substantive is communicable. On the other hand, the final analysis does not inform anything on the acceptability of the general positive discrimination measures. However, while the Advocate General seems to refer only to the possibility of "situational" positive actions in the realm of promotion and appointment, his argumentation seems to suggest that no structural inequality "really" or actually exists or that the structural inequalities, which exist, could be maintained.

Furthermore, as suggested, the Advocate General seems to have made an inductive fallacy in the argumentation. Namely, he does not take into account that the equality of opportunities, evidently existing between two applicants in the case, can be a consequence of many factual and socio-psychological determinants.[869]

3.4.5. Comparative generalities, the paradox, and the use of third law

In point of fact, what one is facing here is generality at two levels; some generality of legislation in Member States (legislative), and the comparable and general constitutional rule of equality (adjudicative). Those laws have been made in support of the corresponding constitutional principles (democracy, equality). What the Advocate General proposes seems to be a test of generality of laws in relation to the generality of the principle of equality. He has two level comparative arguments in use.

Because, according to the Advocate General, they are in conflict, to a certain extent, he actually "finds", against all odds, a comparatively general paradox in the legal systems of some Member States. This is why he is forced to extent his argumentation in order to justify the rejection of the generality of laws.

By this extended argumentation, the Advocate General starts to determine an "institutional" principle of equality as a basis of the justification (i.e. political dimension)[870]. He actually acts as an interpreter of the constitutions, as a kind of a constitutional court. However, at the same time he reads something into the idea of this principle and constitutional traditions, against the idea of transitivity (i.e. the internal paradox of constitutional systems). He also makes use of, in order to support his argument, external (third law) arguments and analysis. He uses the a "third law" the US law to support his "institutional interpretation" of the equality principle. These features are presented by a form of analogical interpretation, and by widening interpretation.

The comparative "generality" arguments and third law arguments, in the Advocate General's justification, reveal the institutionally instrumental thinking concerning constitutional law. From the justification one can note, that the normative message in the argumentation is that the abolition of this type of positive discrimination is considered necessary, despite any circumstances and the legal integrity of any system. It seems to be,

---

[869] These aspects will be analysed below.

[870] There seems to be a genuine conflict between legislative and adjudicative integrity. The fact that the comparative legislative generality is neglected on the basis of socio-philosophical arguments shows, that the question is about this kind of conflict. Here one is not speaking about a relationship between normal "legal" interpretation and their semantic-normative conflict, but rather a conflict, which evidently has to do with basic values.

This fact can be explained by the role of comparative arguments. The comparative value is interpreted against another value, which is, on the other hand, based on a more philosophical analysis of the nature of equality. Here the equality does not correspond with the value represented by the legal systems. The second level analogy between the Community system and the general practices of the States does not "fit". The value, in this case, seems to be based on the "autonomous" philosophical considerations related to the fundamental social context of the arguer.

according to the Advocate General, fundamentally against European law principles[871].

3.4.6. Substantive equality as a cultural argument, the limits of law, and functional law

The Advocate General's strongly principled interpretation leads also to a conclusion that it is determined by the cultural background of the decision-maker. This conclusion is supported also by some ideas presented by the Advocate General.

The Advocate General claims, for example, that discriminatory measures are *"as unlawful today for the purposes of promotion as they were in the past"* (?). Furthermore, some "normative cultural" premises come up in the following way:[872]

> *"In the final analysis, that which is necessary above all is a substantial change in the economic, social and cultural model which will certainly not be brought about by numbers and dialectical battles which are now on the defensive"[873].*

In this sense, the justification seems to suggest quite revolutionary tendencies from the point of view of legal culture.

There is also an explicit reference to the *"limits of law"* idea in this case[874]. On the other hand, one could also claim that because the comparative generality is neglected as a normative premise, one goes beyond the limits of law in this way as well[875].

This *"limits of law"* reference by the Advocate General is interesting. He seems to recognize the value-based nature of the situation, i.e. the fact that there is a choice between two general

---

[871] There could exist an extensive comparative study that has been made concerning these systems. However, in the context of Court's working methods, one can doubt whether any really socially coherent study has really been effected.

[872] One could claim that the Advocate General also attempts to give, in his justifications, some directives for the further interpretation of the Community law.

[873] What is this cultural change? What would be then the structure of this system?

[874] Advocate General maintains: *"Moreover, in this saying this [referring to the acceptability of the measures, para 28] I am not referring only to the limits of the law".*

[875] One of the problems of comparative generalities, in the case, is related also to the instrumental nature of the law in these "social" situations.

One may note that the Advocate General is using a reference to comparative generality. It seems that the Advocate General is making an over-generalization. This type of argument seems to reflect more his *"tertium comparationis"*, i.e., ideology, than a judgment based on the analytical research. The idea of substantial equality refers to practical idea of equality. This practicality is, however, this decision contextualized. In contradiction, every material idea of equality requires its construction on the basis of existing laws and rules of a legal system. That type of equality is generalizable as a legal rule.

It looks as if every time the legal language refers to concepts like freedom or other extreme abstractions ("substantive equality"), one is dealing with the philosophical system, which is referring, on the other hand, to the idea of the stability of a persons world picture and coherent form of life. That is argumentation by authority. On the other hand, one can claim that the argumentation is, however, connected to something permanent. At this stage the legal research becomes part of the anthropological studies. One may start to find the explanations from the personal backgrounds. (For some analysis, see also, Sacco, R., 1991, p.5., also Weiler, J.H.H., 1998, p.44 ff.)

levels (i.e. state and European level). Undoubtedly, the limits of law, in this case, are related to the choice between two orders on the basis of cultural and value-based premisses[876]. Moreover, one of the main limits in European law seems to be related to the cases on the relationship between men and women.

In conclusion, the recognition of the "limit of law" can be associated with the question of how the modern constitutional (functional) legal system can be seen from the point of view of Community law (or in general) and what types of "comparative" alternatives one could construct on the basis of socio-philosophical inspections. This corresponds conceptions of European comparative constitutional law and to the comparative descriptions of European legal cultures. The question is associated also with fundamental institutional arrangements of European law related to these types of functional fields of law[877]. Furthermore, one could predict that this may result in an idea of legal - at least functionally legal - subsidiarity. Regulation of this type of relationship might be left to the realm of orders other than the European legal order, though this would be directly related to market regulation.

It has been suggested here that the Advocate General departs from the legislative (positive) integrity of law, does not keep his distance from constitutional traditions, and ends up in the field of the functional application of law. This way one ends up with different approaches to the functionality of law. Here one could began to identify, in European legal culture, different forms of functional approaches to law.

One may notice that the functionality approach by the Advocate General seems to be related to the deregulative approach, which intends to transfer the discourse on structural inequality to another level of regulation than the state law, towards "informal" measures.

One may wonder if this is the solution for the structural inequalities in society. Isn't it so that normative involvement occurs anyhow at some functional level? In other words, the deregulation of one level encourages regulation at some other level (via some other type of regulation).

On the other hand, from the point of view of the positive legal system, one clearly recognizes the attempt to separate the regulatory relationship between the legal systematic and more informal level.

---

[876] One of the main ideas reflected in this case is the "mate" situation in European law. Namely, it looks as if there are problems in regulating more specifically the relations and positive discrimination in the Community level, because of political and legal-systematic problems. At the same time, regulation made at the national level seems to be *a priori* unacceptable. What is then the way legally to deal with this?
For the changing situation, however, see below.

[877] In a case of philosophical autonomy, we are coming to the edge of legal constitutional culture as such. Here we are faced with really hard cases. Here takes place a disclosure of a "social theory" of law. Here the European Community system comes from the possibility (via analogy with states) into the field of necessity (claiming not a "descriptive" non-comparability, but "normative" one). European law has to interpret here its own premises, and where the states as a possible source of law. Here takes place the interpretation of the European constitution.

It is evident that there is an attempt, in this case, to reproduce one type of approach to the functionality of law. It does not seem to be allowed, legally, to maintain systematic arrangements, which create *"artificial inequalities in order to "correct" the social relationships"* - between men and women and perhaps between some other groups of people as well.

This type of idea may lead to a comparative legal culture, where these types of positive actions cannot be comparatively identified.[878]

3.4.7. A systematic interpretation?

One could claim that the idea of substantive equality expressed by the Advocate General refers to the reflexive nature of European law. The decision based on the doctrine of substantive equality has to be seen as an expression of a non-generalizable norm. This can be explained in the following way.

The recognition of the problem expressed by the German Court, in the realm of Article 177 (the new Article 234) of the Community Treaty, seems to be a recognition of the idea that the law of the German "Land" is contrary to the general principles of law. The German Court seeks the solution of the European Court in reorder to solve the problem, because the internal measures (constitutional provisions and textual and contextual interpretations) cannot justify the deviation from a strict interpretation of the law. The answer to the question by the Community Court is clearly a recognition of this "problem situation".

One may end up with a "reflexive concept" because, as one will see, in some other the Member States at the moment, there is no need to apply the general principle of equality to positive discrimination measures, because the laws effected by the Parliaments concerning positive discrimination are seen to be "constitutional" within these systems. The laws, in democratic systems, represent the "substantive" and political integrity of the system[879].

Consequently, it seems that the comparatively general constitutional principle of equality is an insufficient legal basis, at the European level, for a general prohibition against positive discrimination in all the Member States.

In conclusion, it can be suggested that the European Court, in this example, is more interested in the particular procedural problem-solving, in the particular legal system asking the question, rather than in the general applicability of the European norm.

---

[878] One may maintain, for example, that according to this kind of social ideology of the European law, certain social rights do not belong to the constitutional essentials of the system (discussion on this, see Rawls, J., 1996).

[879] The idea is that women and men, for example, can be substantively equal in different ways. One possibility seems to be a 'natural' equality based on a group identity, another perspective stresses more the discursive equality. The latter stresses more the processes in achieving the equality.

The decision of the European Court could be, consequently, left, as a substantive legal decision, to the realm of the polycentric and reflexive idea of European law, where the law is relativized on a situational basis[880].

3.4.8. Epilogue I: Structural inequality

The reasoning of the Advocate General establishes the grounds for various types of questions. One of the most interesting is the idea of structural inequality and informal reasoning in the society and its regulation. It is not possible to produce here an extensive analysis of this question. However, certain remarks can be made on the basis of the case.

Equal opportunities for female applicants, in general, could be seen as a result of the fact that there have already been, in the promotion processes etc., preferential measures taken. In general, preferential treatment may put women in the situation where they have equal opportunities available and they are able to show their equal qualifications. This idea relates to all types of quotas established in the educational sphere.

On the other hand, one could claim, from the socio-psychological point of view, that women may see their opportunities in the labour markets more realistically, if there is favourable attitude expressed in the legislation, apart from political and socio-cultural spheres. This way, they may apply for jobs, which, in the case of non-existence of the preferential treatment, would be seen somehow, to be necessarily as "mens jobs".

Furthermore, the idea that the promotion by *"education and training"* is the sole basis of equality may be contested. Namely, it seems that training etc., is usually undertaken by persons in order to realize some of the career plans, consciously or unconsciously. Training that does not relate to any plans does not seem to be beneficial training at all. Because of this, women may not choose to take part of any training because they do not see any real possibilities for the realization of their plans. Any choice of training and must be optimal and in accordance with the aim pursued.

In fact, one could even claim that women, not having realistic support from society in the form of strict measures of legislative and political processes, for example, may turn instead towards men-dominated structures ("men's society") and start to treat such structural inequalities as opportunities as such (self-instrumentalization). In this case, women may begin to determine their "life-plans' based on the men's preferential treatment, and attempt to benefit from this by choosing a "life-plan" which can guarantee them the (even very basic) social status which they want to have. This may lead to reinforcement of certain types of

---

[880] The problem of any comparatively reflexive system, using the substantive argument, is transformation of the political reflexivity into institutional reflexivity based on interpretation by its internal professional principles

social structures.

This idea can be developed further. It may be that men also start to orient themselves away from this developing "female social structure", like, for example, from emerging female "family life" and other "non-institutional" activities. This may take place because their opportunities seem to be determined only by their possibilities for participation in organized institutional social life. Thus, the "cumulation" effect can be visible. The organizations with preference men may increasingly accentuate this phenomenon with the outcome of increasing alienation of men from other activities other than that organization. Here one notices a development towards a highly organizationally and institutionally structured society. This type of phenomenon is visible for example in post-industrial societies, where strongly alienated forms of organization demanding unconditional working hours and the demand for relocation appear. In this way, the distinction between groups such as men and women deepens, especially if no corrective measures are available. The cumulative effect is, in this sense, the increasing loss of possibilities for both men and women. This is conditioned "externally" and is not based on discursive forms of 'life-planning".

On the other hand, "women" (in the strong group identity sense) may organize themselves in the "external" sphere of socio-organizational life, whereas men lose their possibilities for turning back to the non-organizational forms of social cooperation. On the other hand, auto-justification, by both groups, turns out to be about the deviating roles in society. They both attempt to justify their role in their own spheres of their social activity. This may destroy all possibilities for discursive compromises between these groups, in both the private and political spheres, and lead to political and social conflicts.

One may also maintain that one of the aims of equality legislation is also to guarantee the existence of certain types of female perspectives in public organizations, which otherwise could be excluded on the basis of prevailing attitudes.[881] In other words, the question may not be only a matter of equality between men and women, but also between different types of female perspectives within the public organization. Discrimination may not be exercised only by men, but, for that matter, by women preferring those women's perspectives which maintain the structural inequality. It is a fact that the real-value perspectives from women's emancipatory movements appear rather from the group of women who are strongly active in the political sense, rather than those organizing their life on the basis of prevailing societal structures[882].

To conclude, it seems that the clear aim of equality legislation of this type, in general, is to

---

[881] On differences between women, Nieminen, L., 1996, pp.30-31.
   This is also related to the fact that it is not only women, which may defend women's rights, but it can be also men who do it.
[882] This idea is in accordance with the development of institutionalization and legalization of politics in contemporary society.

guarantee the security and predictability of female employment in the labour market and in this way to prevent situations of absolute choice (between career and non-career). This would be only encouraged, if stressing the importance of education as a basis for the equal opportunities in the labour market[883]. On the other hand, it may function also as guaranteeing different perspectives in general in public organization.

3.4.9. Epilogue II: a vertical comparative analysis

The starting point of the "vertical" analysis is the observation made by Finnish constitutional Committee on the relationship between positive discrimination and the constitutional principle of equality in the realm of the enactment of the "Law on the Equality between Men and Women"[884]:

"According to Article 9.4. of the Law on Equality Between Men and Women, one cannot consider as discrimination those plan-based measures, which are aiming at a realization of the objectives expressed in this law in practice. The purpose of Article 5 of the Constitution, expressing the general equality norm, has commonly been considered to be the prevention of actions which place citizens or groups of citizens in a relatively better or worse position. The Constitutional Committee has on different occasions expressed the opinion that the general equality principle does not presume that all citizens should be treated similarly in all respects, unless the relevant circumstances are similar. The Committee considered, in its Statement no. 1/1975 vp., that the improvement of welfare opportunities of a certain part of the people, and that way the increasing of societal equality, was not in conflict with equality, even if all citizens did not have similar possibilities to get, with equal conditions, the rights and benefits described in the statute. Because the realization of the equality between men and women, in practice, also by preferring the sex in weaker

---

[883] The interesting fact is, similarly, that the aim of avoiding clear choice situations and guaranteeing the security of women in labour markets may also be based on an idea of cohesion of the legal system, provided by stressing the importance of long paid maternity leave, which try to make the return to the labour markets possible even after longer periods of absence. Many obligations related to this may be directed to the employees in order to secure this type of legislative cohesion. Unfortunately, the liberalization and minimum regulation of social policy and positive action is diminishing this type of thinking, and women, to avoid part time employment and insecurity, are obliged, in contemporary society, to choose between career and the family, for example. This is more striking in the situation, where the rate of employment increasing. It seems that, in modern society, these types of consistencies can be designed only in political processes. Their maintenance does not seem to be possible by any premodern forms of thinking, or by strict natural ideas of equality. (Some analysis of the social law coherence, Bogdan, M., 1996, pp.5-6, and especially, Nieminen, L., 1996, p.27 ff.).

[884] The Constitutional Committee of the Finnish Parliament, Helsinki, 13 May 1986, Statement nro. 1, 1986, p.3.
   The Scandinavian constitutional tradition was not taken into account by the European Court. However, on interesting question may be asked in connection to this statement. Finland and Sweden joined the European Union from 1995, and accepted European case law in the form of *"acquis communataire"*. When accepting the case law, including also the *Kalanke* decision, did the Finnish government, for example, accept also the substantive equality decision unconditionally? On the other hand, if one could claim that the prevailing constitutional doctrine was different in Finland, was there a internal constitutional conflict already in place at the time of the accession? On the other hand, could it be possible to apply a European doctrine of such a kind "retroactively" in order to claim the invalidity of the Equality law, and the invalidity of the Committee's statement too?
   See and compare the Finnish governments intervention in Marschall case (409/95 *Hellmut Marschall v Land Nordrhein-Westfalen* (1997) ECR I-6363 (Judgment of the Court of 11 November 1997, some analysis below).

position, is based on the aim at increasing equality, the proposed statute [the law on the Equality between Men and Women] - in so far as it aims are concerned - is not problematic from the point of view of Article 5 of the Constitution[885]. The Committee pays attention, however, to the fact that, on the individual level, the preferential treatment based on the plans [proposed in the law] may seem to constitute unreasonable discrimination. Because of this, one has to pay special attention to the absolutely undefinable nature of the concept of "plan". This is why one should consider whether there is a need to regulate - separately in the corresponding laws - the planned actions by the public institutions, and whether other types of actions - based on the above mentioned plans - should require a priori acceptance of the Equality Authority."[886]

The analysis of this statement shows clearly that the quota system is not necessarily against the general principle of equality.

Consequently, one may make a distinction made between different welfare state cultures in Europe[887]. This distinction, in turn, can be identified with certain specific questions.

The normative sphere of public "social" action (welfare policies etc.) is strongly related, in Western culture, to the questions on charity. This may be due to the fact that the strong social bonds, which are the underpinnings of social regulation, seem to be connected to some basic systematic normative presumptions[888].

One can maintain that the Nordic tradition of the welfare state has stronger historical roots than usually is proposed, at least in Finnish debate[889]. The traditional approach to the welfare state is usually connected to 19th century nationalism, which rightly brought it into the democratic consciousness in many countries[890]. However, the formation of the ideology can

---

[885] Preferential treatment is not, in principle, in conflict with the idea of general equality.

[886] This is the idea that further discussion and more specific compromises are needed in respect of preferential treatment in public institutions.

[887] See, for example, Kosonen, P., 1996, pp.16-17, pp.150-151, and Rokkan, S., 1981, and Nieminen, L., 1996, p.28 ff. (referring to Esping-Andersen, G., Three Worlds of Welfare Capitalism, 1990 and his distinction between liberal, conservative, Latin, and social-democratic types of welfare regimes)
   On legal philosophical development in this century, see Strömholm, S., 1980.

[888] The social questions are related, because of the different scope of pluralism, to different actors in society. Furthermore, the religious systems in general, in western welfare history, have had their organized forms of care-taking. The ideas on solidarity have had also its pre-Christian religious connotations in Europe.
   The history of trust in England seems to indicate that the changing role of capital had its relation to the emerging state based system during the 16th century reformation in England. Similarly in Scandinavia.

[889] Similarity between Nordic States, and the concept of Nordic, see Trägård, L., 1997, p.263, 282. For the concept of Nordic and development, Östergård, U, 1997, pp.29-71. On Nordic ties legally, see Zweigert, K., Kötz, H., 1987, p.288, 291, 295.

[890] The role of Peasantry etc., Trägård, L., 1997, p.257. Also Stråth, B, Sørensen, Ø., 1997, p.7. The Scandinavian welfare state in general, see (ed.) Nordström, B.J, Dictionary of Scandinavian history, London, 1986, pp.625-627.
   For some considerations on the development in 19th century, see Wieacker, F., 1990, p.61.
   It can be claimed that in Southern Europe the democratic duty and liberty have been associated strictly with the "intermediation" between religion and the secular power, whereas these concepts, in the northern part of Europe, have been part of the internal discourse inside the state or related to nationality. This can be one of the reasons why more instrumentalized forms of social regulation have been accepted in recent history.
   This can be associated with the idea that the state had strong economic role, which, moreover, increased in the age of the nationalism. This caused different functional views of the state to emerge the end of 19th century. One could claim, for example, that the liberal separation of the state and religion resulted in a certain overemphasis of the pure liberal

be traced further behind, to the reformations in the 16th century.[891]
One could say that the real differences in Nordic history as compared to the other forms of welfare histories is related to the fact that the state took over church functions, and these functions were integrated to the functions of the state[892]. On the other hand, development since was characterized by lesser conflicts between the church and state, which was one of the basic issues in many other European countries, and is still (especially in United States and, for example, in Italy)[893].

In general, what one can recognize here is that charity types of thinking in the field of social policy are more typical in the United States and in South European systems, whereas in the highly centralized state system in Northern Europe, political openness and efficiency thinking is more visible.[894] The Northern European systems can be seen as outcomes of particular type of political integrity and the concept of centralized political forces, which was not disturbed by the division between different conceptions of "sovereignty", the more democratic one, and the other more religious one, the latter stressing the importance of liberal principle of non-

---

economic role of the state during that time. Furthermore, this type of economic-political state had a tendency to involve matters of the religious pluralism by propagandist means by claiming the identification of the racial, religious and economic policies, as happened in the post-first world war Europe in many countries. The contrastive religious arguments got involved strongly with economic-political questions, both in "internal" and in international affairs. This was related to the strong discipline of the international legal-economic structures.

In Northern Europe, economic activity has not been so strongly connected to the religious questions internally, but in those states the religious homogeneity has been taken, in political terms, as a self-evident fact. In this sense, the functional forms of law have been developing in the realm of political state. This has also made it possible to unify many family law questions, whereas the integration in continental Europe has started on the basis of political and commercial integration, or by rather contingent comparative influences.

[891] Thorkildsen, D., 1997 (Religious Identity and Nordic identity), Östergård, U., 1997 (The geopolitics of Nordic identity, from composite states to nation-states. Political and religious characteristics), and Aronsson, P., 1997 (Local Politics, The invisible Political Culture, p.173 ff.).

This idea could explain, why the changes and deregulations seem to be difficult for the Swedish society, for example. In Finnish society the deregulation in political sphere seems to be easier, because the Finnish system was in 19th and 20th more or less a result of the modelling according to Swedish system. This type of change in the reflexivity seems to be easier in a situation, where integration is strongly geared towards general European integration.

On the development in Scandinavia since 17th century, see Glendon, M.A., Gordon, M.W., Osakwe, C., Nutshell, 1982, p.28. In general, Gallo, P. Grandi sistemi Giuridici, Torino, 1997, p.219 ff.

On the division in European economic and social structures since 1500, Szücs, J., 1996, p.15.

[892] Trägård, L, 1997, p.260. Also Nieminen, L., 1996, p 32

Reasonable distinctions are made according to the state, not on the basis of the religion. See also, Zweigert, K., Kötz, H., An Introduction to comparative law, II ed., Vol II, Oxford, 1987, p.295. On the formations of states in general, see Wieacker, F., Foundations of the European legal culture, p.49, in: European legal culture.

In England, and the catholic conception, see Jones, G., History of the law of Charity 1532-1827, Cambridge. 1969, pp.3-10

[893] Trägård, L., 1997, p.260.

Concerning the reformation and law England, see Moccia, L., 1981, pp.160-161. On the resistance to "Reception", ibid., p.164.

[894] See, Kosonen, P., 1996. On 19th century policy ideas related to charity in Sweden, see Trägård, L., 1997, p.258. Centrality and functionality approach, idem.. No tested assistance idea (ibid., p.254). Pragmatism in general, Stråth, B., Sørensen, Ø., 1997, p.16. See as well, Zweigert, K , Kötz, H , 1987, p.288.

involvement of the state to "social" and ethical affairs (the principle of subsidiarity)[895].

These modern Nordic ideas can be, for that matter, related also to the gender questions prevailing in these countries[896].

The deregulation of the welfare state is, consequently, not purely an economic or legal-political phenomenon in Nordic countries. One may say that it touches deeply upon the concept and idea of a democratic state, if not even the sovereignty of the democratic parliament[897]. The deregulation of the welfare state seems to be more easily achieved in strongly political or more liberal systems, where the forms of welfare thinking are not so strongly anchored to the concept of state, or in the social-capitalist traditions. One could claim that in the United States, for example, the idea of strong welfare policies has not been taken extremely seriously because of the polycentric nature of the concept of the "political" itself[898].

The importance of the strongly established secularized state in Northern Europe is a phenomenon which importance is not stressed sufficiently when planning integrative actions in the European sphere[899]. The parliamentary state as a socioeconomic actor, owing much its previous religious homogeneity and democratic development has generated forms of regula-

---

[895] For the idea of social integrity in the Swedish context, see Trägård, L., 1997, p.273.
It is not difficult to see, why the basic rights did not achieve such an importance in the modern Nordic states as they did in France, or in contemporary Germany. They seemed to be the third dimension in the tense relationship between church and state, between the European "powers". One could also associate this, historically, with the early existence of the agreements between the land-nobility and king. In fact, Northern European development lacks this type of tension in any politically visible way.
One remarkable feature in the relationship between European Human Rights System and the activities of the Nordic states is the great number of cases dealing with the autonomy of the family from the interventions by state authorities. In both Sweden and Finland, these cases seem to be in the heart of the European intervention. Many times, in the European Human Rights system, there is voting in the legal decision process, and there the South/North separation between opinions is clearly visible.
[896] Trägård, L., 1997, p.274, 278
From the point of political history one make also the observations that, whether one are speaking about social movements in general or in particular gender movements, the northern countries have a more vivid history. The gender movements have been and are strong political movements. The questions of equality and certain preferences are as well part of the politically integrity of the system, which is not the case in southern countries (Gender and Politics in Finland (ed. Keränen, M., Aldershot) 1992). This is kind of a basis of a democratic political peace.
[897] Centrality of State, Trägård, L., 1997, p.283, Stråth, B., Sørensen, Ø., 1997, p.6, also Zweigert, K., Kötz, H., 1987, p.288, no formation analysis, though. Neither in David, R., Brierley, J.E.C., 1978, p.113.
On the post Maastricht welfare state, Bislev, S., European Welfare states: Mechanisms of Convergence and divergence, EUI working papers 97/24, European University Institute, Robert Schuman Centre, 1997, p.2 ff.. p.11, and democracy, p.26. Welfare state and European development, Rhodes, M., Globalization, Labour markets and welfare states: a future of 'competitive corporativism', EUI working papers 97/36, European University Institute, Robert Schuman Centre, 1997.
[898] The United States can be seen as a constitutionally pluralistic society. Religion is not a reasonable distinction. Many questions in USA have been related, however, to the racial questions. These questions have enabled the legal actors to consider and reevaluate the question of social opportunities, when the pluralism has made obstacles to more "holistic" social regulation by the state (Brown case and the subsequent case law).
The United States' system is an example of a system where the function of the liberal state is to secure the pluralistic society. It may be exactly due to this why unable to regulate welfare matters so profoundly. The "care-taking" systems seem to be part of the function of the liberal societal actors ("charity").
[899] Problems in European Union, see Trägård, L., 1997, p.284 ff., Stråth, B., Sørensen, Ø., 1997, p.23

tion incomparable to rest of the Europe. The idea of cultural homogeneity separated from the democratic state, prevailing idea in continental Europe, does not seem to have a strong role in traditional Northern thinking.

Against this background, one may see many problems in understanding the aims of the European integration and deregulation. Namely, European integration stresses the importance of political, religious and even racial questions in economic integration. This must be seen in the context of continental history. The idea is the enforcement of equal opportunities in spite of these features. One could claim that these are the features which in a homogeneous Northern European context are recognized many times irrelevant because of the pragmatism of the political discourse, even if it is recognized that these distinctions are important for the European integration. However, social regulation deriving from the diverse historical context of the Northern European countries definitely has already given space to the continental type of liberalization entering into the traditional forms of Northern systems. As biproducts, one recognizes artificial importance being placed upon the questions of race, religion and ethnic background.

To conclude, one can wonder whether the Nordic countries must give up their traditional forms of welfare regulation and its integrity, or whether this type of comparative aspect will be taken into the European level discussion so as to maintain the idea. The latter alternative would be the best solution in order to maintain the coherence and discursive integrity of European law in general[900].

---

[900] An example of the analysis of the positive social political actions related to the nature of the social relations between men and women in Sweden and Finland, see Tyrkkö, A, Anpassning mellan arbetsliv och familjeliv i Sverige och Finland, In Dilemmaet arbetsliv, familieliv i Norden (ed. Bonke, J) Nordisk Ministerråd, TemaNord 1997:534, Socialforskningsinstituttet 97:5. The article represents the differences in Sweden and in Finland in relation to, for example, the working hours regulation, and the economic insecurity and opportunities for public employment, which result in more asymmetric relationships between men and women in both family and working life (ibid., pp.142-143).

In the field of social regulation, one could also speak of a "capacity" approach adopted in these countries (On the capacity approach, see Sen, A., Inequality reexamined, 1996).

The current discussion on the welfare state, in both political and legal spheres , seems to be contrary to its main idea. The idea of the welfare state is used as a justification for a more liberal approach, and the introduction of the "social law" seems to diminish its role in the political processes as a practical phenomenon. The question seems to be either about the securing of the some acquired benefits, or about their deregulation.

A conceptual turn has also taken place. Now the "welfare state" is "welfare society".

The welfare state, however, seems to be a politically functional phenomenon deriving its nature from democratic compromises and balancing. Any normative idea of the welfare state seems to be strange, as well, on the other hand, any idea of welfare society. The welfare state is a political process, which does not get attached easily to any ideas of principles and construction type of legitimacy.

A curious phenomenon in the contemporary European development is that there seems to be a tendency to deregulate exactly those forms of regulation, which have proved to be the most successful in constructing a socially sensitive democratic nation state. The tendency seems to be towards forms of regulation, which have proved to be problematic from the democratic point of view.

In this connection, attention has been paid also to the Judgment of the Privy Council of The United Kingdom, case *Mataleen v. Pointu* (P.C.) 1997 Nov. 26,27; Dec. I; 1998 Fed., 18, W.L.R. 19, June 1998, p.18 ff (Appeal from the Supreme Court of Mauritius). The judgment of their Lordships was delivered by Lord Hoffman. In this case, there is an

262   CHAPTER 3

3.4.10. Final conclusions

What does the substantive equality really mean?[901]
   It appears as if support for this type of principle cannot be found in the comparative political and legal sphere. There seem to be problems of the comparability of socio-cultural policies. It looks like the idea of substantive equality is related to a non-discursive and quite instrumentalist approach to law. The application of such principle seems to be related to a strict and logical principle of equality. The generality of this type of principle and its application are conditioned by the phenomenological idea of law, which does not seem to comply with more reasonable application of law.

---

extensive analysis of the principle of equality, and its relationship to democracy. See especially, pp.26-27.
[901] The idea of substantive equality is a philosophical problem.
   The analysis of substance has a long history (Leibnitz, Locke and Kant, see Abraham, W.E. Oxford Companion to Philosophy, 1992, pp.358-359, also Grande Dizionario Enciclopedico (Torino) 1936)
   Substance (substantive equality) seems to something extremely resistant to change. In this sense, equality would be the basic norm. However, the questions can be asked; equality of what? Any discussion on substantive equality without a criteria for its relevance other than "human nature" (substance or ratio) seems to instrumentalize, contrary to the 'idea' of substantive equality, human beings as a 'thing' to be discussed without a genuine relational attitude. Ultimately one is dealing with an idea extremely ideal in nature, perhaps about the ultimate form of ideality and determinism. The question is about something which has content and meaning (and equality of that).
   Etymologically history of substance is interesting both from the Latin and Greek perspective. Before the religious and scholastic interpretations were made, the substance was dealt by Aristotle. He saw it as something basic, essence and natural, divided into material and real (*ens quod per se subsistit et sustinet accidentia*). Justice is to treat alikes alike and unalikes unalike, according to their essential difference. This applies to people and things, and situations. The essentially is the problem. For example, the distinction between men and women was seen as essential in theory, as well in practice. One may say that, in this sense, there was a 'thing' character of human beings. This idea was later connected to the sholastic dotrine, based on many "spiritual" arguments on the basis of the hierarchy. Scholastic interpretation saw it as something other than material (Giovanni Scoto Eriugena: *"quod semper id ipsum est vera substantia dicitur"*, De div. Nat. vol I, p.65). For Descartes in the Principia philosophiae *"Per sostanza non possiamo intendere altro che una cosa la quale esiste in modo da no aver bisognio di nessui altra cosa per esistere. E la sostanza che non ha proprio bisognio di alcuna cosa si pu`o intendere solo come unica, il che `e Dio"*. If one makes a distinction between the material and "thinking" type of substance (spirito), one can ask, who`s substance is it (*"res quae solo Dei concursu egent ad existendum"*). Spinoza described it as *"per substantiam intelligo id quod in se est et per se concipitus* (Ethics, Vol I, prop. III), because *"gacies infinitis modis variet tamen semper aedem"* (Spinoza, Epistola, p.64). Kant, by following the scholastic interpretation, discussed substance as an ultimate centre of force used in grounding change-producing actions and causalities One could also make a distinction between material substances and spiritual substances. It has been also maintained that onemay speak about physical arithmetic, something-I-know-not-what (Locke).
   Modern substance may be defined as the the "real nature" and "essence" of the things. The idea prevailed through the centuries in the continental political, religious and legal thinking.
   However, one may pose a question, or formulate it in another way, as to substantive equality. Could one say that the question is not about equality at all, but about inequality? In other words, the modern legal systems, in point of fact, create inequalities too, and also balances them (or, by it the inequalities, as its creation, are balanced in the political discourse) There are no modern legal system which would create equality (Olaus Petri: *"the biggest justice is the biggest injustice"*). The law is not relating to equality, but rather, to inequality and to the balancing inequalities in a politically integrative way. If one would have a principle of substantive equality, one would only have to wait for a "fire from heaven".
   To see the balancing as historically "punitive" is too logical. The question is about the discursive substance as a modern substance. Any informal and substantive equality which prevails societally, must be balanced with public and social considerations in order to avoid structural inequalities. This generates possibilities for a liberating approach to the instrumentalization of human beings.

On the other hand, the idea in *Kalanke* could be interpreted against the contemporary development towards governmental legislation in Europe. If this development is combined with the more political concept of gender equality, it could be true that this political type of equality could threaten and render unpredictable the whole idea of equality. In this sense, some protection of men could be preferable in the way the Advocate General suggested. Then the question is no longer about the discursive form of political equality, but a governmental and non-discursive form.

Furthermore, it has to be remembered that the political type of equality preferred here is also combined with many other forms of legal regulation (coherence of legal system). If these types of regulations are increasingly deregulated, the basis of the political and discursive equality in nation states is difficult to maintain.

In conclusion, the fact that more "procedural", discursive, and reasonable approaches seem to be preferable also in Community law may be related to the recent "change" in the Kalanke -"doctrine" by the European Court of Justice. The Court explained the acceptability of the quota-system in relation to same legal measures as in the Kalanke case in the following terms:[902]

"In paragraph 16 of its judgment in Kalanke, the Court held that the national rule which provides that, where equally qualified men and women are candidates for the same promotion in fields where there are fewer women than men at the level of the relevant post, women are automatically to be given priority, involves discrimination on grounds of sex.

However, unlike the provisions in question in Kalanke, the provision in question in this case contains a clause ('Öffnungsklausel', hereinafter 'saving clause') to the effect that women are not to be given priority in promotion if reasons specific to an individual male candidate tilt the balance in his favour.

It is therefore necessary to consider whether a national rule containing such a clause is designed to promote equality of opportunity between men and women within the meaning of Article 2(4) of the directive"

---

[902] Case 409/95 *Hellmut Marschall v Land Nordrhein-Westfalen* (Reference for a preliminary ruling: Verwaltungsgericht Gelsenlichen, Germany, equal treatment of men and women, equally qualified male and female candidates, Priority for female candidates, Saving clause) (1997) ECR I-6363 (Judgment of the Court of 11 November 1997).
    Also Opinion of Mr Advocate General Jacobs delivered on 15 May 1997. By going through the previous case law, Advocate General Jacobs concluded, however, that the directive precludes such a priority provision of national law. He saw the case as being similar to the *Kalanke* case, contrary to the argument presented by Austrian, Finnish, Norwegian, Spanish and Swedish governments, according to which in this case there was no absolute priority. He also referred to the opinion of Mr. Tesauro, regarding the analysis of 'equal opportunity'.
    An interesting point was raised by the French government. It claimed that the question is about preciseness of the national provision. It maintained that the national provision seems to be against the legal certainty. This idea seems to be quite formal.
    The Advocate General Jacobs recognizes the 'competence' problem in European policy formulations between the legislature and adjudication, and even proposes some kind of a "margin of discretion" for the Member States. The idea remains, however, unclear.
    No comparative observations, like *Kalanke*, were presented. However, the parties referred continuously to international arrangements, where there are provisions on the acceptability of quotas. In a separate analysis, Advocate General Jacobs considered the relevance of these international arguments for the interpretation. He saw them as being extremely vague (?) and unhelpful. Furthermore, they were more permissive than mandatory.

and it continued after examining the Kalanke case and arguments put forward by several parties as follows:

> "Unlike the rules at issue in Kalanke, <u>a national rule which, as in the case in point in the main proceedings, contains a saving clause does not exceed those limits</u> if, in each individual case, it provides for male candidates who are equally as qualified as female candidates a guarantee that the candidatures will be a subject of <u>an objective assessment</u> which will take account of all criteria specific to the individual candidates and will override the priority accorded to female candidates when one or more of those criteria tilts the balance in favour of the male candidate. In this respect, however, it should be remembered that those criteria must not be such as to discriminate against female candidates."
> <u>It is for national court to determine whether those conditions are fulfilled</u> on the basis of an examination of the scope of the provisions in question as it has been applied by the Land."

This type of argumentation does not refer to any legislative integrity of the national legal systems. However, it refers to the idea of the adjudicative integrity of a legal order by proposing a more dynamic interpretation of equality. It contains some observations of the "societal" aspects, which may provide arguments for future cases.[903] On the other hand, it "creates" some kind of comparability between the legal systems in realm of European order, because it solves the problem between basic premises by referring to procedural norms.[904]

Finally, in the renewed Rome Treaty (Article 2: basic principles) the equality between men and women has been taken explicitly as an objective of Community policies. However, unanimity is required from the Council in taking measures dealing with sexual discrimination (new Article 13). Nevertheless, the new Article 13 (and especially the new Article 141.4) may encourage affirmative action. Article 141.4 provides that

> "With a view to ensuring full equality in practice between men and women in working life, the principle of equal treatment shall not prevent any Member State from maintaining or adopting measures providing for specific advantages in order for the under-represented sex to pursue a vocational activity or to prevent or compensate for disadvantages in professional careers".

Consequently, it seems that *Kalanke* remained as a "side-step" in the history of European law.

---

[903] The considerations of the integrity of legal systems could be related to the argumentation of some parties by international treaties.
   It is remarkable how one may arrive to such a different solution in a similar situation. The Court and nor the Advocate General in *Kalanke* gave indication that the situation would have been different if such a procedural rule existed.
   See some analysis of the "societal" aspects, see Ellis, E., 1998, pp.404-406. Holtmaat, K. (The Power of Legal Concepts: The development of a Feminist Theory of Law. In: International Journal of Sociology of Law, 1989, p.499) maintains too:
   "The concept of legal equality and that of equal rights cannot serve as a leading substantive principle and/or strategic concept for the role which law could play in breaking open power relations between men and women."
[904] For the idea that the comparison between formal procedural norms is easier in comparative law, see Kulla, H. 1996 (Referring to various authors (Schwarze, Stark, Madeira, Siedentopf)).

3.5.   Conclusions on the "hard cases"

Before the "hard case" studies it was asserted that the question concerned the internal problems of European law and the relative competences of supranational, national organizations, decided on legal basis by a supranational body. The question was not, evidently, about "easy" cases of comparative "construction", but about a choice of "law", or, one should say, a choice of the preferences of "institutional facts" in European law.

What kind of choices one is talking about?

The analysis could be summarized with the following indicators: Case (Case), Type of Comparative Rationality (CompRat), Norms Compared (NorComp), Result of Comparison (ResComp), Legal Fictions Compared (LFicComp), Preference (Pref), Field of the Subject-Matter (FieSubMat), Legal Principle in question (LePrin). Special remarks (Rem) are made in the end to stress the instability of this idea (the following table).

Case	Comp Rat	Nor Comp	Res Comp	Lfic Comp	Pref	FieSub Mat	LePrin	Rem
Otto Prem-ger	value based	morality / state laws	dispa-rity / dispa-rity	reli-gion - expres-sion	reli-gion	poli-tics? (Poli-tical acting)	Right to reli-gion	dissen-ting opi-nions!
Bach-mann	value based	state laws / internat law	internal system consis.-tency / genera-lity	state - Commu-nity	state	econo-my (taxa-tion)	sove-reignty of a state	fede-ralism or functio-nality?
Hoescht	tradi-tional	state laws (statut./ constit.)	genera-lity	home - company	home	econo-my (bu-siness secrecy)	individ. pro-tection	
Albany	instru-mental	state law third law / principl. of inter-pretation	disparity / genera-lity	collec. agreeing-free compe-tition	collec-tive agreeing	eono-my (so-cial pol-icy	social prote-tion	The Court: "consis-tent and effective interpre-tation"
(Albany, specialist study)	tradi-tional.	state law / constit?	disparity / genera-lity?					"Treaty as a whole"
Kalanke	instru-mental	functio-nal law of states / (statut./ constit./ third law	genera-lity / opposit./ general./ example	men - women	men?	Politics? (Posts in admi-nistra-tion	substan-tive equality	already chan-ged?

What can one say on the basis of such results? Many conclusions could be made. Here, only some remarks are presented.

One could claim that the legal ideological structure or the European institutional legal identity is more or less represented in this diagram. The picture shows how, with a comparison of different types of norm sets, one has been able to confirm a solution in a conflict between different types of institutional legal fictions.

In the hard core of traditional European law there seems to be the economic sphere, which is regulated by the principles of individual protection and state sovereignty. In both cases, Community law, for example, has been refraining from touching them by maintaining the consistency of the state system, or by stating that it respects the legal principle in state systems (the principle of the inviolability of home). Other type of organization (the European Community itself or an economic community) is not able to claim the same type of competence. The Community has confirmed its autonomy also in this "negative" sense.

The margins (or limits) of European level law come up also when approaching the political sphere, where the disparity of state law is confirmed by the principles of substantive or more material equality, and the protection of religious feelings. Here the limits of political action were confirmed in attempts to secure some administrative power by political means, and in attacking the main form of religion in a particular society. In both case, the idea was to change any formal idea of equality to non-politically determined formal equality.

It seems that where one enters from the economic "hard core" of European level law towards more political sphere of action, one arrives at more institutional type of law not really supported by any generality in positive law of the states, or rather supported by extremely instrumental type of comparative reasoning. Here one recognizes also a strong "federalist" attack based on some kind of "informal" idea of equality, against those state polities which are still based on strict formalism and institutionalized discourses.

Nevertheless, religious protection (*Otto-Preminger*) came under heavy criticism, also by the judges themselves in the dissenting opinions. Furthermore, the rule in *Kalanke* case has been changed to a certain extent. The instrumentality in Albany has been "traditionalized" by comparative legal discourse by legal experts and the decision by the Court. On the other hand, one may say that the current discussions on federalism may touch upon the consistency and sovereignty principle of taxation. These tendencies reveal the current instability of these types of discussions.

These observations have been made in the realm of European level institutional law. The hard core of the relationship between state supremacy and individual protection should be studied in the realm of the national legal systems.[905]

---

[905] The recent *Pinotchet* case in the House of Lords (see, above) is definitely such as case. It deals exactly with the relationship between individual protection and the state autonomy, immunity, and supremacy. It seems to make clear that the hard case in international law are not resolved by international law comparison only, but the sovereignty of parliamentary states can be the basis for judging also the relationship between the sovereign and the individual in the political sense. One may note, that the *Pinochet* case was decided by a comparison of various measures of international law, and, on the other hand, by referring to the sovereignty of Parliament

CHAPTER 4

CONCLUSIONS

1. COMPARATIVE EUROPEAN LAW AND EUROPEAN COMPARATIVE LAW

1.1. Preliminary remarks

Basically, there seems to be two dimensions to the European comparative interpretative practice in an institutional sense. The first dimension is the reasonable orientation of legal actors, in legal institutions, and in one form or another, towards other legal systems in an intellectual sense and the use of these observations in legal reasoning, argumentation and justification. The second dimension is related to the "importation" of domestic legal actors to the supranational institutions and the planning of the architecture of these institutions on these basis.[906]

In the first type, the role of comparative law as a legal source depends on the material and intellectual resources of the institution and its actors. Moreover, the adaptation of comparative arguments to the justification requires certain characteristics of the philosophy of the system (the legal-cultural ideology and theory of law).

In the second type of situation lawyers as such function as "comparative" dimensions of the system. The persuasiveness of this type of comparative system depends strongly on the characteristics and qualities of its personnel[907]. Consequently, one may say that the quality of a lawyer, as a domestic and culturally attached lawyer, influences "comparatively" the work of the institution. In this sense, one could claim, that the more the lawyer (a judge or administrator) is attached to the basic cultural values and "customs" of his/her national context, the more influential he/she is in the institution, "comparatively". On the other hand, the more susceptible the lawyer is to foreign ideas, or more he/she is relying on the institutional and organizational authority, the weaker the "comparative" influence is.

---

[906] A good example of this architecture is the recent change in the European Human Rights Court, where the renewed rule of the Convention says that in a case one judge should come from the country under examination.

[907] On the legal traditions and domestic training in the Community system, see Bengoetxea, J., 1993, p.123.

1.2. The intellectual dimension: forms of interaction of arguments and legal systems

1.2.1. General remarks

   As it has been shown, the comparative arguments can emerge in the form of generality, diversity, or exemplification[908]. All these forms appear in the work of the adjudicative institutions.

   The descriptive analysis of the comparison usually consists of the description of the *tertium comparationis* and statements on comparability or non-comparability. The prescriptive part may include the recognition of this generality, disparity, or the example as a legally relevant idea. This is attached to the statement of its acceptability.[909] The norm of the case results from these premises in different ways in interaction with other arguments.

   The method of comparative law can be traditional[910]. Then the legal sources' doctrine, on the basis of the comparison, includes laws and precedents, and scholarly opinions[911]. However, in European level institutions, traditional comparative reasoning seems to be based on restricted idea of sources of law (for example, usually no *travaux preparatoires* are used)[912]. On the other hand, one may observe that in English systems the analysis of case law is the main method of comparative reasoning.

   Comparative arguments usually interact with socio-philosophical and principled legal arguments. They are combined with legal principles, some kind of coherence (consistency) argumentation, moral arguments, and also with other types of legal instruments deriving from the international legal community (such as international law arguments and "third countries" analysis). Furthermore, one may recognize some kind of alternateness between comparative argumentation and the intention of the national legislator. In this sense, they are alternative also in relation to *the travaux preparatoires*. As it has been also indicated, comparative reasoning seems to be related to a quite strict literal interpretation. Tendencies and social

---

[908] It has been claimed that Courts comparative considerations do not lead to real imitation (Bredimas, A., 1978b, p.322., analysing case 7 and 9/54 *Steel industries in Luxemburg* (1955-56) ECR 175, and Advocate General Roemers analysis, opinion on 8 February 1956, p. 210 ff. (*"for all these reasons I therefore consider that comparisons with related features of national law cannot be decisive with regard to the question with which we are concerned"*, ibid., 213).
   This may be so in explicit comparative reasoning. However, the reality seems to be different

[909] Pescatore P. speaks about the *"transpassabilty"* (*"transpassable"*) of legal systems or their rules (1980, p.358).

[910] Bredimas A., claims (1978b, p.323) that comparative law is not traditional because of a lack of common highest or lowest denominator. However, in the tradition of comparative law this could be claimed to be a "rule" also. Furthermore, a certain "creativity" is part of the tradition. (About this creativity, see ibid., p.324.)
   Now, as well as in the international Court, also in the European system the acceptability is considered in relation to the institutional or European institutionally dogmatic opinion.

[911] Bredimas, A., 1978b, p.325. At the theoretical level, one can make a distinction between ought, should, may, and may not sources (Bengoetxea, J., 1993, p.225).

[912] The lack of *travaux preparatoires* can be explained by the fact that they belongs to another type of political discourse, and they appears too functional from the point of view of the European legal level.

contexts are seen extremely holistically in connection to comparative observations.

Even if there is an interaction between comparative arguments and other types of arguments, it appears as if comparative argument has often quite decisive role. However, when comparative arguments are used, the basic normative statements are usually justified, in the end, by strong principles or practical arguments. In this sense, interpretation seems to be determined basically by principles and practical arguments[913]. This is what the legal sciences also emphasize.

As noted, the use of comparative law, in the European legal orders, at least, assumes a vertical comparison. The comparative interpretation of Community norms, for example, means analogizing and comparing the outcomes of the comparative studies in relation to the systematic premises at the Community level[914]. In this sense, it is quite evident that where the interpretation of the principles of the European level systems is supported by comparative considerations, these legal principles, in the context of European law, are different from the principles related to the national discourses[915]. This may be observed, for example, in the *Hoescht* case at the European Community level. In this case the principle was recognized, but because it was considered to be something outside the aims of the Community system, and, consequently, a matter for national legal systems, it was only "respected", but not seen as part of Community law as such. This view supported by traditional comparative studies.

Consequently, many of the comparative principles do not have the necessarily common features with the principles supported by the open national dogmatic legal discourse. In an extreme case, in the European human rights system and in the realm of the *"margin of appreciation"* idea, these institutional principles remind us more of an evaluation of the constitutional and national legal systematic principles as such[916].

---

[913] Internal principles, limiting principles, and substantial principles (Koopmans, T., 1991, p.56 ff.). Some classification, Joutsamo, K., The principles of Community law after the Treaty of Amsterdam (Helsinki) 1999.

[914] Lando O. explains how the system examines the "fitness" of the Community system with regard to the laws of Member States (1977, p.656).

[915] In comparative reasoning, the disassociation of legal arguments takes place. It happens in the transferring of an legal concept, rule of principle, or decision from the national systems to the European systems, from another European system to another European system etc. These different types of legal arguments do reappear, consequently, in another context where they are designed as explained before

[916] Furthermore, the common constitutional traditions, and some principles related to that, must be distinguished from the basic principles of Community law (Pescatore, P., 1980, p.353). These are, for example, the principles concerning structure of the Community law, freedom of movements, and non-discrimination principles. What is meant here by institutional principles are the "common core" principles (good faith, judicial security, proportionality) deriving from national experience (ibid., p.352).

It has been suggested that there are three major reasons for the great expansion of judicial review in Europe today
- the emerge of a new form of government
- the new importance of Human rights
- transnational pluralism

Sound governance is not considered any longer from the view point of the "separation de pouvoirs", but rather from the point of view of "checks and balances". It is claimed to be a safeguards against abuses by the political branches (Capelletti, M., 1990b, p.431 ff.).

Consequently, one could claim that the institutionally principled approach determines the qualitative adoption of the comparative examples and references. One may say, contrary to the "constructivist" idea, that these institutionalist principles are, in the end, the decisive part of prior comparative evaluations and selection in the European level legal interpretation.

Furthermore, may note that an intellectually oriented European institutional comparative lawyer is not trying to achieve the support of a very extensive legal audience.

1.2.2. The analytical quality of comparative arguments, the "stages of coherence", and the legal integrity of systems

When the courts, at the European level, take a step towards analysis of different legal systems, the more coherent, *a priori*, the European law can seem. On the other hand, where the legal systems appear analytically irrelevant, may speak of a weak idea of coherence at the European level.

Furthermore, where the comparative studies play only a contextual role, there seems to be, at the European level, evidently an attempt to avoid the problems within this weak idea of coherence (or even possible incoherence?). At the same time, one attempts to maintain the idea of European level adjudicative integrity. If the national legal systems (principles) and their legislation are extensively analyzed, the idea of legislative integrity seems to prevail. In these cases, the European level is determined strictly by the idea of generality, and the national legal level maintains its relative "authority".[917] As noted, this is not usually the case.

Furthermore, in the case of comparison by opposites, where the comparative analysis and some generalities are explicitly rejected, the idea seems concerned solely with the integrity (functional autonomy) of the European level-orders[918]. Where this type of "adjudicative principle of integrity" is prevailing, the European level institution is making a strong value-based judgment despite the legislative integrity. Here one may recognize a general conflict inside the general idea of the integrity of European law[919]. Here one usually speaks about an ultimate form of non-discursive and instrumentalist approach to European adjudication.[920]

---

[917] See, for example, the examination of the case on the inviolability of home.

[918] In the "cohesion of the legal system" - argument is embedded the idea of incomparability. This is related to the cases which demonstrate the limits of legal systems. The cohesion explains the system as a complete system, both formally and functionally.

In cases of coherence argument, the legal systems, or legal orders, are chosen in the realm of the political integrity.

[919] The problem of comparatively reflexive legal systems is the turning of the political reflexivity into professional institutional reflexivity based on the internal autonomous institutional interpretation.

[920] Judge Pescatore, P. (1980, p.359) speaks about this phenomenon, albeit, in different terms, as follows:
"Mais nous avons vu, que la méthode comparative peut également servir de manière toute différente: lorsque l'analyse comparative révèle les disparités et les contradictions irréductibles, sur certain point, entre les droit des Etats membres, la Cour s'en sert comme d'un "reduction à l'absurde" pour justifier le choix de solutions communes,

1.3. Motives for comparative reasoning in European law

1.3.1. General remarks

In this connection, the focus is on the use of comparative law in European level institutions. The analysis of the possible uses in national legal systems is discussed in the last chapter of this work.

In the European level orders, as it has been noticed, comparative law has different types of functions in legal reasoning. The European "systems" are comparative systems. The nature of these European systems, as comparative systems, is related to the fact that they have been practically "constructing" themselves on the basis of national systems, and they reflect directly the traditions of the national conceptualizations.[921] On the other hand, it clearly makes it possible for them to make "legal choices". It has been noted, on the other hand, that comparative law is used mainly in order to arrive to an interpretative method rather than to a substantive solution as such.

It has been maintained that the function of comparative law in the European orders is to make the interpretation fit within the laws of the states, supply material for the "right" decision, establish the common core of the systems.[922] There is thus *"pressure to compare the elements of national and EC law"*[923].

However, one may ask how important these national legal systems really are as a source of law for the European-level orders? Namely, even if one recognizes that comparative observations function as some kind of basis of solutions for the European systems, one notes that European orders do not have, necessarily, to reflect their aims and objectives and previous interpretations within national legal systems[924]. Furthermore, it is generally known that when

---

destinées à dépasser les contradictions des ordres juridiques nationaux. Les amateurs de philosophie pourraient y trouver une application du schéma de pensée dialectique, en ce sens que les contradictions entre thèse et anti-thèse se résolvent ici dans une synthèse réellement nouvelle.
L'auteur de ces lignes espère avoir pu montrer combien la méthode comparative, qui a déjà montré une extraordinaire fécondité scientifique, se révèle également utile lorsqu'elle est appliquée dans le contexte, très concret, des travaux d'une juridiction de caractère multinational qui, par sa constitution même et par sa vocation, doit être riche diversité des droits nationaux dont elle tire son inspiration."

[921] On the interactivity, see Koopmans, T., 1991, p.53. Pescatore, P., speaks about justificatory, apologetic, and constructive approaches (1980, p.357). Furthermore, he makes a distinction between contrastive ("*repoussoir*") and adoptive ("*réception*") ideas.

[922] Lando, O., 1977, p.657, Bredimas, A., 1978a, p.121.

[923] This concerns many fields of law, for example, environmental protection, and social policy, connected especially to the "exemptions" such as Article 30 and 59 of the Treaty (see, Dehousse, R., 1994, p.7).

[924] As it has been noted, that comparative justifications do, on the other hand, reproduce the state paradigmatic thinking of law. On the other hand, the fact that the decisions reached do have a direct impact to the law of the national legal systems does "resubstantialize" these systems.
See Shapiro, M., 1980, pp.541-542.

one uses many arguments (systems), it is many times a sign that no real confidence is attached to any one of them. Even if, at first glance, and in quantitative terms, it seems that the confidence of the European orders is on the nation state systems, in the so-called "hard cases" a different version of the story is noted.[925]

One may say, in general, that the state systems serve as an analogy as long as they can be instrumentalized according to the basic principles of the European system[926].

Is it possible to identify some characteristic motives for these "instrumentalizations"?

1.3.2. The forms of traditional "self-construction", control of compliance, and integrative interpretation

As maintained, one of the motives appear in the traditional claim that comparative law can be used either to the fill up *lacunae* or to construct some principles for interpretation. Comparative argument, in its open form, seems to be a constitutive argument.

This type of constructive use can be divided into the use of pre-implementation material and the use of post-implementation material.[927]

In the use of pre-implementation material, the Community institutions, for example, attempt to cover legal provisions, on which basis one could be able to justify an interpretation of a general principle in the European system. As one has noted, however, this type of "self-construction" is only a justificatory operation. No real resemblance can be found between the principles at the national and regional levels.

In the case of post-implementation comparison, on the other hand, the law of the Member States is usually considered from the point of view of the effectiveness of the Community measures, or the correctness of the implementation[928].

---

[925] This applies especially to the *Albany* case analysed above.

[926] The external and instrumental point of view to the national systems can be seen, for example, in the idea that the national systems function, to a certain extent, as "*laboratories for the legal solutions*" (Lando, O., 1977, p.645). Interestingly enough, the persuasiveness and the great role of comparative law, at the European level and in the international systems is based on the fact that it functions in finding out "tested" forms of law.

The main features of instrumentality are embedded within the idea that the systems (and its institutions) actions are backed up by an examination of different possibilities and choices of the norm. This means choices, in the European context, between different systems, their norms and their interpretations etc. (Mössner, J.M., 1974, p.220).

[927] In the practice of the Court, the use of post-implementation material seems to contain analysis of the national jurisprudence including elements of Community law. In fact, it has been claimed that the special emphasis in the institutional study is on the cases decided after a preliminary ruling has been given (*Note d'information...*, p.3).

Such traditional self-construction has been identified in questions of legislation, administration, and fundamental rights (Pescatore, P., 1980, p.357).

[928] This is, however, not very easy to determine. To a certain extent, every post-implementation practice must be effecting on the interpretation of Community law, or European Law in general, if the states have some autonomy to maintain the coherence or the margin of appreciation of its own legal system (according to European level systems), and even without them.

However, it looks like the Community Court, for example, has to take into account the post-implementation measures as well, if it is to interpret the national legal systems in an integrative way.

The ultimate means of self-construction seems to be the justification of European-level competencies by identifying comparative tendencies in the sociological and "scientific" sense. This helps the institution to justify its function in the European sphere (for example, by defining the "enemy", which can be tackled only on that level).

1.3.3. Maintenance of "reasonable autonomy", and the role of comparative considerations substituting the "travaux préparatoires"

The question of the non-existence of the *travaux preparatoires* brings up the problem of sensible interpretation. This may be related to the motives for the use of comparative law.

It has been recognized, in the context of the Community system for example, that the non-existence of *travaux preparatoires* and any interpretation by the intention of the legislator guarantees the exclusive and practical competence and possibility for the European Court of Justice to interpret Community law. There are restricted possibilities for traditional dogmatics (based on ideas concerning sources of law) to interpret Community law, whether one is speaking about lawyers of different institutions in general or in national courts. As has been seen, this is not exactly the case in human rights system. There the *travaux preparatoires* play a role. However, also in that system, the role of this material and the "intention" of the Parties is diminished where the situation has changed, and where comparative observations come into play.

The "comparative *travaux preparatoires*", on the other hand, make a reasonable yet autonomous justification possible. The Court may justify the decision in difficult cases by the examination of the comparative pre-implementation material. On the other hand, the parties to the disputes may refer to comparative observations in order to support their main

---

How should one take this into account the implementation material? Could it be used as material in a comparative interpretation?

Basically it is quite impossible to consider post-implementation practices as a source of law, in terms of the traditional theories. Namely, the implementation material is conditioned by how the supranational bodies consider the validity of that law and those legal norms. Furthermore, while most of the rules in the Community system, for example, are teleological. This it means that the states do not really have any exact idea as to the correct implementation. The States cannot claim, according to the system, any correct implementation. If comparative observations are made, it is only for practical purposes.

In the Member States implementation laws comparisons can be made, even if their legal function is quite problematic. Studies could be made to map some alternatives for implementation.

The Commission has some times presented post-implementation material as an argument in a case, relating mainly to the question, whether the Member States have sought to utilize derogation clauses (Directive Article 2(2) of the Directive No 76/207)

Different dimensions of this idea could be worth a separate study.

arguments. The use and evaluation of the comparative material of this kind transfers the question of sovereignty and autonomy to a question of the autonomy of the comparing institution.

It is clear that the reflexive relationship between the regional systems, such as European Community, and state systems would not function in legal terms if the *travaux preparatoires* were too extensive. Namely, the possibility for a reinterpretation of European law would endanger the usefulness of the European norms in the internal regulation within states. On the other hand, the European system would be not able to control this interpretation (on the basis of the Article 177 (the new Article 234), for example). The interpretative competence would be automatically, to a certain extent, transferred to the national level. This possibility of "formative" directing by the Court of Justice in the preliminary ruling process would be endangered.[929]

Consequently, one may say that, for example, the Court of Justice constructs its own *travaux preparatoires* autonomously by means of comparative observations. Comparative law substitutes the *travaux preparatoires*, but in an extremely dynamic way and without any need to have an idea of the legislative intent.[930] This fact underlines - additionally - its autonomy as a legal institution and as an actor of the Community legal system.[931]

Furthermore, it maintains the teleological premises of the system in general. This "reconstructive" approach to the sources of law (i.e. kind of a "functional source of law") leads to a politically and legally dynamic and functional system. The legal "traditionalization" is in the hands of the process in the Court of Justice[932]. As observed before, this leads to institutionalist traditionalization of the comparative law in general.

This feature is related also to another benefit of "comparative *travaux preparatoires*". By the comparative observations the Community Court deconstructs the legal language of the national legal systems, and they become "invaded" by the instrumentalist Community conceptualization.[933]

The question of autonomy can be approached also from another perspective. Namely, the use

---

[929] Millett, T. (1988, p.163 ff.) also maintains that the methods of interpretation of the Court of Justice are conditioned by characteristics of European legislation. If this construction is lost, it would be a risk to the "system".

[930] This may be associated also with the avoidance of national conceptualizations. As seen, one of the basic ideas behind the choices of comparative reasons for the argumentation in the Community system seems to be the avoidance of nationally-loaded expressions. By finding disparity, the Community institution, in a reasonable way, can depart from any particular influences and is able to construct an autonomous European conceptualization.

[931] Concerning the autonomy functions, see Pescatore, P., 1980, p.356.

[932] Comparative law as a source of law seems to move on the same level as the precedents in international and regional legal systems. They seem to be a source of arguments, which complement and balance the institutional self-referentiality of using only case law as a source of law.

[933] On the other hand, because the legal argumentation of the national courts is determined more and more by the Community (and in general, the European) conceptualization, this guarantees the interpretative autonomy of both orders in relations to legal dogmatics. From the discursive point of view, this abolishes the interpretative possibilities of the lower level actors in the Community system.

and making of comparative observations in the justification and even in the dissenting opinions indicates the fact, that comparative observations have been considered. This, on the other hand, gives indication to the national level that comparative considerations have already been made, and that they are not necessary in the implementation of the "supra" national norms. This gives further autonomy to the European-level legal orders.

1.3.4. The implementation of changes in a persuasive way; the strength of the normative solution

The idea of comparative law theory [934] that comparative arguments are used usually in a situation where changes are needed, applies likewise to the European legal orders[935]. A good example of this was seen in the "double comparison" undertaken by the Advocate General in *Kalanke* case, who used the law of the United States to determine the direction of the change, contrary to the "internal comparison" between the Member States of the European Community[936]. By the institutionally qualitative approach the Community institution can direct the change and even propose quite "new" ideas concerning the allowed and prohibited types of legislation in the Community system. One could claim that comparative surveys make feasible teleological justification and formulation of norms and decisions[937].

The ultimate "change" in the comparative "directing" is naturally the "self-construction" or maintenance of the European institutional framework or the re-definition of competencies in the European sphere. In this sense, comparative argumentation does not have to be, in itself, extremely "radical". The disparity in the comparative situation, on the other hand, seems to be related to substantial "conservativeness".

Also the non-justificatory use of comparative considerations makes possible a teleological formulation of the justification, and a possible change. When one knows the features of the existing systems and one knows the dominant arguments used in the systems, one is able to formulate a radical justification, which is more easy to fall in with. It is possible to think that the judges need to observe the context into which the interpretation is "transplanted". This way there is a possibility to take into account the particular features of each legal system, and formulate the justification and the interpretation so that the norm is easier to place within a

---

[934] This is contrary to the regulative ideas concerning normal analogy (see, p.50 ff.).

[935] The fact that internal working methods change and that the styles of discourse in the courts change can hardly be attributed to comparative law as such (Like Bredimas, A., 1978b, p 322).

[936] This particular feature proves how the European system is reflexive also in the "external" legal sense and not only in the "internal" legal sense.

[937] It gives the European judges perspectives upon a legal problem (Pescatore, P., 1980).
    Comparative law is a source of unwritten Community law. It also functions in restricting elements of the case (Bredimas, A., 1978b, p.332).

national system. This often gives the impression that the European Court functions as a forum of *"legal innovation"*[938] (which, is turn, associated with the "precedential" thinking of the European Court[939]).

These ideas also seem to have a relationship to the "contextual" (socio-phenomenological) tendency argumentation.

1.3.5. The stability function: the strength of the argument, the judicial self-restraint[940], and the relative dynamics and stability

Comparative considerations, in connection to an interpretation of a legal norm in the European level institutional context, is a way to evaluate the legal "strength" of the (interpreted) norm in the realm of European law.[941] In reasoning, on the other hand, it seems to strengthen the legal argument, but can be also some kind of a sign of judicial self-restraint. This latter feature is visible especially in the European human rights system.

In this sense, the use of comparative law can be, to a certain extent, associated with the recognition of the "intentions" of the states, at least formally. Every time one deviates from the "autonomy" of the supranational European system, the question is about recognition of the states as legal actors[942]. In this sense, comparative reasoning seems to be used, where the aim of the system is to "translate" the normative idea into the language of the traditional national

---

[938] Pescatore speaks even about linguistic reformulations in order to find a persuasive formulation (1980, p.356).
   This can be the process of creating also an artificial language (see Sacco, 1991, p.18). That is to say, the role of the interpreter is becoming extremely central, even linguistically.

[939] See, Pescatore, P., 1980, pp.356-357.

[940] See also, Doetring, K., 1987, p.58. Wiklund, O (EG-domstolens tolkningsutrymme, Stockholm, 1997) has made a study on the judicial discretion of the European Court of Justice and its limits. He starts from "realistic approach", which takes into account the structure of norms and the division of powers between states and EEC as the basic determinants of the limits of this discretion. The study is "institutionally realistic" ("political" and "moral") rejecting a "positivist" approach.
   Wiklund emphasizes the (institutional) problem of division of powers as the basic problem. He notices the strong role of the European institutions in the integration process, but rejects the doctrine of supremacy of European law. He claims that the extensive use of discretion (pragmatism and effective protection of private individuals) by European Court has led to restrictions of the procedural and constitutional autonomy of the Member States. He claims that the critical legal scholarship should be activated in relation to the law-making activity of the European Court in order to secure the legitimacy of the European Court
   It looks like Wiklund, quite formally, underestimates the "coordinative" function of the European institutions, and "equalizes" the functions of national and European levels. He does not seem to accept any distinction between the issues of regulation. He also considers the concept of norm and the constitutionality in quite "holistic" way in the European legal discourse Furthermore, he seems to emphasize the maintenance of the legitimacy of the European Court as an objective in itself.

[941] Pescatore, P., 1980, pp.355-366

[942] The European comparative argument is extremely conservative (as are comparative legal studies in general). Many substantive questions seem to be beyond the comparative legal research. The comparative argumentation is strictly positively oriented This "equality of legal systems" oriented research cannot go beyond the "diplomatic" recognition of states, cannot be analytically open, and cannot sometimes even express studies openly.

lawyer in order to persuade that audience. This traditional audience is persuaded (or at least tried, although sometimes superficially) by this establishing of an relationship and identification of the state legal systems. In this sense, comparative law at least looks like an argument for the maintenance of the integrity of the state legal systems.[943]

This idea can be associated with another phenomenon.

There seems to be, in some fields of law, a strong priority given to the national legal systems. This may have to do with the regulated use of comparative law in certain fields of law. As noticed, comparative law is a legally-regulated source in the field of international law in general[944], and in the European Community system in the fields of responsibility questions (Article 215). On the other hand, Community law recognizes the possibility of using - comparative observations in certain cases relating to constitutional traditions (Article F, the new Article 6, and the case law). What does this tell us about comparative law in this legal order or such legal orders in general?[945]

One could claim that the source nature of comparative law is legally recognized in the fields of law where the system should, basically, be convinced not only of the particular correctness of the solution, but, for that matter, on the general correctness of the solution too. In other words, these fields of laws are the most sensitive areas of law. They seem to be the most universal fields of the contemporary modern legal system, close to the fundamental legal identity.[946]

On the other hand, the idea of including comparative law within the regulated sources seems to also introduce some dynamics into the system. This dynamism is designed to guarantee the idea that the system takes into account the general development of law (comparative law opinion), and constantly corrects itself in relation to these developments or undevelopments. In other words, this regulation is the normative functional arrangement in the realm of functional legal systems. It introduces an idea of relative dynamics in these fields of law.

In reality, however, the legal basis approach does not necessarily function in this manner. The legal basis seems to be only an *a priori* recognition of the generality. In fact, it may generate more institutionalized instrumentalization of law.

---

[943] This takes place, for example, by revealing fundamental differences between the legal systems (Pescatore, P., 1980, p.359).

This is the idea of the relative stability for the European order in relation to the national legal systems.

It is quite clear why the use of comparative law concentrates on the European States. This is determined by the legal and political integrity and equilibrium demands. It is, as well, rhetorically persuasive. The use of comparative law is not determined by the interest to information and new models.

On the other hand, the fact that United States appears a model, in many decisions, seems to be the outcome of the earlier adaptations of law. Furthermore, it is used settling problems of strong value conflicts.

[944] Comparative law can be associated with the recognition of the intentions of the states Every time one deviates from the autonomy of the supranational European system, the question is about recognition of the states as legal actors.

[945] Some analysis of the question already in 1944, see Gutteridge, H.C., 1944, p.8.

[946] See also, Galmot, Y., 1990, p.259.

On the other hand, in those fields of law, where the use of comparative law seems to be only practical, the interest seems to be only to guarantee the effective justification of the solution, or to design the context of implementation or to persuade the parts of the audience (such as like parties) as maintained before.

The fact that the European courts do not so openly interpret national systems may be also related to this idea of relative functionality. Because comparative observations are mainly a matter of the institutional context of justification, and the relative dynamics-approach does not seem to function, it is possible to claim that the relationship between national and European-level orders is increasingly determined by an idea of legal institutional balancing.[947]

1.3.6. Comparative reasoning directing future interpretations in national and European legal systems

One of the functions of the use of comparative observations may be seen in the attempt of the European courts to direct, "contextually", the future interpretations of the national courts[948]. Namely, the explicit reference to some national systems, or to the conceptualization deriving from them, may direct the national judges (or even legislatures) to look to these systems in the future interpretations (in legislation, for example).[949] This can be recognized also from the tendency type arguments appearing in connection to the comparative legal (and socio-phenomenological) arguments[950].

---

[947] This corresponds the way the national courts balance the national legislature by relying on comparative observations, as explained before.

[948] For some indications of this type of strategy, see Pescatore, P., 1980, p.354. This type of function is seen by Pescatore as "rationalization".

In this connection, the idea is about the intentionally strategic argumentation by the European courts Here I do not mean the evolutive aspects, which may be identified in relation to the dissenting, partly dissenting or Advocates General's opinions.

[949] Comparative law is "legal cooperation". It makes the cooperation between courts much easier, for example, in the realm of the Article 177 (the new Article 234) in The European Treaty (Pescatore, P., 1980, p.359).

It has been even suggested that national courts should look the comparative studies presented by the European Court of Justice on several issues in considering the interpretation of law. The national courts should benefit for the stock of comparative studies in European context (Galmot, Y., 1990, p.261).

It is also interesting to ask, what role could the interpretations of the state legal systems have in the dogmatic interpretation of the particular systems of Member States' rules and norms in national legal discourses. Could the description of the European Court be used as an argument in the national dogmatics as a legal argument? As one has noted, this has been done by the English Courts. The question is also about the role of institutional comparative legal studies in the national legal discourses.

[950] In fact, one could claim that the tendency types of institutional, phenomenological and professional arguments are the ultimate forms of comparative arguments. The question always remains: are there really tendencies? Can tendencies be imposed? Tendency type arguments seem to be narratives of the contemporary European world (or about the past?).

It is also another question as to what purposes this tendency information is put. Does one really attempt to maintain the integrity of the legal systems, or is the "tendency" information based on attempt to find out more persuasive forms of argumentation and more "adaptable" and "attractive" solutions.

This type of rationale may apply also to the discourse between the 'political' and the 'legal' at the European level. As has been noted, the European Court of Justice, for example, has had a fruitful discourse with the European legislature in cases, where legislative measures were needed.[951] The Court can, by comparative perspectives, indicate the direction for the legislation without having to adopt an "external" interpretation as such or to function as a legislature.[952]

1.4. The institutional dimension: some analysis of the function of institutional comparative law in European law

1.4.1. Institutional reasoning in European law

Comparative reasoning in the European Community institutions - and this applies, to some extent, to the European human rights system and national legal systems as well - seems to be based on the "common legal cultural tradition" assumption[953]. This can be noted from the fact that, in relation to comparative studies, no general sociological, cultural, or political studies (neither examinations of *travaux preparatoires)* are made. These types of comparative observations often relate to the phenomenological observations of law by the persons in organizations and decision-making institutions. European comparative reasoning is the "institutional professionalistic" and value-based comparative reasoning[954].

However, there is also a possibility that "tendencies" actually represent and define the basic values to be taken into account in the future. With these types of arguments the decision-maker defines its basic distinction. In this sense, the tendency functions also in teleological perspective, and makes one able to structure the reasoning in the future, without making it necessary to refer to any historical considerations. Furthermore, the legal sovereign may, on these basis, actual define its basis and scope and function, an even its fundamental meaning (the institutional existence) as such.

[951] See, Berlin, D., Interactions between the law maker and the judiciary within the EC. In: Legal Issues of European Integration, 1992 (17-48)

[952] This seems to apply also to the *Pinochet* case

As seen, the comparative argument does not have to play always a direct and decisive role. The comparative argument may be a form of a legal soft rule.

It seems also to be quite clear that the comparative reasoning cannot have a great role in a situation, where the law - which should be compared - seems to be instrumental itself. The forms of law, which are designed either to correct or change etc. unwanted situation (social engineering) - or to delegate competences - are problematic. These types of rules are related to rules containing general clauses etc. In these cases, it is problematic to identify any general - or even particular - features of law. One has to identify the system as a whole

[953] The effectiveness of this argument derives exactly from this fact. It assumes, and its addressees (audience) assume, a holistic understanding of the different dimensions of European discourses.

[954] Also Koopmans, T. on "institutional specialism" (1996, p.546). Concerning the "phenomenology" of comparative law, see Pescatore, P., 1980, p.338 ff. On the "pre-institutionalized" form of this type of "comparative law", see Gutteridge, H.C., 1944, p.9.

As has been claimed, value-based decisions can be seen especially in cases, where the comparative generality is neglected as a legal basis. This is so because then the question concerning a particular problem is generalized being connected to all legal systems of the Member States. Here the whole orientation of the tendency is declared unacceptable, and not only the rules of the particular system as such. Here the comparative influences are strongly determined by the traditional orientation

The value-based and institutional-phenomenological nature of European comparative reasoning may be related to certain communicative problems. First of all, the argumentation, in institutions by institutional actors, may be based on an incomplete understanding of the integrities of the overlooked systems. This may be a result of the lack of information on the relevant elements in legal systems. On the other hand, the incompleteness of the information may be accepted intentionally. This may be due to the effectiveness demands of the legal order, but also a result of the pathological tendencies in the organization ("attempt to avoid problems"). Thirdly, the value approach may come into a play because of the exclusion of the comparative information as relevant information as such.[955]

In these types of cases the justifications become extremely affective.

1.4.2. The structure of the European level institutional comparative law

To explain the phenomenon of institutional comparative law, one could make a distinction between different arguer-audience relationships internal to the European level legal institutions. One can consider these audiences as parts of the formation of the institutional opinion.

First of all, it looks as if the judges are the audience for determining the correctness of the expertise (internal-institutional or external institutional) comparative studies (including Advocates General's comparative opinions). Furthermore, all comparative reasoning presented by the parties is directed to the judges.

This means, for example, that, in the European institutions, the final discourse on the acceptability of the relevance of the comparative information takes place in the internal discourses among the Court members.[956] The European Court of Justice in particular restricts

---

of certain systems

[955] If vertical comparability is neglected, it means, in a way, that the systems regulated are not seen as equal any longer. Because of some traditional context, the models must arrive from one context, which remains, in this sense, superior to others.

This explain for example the fact, why the US system is taken as a comparable and referential system in the cases where the vertical comparability is neglected. The US system hides the fact that one of the internal systems, where the model is coming from, is the contextual basis of justification (see *Kalanke* case).

[956] It can be claimed that the principle of confidentiality, some courts, concerning the availability of the comparative information makes it quite impossible to evaluate the influences deriving from different systems (the "diffusions of law"). However, what one may do is to evaluate influences based on other arguments related to comparative legal evaluations.

One may assume also that the idea of restricting the publication of comparative material is based on the interest of limiting the possibility of an impression that a system is a direct source of the solution.

Also questions about different cumulative effects, in the interpretations, seems to be hidden. For example, it seems to be impossible to know about the further implications of the comparative observations in subsequent case law. This is related to the problems of interpreting decisions in general, and their aims. Consequently, the "best argument" remain unknown.

On the other hand, the role of the institutional relationships is difficult to grasp.

It might be exactly the consequence of the informal and instrumental use of the comparative observations, why the relationship between the Community law and national legal systems is difficult to establish in legal research (On this difficulty,

clearly and effectively the use of comparative observations, even if it sometimes expresses the influences explicitly in a shortened and rather simplified way. As noticed, the Advocates General and members presenting the dissenting or partly dissenting opinions are able to make more open statements[957].

The transitivity relationship between national dogmatics and the institutional (external or internal) experts is indirect. This is exactly one of the reasons why one cannot speak of a direct communicative relationship between national and institutional actors. However, the information still flows from the national dogmatics to the expertise institutions. The specialized expertise-institutions function as an institutional expertise opinion. The experts regulate what is considered to be correct, acceptable and relevant information for argumentative purposes internal to the institution.[958]

Where the European level courts rely on either the expert studies (whether internal or external), or on the relatively contingent observations by the judges themselves, it means that the relationship between the Court and the national dogmatics is not systematically direct either. Courts are not the direct audience of the national dogmatics.

Institutionalistic comparative law guarantees the efficiency of such studies. On the other hand, the information is under the institutional control. This way the court, for example, goes beyond the criticism of misinterpretation of national or comparative discourses. This is a form of the reflexivity between these two levels of legal orders. Furthermore, in having the comparative discourse institutionalized, the choices of the persuasive way of reasoning can be selected more efficiently. One is able settle on the type of argumentation which is most suitable for the interested audience.

Now, some special remarks have to be made concerning the relationship between the Advocates General and the Court of the European Communities and on the European system of human rights.

More "qualitative" generality and divergency arguments can be found in the justifications by the Advocates General. However, it is not self-evident that these analyses have a normative value for the Court. They can be adopted or not. In point of fact, it looks as if some of the reasons, and especially the comparative observations presented by the Advocates General, do not appear in any form in the justification of the Court, even if the normative conclusion is the same. Clearly, the reasoning of the Court seems to be extremely formal.[959]

This does not, however, mean that the comparative observations would not have any impact on the normative conclusions of the Court, or that they have not been used in the internal

---

Bredimas, A., 1978a, p.103).

[957] It seems, however, that in the earlier days of the Community order, for example, the practice of autonomous use of comparative material seemed to be more casual and common.

[958] See the analysis of the case *Albany* above.

[959] For some analysis of this relationship, see Pescatore, P., 1980, p.346.

discussions. On the contrary. It seems that the comparative observations are relevant arguments and that the Court has different types of principles and sees the functions of the reasoning differently.

However, it is quite difficult to find any general features of the influences of the contextual comparative law upon the justifications of the European Court of Justice. It seems that the success of the comparative analysis is related to its concordance with the accepted 'internal' principles more than to the idea of "direct derivation"[960]. It seems clear that the Court attempts to maintain the autonomy of the order by interpreting the comparative observations in accordance of the principles of Community law (its aims etc.).

In this sense, the relationship between the Advocate General and the Court appears also normatively transitive. In cases, where the solutions are the same, the comparative observations by the Advocates General are likely to be agreed with. However, if the Advocates General enter too strongly into the comparatively based observations, the Court may neglect the comparative analysis as irrelevant or unacceptable. This rejection could be based, one could imagine, on too much emphasis on the "one-country-as-a-source" idea (also methodologically). Too much significance attached to one country in the comparative analysis can be contrary to the principles of the Court. These types of analyses may be taken into account, but they are not, as such, seen in the reasoning as an explicit reference to one legal system.

On the other hand, one could claim that, in some cases, the material norms referred to just do not seem to be suitable to the European context. The restrictions, based on this substantial inacceptability, are usually made in the context of the institutional framework (the internal discourse), or in the consideration of the relevancy by the Advocates General. However, it is interesting to note, that also the Court, in a substantial sense, may reject the proposals of the Advocates General based on comparative studies.

In the European Court of Human Rights the situation seems to be slightly different from the European Court. It seems that the comparative observations by the Commission and parties have generally a great impact upon the justification of the Court. This has evidently to do with the "balancing" role of the Court. On the other hand, the comparative analysis, in the dissenting opinions, seems to represent reasoning, which has been presented already in the "internal" discourses. In the dissenting opinions, judges are more free to take examples from different national systems. They tend to represent the alternative possibilities in legally reasonable way, which may be contrary to the general case law or against the interpretation of the Court in that particular case. This seems to indicate that also in the internal discourse

---

[960] One interesting subject, in Community legal research, would be the idea of how the opinions of the Advocates General are used, as legal formants, in different decisions over a certain period of time. In general, this would be a study of the role of different institutional sources. These types of studies do not appear in the traditional dogmatic approach to the Community law. The rule oriented studies do not reveal anything on the argumentative strategies.

of the European Court of Human Rights, comparative analyses are discussed, but that the Court does not wish to bring these observations to light as a matter of principle.

On the other hand, the fact that these observations appear many times in the dissenting opinions seems to suggest that the comparative observations are presented exactly in the situations, where there is a strong disagreement. This can be supported as well by the fact that the parallel justifications agreeing with the main justification and solution do not seem to include extensive comparative observations. It seems to be clear that by comparative observations the judges, having separate opinions, seek the adherence of the traditional national audience or the comparative opinion as an alternative to the institutional opinion. This way these types of comparative law observations may give dynamism to the system in an evolutive sense.

The relationship between the Advocates General and the European Court of Justice is especially interesting from the point of view of argumentative functionality. One could see different types of discursive principles behind their justifications, or even two types of discourses. The Court is stressing clearly the efficiency and the autonomy of the European legal order. On the other hand, Advocates General tend to be more oriented towards the Member States and represent the Member States in the Community level.

Even if the function of the Advocate General is to give an advisory opinion to the Court, his opinions are public, and one can hardly overestimate their function also as justifications of the cases, as it has been maintained. However, they have also the function of achieving the adherence of the general legal and general public audiences, and they do not function only in convincing the Court as to the acceptability of some solutions[961]. Here one comes to an interesting point.

To a certain extent, the role of the Advocates General, in arguing to the comparative, and even national audiences, can be seen as a way of avoiding the criticism against the Court itself in a particular way. Namely, it seems to persuade the audience by explaining that the comparative observations have been made, and that the decision is not based solely on institutional principles. Furthermore, it is quite evident that the effectiveness of the Court's argumentation is related to its shortness in relation to the justifications made by the Advocates General. As seen, the relationship between Advocates General's argumentation, in relation Courts argumentation, is also less persuasive because of the breaks and jumps in the analysis. Its shortness and reduced analytical nature make Court argumentation seem more compact. The fact that the Court is making value-based limitations upon the argumentation, and that seems to analytically examine the Advocate General's statements and evaluate them normatively, increases the formal authoritative force of the Court's argumentation. It then looks like the outcome of more careful consideration rather than a mechanical adaptation of reasons. This

---

[961] In this sense, it seems to be acceptable to study of the role of these opinions in the justificatory processes, and to examine the functions of the differences and similarities of these opinions and the Court's judgments

can be seen exactly in the cases of the comparative reasoning in the European Court (likewise in the Court of Human Rights)[962].

In conclusion, however, one may say that Advocates General do seem to have in mind a larger audience, at least they seem to strive towards it, sometimes with success, sometimes not. The Court, on the other hand, seems to be institutionally and procedurally (formally) closed, and it attempts to maintain the authority and integrity of the system. If the Court does discuss the question on a comparative basis, it does so restrictively. However, the combination and interaction of these two institutional actors produce a reasoning related to same large audience as in the case of the Advocates General.

1.5. Conclusions

1.5.1. The function of comparative law in the evolution of European law

As one may notice, European level systems seem to have an idea of "evolutive" interpretation. The systems tend to keep open changes by identifying, on a situational basis, the disparity and generality existing in the systems. This is part of the "legal functionality". This means that the "stages" of European legal development are examined all over again by comparative means. The idea is to establish well functioning norms in each stage of the evolution. The comparative observations function in checking the "evolutionary" stage of European law[963].

Furthermore, comparative law is an extremely important factor in the legal drafting of situationally determined European rules. Moreover, one could see similar functions in the dissenting opinions, and Human Rights Commission and Advocates General argumentation, which may be used as a store of alternative arguments.

Comparative law seems to function as a means of coupling of a system to another system. This coupling takes place in a process where the terms and the solutions of some "transferring" systems are translated into the language of the "receiving" systems.[964] This is true especially in a situation where the comparative examination is contextual, and where the comparative examinations are followed by a norm selection. In an extreme form, comparative law functions as a means for the construction of the European-level system architecture. This way institutions transfer the different traditions of the European state paradigm to the European level. On the other hand, the European systems function as a kind of normative

---

[962] The analysis of the comparative observations can be rich, but not that rich. As is well known, the persuasiveness can be diminished where the analysis is too long. This is related to the restriction of the analysis of the legal systems to the traditional basic legal sources.

[963] See also, Schermers, H.G., 1979, p. 169 ff., and Galmot, Y., 1992, p.258.

[964] On the use of receiving and transferring, see Kamba, E.J., 1974, p.23.

"implanters" of various solutions in national systems to different systems[965], at least in a formal sense. As seen, different reflections transform the European legal systems in different way, and different national legal systems adopt influences in different fields of law etc. This depends upon the general orientation of the institutional actors too, as has been mentioned.

On the other hand, where the changes in European law, through the comparative law of the Member States, can be seen as less "integrative" and the argumentation less "persuasive", so-called "third law" comparisons may appear relevant in justifying the drastic changes to the European legal systems[966].

1.5.2. Problems of evolution?

The function of the comparative interpretation, in a positive sense, is to reveal the heterogeneity of the European legal language, and in this way to provide a context for the justification of the normative choices. However, as the study of the European-level adjudication indicates, the comparative studies are not often revealed.[967] This leads to the observation that it is quite impossible to understand the normative choices of the courts. The courts' decisions have to be interpreted "autopoietically", in relation to the jurisprudence found in its own case law.

In this sense, the European legal jurisprudence seems to be discursively oppressive. It determines the "traditional" use of language by imposing its "legal language" upon the national, comparative and general legal discourses in general, but maintains the understanding (or non-understanding(!)) of the "real" normative reasonable (?) choices in its internal sphere. In this context, one is discussing the normative choices of the models on which the Court builds up its interpretation.

Why would this be important? Why would it be important to know, which comparative choices the Court has made in the institutional context?

The idea behind this interest is that the European jurisprudence is extremely dynamic. To a certain extent, the decisions, in many cases, are not "permanent". The preliminary material consists of possible premises for system-understanding. The study of these internal

---

[965] Concerning the spill-over effects, see Schwarze, J., 1991, p.15 ff., Gordon, A., 1998, pp.255-256. Also, Galmot, Y., 1990, p.261.

What one has to remember is that the question is not only about implanting some positive formulations, but also implanting new approaches to law (some methods of interpretation, for example, teleology) and certain type of institutionalism and division of powers, and, in the ultimate sense, the ideas on social justice.

[966] It seems to be clear, in relation to the *Kalanke* case, for example, that when the "internal" comparison does not result in a principally accepted form of legal basis, resort is then to external comparison. This may be associated with the idea that a legal order seems to be obliged, in European law, to make decisions and to reproduce itself as a superior order.

[967] Pescatore, P., only the *"iceberg"* (1980, p 358).

comparative explanations and descriptions would be important, because they have a tendency to remain and to become "ontologized". This is why the context of the explanations behind the normative decisions must be revealed so that there remains a possibility to reconstruct also other types of comparative explanations, and to reveal the possible misunderstanding internal to the institution[968]. Another method to realize this could be the system of dissenting opinions[969]. That would make it possible to evaluate "contextually" the possible alternative ideas of the role of comparative law. Nevertheless, that would be, I think, only secondary method.

On the other hand, the validity of the use of comparative legal observations in the European Courts is related also to the interpretative status of the judge. The basic idea is, as one knows, that the European judges should not normatively interpret the legal systems of the Member States. In fact, however, this type of interpretation is unavoidable. Furthermore, one knows that the judges have a tendency to interpret comparative material based on their phenomenological understanding and also quite "politically".[970] Here the question of the nature of the comparative studies becomes relevant, if one has to examine the ability of the administration to really present correct interpretations of the national systems, even with regard to their own national systems. There is always the possibility of a "wrong" interpretation, especially, if one thinks about the "tendency" analysis, which seems to be part of the socio-political comparative observations also[971]. I think this idea has been reflected, to a certain extend, in the comparative legal discourse in the context of *Albany* case.[972]

To conclude, there seems to be, in general, reluctance to have the genuine comparative discourse within the European legal institutions. One could even claim that the idea is to avoid scientific discussion of the issue. At least, the European institutions do not encourage the development of the comparative legal discourse in Europe. This seems to be strange, especially because the issues of comparative law, which are many times instrumentalized, are usually somehow "unclear" from the legal scientific point of view.[973] Consequently, no critical and

---

[968] If it is so that the comparative argument is related to the inventive side of law, and, as seen, the organization uses it in the internal discourse rather than in the external justificatory discourse, it is a case in point of autopoietic organization. It changes and develops the law by closing itself normatively.

[969] Proposed, for example, by Weiler, J.H.H. (Helsinki European Law seminar "The Future and Function of European Law, 1999).

[970] See also the discussion of Weiler, J.H.H., 1998.

[971] For some aspects, see Hunnings, 1996, p.171. For an indication of the strong value-based method of comparative interpretation in general by European judges, see Mancini, G.F., 1998 (especially the comparative observations on pages 33-39).

[972] See, discussion in ColCom, Final Report (Jari Hellsten), 3.7.2000.

[973] The idea of *ad hoc* requests for comparative studies from different scientific institutions indicates that some scientific "correctness" is wanted.
   However, one has to remember that the comparative observations are still made in the organizations, and these studies are not necessarily revealed to the public or to researchers.

analytical perspectives are usually available in everyday discussion. This means, on the other hand, the disappearance of a genuine attempt at a scientific comparative discourse. At the same time, one is not able to take comparative law seriously as an argument. The lack of internal and analytical comparative law discourse causes a lack of persuasiveness of these arguments. This, in turn, generates a lack of an essential dimension for the development of the national legal systems.

2. CONCLUSIONS ON EUROPEAN LAW

2.1. General remarks: toward a "reflexive" theory of European law

One could easily come to the conclusion that the only way to have really genuine "European legal studies" would be to undertake sociological studies on the institutionalized forms of legal decision-making in Europe. However, the legal system(atization) approach is preferred, in this connection, and some remarks can be made on the legal dimension of institutionalized comparative law in general, from the point of view of the legal discourse theory.

The identity of European law may be seen in the "comparative formations", as it has been maintained. This legal identity is not necessarily related only to the normative outcomes of the comparisons, but, for that matter, to the types of comparative processes and comparative formulations themselves attached to these processes. This kind of concept of European legal identity deviates from the traditional "paradigmatic", ideological, dogmatic, and political ideas of identity.[974] It is based on the idea of the discursive identity. Consequently, when one speaks about the European legal orders, one seems to speak about <u>relatively autonomous orders and legal cultures.</u>

This comparative relationship between different European legal orders can be, moreover, characterized as reflexive. In the realm of this comparative reflexivity, there seems to be linguistically (performatively) formalist systems, which, on the one hand, are flexible in their historical interpretation of law. At the same time, there seem to be systems where the linguistic formalism refers rather to the weak role of "common language" as a legal measure, and, similarly, sticks strongly to the legal-historical and dogmatically defined conceptualism (and "substantialism").

To make it possible to merge these types of systems, for example, into one "European" perspective requires the idea of discursive reflexivity. This way one ends up with the idea of

---

[974] Compare, for example, Brusiin, O., Zum Ehescheidungsprobleme (Hyvinkää) 1959, p.17 ff.

comparative discursive reflexivity of legal systems. This comparatively discursive reflexivity can be explained in the following way.[975]

First of all, the systems seem to identify each other mainly via their institutional margins of law. This seems to be due to the fact that legal institutions are, at the same time, liberative (opening) and deliberative (closing). They interpret their "own" rules and formulate norms, but are open also to "external legal information" in quite a "genuine" sense (independent or dogmatic academic comparative law studies are not always that). On the other hand, when institutions are using comparative law as a source of law, they are not always able to be open in relation to public discourse (i.e. to be discursively liberative). In general, as it has been stressed, in the using of comparative observations, the discursively liberative aspect gets diminished. In fact, any use of comparative observations seems to lead to institutional legal conducting mechanisms, even if, from a purely formalist legal point of view, the use of comparative law seems to be important for the continuity of the legal system as such. This idea is also related to the fact that comparative observations are strongly directed only to the institutional legal audience. The problem is that there seems to be a gap between legal professionalism and other types of audiences.

If one would maintain the centrality of this institutional dimension, one would have to centralize this type of discursive reflexivity also. Consequently, one would have to also give preference to legally professionalist and instrumental institutional systems. However, it is argued that European law cannot be (also from the point of view of the democratic theory) institutionally centred, and the gap between the general public (legal) discourse and the institutional professionalist discourse has to be avoided. One must consider the European comparatively reflexive discourse as a discourse in the margins of law. This type of institutional discourse takes place in the following way.

It can be maintained, firstly, that comparative law may be used only in hard cases, if parties accept and demand the use of comparative analytical observations and the decision-maker chooses to do so or, as in European Community law, where there are institutional forms for this type of use. When this use is not demanded (i.e. where the argumentation by parties is based mainly on extremely "common sense" reasoning by practical-teleological arguments), the decision-maker may not use them. On the other hand, when the comparative analysis is considered sensible and reasonable approach in the given situation, it may be included within the justification. The use of comparative law is, in this sense, an alternative and a marginal phenomenon.

One may also challenge the centrality of the hard cases of law (related to these comparative

---

[975] Some suggesting a strictly normative theory on the relationship have used concepts of "parallel" and "exclusive" powers, see, Bieber, R., 1988, 147 ff. It seems that in this theory, the distinction between order and system is not analytically relevant. It also assumes strong "commonness" in relations to concepts and norms.

For the problem of "commonness", see Legrand, P., 1996, p.54 (especially p.56).

observations) - from the point of view of an idea of legal culture - in the following way.

In "normal" legal decision-making, judges decide cases by making interpretations based on usually quite well-justified, albeit conflicting, opinions of the parties of the case. However, if one is not able to find, on the basis of the parties reasoning, the essential elements for an interpretation and there is a problem in the reasonability of interpretation, one may take up - in the absence of other "new" material - comparative observations. However, at the same time one steps out of the hard core of the positive formal legal culture, as it has been maintained. Moreover, if comparative argument is taken up as a best argument, the decision-maker clearly moves in the margins of any legal cultural perspective, at least in a formal way.

When one has an "easy case", to be decided on a conventional (legal traditional) basis, the parties are usually not discursive in any traditional sense. On the contrary, in these types of cases the parties seem to be extremely instrumental in their legal argumentation. The established forms of reasoning and doctrines are maintained as best arguments. In fact, then the cultural (institutional) contextuality is more decisive, and one may even claim that the societal structures of authority are decisive for the "substance". Here the "easiness" of the case appears only from the institutionalist point of view.

In this sense, it seems interesting that a certain degree of (political) instrumentality seems to be a phenomenon on the hard core of the legal culture. Thus, one could identify legal culture as politically (ideologically) contextualized social phenomenon. One actually could speak about an instrumental game of law as a hard core of a legal culture. However, this does not seem to be correct. Namely, one easily comes back, in this type of institutionalist legal theory, to the margins of law.

However, in the realm of the discursive theory of law, one could instead replace the idea of the "political" with the idea of finding finer meaningful distinctions. In this sense, the hard core of the legal culture seems to be a search for the distinctions relevant to the interpretation of law. The extent to which this can be done is determined by the discursive sensitivity of the parties and judges, but also on their idea of discursive integrity. This will be dealt with later on. Nonetheless, in this connection one may say that if one really tries to grasp the idea of how the coherence of law, legal systems, or cultures seem to be maintained, one may adhere to the idea that this process takes place within the discourses in a equal and integrative way. Within this type of maintenance, the "legal" parties justify analytically their opinion (in a reasonable way). In fact, the task of the judge, in these types of cases, may be determined by the task to "guard" that the legal discourse deals also, and mainly, with the hard core of the traditional legal opinions presented and prevailing. In the traditional legal sciences, this seems to be the role of legal dogmatics and also legal theory.

The idea in this kind of integrative and equal discourse seems to be, consequently, to interpret legal culture as a discourse. The institutional discourse may, in this sense, show itself only as an institutional hard core of the legal culture. In this type of institutionally "marginal" interpretation, however, one may move towards the hard core of the legal culture as such. The institutional discourse may be instrumentalized as such.

Now, in this type of institutional discourse, comparative arguments may have an open role. However, these institutional discourses are still at the "margins" of the legal culture in any substantive sense. They are marginal from the point of view of the general legal discourse, and their role is to be decided on the basis of further development, discourse in dogmatics and legal theory etc. Furthermore, from the point of view of the traditional theory of legal discourse this should be so. One does not aim to speak to a more general audience than to the quite-restricted legal audience.

In this sense, to conclude, one may remain in the realm of the comparatively discursive reflexivity of law.

How could the hard core of European law could be seen from this point of view? How could we apply these ideas to European law in general.

Because European-level norms are more or less comparatively (and institutionally) constructed, no real "hard core" seems to exist. In the realm of the European norms, one seems to be unable to reach any self-sufficient clarity. European level law is reflexive law as such. Also the institutionally determined comparative interpretation seems to indicate this. The process is not an analytical discourse based on comparative analysis, but institutionally and, at most, traditionally determined <u>comparative</u> justification. It is very difficult to reach the traditional sphere of law in general. The comparative observations do not seem to go towards any finer sensitivity of the legal situation analysed in an equal and integrative discourse. On a contrary, the comparative analysis shows itself in many ways as an superficial confirmation of the homogenized legal past, which is intrumentalized by means of institutional authority. In this sense, it moves in the margins of law.

Could one claim, however, that the European legal principles could be some kind of central (cultural) "structurants" of European-level law?

The scope of European legal principles is not clear. Their use seems to represent a hard case, as one may see also from the extensive but, nevertheless, traditional use of comparative law in their interpretation. The "discursive game" seems not to be about finer distinctions, but usually about the European self-construction or the "balance" between these spheres as an aim as such. The political game seems to be also seen as a game of statal and governmental self-recognition. The change of the "spheres" from national to European takes place many times in this interest (one is able to see the state systems holistically, and to avoid genuine discourses).

However, this type of legal-political game is not, in any way, linguistically or culturally contextualized in the traditional discursive sense.[976] It is institutional-professionally

---

[976] Pescatore, for example (1980, p.358) speaks about discursivity, but seems to refer only to the institutional discourse as a discursive approach.

determined. The institutional self-reproduction seems to be exactly in the hard core of the European law. The European level fills up the *"lacunae"* of the national legal systems and their hard cases by its institutional appearance. One discusses, on these bases, something, which has not been taken up in national legal systems as a relevant subject.

Consequently, in many ways, European level law moves in the margins of discursively conditioned games of legal interpretations. Its principles are in the margins of law. In a best situation, when dealing with comparative aspects in these processes, one may come to a value-based discursive legal process. Nevertheless, these institutionally conducted processes do not seem to strive towards the hard core of law or traditional legal culture in this sense. They are not discourses on the hard core of value-based language.

The hard core of European law and legal culture is in its institutionalist possibility.[977] Comparative law is a legal source in European principled institutional decision-making, because it is considered a balancing element in the very strong institutional performances in the case there is no hard core linguistic or any other type of sources for the discourse. The use of comparative law attempts to balance the principled institutional decision-making, but many times fails to do so because of its incomplete understanding of comparative law (seeing it not as a discourse, but a form of conceptual framework).

On the other hand, where the European institutional law is directed to the national legal systems, it is redefined in the terms of the national legal conceptualization and interpretation of the national legal institutions and dogmatic discourses.[978] The arguments deriving from the European regional discourses interact with the arguments in the legal-political discourse of rule creation and legal discourse of rule application, the results of which depend on the internal discursive culture of the adapting system. However, in the factuality of a system or systems, the descriptions cannot be genuine arguments for they do not represent a basis of a consensus as an immanent form but rather, as mentioned before, they are quite contingent adaptions. If the factuality of legal systems enters into the legal discourse of another system, it has to be rerationalized in its own discourse. This is the other side of this reflexivity.[979]

---

[977] This is maintained, for example, by Weiler, J.H.H., 1998, analyzing Mancini, G.F., 1998.

[978] Reflexivity is a simple result of the fact that all norms at one level (international-EC, EC-national etc, national-national) have to be transformed in the formal and substantial level of the system concerned (domestication/internationalization).
  See the concept of domestication, de Boer, Th.M., 1994, p.18. This is kind of a "logical process".
  Some discussion on the influences of European Community law to national legal systems, see Koopmans, T., 1991, pp.505-507.

[979] In this sense, one may understand, for example, why the European Court speaks about the autonomy of the European legal order, and not about the autonomy of the European legal system. Even if the European legal order (Community law) can be normatively considered to be as an autonomous order, it is not so conceptually, procedurally, organizationally, and, in addition, jurisdictionally. The idea of "legal order" seems to be an explanation for the fact that the legal "system" is unsystematic in nature, and that the systematization itself takes place in genuine legal discourses. The Community order uses these discourses instrumentally. This way the autonomy can be defined as instrumental autonomy. This idea suits well to the idea of the nature of European legislation as instrumental and teleological legislation. For the nature of interpretation in Community order and legal system, see Daig, H-W., 1981, p.402 ff.. There has been also use of the expression "Le

2.2. Is there any justification for the (institutional) non-discursive reflexivity?

It may be asked whether the closed comparative reflexivity of European legal institutions could be justified in legal terms?

Some reasons for it at the European level has already been found. For example, one may emphasize the idea that the European level orders close themselves mainly because there is an attempt at its reproduction as the <u>only</u> legitimate authority (the argument of institutional integration). The clear references to state legal systems and, moreover, the analysis of particular legal social systems, would drop off the force of its interpretation to the extent that the system would lose its reproductive status in the social system. In other words, the "legal sovereignty" idea may serve the purposes of integration. Non-referentiality at the national level may also be based on this idea, but in an extremely formal sense.

In the case of European Union law this is particularly visible. The only way to establish a "new" legitimate order is to maintain some degree of closeness in the situation, where the social system seems to be, in many ways, disintegrated. In this way it is possible to weight up effectively (in political discourse) the conflicts internal to the European systems, and to maintain relatively acceptable solutions and argumentation. The disparity of discourses and the non-existence of the general European discourse can function as a legitimation of this instrumental closeness.

On the other hand, one justification could be derived from the idea of the internal problems of the balance of power in the national legal systems, as it has been maintained. The national adjudication has to, increasingly, follow the globalized legislature to that same sphere of rationality. One could say that any method of balancing this development is justified. In national legal institutions, the idea may be related also to the "internal" balances. Namely, by the closed use of comparative material one tries to reproduce the idea of the traditional "material" supremacy of parliament.

Another justification is related to the nature of legal justification as such. This will be dealt in the last chapter more thoroughly.

However, it is exactly these features which speak also for a relatively open comparative

---

systéme juridique communataire", see for example, Wilmars de, J.M., 1991). For the autonomy, see Mortelmans, K , Community Law: More than a functional area of law, less than a legal system. In: Legal Issues of European Integration, 1996/1 (23-49) maintaining that the national legal systems do not fulfil all the criteria set by legal theoreticians (referring to Bengoetxea, J., who sees, on the other hand, the Community system not fulfilling the criterion of a legal system). Also, Schilling, T., The Autonomy of the Community legal Order: An Analysis of Possible Foundations. In: Harvard International Law Journal, 1996 (389-409), who studies the autonomy of the Community law on the basis of the original Treaties, its further development, its natural law status, its international law status, and comes to the conclusion that international law functions as the only basis justifying the autonomy of the Community legal order from the national legal systems, which also seem to function as the *Kompetenz-Kompetenz* instances of this melée.

reasoning. Firstly, one could say that the general legal discourse is the only way to harmoniously develop the European legal systems. If the substantial comparative reasons and analysis are exposed to the light, the discourse on them creates the dynamics essential for the development of the European legal sphere. Secondly, re-founding the traditional forms of legal sources, the states and perhaps the normative social subsystems, functions to stabilize the legal framework of Europe before it becomes heavily overloaded by instrumental and ideological afflictions [980]. Here one could claim that even if the reflexive relationship between systems would seem only to maintain the autonomy of the legal systems and orders, and even if the relationship would be legally indirect, it still would be based on the principle of the adjudicative integrity of law.

In the end, one may claim, from the point of view of legal theory, that "European institutional" law is, in relation to its comparative approach, deliberative in general. The general discursive coherence is not, and does not seem to be able to be the main aim and principle of European adjudication.[981] The legal theoretical perspective is in many ways restricted. There is no attempt to create a more discursively extensive analysis of the system in general. The adjudication of this kind, apart from the English approach, does not aim to relate itself to the "total" system. This type of legal theoretical idea leads to the fact that no liberative perspective exists. At the European level, this, on the other hand, results in a non-discursive approach to legal adjudication and has its influence also within national systems oriented to a formal use of European-level decisions.

2.3. Integrative reflexivity and European comparative rules

Even if the coherence of a legal discourse is the basic theoretical normative premise of European law, the evolution of law and legal systems is a continuing process, and the idea of coherent closeness of legal systems and the law, as a discourse, does not exclude the possibility that the perlocutionary sphere of social normativity ("results of law") is taken up to be a question for the legal discourse. These normative "perlocutions" of legal systems can be adapted also to the political discourse and, in the global sphere, to the discourse of international and regional systems. These latter systems, in particular, create their immanent propositions in relation to genuine legal discourses *a posteriori*.

The basis of this rationalization of the "factuality" of another legal system takes place, as seen, in the realm of the comparative legal discourse. The comparative law discourse is an

---

[980] It can be noted how comparative observations are sometimes related to the legal "sub-systems" too. In some cases, there has been a comparison between the rules of the lawyers associations. These sub-systems maintain a relative autonomy in deciding on their internal rules.

[981] In relation to the English system one may have, however, also a contrary opinion.

attempt to rationalize the adopted arguments, and even their choice and reformulation, and generality conclusions. This way there seems to be a creation of a "hypothetical comparative rule" for the use of the regional or domestic legal discourse, which can, consequently, function as a basis of a consensus.

One could claim that the basic ideas behind the <u>application</u> of the comparative rule, as a hypothetical legal rule, which can enter into a legal system as a rational legal argument, are constructed in a process based on the principle of discursive integrity of the particular legal-political community. The social and legal consensus is on this principle. On the other hand, the study of the application of this legal principle of discursive integrity, and the comparative legal discourse, explains, how the legal normative principle of integrity can be seen in different legal systems of regional or international communities. The legal discourse may "socialize" the integrity principle by explaining the normative nature of this integrity in legal terms (the nature of the comparative rule), and by explaining the intentional forms of integrity as a teleological aim of a system. In this sense, it looks like the comparative discourse aims at a common legal understanding of the legal and social nature of integrity as a comparative law principle. This is what has been attempted in this book.

On the other hand, in the realm of the legal discourse, one finds also the limits and nature of the consensus on this integrity. The legal discourse rationalizes the comparative rule of integrity and the comparative legal rule so that it can be seen to be rationally adaptable (or non-adaptable) in different regional and domestic discourses of law as argument of law.

Consequently, there is the possibility to arrive at an immanent form of law as the premises for an interpretational process. The legal discourse brings to the light the existence of an integrative rule of law, which can serve as a legal basis in a particular legal system. This way the comparative legal integrity could be used even as an argument in the practical legal discourse of application as such[982].

Consequently, one could maintain that the idea of the European comparative dogmatics, founded on the examination of the European legal integrity, consists in the identification of hard cases, and marginalities as the basis of the decisions, and identifications of the fallacies of the problems of comparative reasoning in legal decisions-making[983]. This is discussed more thoroughly below.

There is also another factor. In the field of legislation, the transfer of sovereign powers from national systems to the European Union creates obstacles for national parliamentary systems to regulate certain fields of law. However, the fact that comparative law is embedded in the instrumental work of the European Court, and to the work of European institutions has certain

---

[982] One could say that where the aims of a general system starts to determine the aims of the sub-systems, rationality is not the basic determining factor in the relationships of the sub-systems of general system.

[983] This will be discussed more thoroughly in the end of the work, but here one can say that the comparative dogmatics of this type seems not to have possibilities to really propose legal solutions as such.

consequences.

The legal and customary basis of the use of comparative law, in European law, gives the states the possibility to exercise their own "option" or "flexibility" policy in a legal sense, and even to have an effect at the European level, based on the respect the principle for legal integrity in its legislative form. If the states are able to regulate, for example, the constitutional way their own normative system, they can have an impact upon the marginal observations of the European Union system (by, for example, introducing aspects deriving from the "*traditions*" and even "*identity of the Member States*").

On the other hand, many other unofficial aspects may have an impact upon the European system. By regulating the margins of their own system, they are able to regulate the European system too. This can be seen already, and especially, in these countries with special constitutional controls strong enough to regulate the law. In other words, because the legal orders at the European level seem to be relatively dependent on states and their legislative integrity in comparative terms, it means that states may shape the European level only by shaping their own legislative and adjudicative systems. It is not only the constitutional traditions, which are on the basis of the possible influences, but other types of regulations may become relevant for comparative law as well.

This means that the only way to regulate the European system is not by external (political) regulation but also the internal (comparatively legal) one or by givin up the integration process on the basis of the "*flexibility*".

The two spheres of systems, national and European, function, in other words, in a relationship of a mutual co-variation based on the principle of legal integrity.

In conclusion, as it has been maintained, these ideas of comparative reflexivity and legal integrity lead to certain scientific pressures for comparative research, and some rethinking of the role of comparative legal research. One could maintain that the comparative discourse has to be found again as a scientific discipline. Traditional comparative law is needed. The instrumentalization of comparative law in the European institutional architecture is, to a certain extent, a supportable element of modern comparative law. However, one has to maintain the traditional concept of European law, where the different socio-cultural and systematic aspects are taken into account. As it has been suggested, this approach can be called critical comparative law. This type of idea is strongly related to the comparison of social policies, to the "instrumentalist" sphere of modern law.

On the other hand, one could propose that different legal institutions should increase the use of consultative forms of scientific research external to their internal institutional arrangements, and, in other ways, create an impact upon the comparative legal discourse in Europe. This should take place especially in the realm of the forms of social law. Another possibility is that comparative research is taken more seriously in the internal work of the institution.

2.4. European comparative dogmatics and vertical comparisons

Questions of "comparative dogmatics", described above, are strongly related to the idea of "vertical comparison". The idea (presented, for example, in the Community legal order) that comparability does not have to be quantitative but qualitative[984], functions already as a premise for vertical comparison.[985] Namely, one may ask, how could it be possible to have a dogmatic and theoretical discourse on European law and its function if vertical comparisons are ruled out and considered unacceptable, at the same time the European institutions and legal decision-makers do utilize comparative legal observations in defining different vertical relationships?

One may contend that it is not possible to exclude vertical comparative research from contemporary European comparative legal research. It seems that vertical comparisons have to be included within the comparative law framework in order to produce some useful knowledge on the functioning of European law, and to be able to critically look over law in its contemporary form as a comparative legal discourse. This is so in its educative, legislative and adjudicative form of legal discourse.[986]

How could this be done?[987]

Now, the restrictions, in comparative law studies, are restrictions upon the relevant and essential legal systems (or orders), and the conclusion of the comparative argument is the choice of a doctrine. From that choice the legal order derives the legal solution. Even if, from the point of view of comparative law, the legal systems cannot be chosen (there are binding legal systems, and non-binding legal systems), legal systems (and their rules and interpretations) may be chosen as arguments against some other systems, or in order to establish a critical relationship internal to a (European) legal order.[988]

---

[984] As, for instance, was maintained in case 5/55 *Assider* (1954-56) ECR 135 per Advocate General Lagrange. A general principle is not necessarily the solution accepted in the highest number of states (very detailed analysis of some national and international orders, pp.147-149, some analysis, Bredimas, A., 1978a, p.120). The idea is to avoid imitation and mechanical observations, and even evaluate and shape systems (idem).
      The question is claimed to be a matter of fundamental and technical differences (Bredimas, A., 1978a, p.121).
[985] On the problems of comparability, see Dehousse, R.,1994, p.17. For some theoretical remarks, see Sacco, R., 1991, p.7.
[986] See some analysis on the interpretation of ECHR precedents on national systems, Martens, S.K., 1998, p.13.
[987] A practical example, see ColCom 3.7.2000, by European labour law scholars.
[988] As noticed, comparative argument in itself is a form of establishing the authority of its user. As in all arguments, the arguer uses the authority of the legal systems in justifying its decision and convincing the recipient of the acceptability of his decision and his authority. However, unlike in any other type of legal argument, the legitimacy of these legal systems is related to their binding character in particular. In generalizing this binding character of some systems via itself, the system establishes a two pole system of bindingness, where it is itself binding as a adjudicative system, and the other systems as legislative systems.
      This feature creates a polycentric system of European law in the long run. Certain rules are binding both in national legal systems, and also in the European level. Furthermore, they are *a priori* identical in both systems. In other words, this

Where the dogmatics would not comply with the type of comparative coexistence chosen by the court, it may have to examine the harmony all over again. This is the basis of European legal dogmatics, the comparative dogmatics of European law. Furthermore, the comparative dogmatics can suggest "hard core" norms based on "generality" or disparity. On the other hand, the European courts may either accept or neglect these arguments.

The task of this comparative dogmatics seems to be examination of the legal quality of decisions in relation to the use of traditional legal sources. On the other hand, in case the justification is restricted to the internal use of the institution, the only possibility is to examine the acceptability of this restriction, and to take a more system oriented approach. This way the dogmatics may orient itself to a more critical examination of the philosophical, sociological or political premises of the courts. Only this way can the dogmatics establish its opinion on the hard core of European law.

This serves also national decision-making, legislation, and dogmatics. By knowing the discursive quality of the hard core standpoints made by the European level institutions, national dogmatics, legislation and legal decision-making can establish its opinion on the issue, evaluate those aspects in discourses on that level, and use the outcomes of this discourse critically as the basis of its interpretative function in a coherent way. In this way there is a discursive maintenance of the coherence of the whole European law[989].

As one can see, the transformation of the rules from one level to the other takes place after a comparative discourse. This is to say that the comparative discourse is a legal transformative discourse, which seems to be a neutral (descriptive) discourse on the comparability and the substance of the general norm, without an idea of direct applicability of all general norms at the international level. The comparative discourse is a discourse where the integrity of all the legal orders is taken into account.[990]

2.5. Conclusions

Many conclusions on the basis of this work relating to the incomplete nature of the European concept of law, to the teleological nature of European law in general, to functional subsidiarity and liberal equality, to the nature of individual protection, to the European legislative and adjudicative integrity, to the "autopoetics" of the European institutional discourses, to

---

establishes also the European system as a two level system. In these fields of law, there are no conflicts between the different levels of law. These fields of law are, in fact, the hard core of the European law.

[989] It is clear that because this relationship between these systems is reflexively regulated (European law), the use of these interactive elements of comparative law is difficult to analyse. The reflexive relationship, between these systems, is sometimes instrumental, sometimes traditional, etc.

[990] Future comparitivist are claimed to be economists, sociologists, statistician, etc, in order to find the relationship between law and existing social needs. See Lando, O., 1977, p.651.

polycentrism, to the tendency of minimum regulation visible in European law, to the distortions of communication in the European legal discourse, and basically, to different political philosophies and concepts of democracy. These topics will become more important in the realm of the possible deepening and enlargening of the integration in Europe, European Monetary Union and expected institutional changes[991].

Real suggestions are not made, even if there has been criticism and prospects for a change, which may set a scene for various proposals. They are also matters of separate studies.

Nevertheless, some aspects may come up in the epilogue. Furthermore, one may briefly summarize the main concrete problem related to these aspects.

One could maintain that the problem of modern European law is not solved by the "reluctance" of the European Courts, by the fear of judicial activism and an attempt to guarantee the position of the European institutions on a "federal" basis.[992] European law needs "radicalized processes", which are beyond seemingly radical, but basically conservative, political ideas in contemporary European law. The problems of functional law and its role in "comparative systems" like European law must be resolved by functional means if the political sphere does not do so. Moreover, because one is moving in the realm of institutionalized comparison, the functionality has to be connected to the institutional functionality. This may be, however, too much to ask.

Related to this, it is generally agreed that the current problem of the legitimacy of the European Union system is dependent on its ability to take into account any social rights in its decision-making. Furthermore, the basic problem of the system is the increasing democratic deficit of the state systems in the Union, which is reflected also in the European level democratic deficit. This is due to the fact that governmental legislation is gaining a central role and the national parliaments are becoming administrators of Union law. [993] Furthermore, Union law is increasingly, especially in the case of monetary Union[994], thus Europeanizing

---

[991] For some analysis of the post Maastricht crisis, see Weiler, J.H.H., 1995.

[992] See, for example, Mancini, G.F., 1998, and commentary, Weiler, J.H.H, 1998.

[993] In general, Cirdell, K., 1991, p.718. See also, Mancini/Weiler discussion 1998.

One may claim that the constant normative tension between two spheres of regulation, state and Community, waters down many progressive developments in the field of social rights. This tension causes the inability to take seriously social improvements, and may, in the long run, lead to frustrations.

The following analysis is based on the idea, that the implementation of European law has to be considered as legal administration. The ideas on administration can be applied to the analysis of the phenomenon.

The powers of government do not increase only in the field of the traditional legislation. They do also, by "semi-comparative" considerations and arguments, define, in the European Courts, the idea of national legal systems (as seen in the *Bachmann* case in the European Court of Justice). This is related to the system of intervening in the legal processes. Governments are the ones which "systematize" national legal systems in these European legal institutions by explaining what is, and what is not, relevant in that particular connection.

[994] The following ideas are based also upon assumption that European Union law becomes increasingly central because of Monetary Union.

national legislation.[995] Monetary Union is also likely to lead to some kind of federal structures. The openness of the institutional decision-making is part of this problem.

From the point of view of the welfare system, this question is apparently central. Liberalization and deregulation are not checked from the point of view of the legislative integrity and continuity of the system, but the governmental proposals can break drastically new ground for the national systems in relation to the implementation. On the other hand, it is difficult for the parliament to look over the nature of the expert governmental proposals connected to the implementation of the laws. The validity of these proposals is based on the implementation of European law, control over which is not within competence of the Parliament.

Some words can be said on these above mentioned aspects also in the context of the changing architecture of the European Union.

The effectiveness of the court system is frustrated by the enormous workload. Part of this workload is the comparative law work in the courts.

In the context of the institutional changes - concerning also European court system - there has been discussion on the transfer of powers of Community institutions to national level (right to interpret), specialization of the chambers (especially in the Court of First Instance), and different filtering mechanisms (concerning the case coming to European Court). With these changes one aims at speeding of the court processes and effectiveness of the legal order in general.

If national institutions are to have a bigger role in the European law, the role of comparative law will get bigger. On the other hand, the specialization of some chambers and the court system in general (in European level) would entail also specialization of the prior investigation methods and the staff in the internal research. It is clear that by the increasing and focussing the internal research the quantitative and qualitative aspects of the Community legal order will get improved. This would require also some opening up of the internal documentation.

If the role of national courts will be restricted in the realm of the Article 234 (preliminary ruling), it could mean that the Community law application in these lower courts will be intensified and, consequently, the comparative law aspects would be considered more carefully in the Community law interpretation by these lower courts.

Another question relates to expansion of the Union in general. Where the amount of Member States increases, the comparative workload may increase. What does this mean? Do some systems come more decisive and some systems institutionally restricted from the scope of the comparative studies? Are the European Courts granted new resources to maintain their comparative function?

---

[995] It is problematic to evaluate the "increasing" Europeanization of the national laws. There are always the qualitative and the quantitative aspect to this. However, if 80% of the volume of the national legislation is based on European regulation, there must be something correct in the Europeanization thesis (See, Mancini/Weiler discussion 1998).

The final remarks are related to comparative law and the comparative arguments in legal justification.

EPILOGUE

1. CONTEMPORARY COMPARATIVE LAW

Comparative law has to do, on many levels, with constituting elements of law. Historically one can see how comparative law had an extremely important role in the construction of the identities of the state legal systems and a stabilizing function in the legal consensus-creation on the question of the nature of legal systems. Contemporary comparative law moves in the realm of this structure of the state paradigm of law. This state paradigm of law, at the moment, consists of both states as a legal system and of the international systems as legal orders. These legal orders are the marginal subsystems in the state paradigm of law.

On the other hand, the disparities and generalities in the realm of comparative law have been made normatively relevant by reflecting them within the *a priori* institutionalized general principles and common traditions, and to concepts like coherence, morality and substantive equality or by just practically accepting them by institutional actors[996]. The comparative approach has shown its alternative nature in relation to any "sovereignty" ideas ("will", "intention", etc.).

The uses of comparative observations have resulted in definitions and the establishment of institutional arrangements, but, for that matter, the maintenance of the relative autonomy of the state legal systems as relevant systems in determining the questions of economic, social, human rights policies at the European level. Furthermore, by comparative reflections one has been able to solve different competence questions.

The internationalization and the Europeanization of law seems to increase the relevance of comparative law. This is due to the fact that one increasingly arrives at "system-selection" situations, where several "competent" systems exist, and where the competencies have to be defined. Some remarks on this have been made before.

Comparative reasoning has, as shown, a kind of mediating function between systems. Comparative law within legal reasoning makes it rationally, i.e. reasonably, possible to make legal choices in cases where the systematic legal arguments (deductive-logical measures) do not provide answers to the particular legal question. Comparative aspects determine - contemporary Europe, for example - the basic procedural, conceptual and jurisdictional ideas. The constitutional ideas in Europe are based on comparative aspects, and they are dynamically interpreted this way. Comparative law has a function in defining the hard cases of the contemporary legal systems, cases dealing with basic problems of the society. The normative results, however, appear quite conservative.

---

[996] For common traditions determined by the Roman law origins of a common tradition, for example, case 23/68 *Klomp v Inspectie* (1969) ECR 43.

On the other hand, states in many ways confirm their international identity as legal systems (and their own limits of sovereignty) on comparative legal basis. This concerns likewise the relationship between systems such as the European Union and the United States.

Comparative law is, consequently, functioning in the constant rejustification of the law on the basis of foreign experience.

There are, in other words, several "cases" of comparative law[997]. In a legal case, comparative law functions as a source of law. In a "new case" comparative law is a practical argument. In an "existential case" comparative law is the basis of the creation of the identity of the system as a procedural entity and a linguistic system. In an "authority" case the subsidiarity and "substantive" issues are examined.

The basic premise of the use of comparative law in substantive norm construction is difficult to define because of the closed nature of its use. It is, in many ways, a subjective and institutional method of reasoning. Furthermore, the increasing flow of information, also in the field of comparative law, has resulted in a tendency toward the sketchy use of comparative information. As noticed, because of the increasing possibility for quick transmission and receiving information the traditional seekers of legal and legally related information, including comparative law, have come to be replaced by institutional self-sufficiency. The doctrinal analyses are left out, and the legal decision-making institutions collect and analyse the information themselves. The law in these institutions becomes a professional enterprise, and the institutions close themselves normatively. The discursive analyses disappear. This is one of the basic problems of comparative law at the moment. The comparative information gets instrumentalized more easily. The comparative information becomes merely practical information.[998]

On the other hand, one could claim that different legal subsystems are also entering into the sphere of comparative law. This means that comparative law will be opened up, and may become more than traditional comparative contract law or comparative constitutional law. It would consist of various forms of national and international processes. This is a real breakthrough for comparative law. Comparative law can be understood also to be comparative research of differentiated legal procedures in a certain global area.

Moreover, what one may note, in the case of institutional comparative law, is the

---

[997] These can be called the "hard cases" of European law.

[998] This is also connected to the "data processing" of the comparative information. For traditional approach, see Cottin, S., 1996, p.403. The Recommendation No. R (92) 15 and the explanatory memorandum (Council of Europe, 1994) does not really discuss the legal problems of data-processing, but only the technical aspects. The legal aspects should be taken more seriously.

In general, because of the speed of different information channels, one seems to be able to reproduce, as an historical entity, all kinds of systems. In this process, however, one emphasizes particular and simple systems, the role of the pure normative systems. This is so, because they are the only systems, which do not cause frustrating analysis, or "unpractical" historical reproductions.

phenomenon of the institutional systematization of legal systems.

Consequently, one could maintain that contemporary comparative law is institutionally controlled. Comparative receptions are controlled and reflected with regard to functionality of the supranational systems. The supranational institutions define and redefine comparative generalities and divergences. The comparative adaptions take place according to the conditions established by the supranational legal institutions. Generalities are adaptable and acceptable, and the divergences maintain comparative divergency. Comparative law has come from autonomous, institutionalized and academic comparative law towards institutionally-controlled comparative law.

Comparative law, in this more "post-modern" form in differentiated discourses, may have an extremely important role in the legal discourse when differentiated particular discourses start to assert their identity and essential features in a more analytical way. In this process, the state law and particular legal "sub-systems" in society may become closer to each other. However, the main condition of this is that one comes clean with change in the idea of comparative law, i.e. that comparative law corresponds more to the general development of differentiation of functional systems, and does not remain a system of national legal systems only.

This idea is not devoid of empirical data. For example, "comparative international law" - comparison of international treaties and their provisions - seems to be a useful method in resubstantiation of national law at the moment. By collecting comparative evidence from the international and its implementing legal orders one seems to be able to arrive to a kind of an idea of international legal community. This development is still in an evolutive stage, but one can notice that pure comparison of national systems in interpreting national or international rules is not the only method particularly where "new" cases come into question. Traditional comparative law, based on state-paradigmatic assumptions, seems to be, in fact, a conservative attempt to maintain the traditional structures and doctrines in the internationalized law. Comparative international law, on the other hand, provides effective means to justify, for example, the deviation from the strict interpretation of the doctrine of state sovereignty. In this sense one could maintain that there is currently a transitional period. This idea needs, however, further development, which is not made here. What one could say is that it seems to be based on an extremely strict internationalized positivistic approach. It assumes a very common sense interpretation of international treaties and conventions. On the other hand, it seems to be able to react to societal needs and changes taking place in the international sphere and internationalized legal thinking.

What one can say in the end is that comparative law discourse has to find its relative autonomy from the contemporary international, national and supranational discourses by beginning to consider itself as a part of the legal discourse as a legal argument and as a legal source. This takes place by newly establishing connections with the legal philosophical, legal sociological and legal historical discourses and reasoning. This way law can maintain its character as a possibility in the contemporary "Europeanization" and "internationalization" of law. If this is not done, the internationalization, related to the closing up of the institutional considerations in the realm of increasing flow of information, closes the national legal systems from each other as forms of discourse. One may call this some kind of a "blocking effect".

A concrete aspect of the opening-up is also the inclusion of the "vertical" studies into the function of comparative law in the realm of the principle of discursive integrity, as it has been suggested in this book. This would mean critical examination of comparative law, not only in scientific sense and national legal discourses, but also in international and regional legal systems.

Finally, one may claim that the "highmodern" comparative law is no longer about the Germanic, Latin, Anglo-Saxon, or Nordic traditional distinctions or about a common European legal culture based on these types of classifications, but that something else is essential in this respect[999]. It seems that the key distinction can be found from the idea of the discursive concept of law. As it has been identified, there are different types of legal discourses, and they are emphasized in different ways in various legal systems.[1000]

On the other hand, the second integral criterion in comparative law is evidently related to the distinction between the systems, which stress liberal aspects and make a clear distinction between informal and formal regulation and those systems where these characteristics are not so much emphasized. As indicated, the differences may be associated with the differences in historical development. In some systems, there is no "homogeneity" idea. They consist of different levels of regulation, as the all-encomposing principle of subsidiary indicates[1001]. On the other hand, the Nordic legal cultural features, for example, seem to be related to the idea of a legally homogeneous state, which, on the other hand, is related to the strong legalistic tradition and social functionality of law (some kind of legal "realism"). In spite of the continuing liberalization taking place in the Nordic society, I do believe that this idea of law is still prevailing. The only problem is how to define it in the future, instrumentally or in a value based way.

Furthermore, the idea that certain types of policies are possible only in certain types of social systems and in the realm of certain type of constitutional though, is not very far from the consideration of this last idea. It seems that Nordic constitutional thinking may entail more functional constitutional thought concerning political integrity than in most of the European states.

---

[999] On the "Kulturvergleichung", see Häberle, P., 1994, p.16.
[1000] See the book Interpreting Statutes (Dartmouth) 1991.
[1001] In this context, see Stråth, B., Sørensen, Ø., 1997, p.12

2. WHAT KIND OF INSTITUTIONAL JUSTIFICATION IS
COMPARATIVE LEGAL JUSTIFICATION?

In the end, one could try to formulate some regulative ideas for the comparative legal justification in the context of institutional law. Here one comes to some ideas on the relationship between comparative discourse and the institutionalized legal procedures in general.

The inclusion of comparative law to the sources of law (regulated by standards of reasoning) has been discussed already in the chapter on the theory of comparative legal reasoning. However, questions remain; for example, what kind of legal justification is comparative legal justification?

Where the source of law doctrine and the standards of reasoning deal, basically, with the acceptability of comparative argumentation and its role in legal justification on traditional basis (i.e. traditional legal discourse theory and traditional comparative law), the analysis of its justificatory aspect refers, one may say, to its basic conditions in relation to discourse ethics as such. In other words, where the traditional theory of legal justification replaces it in relation to the traditional method of legal justification, the value-based theory speaks about the relationship between comparative justification and general "discourse" ethics.

This latter "value" analysis is possible only in the context of the empirical data presented above. This is why this analysis is replaced after the empirical survey and analysis of the functionality of comparative law in contemporary legal orders. Only in this way is one able to confirm and augment this theory of comparative legal justification in a critical way.

In practice, as one can note on the basis of the empirical survey and the traditional approach to comparative law, the reasons for the use of comparative law as a source of legal arguments has been related to many types of "integrations", to plain "utility", or to substantial or formal authority. However, these types of justifications for the use of comparative law, observed in the empirical study, have not yet - one may say - told us anything about the reason why comparative law really should be used as a reason in justification. The idea of integration and utility - as well as the ideas of "substantialization" and "authority to qualify" - seem to be extremely situational, practical, and functional justifications of its use, as maintained already before. In fact, on these basis one could still easily claim that comparative law does not have, whatsoever, the nature of a real legal source.

However, as maintained, the use of comparative law in the institutional legal justification seems to indicate that the user of these types of arguments has moved towards a theoretical level of the legal phenomenon and also towards a general legal discursive sphere. However, a traditional comparative listing of legal systems and their description in rather mechanical way - by using exclusive generalizations - seems to be based on the extremely state-paradigmatic, "natural", and traditional (cultural)"contextual" premises. In this type of traditionality other systems seem to be only instruments of the classification and systematization, and it looks as if, by this type of approach, one does not really take part in the legal discourse, but actually tries to avoid any legal analysis. The same seems to apply also to the sketchy use of comparative observations in legal decision-making.

Any institutional and instrumental (non-discursive) use of comparative law, on the other hand, does not seem to guarantee the rationality of the legal order. On the contrary, it in many ways leads to irrationality at least from the point of view of the legal discourse, because it means effective exclusion of, for example, national legal discourses, and results in, and is based on, strict hierarchical forms of institutional organization. The institutional forms of the use of comparative law do not prove anything about the flexibility, informational openness, susceptibility, and sensitivity of the institutional legal order. In fact, it seems that more unsystematic and inspirational forms of the use of comparative law in a legal organization seem to indicate more discursive flexibility of an order.

The use of analytical comparative exemplifications seems to, nevertheless, relate more to the discursively "jurisprudential" and legal theoretical perspective. Namely, in this type of use there is an attempt to arrive at theoretical understanding of the legal phenomenon in question (vs. a specific national dogmatic contextualization) and, furthermore, the legal phenomenon is related to the "total system" of theoretical perspectives.[1002] Moreover, one may say that in an analytical exemplification by comparative arguments, the decision-maker approaches the "common sense" analysis, and explains more clearly the value-based issues involved in his thinking.

One may try to formulate an analysis in the context of the questions asked above. The method of this analysis is following. Firstly, this is made in the light of some rules of value-based theory of legal argumentation[1003], secondly, from the point of view of the idea of utility, and thirdly, as a philosophical analysis of the institutional discourse as such.

From the (value-based) legal theoretical point of view (the value-based regulative dimension) it has been maintained that *"every speaker may only assert what he or she believes"*. In this sense, in using comparative legal arguments, one has to believe firmly that one sincerely understands the idea of these foreign norms. This can be related also to generalizability. One has to be ready to apply generally the comparative rules achieved. Problems may be noted, however, if one asks the question "to what audience is one really arguing?".

On the other hand, the fact that comparative arguments strive to a more "theoretical level" or are plain linguistic-analytical arguments is also justified according to rules of justification. This can be the case at any point of the legal discourse. Naturally, one could also challenge

---

[1002] On the "total" system, see, Brusiin, O (1953) and note 13.
[1003] Alexy, R., 1989, pp.297-302.

the legal source nature of the comparative law in any form of an argument on any stage of the discourse.

Furthermore, because everyone taking part in the discourse should also *"give reasons…when asked to do so, unless she can cite reasons which justify a refusal to do so"*, the claim of not really knowing the content of foreign norms can be a justification for a refusal to carry on in the analysis of the foreign system.

Comparative observations may also be problematised at any point of the discourse. They are not any "final" arguments. If the justification is carried on by comparative arguments and their use is challenged, a full statement of reasons must be given in order to justify the use of comparative law as a legal source. This is related to the nature of comparative law arguments as "special" arguments[1004]. However, as one may understand, this may result in unbearable problems to the rationality of the discourse (efficiency etc.).

Because the question, in the introduction of comparative premises, seems to lead to unequal treatment of persons, justifications for their use has to be presented also on these bases. This relates to the use of comparative observations in general. They are not really the (norm) topics under discussion in a process of discourse. In general, it seems that, in a legal discourse, the maker of comparative observations has an extremely strong burden of proof.

The use of comparative arguments may be justified also by the fact that at least *"one universal norm must be adduced in the justification of a legal judgment"*. This seems to be the case of with "hard cases" lacking sensible reasons deriving from the traditional sources of law. In another context, there has been already some discussion about the exhaustion of other sources before comparative observations may be used. This seems to be a firm rule for comparative justification.[1005]

Foreign precedents seem to be at the heart of the exemplified comparative justification. Consequently, from the point of view of some rules on the use of precedents, the question can be asked, whether foreign precedents should be used, if one's "own" precedents do not exist?[1006] Firstly, it is not asserted that a deviation from a foreign precedent should be justified. The burden of proof is on the other side, on the one explaining the content of the precedent. However, one could claim that a general rule that *"precedents should be cited"* does not seem to apply as such. Nevertheless, one could produce some justification for the use of foreign precedents. For example, it must be maintained that the analytical quality of the reasoning may be better achieved by an analysis based on precedents. This is especially the case, if no

---

[1004] *"Special legal argument forms must have the reasons for them stated in full, that is, must achieve saturation"* (Alexy, A., 1989, p.302).

[1005] *"Whenever dogmatic arguments are possible they should be used"*, even if *"every dogmatic proposition must be able to stand up to systematic testing in both the narrower and the wider sense"* (Alexy, R., 1989, p.301).

[1006] Alexy, R., maintains that *"if a precedent can be cited in favour of or against a decision it should be so cited"*, and that *"whoever departs from precedent carries a burden of argument"* (Alexy, R., 1989, p.302).

precedents or doctrinal analysis exist in the one's "own" legal context.

This is related to the following question: "why are comparative observations utilizable?" (the utility dimension).

As it has been already indicated in the remarks on the analogical argument in general, comparative observations, according to our opinion, seem to help the decision-maker to "structure" his legal reasoning (schemes).[1007] Comparative arguments function as some kind of "beginnings" for the reasoning and provide starting points for the structuring of reasoning. One may say that they help the decision-maker to conceptualize the legal situation. This takes place in relation to analytical comparative considerations, and may be based on some historical or other reasons which associate comparative observations "rationally" with systematic reasoning. Then also the legal audience may understand, what one is speaking about. However, this is a strongly value-based situation.[1008]

This type of "structuralist" utility has to do usually with the fact that other legal systems and orders may be the only legal instances, where such a legal question (a new question) has been asked and resolved. In this sense, comparative observations function as a source of information in a case where the "orthodox" sources of the system do not explicitly give any answer. This may be the case where no statutory law has been enacted, for example.[1009] Secondly, the utility may be related to the fact that the comparable decision-maker, which is considered, may be a authority on the question for some reason. This could be a case, for example, even if the dogmatic of legal scientific authorities have been dealing with the problem.

In general, one could say that the value-based rules of legal justification do not seem apply satisfactorily for the phenomenon of the comparative legal justification. The utility idea may, however, function as some kind of a basis, even if it seems to lead to extremely subjective standards.

It seems that in the comparative justificatory processes one may easily enter into a separate comparative law discourse in the realm of the legal process, which cannot be prohibited as such, but may easily be rejected on the basis of procedural economic premises (efficiency demand). On the other hand, if such a separate discourse is effected, the task of the procedural supervisor (the judge) seems to be only to maintain the centrality of the "internal" premises,

---

[1007] See also, for example, Varis, M., 1998, p.101 ff.

[1008] This is not disproved by remarks made in this book that comparative observations appear usually in dissenting or similar types of argumentation. In fact, one may claim that the dissenting opinions have an evolutively structuring role in the evolution of the case law. The dissenting opinions may help the decision-making institutions to start their line of argumentation in a next case based on observations by the dissenting judge, for example. Furthermore, if he has been arguing analytically by comparative remarks, the decision-making institutions has in fact already a "stock of arguments" for its use. Furthermore, the parties may start also from these premises.

[1009] It could be claimed that comparative law has, and actually can have, a role in systems where no *travaux preparatoires* are available or in general use.

and ask, for example, questions like "cannot one find these types of ideas also in our own legal system (or in our own legal discourse)?"

One may try to perceive the idea of comparative legal justification exactly in this type of discursive context (the discursive dimension). Namely, one can start to analyse the legal justification process (the legal institutional process) from the point of view of the use of comparative observations. The empirical observations made may give us valuable indications.

Let us imagine two persons come to a court with their conflicting claims. One may say that the more intense the conflict is, i.e. more interests and values are involved, the less the other party may be ready to try to find the "correct traditional interpretation of law" on the basis of a complete collection of traditional legal sources. This is so, because, even if he recognizes the line and the logic of the traditional interpretation, he may feel that the traditional interpretation is not satisfactory for him. His aim is to win the case.

In this type of strong value conflict, one may try to claim a special character of the case, and that something deviating exists in relation to former cases and traditional interpretation of traditional legal sources. On the other hand, usually, in this type of case, the other party to the dispute argues strongly for the traditional sources and for a traditional interpretation.

One could actually identify this situation as a kind of a strong *a priori* "inequality" in front of the law. Namely, the first party may recognize *a priori* the traditional line of interpretation, but he feels that the case is important and his interests are immense and that there is a difference in situation from the existing "similar" cases. However, at the same time, he trusts the intellectual institutional legal order and its ability to recognize the difference between his situation and other previous cases.[1010]

Consequently, the need for an analytical approach is stressed by the first party. In this situation, he may take up examples from comparative law to prove his point. He wants, in order to feel as if treated in an integrative way, an analytical approach to the largest possible extent.[1011] In this type of situation, the claim is that the legal situation should be "changed"

[1010] This seems to indicate, for example, that a strongly normative, value-based- theory of legal justification assumes a strong institutional attachment.

[1011] In fact, the idea of inequality of this type corresponds quite well with the situation, where one is dealing with any accusatorial cases (for example criminal cases). <u>Procedurally</u>, the defendant or the accused is more or less required to establish a justification for the act he is alleged to have committed, and that the accusation is unfounded. This is, for example, the reason, why in criminal law the principle of the presumption of innocence exits as a premise imposed by most civilized legal systems. It tries to diminish the influences of an oppressive situation (individual against a legal system as a whole) and bring the defendant to a more or less equal situation with the accusatorial system (or with the public sphere). Furthermore, the burden of proof is on the public side.

In other words, in our case the inequality before the law arises on the basis of established case law or prevailing interpretation (legally intellectual situation). In criminal law cases, usually, the law is strongly established (moreover, even defined by restricting principles like *nulla poena sine lege* or the principle of legality). This means that, in criminal cases, the <u>justification</u> of the case is <u>legally</u> quite simple (and also that the emphasis is usually in the proving of facts). The legal justification, the findings of law, are usually accepted to be quite straight forward. Even the loser of the case usually accepts the authority of the positive law *a priori*.

analytically, because it is felt that the traditional forms of interpretation (and sources: statutes, cases, doctrinal analysis) do not bring the "correct" solution in that particular case.

This brings us to another idea, which may relate the to interests of analysis in general. Namely, it is possible that intellectually-oriented lawyers, for example, may recognize an idea of "reasonable equality" as a main principle of procedure. This means that they may accept the idea of discursive law, and more than that, the idea of discursive integrity of law. In this type of situation, the parties are willing to analyse the traditional sources of law, and - in addition to that - other types of sources, if they provide better or more reasons and more analytical approaches for the deciding of the case. This, in fact, means that they are willing to discuss the case analytically, and not to rely only on traditional sources, which, with a method of analogy or enlarging method, may bring a result to a question. However, they want a discussion on the subject related exactly to the subject, and they want to have the case reasonably justified in order to be able to, firstly, accept the solution as rational, and secondly, in order to maintain the discursive integrity of law.[1012]

It may be asked, in what type of situations would one start to think these two last premises?

One could say that in these types of situations, the parties take some kind of a risk in trusting the institutional system and its value-based analytical capacity (institutional law). On the other hand, they also trust in their ability to provide material for the discussion. It means also that these premises may come up in extremely difficult and unclear situations. However, the essential idea is that, in these types of cases the parties are, to a large extent, transferring the authority to the institutional decision-maker letting it ultimately speak about its values. However, they trust it because it takes into account any arguments put forward by the parties, and is not institutionally and instrumentally oriented, but applies the idea of discourse ethics.

Now, as noted, those cases where comparative observations appear more than relevant, are the "hard cases" of equality questions and those pertaining to fundamental values. Furthermore, they are often cases, where, procedurally, the parties' and all represented interests' (for example, in a form of intervention) integrity is attempted to maintain. This seems to indicate that in the use of comparative observations one is faced with integratively discursive cases.

In these types of cases, one demands an intensely reasonable approach from the decision-maker, and consequently, a clear expression of the value-based premises. It seems that this type of process is based on some kind of discursive "*saturation*"[1013] rather than only upon systematic saturation. On the other hand, in these discursively equal and integrative processes, the demand for reasoning may be satisfied only by going beyond all the exhausted

---

[1012] This relates to the idea of "finer distinctions -search" explained above in the previous chapter on European law.
[1013] On this, see, for example, Alexy, R., 1989.

traditional sources. There has been already some kind of systematic *"saturation"*.[1014] When reasonableness is demanded from the decision-maker, he has to make comparative observations in order to maintain the integrity of the loser of the case, but also the discursive quality of the decision and justification in general (institutional opinion).

In fact, if the comparative observations would be accepted by the parties in their argumentation, and the decision-maker, in his justification, would not consider them, it would be likely that the decision-maker did not convince the parties in a reasonably way and neither treat them integratively. In order to avoid this type of situation, one should make at least a reference to the national discourse on the subject and to the differences related to the compared systems on some essential point when rejecting parties' comparative arguments as relevant. Where even the loser of the case seems to know the law and its line of reasoning, it is extremely difficult to convince him on the basis of an unanalytical (perhaps domestic analogical) approach. Only in this way may one maintain the intellectual and substantial authority in a case.

Consequently, one may note, how in some cases and in some types of systems, the "saturation" in legal justification may be achieved only by including comparative legal observations in the justification (or argumentation). In order to maintain the discursive integrity of the party, but also the legal order, one may be obliged to go beyond the traditional sources, and use arguments which structure and reflect the essential question to be considered. As one may also notice, these types of comparative considerations may be taken up in cases where one is dealing with a hard question but, moreover, also with parties willing and obliged to discuss the situation in a reasonable way (also with comparative observations). This explains why one is usually looking into a legal discourse between professional lawyers or, more commonly, into a discourse in realm of a scientific-analytical philosophy of legal dogmatics.

This means, basically, that even in a systematic approach to law, there may be a place for comparative law arguments and a kind of a priority of foreign precedents, especially in cases where domestic precedents do not exist.

In conclusion, one may say that the situations where comparative law may be used or even should be used as arguments of justification are those situations of discursive processes of hard cases where the integrity (and equality) of law is attempted to maintain on many levels. In these types of discourses, one attempts, reasonably, to balance systematic, coherent, logical, and extremely well-justified points of views. Furthermore, the parties taking part in these kinds of cases have a discursive attitude. In these types of hard cases, where parties seem to agree about the need for a reasonable solution - for example, by bringing the comparative observations into the discourse themselves - the decision-maker may have even a weak

---

[1014] As known, in European-level legal orders this exhaustion takes place quite quickly because of the strong formality.

obligation to use comparative law in justification.

This is why it may be said that comparative law, as a method of justification, seems to be a kind of an "optional", "consensual" and "discursive" method of legal justification - apart from being a special case of allowed legal sources. Furthermore, if one is to have a discursive point of view upon the law, one may also consider it as an "institutional" source of law. However, this does not mean that it is an institutional source in a sense of discursively closed systems.[1015]

Nevertheless, it has to be stressed that the source and justificatory value of comparative law cannot be considered - as many comparative lawyers seem to do - on the basis of balancing, integrating, or choosing legal systems etc. This is why one has also to emphasize the idea that if the situation is not "consensual" in the way just described, i.e. the need to make comparative observations does not arise from the discursive quality of the process itself (in the way explained above), the decision-maker - using comparative observations - must at least justify the use of these types of methods of justification by considering, at a minimum, the standards of reasoning developed in this work.[1016] This is due to the unsystematic nature of this type of source.

Finally, one could ask, does one even have to go to comparative law as a source of law. One could discuss the issue on the basis of moral or other types of practical arguments? These two types of reasoning (justifications) seem to be, to a certain extent, alternatives. The answer to the question seems to be that the former leads to a discourse on law. The use of comparative law seeks to give an answer to the question of "what is the law?", and not to the question "what is moral and practical?".

Consequently, and in conclusion, one may summarize the main argument and the philosophy of this book on the comparative legal reasoning - the discursive integrity - with the answer received to the question *"To whom do you think one justifies the decision"*[1017]:

[1015] This idea seems to relate to legal formalism in a strongly linguistic and procedural sense, and not to legal formalism as legal systematic terminology.

[1016] This seems to correspond to the Alexian rule regarding special justification of the changes in the method of justification.

[1017] Lord Justice Schiemann, Court of Appeal, 25.3.1997.

"I always think
that the most important person is the person
who is going to lose the case
I feel I ought to explain
to one who has lost,
why a judge,
who has ever met either of these parties before
has come down on his opponents side.
This is the person who wonders,
why he got the judgment
wrong"

Literature

Aarnio, A, The rational as reasonable: a treatise on legal justification (Dortrecht), 1987

Aarnio, A., Interpreting statutes in Finland (Dartmouth) 1991 (123-171)

Aarnio, A., Reason and authority. A treatise on the dynamic paradigm of legal dogmatics(Dartmouth) 1997

Agostini, È., Droit comparé (Paris) 1988

Ajani, G., By change and prestige: Legal Transplants in Russia and Eastern Europe. In: Am Jour.Comp.Law 43, 1995 (93-117)

Alexy, R., A theory of legal argumentation: the theory of rational discourse as theory of legal justification (Clarendon) 1989

Alexy, R, Interpreting statutes in the Federal Republic of Germany. In: Interpreting statutes (Dartmouth) 1991 (73-123)

Ancel, M., Le role de la recherche comparative dans la cooperation juridique international. In: De Conflictu Legum, Leiden, 1962 (Essays to Kollewijn, R.D., Offerhaus, J.) (31-37)

Ancel, M., Utilité et méthodes du droit comparé (Neuchatel) 1971

Ancel, M., Les Grands étapes de la recherche comparative au Xxe siècle. In Rechtsvergleichung (Darmstadt) 1978 (350-360). Also in Studi in Memoria di Andrea Torrente I. (Ed. Giuffré, A., Milano) 1968 (23-32)

Aristotle, Nichomachean ethics, book X, chapter 10, Beckers, 1931 addition Endevion ethics, On virtues and vices, Harvard University Press (Cambridge) 1952

Aristotle, Nicomachean ethics. The Ethics of Aristotle. The Nicomachean Ethics, trans. Thomson, J.A.K. rev. Tredennick, H., intr. Barnes, J., Peguin) 1953

Aristotle, The Athenian Constitution (transl And intr., Rhodes, P.J. Rodes, P.J Penguin) 1984

Aristotle, Rhetorique (trad. Ruelle, Rev. Vanhemelryck, P., Com., Timmermans, B., LGF) 1991

Aristotle, The Politics (trans. Sinclair, Rev Saunders, T J , Penguin) 1962 [Commentary, Finnish translation 1991, Sihvola]

Aubin, B , Die rechtsvergleichende Interpretazion autonom-internen Rechts in der deutschen Rechtssprechung (The Comparative Interpretation of National Law by German Courts (Summary)). In: RabelsZ 34, 1970 (458-480)

Bankowski, Z., MacCormick, N., Interpreting statutes in United Kingdom (Dartmouth) 1991

Bates, F., Comparative Common law and justification. In: XIV SILSA, 1981 (259-.277)

Baxter, L.G., Pure comparative law and legal science in mixed legal systems. In: XVI SILSA, 1983 (86 ff.)

Bell, J., Comparative law and legal theory, In: Prescriptive formality and Normative rationality in Modern legal systems, Festschrift for Robert S. Summers (ed. Krawietz, W., MacCormick, N , von Wright, G.H Duncker&Humboldt, Berlin) 1994

Bell, J., The Acceptability of Legal Arguments. In: The Legal Mind. Essays for Tony Honoré (eds. MacCormick, N., Birks, P., Oxford) 1986 (45-65)

Bell, G.J , Commentaries on the Law of Scotland and on the Principles of Mercantile Jurisprudence [1810] (new 7th ed., Edinburgh) 1870

Bell, G.J , Inquiries into the contract of sale of goods and merchandise judicial decisions and mercantile practice of modern nations (Edinburgh) 1844

Bennet T.V., The application of customary law in Southern Africa. The conflict of personal laws (Cape Town) 1985 (250 ff.)

Bengoetxea, J., Legal reasoning of the European Court of Justice. Towards European Jurisprudence (Oxford) 1993 (124-139)

Benos, G., Practical debt of the Community law to comparative law. In: Rev. Hellénique Droit Int'l 37, 1984(241-254)

Bézard, O., Les magistrats francais et le droit compare. In: Rev.Int.Dr.Comp., 1994 (776 ff.)

Bieber, R , On the Mutual Completion of Overlapping legal Systems: The Case of the European Communities and National legal Orders. In: European Law Review, 1988 (147 ff.)

Biscaretti di Ruffia, P., Diritto Constituzionale XV ed (Napoli) 1989

Bodin, J., Les six livres de la republic (Paris) 1955a, 1986 [1583]

Bodin, J., Six Books on Commonwealth (Abr. and transl. Tooley, M.J.) 1955b

318   LITERATURE

Bodin, J., Six Bookes on Commonweale (N.Y.) 1979 (Reprint of the ed. Cambridge, Mass., which was edited by K. D. McRae N.Y.) 1979, c1962. [translation of Les six livres de la République] Other authors: McRae, Kenneth Douglas)

Bodin, J., Colloquium of the Seven about Secrets of the Sublime, Colloquium Heptaplomers de Rerum Sublimium Arcanis Abditis (trans. with intr., ann., critical read. by Kuntz, M., L , D., Princeton) 1975

Bodin, J., Methodus ad facilem historiarum cognitionem [1566, 1606, 13 editions 1566-1650] Method for the Easy Comprehension of History by Jean Bodin (transl. And foreword, Reynolds, B., Columbia University press, New York) 1945

Bogdan, M., Comparative Law (Göteborg) 1990

Bogdan, M , Jämförande juridik - vad, varför, hur?. In: In: Comparative law: what, why, and how?[Jämförande juridik, vad varför hur?] (Meddelanden från ekonomisk-statsvetenskapliga fakulteten vid Åbo Akademi, Åbo) 1996

Bognetti, G., Introduzione al diritto constituzionale comparato - il metodo (Torino) 1994

Boult, R., Aspects des rapports entre le droit civil et la "common" dans la jurisprudence de la Cour suprême du Canada. In: Can. Bar. Rev. 4, 1977 (738-770)

Bredimas, A., Methods of interpretation and community law (Amsterdam), 1978a (esp. 124-140)

Bredimas, A., Comparative law in the European Court of Justice of the European Communties. In: Yearbook of World affairs, 1978b (320-333)

Brierly, J.E C , Major legal systems in the world today. An introduction to the Comparative Study of Law (London) 1978

Brusiin, O., On legal comparison [Oikeusvertailusta]. In: Lakimies, 1953 (434-466)

Brusiin, O , Methodological aspects of legal theory. In: Studi in onore di Emilio betti (Milano) 1962 (43-48)

Brusiin, O., The legal reasoning of judge in the absence of norm [Tuomarin harkinta normin puuttuessa] (Vammala) 1938

Bruun, N., Hellsten, J. COLCOM Final Report. Collective Agreements on the Competitive Common Market. A Study of Competition Rules and Their Impact on Collective Labour Agreements (Helsinki) 2000. To be published: "Collective Agreements and Competition Law in the EU" (Copenhagen) 2000

Buergenthal, T., The effect of the European Convention of Human Rights on the internal law of Member States. In.The European Convention of Human rights, 1965

Buxbaum, R.M., Die Rechtsverglaichung zwischen Nationalen Stat und International Wirtschaft. In: RabelsZ 1996 (202-230)

Cirdell, K., European Union and the nation state. The politics of hope encounters the politics of experience. In: European legacy 31, 1998, nr 2

Calhoun, G.M., Introduction to Greek legal science (Oxford) 1944

Calhoun, G.M., Working bibliography of Greek law (by Calhoun, G.M., Delamere, C., Amsterdam) 1968

Capelletti, M., In Honor of John Merryman In: Comparative and private international law. Essays on Honour of John Henry Merryman on his 70th Birthday (ed. Clark, D S., Berlin) 1990a (1-7)

Capelletti, M., Balance of powers, Human Rights and Legal integration. New challanges for European judges. In: Comparative and private international law. Essays on Honour of John Henry Merryman on his 70th Birthday (ed. Clark, D.S., Berlin) 1990b (341-352)

Capelletti, M., Le droit comparé et son enseignement face à la société moderne. In: Rotondi Inchieste diritto comparato, 2, Scopi e metodo del diritto comparato - Buts et Méthodes du droit comparé - Aims and methods of comparative law (Padova-N.Y.) 1973 (57-75)

Capelletti, M., Judicial process in comparative perspective (Oxford) 1989 (1-417)

Cardoso, B., The nature of judicial process. In: selected writings of Benjamin Nathan ardoso (ed. Hall, M.E. and Patterson, E.W.) 1947 [1921]

Cicero, De re publica, De Legibus (trans. Keynes, C.W., London, Loeb) 1970 (ed. and comm. Rudd, N., Wiedemann, T., Bristol) 1987

Cicero, On government (trans. Grant, M., Penguin) 1993

Cicero, Oratorio Pro Sexto Roscio Amerino, xxv, 70 (Loeb) 1930
Cicero, De Inventione, ii.40.116-51 154; Topica, xxiv.92 (Loeb) 1945
Cicero, De Oratore, I:xliv, 197 (Loeb) 1942
Cohler, A., M., Introduction to Montesquieu's The Spirit of Laws (Cambridge) 1989
Coing, H., The Roman Law as Ius Commune on the Continent. In: 89 L.Q P, 1973 (505-517)
Constantinesco, L-J., Rechtsvergleichung, band I, Einführung in die Rechtsvergleichung (Köln) 1971,
    band II 1972
Cooper, T.M., The common and civil law - a Scot's view. In Harvard Law Rev., 1950 (468 ff.)
Cottin, S., Les possibilités de l'informatique en matiére de documentation. In: Rev.Int. Dr.Comp. 2, 1996
    (403-417)
Daig, H-W., Zu Rechtsvergleichung und Methodelehre im Europäichen Gemeinschaft. In: Festschrift
    Zweigert, 1981 (396-415)
David, R , Traite élementaire de droit civil comparé (Paris) 1950
David, R., Sources of Law. In: International Encyclopedia of Comparative Law (The Hague) 1981
David, R , Jauffret-Spinosi, C., Les grandes systemes juridiques (Paris) 9me édition, and edition 1995
David, R., Brierly, J E C., Major legal systems in the world today.
    An introduction to the comparative study of law, 3d ed. (London) 1985 [1978]
Davis, F., Comparative law contributions to the international legal order, Common Core research. In:
    Am.Jour.Comp.Law 37, 1969 (615-633)
de Boer, Th.M., Missing link. Some thoughts on the relationship between private international law and
    comparatiove law In: Comparability and evaluation, Essays on comparative law, private
    international law, international commercial arbitration in honour of Dimitra Kokkini-Iatridou (ed.
    Voele, K , Woelki, V., et all, The Hague) 1994 (13-25)
de Groot, G-R., Schneider, A, Das Verurteil in der Rechtsvergleichung Die Suche nach dem besseren recht.
    In:Comparability and Evaluation (eds. Voele, K , Woelki, V., et all, The Hague), 1994 (53-68)
de Gruz, P., A Modern approach to Comparative Law (Deventer) 1994
Dehousse, R , Comparing national and EC law The problem of level of analysis (European University
    Institute) 1994
Demas, G., Practical debt of Community law to comparative law. In Revue Hellenique de droit
    international 37, 1-4, 1984
de Tocqueville, A., Democracy in America (Trans. Reeve, h., rev. Bowen, F., Intr Renshaw, P
    Wordsworth) 1998
de Wilmars, J M., La droit comparé dans la jurisprudence de la Cour de Justice des Communautés
    européennes. In: Journal des Tribunaux, 19 Jan 1991
Doehring, K., The auxiliary function of comparative law for the interpretation of legal rules of national and
    international law. In· International law at the time of its codification: essays in honour of Roberto
    Agom IV (Milan) 1987 (47-62)
D'Oliveira, H.J., La méthode comparative et le droit international privé. In: General reports to the 10th
    international congress of comparative law (eds. Péteri, Z , Lamm, V , Budapest) 1981(51-73)
Drobnig, U., The International Encyclopedia of Comparative Law. Efforts towards world a wide comparison
    of law In: Cornell International Law Journal Vol.5, 1972 (113-129)
Drobnig, U , Methods of the sociological research in comparative law. In: 1971 RabelZ 35 (496-504),
    Deutcher Landesbericht zum VIII. Internationalen Kongress für Rechtsvergleichung Pescara) 1970
Drobnig, U., Rechtsvergleichung zwischen Rechtsordnungen verschiedener Wirtschaftssysteme. Zur problem
    der intersystemaren Rechtsvergkeichung . In. RabelsZ 1984 (233-244)
Drobnig, U., Methodenfragen der Rechtsvergleichung im Lichten der ´International Encyclopedia of
    Comparative Law"´ In Ius Privatum Festschrift für Max Rheinstein, vol 1 (eds. Caemmerer, von
    E., Mentschiloff, S , Zweigert, K., Tübingen) 1969 (221-223)
Drobnig, U., Rechtsvergleichung in der deutchen Rechtsprechung. In. RabelsZ 50, 1986 (610-630)

320 LITERATURE

Drobnig, U., The use of Foreign law by German Courts. In: German National Reports in Civil Law Matters for the XIV th Congress of Comparative Law in Athens, 1994 (5-24)

Dworkin, R., Law's Empire (London) 1986

Ellis, E., Recent developments in European Community sex equality law. In: Common Market Law review 35, 1998 (379-408)

Ereciński, C., Application of foreign law in socialist states. In: Law Yearbook. International legal studies (London) 1978 (201-216)

Eörsi, G., On the problem of the division of legal systems. In: Rotondi Inchieste diritto comparato, 2, Scopi e metodo del diritto comparato - Buts et Méthodes du droit comparé - Aims and methods of comparative law (Padova-N.Y.) 1973 (181-209)

Fentiman, R., Foreign law in English courts. In: Law Quarterly Review, 1992 (142-156)

Flécheux, G., Israël, J.-J., La situation en France: Le point vues des professions juridiques. In: Rev.Int.Dr.Comp. 2, 1996 (319-325)

Frankenberg G., Critical comparison: Re-thinking Comparative Law. In: Harvard International Law Journal Vol. 26, 1985 (411-455)

Friedmann W., The teaching of Comparative jurisprudence. In: Rotondi Inchieste diritto comparato, 2, Scopi e metodo del diritto comparato - Buts et Méthodes du droit comparé - Aims and methods of comparative law (Padova-N.Y.) 1973 (225-232)

Friedmann, D., Infusion of the common law into the legal system of Israel. In: Israel law review, vol 10, 1975 (350-355)

Friedman L.M., The legal system. A social science perspective (N.Y.) 1975

Gaillard, E., The use of comparative law in the international commercial arbitration. In: Sanders, A. (ed.) Arbitration in settlement of international commercial disputes involving the Far East (Deventer 1989) (283-289) Also, In: Arbitrartion 55, 1989 (263-267)

Galmot, Y., Réflexions sur le recours au droit comparé par la Cour de justice des Communautes européennes. In: Rev, Fr.Droit.Admin., 1990 (255-262)

Glendon, M.A.Gordon, M.W., Osakwe, C., Comparative legal traditions (Nutshell) 1982

Gordon, A , Community Law and the development of UK Administrative Law: Delimiting the 'Spill-over' Effect. In: European Public Law 4, 1998

Gorla, G., Short history of comparative law in Europe and Italy during modern times, 16th and 19th century, Italian National reports to the XII International Congress of Comparative Law, 1986 (66-86)

Gorla, G., Bell, One of the Founding Fathers of the "Common and Comparative Law of Europe" during the 19th century, In: The Jurid. Rev. N.S. 2, 1982 (121-138)

Gorla G., Moccia, L., A 'Revisiting' of the Comparison between 'Continental law' and 'English law' (16th -19th Century). In: Journal of Legal History 2, 1981 (143-157)

Gorla, G., Prolegomeni ad una storia del diritto comparato europeo. In: L'apporto della comparazione alla scienza giuridica (Milano) 1980 (268-298)

Goutal, J.L., Judicial style· French and British. In: European legal cultures (ed. Gessner, V., Hoeland, A., Varga, C., Sydney) 1996

Grabenwarter, Ch., Filmkunst im Spannungsfeld zwischen Freiheit der Meinungäußerung und Religionsfreiheit. In: Archiv des öffentliches Rechts, 1995 (128-165)

Granger, R , La tradition en tant que limite aux réformes du droit. In: Rev.Int.Dr.Comp., 1979 (37-125)

Graveson, R.H., Philosophy and Function in Comparative Law. In: International and Comparative Law Quarterly, Vol. 7, 1958 (649-658)

Graveson, R.H., The contribution of private international law and comparative law to international harmony and understanding. In. essays in International law in Honour of Judge Manfred Lachs. Makarczyk, J. (Ed.) (The Hague) 1984 (109-120)

Graveson, R.H., Methods of comparative law in common law systems, In: Rotondi Inchieste diritto comparato, 2, Scopi e metodo del diritto comparato - Buts et Méthodes du droit comparé - Aims and methods of comparative law (Padova-N.Y) 1973 (299-316)

Green, L.C., Comparative law as a source of international law. In: 42 Tulaine Law Review, 1967 (42-66)

Gutteridge, H.C., The Value of Comparative law, JSPTL, 1931

Gutteridge H.C., Comparative law and the law of nations. In: In: Brit.Yearb.Int.Law 21, 1944 (1-10)

Gutteridge H.C., Comparative law. An introduction to the comparative method of legal study and research, 2d ed. (Cambridge) 1949 (London, 1971)

Gyselen, L., Review of the Albany case. In: Common Market Law Rev. 37, 2000 (425-448)

Hamza, G., Comparative law and antiquity, Akadémiai Kiadó (Budapest) 1991

Hartley, T.C., The foundations of European Community Law (3d. Ed. Oxford) 1994

Hartley, T.C., Pleading and proof of foreign law: The major European systems compared. In: International and Comparative Law quarterly 45, 1996 (271 ff.)

Hawk, B.E., United States and Common Market and international anti-trust. A comparative guide (Englewood Cliffs) 1990

Hazard, J.N., Comparative Law in Legal education. In: U Chi LR 18, 1951 (273 ff.)

Hazard, J.N., Comparison in preparation for statesmanship. In: Rotondi Inchieste diritto comparato, 2, Scopi e metodo del diritto comparato - Buts et Méthodes du droit comparé - Aims and methods of comparative law (Padova-N.Y.) 1973 (357-367)

Heide, H., Les professions juridiques et le droit comparé en allemagne. In: Rev.Int.Dr. Comp, 1994 (730-733)

Heldrich, A., Sozialwissenschaftliche Aspekte der Rechtsvergleichung. In RabelZ, 1970 (427-442)

Herczegh, G., La place de l'etat dans l'ordre juridique international (La Communauté des États et lec "jus cogens". In: Comparative law (ed. Szabó, I., Péteri, Z.) Budapest 1978 (73-84)

Herman, S., Quot judices tot sententiae: A study of the English reaction to continental interpretative techniques. In: Legal Studies, 1981

Hill, J., Comparative law, law reform, and legal theory.In: Oxford legal studies 9, 1989 (101-115)

Hill, E., Comparative and historical study in modern Middle-Eastern law. In: vol 26, Am.Jour.Comp.Law, 1978 (279-304)

Holdsworth, W.S., Sir, History of English Law, 3d ed., 1923 [[1956, London]

Hondius, E.H., Teaching and research in comparative law in the Netherlands. In: Netherlands Int. Law Rev. Essays on International Law and relations in honour of A.J.P. Tammes (eds. Meijers, H., Vierdag, E.W., Leyden) 1977 (560-567)

Hug, W., The history of comparative law. Harv.L.Rev. 45, 1932 (1027 ff.). Also in: Rechtsvergleiching (Darmstadt) 1978 (109-161)

Hunnings, H., The European Courts (London) 1996

Häberle, P., Europaeishe Rechtskultur (Baden-Baden) 1994 (22-23)

Igarashi, K., Die Bedeutung der Rechtsvergleichung bei der Juristen Ausbildung. Die Japanishen Erfahrung - Gestern heute. In: Recht in Japan 22, 1977 (36-42)

Irvine of Lairg, Lord, The Development of Human Rights in Britain under an Incorporated Convention of Human Rights. In: Public Law, 1998 (221-236)

Jacobs, F.G., The European Convention of Human rights (Oxford) 1975

Jacobs, F.G., The uses of comparative law in the law of the European Communities. In: Plender, R. (Ed.) Legal history and comparative law (London) 1990 (99-111)

Jamieson, M., Source and target oriented comparative law. In: Am.Jour.Comp.Law XLIV, 1996

Jennings, R.Y., The judiciary, international and national, and the development of international law. In: Int. and Comp. L. Quarterly 45, 1996 (1-13)

Jescheck, H-H. Rechtsvergleichung als grundlage der strafprozess reform, In: Auslands Der zeitschrift für die gesammtes strafrechtswissenschaft, Max Planck (Freiburg) 1974. Band 86 (761-782)

Jolowicz, J.A., Les professions juridique et le droit comparé: Angleterre. In: Rev.Int.Dr.Comp., 1994 (747- 755)

Joutsamo, K., Perspectives to European Community Law [Näkökulmia EY oikeuteen]. In: Oikeus Journal,1997:3

Jyränki, A., The Law of Laws: Constitutional law and its bindingness in European and North American legal thinking from the great revolutions to the second world war [Lakien laki] (Helsinki) 1989

Jyränki, A., "Im fremden Spiegel" - tankar im jämförande rättsforskning. In: Comparative law: what, why, and how? [Jämförande juridik, vad varför hur?] Meddelanden frän ekonomisk-statsvetenskapliga fakulteten vid Åbo Akademi, Åbo) 1996 (9-16)

Kahn-Freund, O., Comparative law as an academic subject. In: LQR, lxxxii, 1966, Also in: Rechtsvergleichung (Darmstadt) 1978 (307-333)

Kahn-Freund, O , On uses and missuses of comparative law. In: Mod.L.Rev. 3, 1974 (1-27)

Kahn-Freund, O., General problems of private international law (Sijthoff) 1976

Kamba, E.J., Comparative law. A theoretical framework. In: ICLQ, 1974

Kelsen, H., On the theory of interpretation. In: Legal Studies, Vol 10 No 2, July 1990 (132-135)

Kelsen, H., General theory of law and state (Harward) 1946

Kelsen, H., Pure theory of law (trans. Knight, M., Berkeley) 1967

Kelsen, H., Introduction to the Problems of Legal Theory (trans, Paulson, B.L., Paulson, S.L., Oxford) 1992

Kiikeri, M., Theory and practice of comparative legal reasoning. From inspiration to rational legal justification. Doctoral thesis in European University Institute, Florence, 1999

Kisch, I., Statutory construction in a new key. "Harmonizing interpretation". In: 20th century comparative and conflict law (1961) (262-276) (also, OUJ offenbare ort rechtsver oppstellen aan geboden kaan, Zwolle, 1975, and Uitgelezen opstellen. Een bloemlezing iut het werk van Prof. Mr. I. Kisch, ed d'Oliveira, J.H.U., Zwolle, 1981 157-171)

Klami, H.T., Comparative law and legal Concepts In: Oikeustiede-Jurisprudentia XIV, 1981 (67-165)

Klami, H.T , Methodological Problems in European and Comparative Law. Publications of the Institute for Jurisprudence, 2nd ed., Helsinki, 1997

Koopmans, T ,The birth of European law in the crossroads of legal traditions. In: Am.Jour.Comp. Law 39,1991

Koopmans, T., Comparative Law and Courts. In: International and Comparative Law Quarterly, July, 1996 (545-556)

Koopmans, T., European Public law. Reality of Prospects. In: Public Law, 1991 (53-63)

Koskenniemi, M., Preface. In: Nordic Journal of International Law 65, 1996 (337-340)

Kosonen, P., European Integration. The welfare state perspective, University of Helsinki. Sociology of law series 8, 1996 (16-17, 150-151)

Kropholler, J., Comparative law, function and methods. In. Encyclopedia of Public International Law vol. I (Amsterdam) 1992 (702-707)

Kulla, H., Comparison of laws and European administrative law. In: Comparative law: what, why, and how? [Jämförande juridik, vad varför hur?] Meddelanden frän ekonomisk-statsvetenskapliga fakulteten vid Åbo Akademi, Åbo) 1996 (39-51)

Lambert, É., Conception général et définition de la science de droit comparé, sa methode et son histoire de droit comparé et l'enseignement du droit. In: Rechtsvergleichung (Darmstadt) 1978 (30-51). Also, Congrès International de Droit comparé. Tenu à Paris du 1900. Tome premier. Paris: Librairie Générale de Droit et de jurisprudence 1905

Lambert, J., La contribution du droit comparé à l'etude des problèmes du sous-développement.In: Problèmes Contemporaires de Droit comparé. Tome II (Tokio) 1962 (177-187). Also In: Rechtsvergleichung, 1973 (270-281)

Lambert, J , L'idé d'une science universelle du droit comparé (droit comparé et culture générale). In: Études de droit contemporain (Contributions Francaises aux IIIe et Ive Congrès internationaux de Droit Comparé (Sirey) 1959 (271-288)

Lando, O., Komparative ret. Kort Införing (Köpenhamn) 1986

Lando, O , The contribution of comparative law to law reform by international organizations, Am.Jour.Comp.Law 25, 1977 (641-657)

Lash, S., Modernity or modernism? Weber and Contemporary Social theory In: Max Weber, rationality and modernity (eds. Lash, S , Whimster, S., London) 1987 (355 ff.)

La Torre, M., Rules, Institutions, Transformations, Considerations on the "Evolution of Law" Paradigm. In: Ratio Juris 10, 1997 (316-350)

La Torre, M., Pattaro, E., Taruffo, M., Statutory interpretation in Italy. In: Interpreting statutes (Dartmouth) 1991 (213-257)
Lawson, F., Comparative judicial style, Am.Jour.Comp.Law 25, 1977 (364-371)
Lecourt, R, L'Europe des judges (Bruxelles) 1976
Legall, J-P., Dibout, P., La fiscalite des fusions d'entreprises communataires.In: Semaine Juridique 65/2, 1991
Legeais, R., L'utilisation du droit comparé par les tribunaux. In: Rev. Int. Dr. Comp., 1994 (347-358)
Legrand, P., Comparér, Revue Internationale de droit comparé, nro 2, Avril-Juin, 1996
Legrand, P., European legal Systems are not Converging. In: International and Comparative Law Quarterly, 1996 (52-81)
Lobban, M., Was there a Ninteenth Century 'English School of Jurisprudence'? In: The Journal of Legal History 1, 1995 (34-62)
Loussouarn, Y., La méthode comparative en droit international privé. In: General reports to the 10th international congress of comparative law (eds. Péteri, Z., Lamm, V., Budapest) 1981 (127-144)
MacCormick, N., Weinberger, O., An institutional theory of law: new approaches to legal positivism (Dortrecht) 1986
MacCormick, N. and Summers, R.S , Interpretation and justification. In: Interpreting Statutes (Dartmouth)1991 (511-545)
Machiavelli, N., Prince (trans. Detmold, C.E., Intr. Kekewich, L.M., Wordsworth) 1997
Mádl, F., A comparative law theory on developing norms in private international law. In: Comparative law (eds. Szabó, I., Péteri, Z., Budapest) 1978 (85-106)
Mádl, F., Comparative law synthesis theory v. private transnational law as a new concept in private international law In: Comparative law Yearbook 2, 1978 (1-46)
Maine, H S. Sir, The effects of observation of India on modern European thought" (the Rede lecture, London) 1875
Maine, H.S. Sir, Ancient Law (Intr. Morgan, J.H., London) 1954 (1861)
Maitland, F.E , The constitutional history of England : a course of lectures delivered by F E. Maitland (Cambridge) 1908
Mancini, G.F.,Europe: The Case for Statehood. In: European Law Journal 4, 1998 (29-42)
Markesinis, B., Comparative law - a subject in search of an audience In: Mod.L.R 53, 1990 (1-21)
Markesinis, B., Judge, Jurist and the Study and Use of Foreign Law. In: Law Quarterly review, 1993 (622-635)
Markesinis, B., Foreign Law and Comparative Methodology (Oxford) 1997
Marsh, N.S , Comparative law and law reform. In: RabelsZ, JG, 41, 1977 (649-668)
Marshall, G., Interpreting interprpetation in the Human Rights Bill. In: Public Law, 1998 (167-171)
Martens, S.K., Incorporating the European Convention: The Role of the Judiciary. In: European Human Rights, 1998 (1-14)
Martines, T., Diritto Constituzionale 2. Ed (Milano) 1981
Mathijsen, P.S.R.F., A guide to European Community Law (London) 1990
Mayda, J., Some critical reflections on contemporary comparative law. In: Rechtsvergleichung (Darmstadt) 1978 (361-394)
McRae, K.D., Introduction to Bodin, Jean (1530-1596) The six books of a commonweale. A facsimilereprint of the English translation of 1606, corrected and supplemented in the light of a new comparison with the French and Latin texts. Edited with an introd. by Kenneth Douglas (Cambridge) 1962 (Out of the French and Latine copies, done into English, by Richard Knolles (1550?-1610). "A bibliography of the République": (A78-A86) Also 1979 version
Merryman J.H., Comparative law and social change On the origins, Style, decline and revival of the law and development movement. In. Am.Jour.Comp.Law 25, 1977 (457-491)
Miller, N.E., and Dollard, J., Social learning and imitation (New Haven) 1941
Millett, T., Rules of Interpretation of EEC legislation. In: Statute Law Review, 1988
Moccia, L., English Law attitudes to the 'Civil Law' In: The Journal of legal History 2, 1981 (157-168)

LITERATURE

Moccia, L., Les bases culturelles du juriste européenne: un point de vue continental. In· Rev.Int.Dr.Comp., 1997 (800 ff.)

Montesquieu, The spirit of laws (trans. and ed. Cohler, A.M., Miller, B.C., Stone, H.S., Cambridge) 1989

Montesquieu, L´esprit des lois 1-2 (chr., intr., bibl. Par Goldschmidt, V., Paris) 1979

Morgan, J.H.,Introduction to Maine´s Ancient Law, 1954

Mössner, J.M., Rechtsvergleichung und Verfassungsrechtssprechung. In: Archiv des öffentliches rechts 99, 1974 (193-242)

Mouly, C., Le droit peut-il favorise l'integration européenne?. In: Rev.Int.Dr.Comp, 1985 (895-947)

Neumeyer K.H., "Law in books, law in action" et le methodé du droit comparé. In: Rotondi Inchieste dıritto comparato, 2, Scopi e metodo del diritto comparato - Buts et Méthodes du droit comparé - Aims and methods of comparative law (Padova-N.Y.) 1973 (505-523)

Nieminen, L., The special problems related to the comparison of social rights [Sosiallisten oikeuksien vertailuun liittyvistä erityisongelmısta. In: Comparative law: what, why, and how? [Jämförande juridik, vad varför hur?] Meddelanden från ekonomisk-statsvetenskapliga fakulteten vid Åbo Akademı, Åbo) 1996 (25-36)

Peczenik, A., On Law and Reason (Dordrecht) 1989

Peczenik, A., Law, Morality, Coherence and Truth. In: Ratıo Juris 7, 1994 (146-177)

Peczenik, A., Bergholz, G., Statutory interpretation ın Sweden In: Interpreting statutes (Dartmounth) 1991(311-359)

Pegoraro, L., La Corte constituzionale e il diritto comparato nelle sentenze degli anni ´80. In: Quaderni constituzionali, Aprile 1987 (601-613)

Perelman, Ch., Olbrechts-Tyteca, L., Traite de l'argumentation : la nouvelle rhetorique (4 ed., Bruxelles) 1983

Perelman, Ch., Olbrechts-Tyteca, L., New rhetoric . a treatise on argumentation (Notre Dame) 1969 [Trans. from the French La nouvelle rhetorique : Traite de l'argumentation Perelman, Ch., Olbrechts-Tyteca, L., Bruxelles, 1958]

Pergola, La, A., The role of comparative law in the legal system of regional organizations. In: Italian national reports to the Xth International Congress of Comparative law, Budapest, 1978, Milano (77-96)

Pescatore, P , Quelques réflexions sur le fondement du droit comparé. In: Aspects noveaux de la pensée juridique. Recueil d´études en hommage à Marc Ancel, vol 1 (Paris) 1975 (23-41)

Pescatore, P., Le recour dans la jurisprudence de la court de justice de communaté Européen à des normes deduité de la comparation de droit des etaits membrés. In: Revue international de droit comparé, 1980 (337-359)

Peteri, Z., Goal and methods of legal comparıson, In: Péterı, Z. (Ed.): The comparison of law (Budapest) 1974 (45-58)

Péteri, Z., Comparative law applied for state phenomenon. In: Socialist approach to comparative law (eds Szabó, I., Péteri, Z., Leyden) 1977 (95-130)

Pizzorusso, A., Corso dı dırıtto Comparato (Milano) 1983

Prott, L.V., Judicial reasoning in the common law and code law systems. In: Archiv für Rechts- und Sozialphilosophıe, 1978

Pugliese, G., L'importance du droit comparé dans l'enseignement jurıdique en Italie. In: Italian natıonal reports to the Xth International Congress of Comparative law, Budapest, 1978, Milano (97-108)

Pugliese, G., Ius Honorarium and English Equity. In Essays ın honor of John Henry Merriman (Berlin) 1990 (275-282)

Póyhónen, J., Basic Misunderstandings in Comparative Law. In· Changıng Europe and Comparative Research (Suomen Akatemia) 1992 (60-68)

Rabel, E., Aufgabe und Notwendigkeit der Rechtsvergleichung, In: Rheinische Zeitschrift für Zivil- und Prozessrecht, 1924, Also in Rechtsvergleichung (Darmstadt) 1978 (85-108)

Rasmussen, H., On the law and policy in the European Court of Justice (Dortrecht) 1986

LITERATURE 325

Rawls, J., Political liberalism (New York) 1996
Rawls, J., A Theory of Justice (Cambridge) 1971
Raz, J., The Politics of the Rule of Law. In: Ratio juris 3, 1990 (331 ff.)
Raz, J., The identity of legal systems. In: Cal.L.Rev. 59, 1971 (795-815)
Ress, G., Die Bedeutung der Rechtsvergleichung für das internationaler Organisazionen. In· Zeitschrift für ausländische offentliches Völkerecht, 1976 (227-279)
Reuter, P.,Introduction to the Law of Treaties (London) 1995
Riles, A., Wigmore's Treasure Box· Comparative Law in the Era of Information Harvard International Law Journal 40 (1999) (221-285)
Rokkan, S., The growth and structuring of mass politics, in. Erik Allard et all (ed.), Nordic democracy. Det danske selbskab (København) 1981
Rotondi, M , Technique du droit, dogmatique, et droit compare. In: Rotondi Inchieste diritto comparato, 2, Scopi e metodo del diritto comparato - Buts et Méthodes du droit comparé - Aims and methods of comparative law (Padova-N Y.) 1973 (557-577)
Sacco, R , Legal formants: a dynamic approach to comparative law, AJCL 39, 1991 (1-34, 343-401)
Sacco, R , Le formation droit comparé l´experience italianne. In: Rev .Int. Dr. Comp., 1994 (273-278)
Sacco, R , Les buts et les méthodes de la comparaison du droit. In: Italian national reports to the Xth International Congress of Comparative law, Budapest, 1978, Milano (113-119)
Sanders, A.J.G.M., The role of comparative in the internal conflict of laws. In. Sanders, A. (Ed.) The internal conflict of laws in South Africa (Durban) 1990 (57-65)
Scheuner, Ch., Comparison of the jurisprudence of national courts with that of the organs of the Convention. In: Human Rights in National and International Law (ed. Robertson) 1968
Scheuner, U., Der Einfluß des französischen Verwaltungsrechts auf die deuctshen rechtsentwicklung. In: Die Öffentliche Verwaltung, 1963 (714-719)
Schlesinger, R.B., Die Behandlung des fremdes Rechts im americanische Zivilprozess. In: RabelZ, 1962/63 (54-72)
Schlesinger, R.B. (ed.) Formation of contracts. A study of the common core of legal systems (Dobbs-Ferry-London) 1968
Schlesinger, R.B., The Uniform Commercial code in the Light of Comparative Law. In. Inter-American Law Rev , 1959
Schlesinger, R B., Comparative law. Cases-Text-Materials (4 ed., New York) 1980
Schlesinger, R.B., Past and future of comparative law. In: Am.Jour.Comp.Law 43, 1995 (477-478)
Schlesinger, R.B., The Common core of legal systems. An emerging subject of comparative study In: ACJL, 1968 (65-79). Also In: Rechtsvergleichung (Darmstadt) 1978 (249-270)
Schermers, H.GWaelbroeck, D , Judicial protection in the European Communities (4th ed., Deventer) 1987
Schermers,H G., Application of international law by the Court of Justice of the European Communities. In: European law review, 1979 (169-179)
Schmitthoff, C.M., Unification or harmonization of law by means of standard contracts and general conditions. In: International Comparative Law Quart. 17, 1968 (551-570)
Schmitthoff, C.M., The Science of Comparative Law. In· Cambridge L J 7, 1939 (94-110)
Schreuer, Ch., The waning of the sovereign state· towards a new paradigm for international law. In: European Journal of International Law 4, 1993 (447-471)
Schreuer, C.H., The interpretation of Treaties by domestic courts. In British Yearbook of Internaltional law 45, 1971 (255-301)
Schwind, F., Rechtsvergleihung in Österreich. Probleme, ziele, methode. In: Rotondi Inchieste diritto comparato, 2, Scopi e metodo del diritto comparato - Buts et Méthodes du droit comparé - Aims and methods of comparative law (Padova-N Y.) 1973 (624-632)
Sen, A, Inequality reexamined (Oxford) 1997
Shapiro, M., Comparative law and comparative politics, Sourthern Cal.L. Rev. 53, 1980 (537-542)
Shapiro, M.,Courts. A Comparative and Political Analysis (Chicago) 1981
Sihvola, J., Commentary. In: Aristotle, Politics [Politiikka] 1991

LITERATURE

Stern, K., Der Staatsrecht der Bundesrepublic Deutchland, vol 2 (München) (1971-) 1980

Stone, J., Human law and Human Justice (Stanford) 1968

Stone, F.F., The end to be served by comparative law. In: Tulaine LR 25, 1951 (325-333). Also in
    Rechtsvergleichung (Darmstadt) 1978 (211-225)

Sørensen, Ø., Strath, B., Introduction: The cultural construction of Norden. In: The cultural construction
    of Norden (eds. Sørensen, Ø., Strath, B., Oslo) 1997 (1-25)

Strömholm, S., Comparative legal sciences. Risks and Possibilities, In: Law under Exogenous Influences
    (ed. Suksi, M., Publications of Turku Law School, V.1) No.1/1994

Strömholm, S., La philosophie du droit scandinave. In: Rev.Int.Dr.Comp., 1980 (5-16)

Strömholm, S., Har den komparativa rätten en metod? [Is there a method of Comparative Law]. In: Svensk
    Juristtidning, 1972 (458-465)

Sulkunen, O., Trade union rights in the law of the European Communities [Ammattiyhdistysoikeudet
    Euroopan yhteisön oikeudessa. Publications of the Labour Law Association [Työoikeudellisen
    yhdistyksen vuosikirja] 1999-2000 (Helsinki) 2000

Summers, R.S., Statutory interpretation in United States. In: Interpreting statutes (Dartmouth) 1991
    (407-461)

Summers, S., Taruffo, M., Interpretation and comparative analysis.In: Interpreting statutes (Dartmouth)
    1991 (461-511)

Szűcs, J., The Three Historical Regions of Europe. In: European legal cultures (ed. Gessner, V., Hoeland,
    A., Varga, C., Sydney) 1996

Terrill, R.J., The Application of the Comparative Method by English Civilians: The Case of William
    Fulbecke and Thomas Ridley. In: The Journal of legal History, 1981 (169-185)

Teubner, G., Law as an autopoietic system (Oxford) 1993

Thorkildsen, D., Religious Identity and Nordic identity. In: The cultural construction of Norden (eds.
    Sørensen, Ø., Strath, B., Oslo) 1997(138-160)

Trindade, A.A.C., La méthode comparative en droit international. Une perspective européenne.
    In: Rev.Dr.Int. Oct. 1977, nro 4 (273-288)

Troper, M., Grzegorczyk, C., Gardies, J-L., Statutory interpretation in France. In: Interpreting statutes
    (Dartmouth) 1991 (171-213)

Trägårdh, L., State individualism: on the culturality of the Nordic welfare state. In: The cultural construction
    of Norden (eds. Sørensen, Ø., Strath, B., Oslo) 1997 (253-286)

Tunc, A., La contribution possible des etudé juridiques compatatives. A une meilleur comprehension entre
    nations. In: Rechtsvergleichung (Darmstadt) 1978 (282-306) Also in: Rev.Int.Dr.Comp.
    19 1964 (47-63)

Tunc, A, On the possible contribution of comparative legal studies to the understanding between nations.
    In: Int. Soc. Sci J. 16, 1965 (413-419)

Unger, R.M., Law in Modern Society (NY) 1976

Usher, J.A., The impact of EEC legislation on the United Kingdom Courts. In: Statute Law review, 1989

Usher, J.A., The influence of national concepts on decisions of the European Court. In: European Law
    review, 1/1976

Valladão, H., Private international law, uniform law and comparative law. In: 20th century comparative and
    conflicts of law, 1961 (98-113)

van der Meersch, W.J.G., La référence au droit interne des ètats contractants dans la jurisprudence de la cour
    européenne des droit de l´homme. In: Rev.Int.Dr.Comp., 1980 (318-335)

von Mehren, A.T., Choice of law theories and comparative law problem. In: Am.Jour.Comp.Law vol 23,
    1975 (751-758)

Vousden, S., Review of the Albany vase. In: Industrial Law Jour. 29, 2000 (181-191)

Ward, I., The Limits of Comparativism: Lessons from UK-EC Integration. In: Maastricht Journal of
    Eur.Comp Law, 1995 (33)

Watson, A., Legal Transplants . An approach to comparative law (Charlottesville Va.) 1974 (16-20)

Watson, A., International law in archaic Rome : war and religion (Baltimore) 1993

Watson, A., Sources of law, legal change, and ambiguity (Philadelphia) 1984
Watson, A., From legal transplants to legal formants. In: Am.Jour.Comp.Law 43, 1995 (469-485)
Watson, A, Comparative law and legal change. In: Cambridge Law Journal 1978a (313-336)
Watson, A., Two tier law. A new approach to law making. In: Int.Comp.law Quar. 27, 1978b(552-575)
Watson, A., Legal transplants and law reform. In: L.Q.R., 1976 (79-84)
Watson, A., Aspects of Reception of Law. In: The American Journal of Comparative Law, 1996 (335-352)
Watson, A., Evolution of law. In: L& Hist. Rev. 5, 1987 (537-570)
Weber, M., Economy and society : An outline of interpretive sociology (eds. Roth, G., Wittich, C., trans.
    Fischoff, E., 2 vols. Berkeley) 1978 [Trans. from the German Wirtschaft und Gesellschaft,
    Tübingen, 1972]
Weber, M., On Law in Economy and Society. In: 20th century legal philosophy series vol. IV(ed. Rheinstein,
    M., Cambridge) 1969 (284-321)
Weiler, J.H.H., Fin-de-siecle Europe: On Ideals and Ideology in Post-Maastricht Europe. In: Institutional
    dynamics of European Integration. Essays in honour of Henry G. Schermers (Eds. Curtin, D.,
    Heukels, T., Dortrecht) 1995 (23-41)
Weiler J.H.H., Legitimacy and Democracy of Union Governance. In: The Politics of European Treaty
    Reform (eds. Edwards, G., Pijpers, A.) 1997 (249-288)
Weiler J.H.H, Missing view of the cathedral. The private law paradigm of European integration, Harvard
    Jean Monnet Papers, 2/96, 1996
Weiler, J.H.H., Europe after Maastricht. New clothes of the Emperor. Harvard Jean Monnet Working Papers
    12/95, 1995
Weiler, J.H.H., Europe: The case Against the Case for Statehood. In: European Law Journal 4,
    1998 (43-62)
Weinberger, O, Basic Puzzles of Discourse Theory. In: Ratio Juris 2, 1996 (172-181)
Weinberger, O., Interpretation and analogy re-considered in the mind of neo-institutionalism. In: Seminar:
    Building the legal system. Limits of analogical interpretation and concurring rules, 1997
Weinberger, O , Conflicting views on Practical Reason Against Pseudo-Arguments in Practical Philosophy.
    In: Ratio Juris 3, 1992a (252-268)
Weinberger, O., Basic puzzles of discourse philosophy. In: Ratio Juris vol 9, 1992b (172-181)
Weinberger, O., Habermas on Democracy and Justice. Limits on a Sound Conception. In: Ration Juris 7,
    1994 (239-253)
Wieacker, F., Privatrechtsgeschichte der Neuezeit, 2 aufl. (Göttingen) 1967 (496-513)
Wieacker, F., Foundations of the European legal culture. In. Am. J.Comp. L. 38, 1990 (1-29) (also in:
    European legal cultures, 1997)
Wiegand, W., The Reception of American Law in Europe. In: Am. Jour. Comp. Law 2, 1991(229-248)
Wilhelmsson T., Jackin-the box theory in the European Community Law [vieteriukkoteoria
    EY-oikeudessa]. In: Aulis Aarnio, Oikeustiede-Jurisprudentia XXX, 1997
Wihelmsson, T., More about The Jack-in-the-box theory, Oikeus Journal, 1997:3
Winterton, G , Comparative Law Teaching. In: Am.Jour.Comp.Law, vol 23, 1975 (69-118)
Yntema, H.E., Legal science and reform. In: 1934, 34 (KL) Col.L review
Yntema, H.E., Comparative law and Humanism, Am.Jour.Comp.Law 7, 1958 (493-499)
Yntema, H.E., Roman law as the basis of comparative law. In: Rechtsvergleichung (Darmstadt) 1978
    (162-185)
Zagrebelsky, G., Considerazioni sull'uso della comparazioni negli studi di diritto constituzionale italiano.
    In: In: L'apporto della comparazione alla scienza giuridica (Milano) 1980 (85-112)
Zajtay, I , Réflexions sur le probleme de la division des familles de droits. In: RabelsZ, 1973 (210-216)
Zajtay, I., Reflexions sur l'évolution du droit comparé In: Festschrift Zweigert, 1981 (595-601)
Zaphiriou, G.A., Use of comparative law by the legislat. In: Law in the U.S.A. for the 1980s. Reports from
    the United States for the XI Congress of the International Academy of Comparative Law, 1982
    (suppl. Am.J.Comp.L., vol. 30) (71-93)

LITERATURE

Zimmermann, R., Roman and Comparative Law: The European Perspective (Some remarks apropos a recent
    controversy). In: The Journal of Legal History 1, 1995 (21-33)
Zweigert, K., Methodological problems in Comparative law. In: Isr. Law. Rev 7, 1972 (465-474)
Zweigert, K., Méthodologie du droit comparé. In: Mélanges Mayry (Paris) 1960 [Method of
    comparative law]
Zweigert, K., Des solutions identiques par des voies différentes, 1966. In: Rev.Int. Dr.Comp. 17 (5-18)
Zweigert, K., Rechtsvergleichung als universale interpretazione. In: RabelsZ, 1949-50 (5-21)
Zweigert K., Lehre von der rechtskreises, XX century Comparative Conflicts of law Conference, Legal
    essays in honour of Hessel E., Yntema (Leiden) 1961 (42-55)
Zweigert, K., Die "praesumptio similitudis" als Grungstatzvermutung rechtsvergleichender Methode. In:
    Rotondi Inchieste diritto comparato, 2, Scopi e metodo del diritto comparato - Buts et Méthodes du
    droit comparé - Aims and methods of comparative law (Padova-N.Y) 1973 (735 ff.)
Zweigert, K., Kötz, H., Einführung in die rechtsverleichung auf dem Gebiete des Privatrechts vol. 1-2
    (Tübingen) 1971
Zweigert, K., Kötz, H., An Introduction to Comparative Law. The Framework I (Trans. Weir, T.,
    Amsterdam) 1977
Zweigert, K., Kötz, H., An Introduction to Comparative Law (Trans. Weir, T., Oxford) 1987
Zweigert, K., Siehr, K., Ihring's Influence on the Development of Comparative method. In: American Journal
    of Comparative Law, 1971 (215-231)
Zweigert, K., Puttfarken, H-J. (eds.) Rechtsvergleichung (Darmstadt) 1978
Östergård, U., The geopolitics of Nordic identity - from composite states to nation-states, Political and
    religious characteristics. In: The cultural construction of Norden (eds. Sørensen, Ø., Strath, B ,
    Oslo) 1997

Interviews (1995-1996)

European System of Human Rights:
- Mr. Leif Berg, Clerk in the *Commission of Human Rights*
- Mr. Matti Pellonpää, Member of the *European Commission of Human Rights*
- Mr. Raimo Pekkanen, Judge in the *European Court of Human rights*

European Community:
- Mr. Leif Sévon, Judge in the *European Court of Justice*
- Mr. G. Federico Mancini, Judge in the *European Court of Justice*
- Ms. Benita Broms, Clerk in the *European Court of Justice*

Germany:
- interview in the Supreme Court (*Bundesgerichtshof*)
- Ms. Helga Seibert, Judge in the Constitutional Court (*Bundesverfassungsgericht*)

Sweden:
- Mr. Hans Danelius, Judge in the Supreme Court (*Högsta Domstolen*), Member of the European Commission of Human Rights
- Mr. Anders Knutsson, Judge in the Supreme Court (*Högsta Domstolen*)

Finland:
- Mr. Gustaf Möller, Judge in the Supreme Court *(Korkein oikeus)*
- Mr. Per Lindholm, Judge in the Supreme Court (*Korkein oikeus*)
- Mr. Juhani Walamies, Clerk in the Supreme Court (*Korkein oikeus*)

United Kingdom:
- Lord Justice Schiemann, Judge inf the *Court of Appeal*
- Mr. Andrew Mckowen, Clerk in the *House of Lords*

Italy:
- Mr. Massimo Bonomo, Clerk in the Court of Appeal and Supreme Court (*Consigliere in Corte Cassazione*)
- Ms. Elisa Bianchi Figueredo, Clerk in the Constitutional Court (*Corte Constituzionale*)

France·
- Mdm. Sylviane Dayant, Clerk in the Supreme Court (*Magistrate Auditeur á la Cour de Cassasion*)

Index

Law and Philosophy Library

1. E. Bulygin, J.-L. Gardies and I. Niiniluoto (eds.): *Man, Law and Modern Forms of Life*. With an Introduction by M.D. Bayles. 1985   ISBN 90-277-1869-5

2. W. Sadurski: *Giving Desert Its Due*. Social Justice and Legal Theory. 1985
                                                                            ISBN 90-277-1941-1

3. N. MacCormick and O. Weinberger: *An Institutional Theory of Law*. New Approaches to Legal Positivism. 1986   ISBN 90-277-2079-7

4. A. Aarnio: *The Rational as Reasonable*. A Treatise on Legal Justification. 1987
                                                                            ISBN 90-277-2276-5

5. M.D. Bayles: *Principles of Law*. A Normative Analysis. 1987
                                                    ISBN 90-277-2412-1; Pb: 90-277-2413-X

6. A. Soeteman: *Logic in Law*. Remarks on Logic and Rationality in Normative Reasoning, Especially in Law. 1989   ISBN 0-7923-0042-4

7. C.T. Sistare: *Responsibility and Criminal Liability*. 1989   ISBN 0-7923-0396-2

8. A. Peczenik: *On Law and Reason*. 1989   ISBN 0-7923-0444-6

9. W. Sadurski: *Moral Pluralism and Legal Neutrality*. 1990   ISBN 0-7923-0565-5

10. M.D. Bayles: *Procedural Justice*. Allocating to Individuals. 1990   ISBN 0-7923-0567-1

11. P. Nerhot (ed.): *Law, Interpretation and Reality*. Essays in Epistemology, Hermeneutics and Jurisprudence. 1990   ISBN 0-7923-0593-0

12. A.W. Norrie: *Law, Ideology and Punishment*. Retrieval and Critique of the Liberal Ideal of Criminal Justice. 1991   ISBN 0-7923-1013-6

13. P. Nerhot (ed.): *Legal Knowledge and Analogy*. Fragments of Legal Epistemology, Hermeneutics and Linguistics. 1991   ISBN 0-7923-1065-9

14. O. Weinberger: *Law, Institution and Legal Politics*. Fundamental Problems of Legal Theory and Social Philosophy. 1991   ISBN 0-7923-1143-4

15. J. Wróblewski: *The Judicial Application of Law*. Edited by Z. Bańkowski and N. MacCormick. 1992   ISBN 0-7923-1569-3

16. T. Wilhelmsson: *Critical Studies in Private Law*. A Treatise on Need-Rational Principles in Modern Law. 1992   ISBN 0-7923-1659-2

17. M.D. Bayles: *Hart's Legal Philosophy*. An Examination. 1992   ISBN 0-7923-1981-8

18. D.W.P. Ruiter: *Institutional Legal Facts*. Legal Powers and their Effects. 1993
                                                                            ISBN 0-7923-2441-2

19. J. Schonsheck: *On Criminalization*. An Essay in the Philosophy of the Criminal Law. 1994
                                                                            ISBN 0-7923-2663-6

20. R.P. Malloy and J. Evensky (eds.): *Adam Smith and the Philosophy of Law and Economics*. 1994   ISBN 0-7923-2796-9

21. Z. Bańkowski, I. White and U. Hahn (eds.): *Informatics and the Foundations of Legal Reasoning*. 1995   ISBN 0-7923-3455-8

Law and Philosophy Library

Law and Philosophy Library

44. M. Friedman, L. May, K. Parsons and J. Stiff (eds.): *Rights and Reason*. Essays in Honor of Carl Wellman. 2000   ISBN 0-7923-6198-9

45. G.C. Christie: *The Notion of an Ideal Audience in Legal Argument*. 2000
          ISBN 0-7923-6283-7

46. R.S. Summers: *Essays in Legal Theory*. 2000   ISBN 0-7923-6367-1

47. M. van Hees: *Legal Reductionism and Freedom*. 2000   ISBN 0-7923-6491-0

48. R. Gargarella: *The Scepter of Reason*. Public Discussion and Political Radicalism in the Origins of Constitutionalism. 2000   ISBN 0-7923-6508-9

49. M. Iglesias Vila: *Facing Judicial Discretion*. Legal Knowledge and Right Answers Revisited. 2001   ISBN 0-7923-6778-2

50. M. Kiikeri: *Comparative Legal Reasoning and European Law*. 2001   ISBN 0-7923-6884-3

Printed in the United States
21855LVS00003B/11

9 780792 368847